Letters to Louise

Letters
to Louise

Russell J Jewett

Copyright © 2010 by Russell J Jewett.

Library of Congress Control Number: 2010908119
ISBN: Hardcover   978-1-4535-1301-9
               Softcover   978-1-4535-1300-2
               Ebook   978-1-4535-1302-6

All rights reserved. No part of this book may be reproduced or transmitted in any form or by any means, electronic or mechanical, including photocopying, recording, or by any information storage and retrieval system, without permission in writing from the copyright owner.

'Unless otherwise noted all photos used in this book is own by the author.

This book was printed in the United States of America.

To order additional copies of this book, contact:
Xlibris Corporation
1-888-795-4274
www.Xlibris.com
Orders@Xlibris.com
79695

Contents

Acknowledgments 9
Preface 11

Chapter 1:   How It Began: Family History 15
Chapter 2:   How It Began: Growing Up 19
Chapter 3:   How It Began: Swimming 23
Chapter 4:   Navy Reserve 25
Chapter 5:   Louise 28
Chapter 6:   Boot Camp 34
Chapter 7:   Going Regular Navy 39
Chapter 8:   Graduation 44
Chapter 9:   Flight to Japan 50
Chapter 10: First Day in Yokosuka 56
Chapter 11: Daily Life in Japan 62
Chapter 12: Marine Casualties from Vietnam 68
Chapter 13: Reunion of Homeboys 72
Chapter 14: Italian Gardens 76
Chapter 15: Busted 80
Chapter 16: Nagasaki 86
Chapter 17: Mount Fuji 90
Chapter 18: Yokohama Dreamland 93
Chapter 19: Back to California 98
Chapter 20: Field Medical Service School 101
Chapter 21: Okinawa 109
Chapter 22: Da Nang 112
Chapter 23: Third Shore Party 117
Chapter 24: Dong Ha 121
Chapter 25: Boat Trip to Thuan An 130
Chapter 26: A Shau Valley 135
Chapter 27: MACV-I 140
Chapter 28: Hue Hospital 144
Chapter 29: 3/3 Dong Ha 149
Chapter 30: Lima Hill 152
Chapter 31: The Razorback 162

Chapter 32:	Payable	176
Chapter 33:	Friendly Fire	181
Chapter 34:	Lima Company to the Rescue	190
Chapter 35:	Ripley's Raiders	192
Chapter 36:	Seeing Old Friends	227
Chapter 37:	The Rest of March	232
Chapter 38:	Ca Lu Mountain	239
Chapter 39:	Ca Lu	244
Chapter 40:	Ambush at the L	249
Chapter 41:	Indigenous People of the Area	253
Chapter 42:	Rough Rider	257
Chapter 43:	R&R	261
Chapter 44:	Rocket Attack on Dong Ha	264
Chapter 45:	Rat Catcher	268
Chapter 46:	Battalion Aid Station Forward	271
Chapter 47:	Malaria	276
Chapter 48:	Dr. John Miller	279
Chapter 49:	Cam Lo MedCAP	282
Chapter 50:	Nick Longo	285
Chapter 51:	The Long Hot Summer	288
Chapter 52:	Ambush on Highway 9	295
Chapter 53:	Another Ambush on Highway 9	300
Chapter 54:	BAS Rear	305
Chapter 55:	New Orders	309
Chapter 56:	Smoking Pot	314
Chapter 57:	China Beach	316
Chapter 58:	Getting Short	321
Chapter 59:	Graves Registration	324
Chapter 60:	Orders Home	325
Chapter 61:	Home at Last	330
Chapter 62:	My Last Duty Station	332

Epilogue	335
Glossary	341
Index	401

Dedication

To Ripley's Raiders and our fellow warriors who paid the ultimate price for freedom. Semper fi!
To all combat veterans, including their wives and families who equally suffer from the devastating effects of PTSD.

Acknowledgments

JOURNALIST JOHN CATHY for his encouragement in 1998 for me to document my memories, resulting in the creation of my photo essay on the Internet and evolving into www.gruntfixer.net.

Vietnam veteran Marine Tom Smith for seeking treatment for his symptoms of PTSD through local Veterans' Services and encouraging me to do the same.

World War II Marines Beans Minor and Paul McNabb and the other WWII and Korean era veterans who still meet on Monday night group therapy meetings dealing with living with PTSD.

World War II veteran Guy Grenny, PhD, for his concern and care of veterans on the Mendocino Coast and his assistance in documenting and submitting my stressor reports to the Veteran's' Administration.

Chris Hoy, MA, for assisting Dr. Grenny with group therapy for veterans and providing me with guidance during personal counseling sessions for the past five years and his ongoing encouragement for me to write and publish this book.

My former wives Jeri, Pene, Dorothy, and Susan.

Louise Johnson Ebling for saving all my letters and allowing me to scan all of them. To her husband, Gordon, for the interruption to their life that ensued.

Former Associated Press correspondent Ron Deutsch for his service with the AP in Saigon, who I met forty years later at Piaci. Thanks for all your support, encouragement, and the pizza and beer.

Jim Jackson, Esq., for patiently reading and editing my original manuscript not just once, but twice.

Vietnam veterans Richard Banks and John P. Miller, MD, for providing additional photo images to illustrate my manuscript.

The Xlibris team for helping with professional guidance and services to publish this book.

Preface

AT THE AGE of twenty, I served as a combat medical corpsman in an infantry unit of the Fleet Marine Force deployed to Vietnam I (eye) Corps near the DMZ. From January to June 1967, I had the good fortune to work and live with an outstanding group of Marines under the leadership of Captain John W. Ripley, company commander of Company L, Third Battalion Third Marines. The combat I experienced back then still affects me today.

After discharge from the navy in 1968, I spent uncountable hours looking at my photos of Vietnam and knew everyone's names and the details of every picture. I believed those names would never fade. After getting on with my life, I put the photos in the attic, and most of the names did fade, but a few did not. One of those names sticking with me was that of Corporal Leslie B. Johnson from Kentucky. Not only was LBJ an outstanding squad leader, but also his initials were easy to remember.

April of 1999, I decided to get a broader understanding of exactly what Third Battalion Third Marines role had been while I was with them. Most of the books on the Vietnam War had very little to say about the year of 1967. I did a Google search on Marine units in Vietnam and turned up a number of sites, which included the Third Battalion Third Marines Vietnam Era Vets Association Web site. Their Web site included a Wall of Honor listing in chronological order the members of 3/3 who never made it back to the world. This experience was very moving and brought back some of the lost names that had slipped away from my consciousness over the years.

On their Web site, they also had a guest book. After signing in at around visitor number 945, I started reading backward, checking out the names of all the others who had made entries, hoping to run across a familiar name. Several hours later and somewhere in the entry numbers under 100, I ran across LBJ's e-mail address with an entry he made. I was elated at seeing a familiar name. I quickly scanned a picture of him standing in the middle of the bridge near Ca Lu on Highway 9 in Vietnam, attached it to an e-mail to him, and sent it off. I received a response from Les the next day. He expressed his happiness at hearing from me and stated that after he was wounded and medevaced on 21 August 1967, none of his personal effects had followed him. The photo I sent him was the only one he now possessed from his tour in Vietnam. Other than his scars and personal memories, Les had no real mementos of one of the most influential periods in his life. I happily scanned and e-mailed fifty photos of the times we had in common when we were both part of the same platoon.

LBJ shared information with other members of 3/3 with whom he still had contact. It wasn't long before Kevin MacDonald, a college athletic director back in Massachusetts, called. Kevin informed me he had been a PFC in Third Platoon. Though I had no recollection of Kevin, he and I had several mutual experiences and knew several of the same people. Kevin and LBJ had attended a 3/3 reunion in 1998. Since then, they had talked frequently on the phone. Les told him about my contact. During our conversation, he suggested that I get a copy of Otto J. Lehrack's book *No Shining Armor*. Otto Lehrack, who served as the battalion logistics officer in 1967-68, documented the history of 3/3 in Vietnam from when the battalion landed at Chu Lai in1965 to 1969 when they returned to Hawaii. I immediately purchased a copy.

Kevin mailed a packet of copies of photos and personnel rosters of Lima Company for January through April '67. Included were two excellent pictures of himself and third squad of Third Platoon on top of the Rockpile, taken by author Bernard Fall, a prominent war correspondent, historian, political scientist, and expert on Indochina during the 1950s and 1960s. He also included another photo taken by Father Guy MacPartland, 3/3s chaplain, LBJ, and Second Platoon on top of the Razorback, Christmas Eve 1966.

Soon, others began contacting me. Bruce Smith who served with Kilo Company of 3/3 was on the convoy ambushed by the NVA on Highway 9 on 21 August 1967. The ambush produced a great number of casualties I helped process and treat at the Battalion Aid Station that day.

Byron Perkins, a former navy corpsman with 3/3. Byron survived a rocket attack on Dong Ha that killed or wounded all the corpsmen at the BAS after midnight on 18 May '67. John Kelsey, Lima Company's senior corpsman (wounded twice in March of '67), gave me additional valued input.

Don Wolfe, a soldier on a Duster (a small tank with naval twin 40s guns). His unit (the 1st/44th) was attached to 3/3 and participated in much of the action we saw on Highway 9.

Further searching on the Internet, I ran across some great pictures of the Rockpile and Razorback taken by David Althoff, lieutenant colonel (retired), a Marine helicopter pilot. Colonel Althoff was CO of HMM-262, a unit of CH-46 helicopters, in Quang Tri in 1968 and had posted his photos on their Web site. Several of his photos actually showed an aerial view of Lima Hill and the muddy area we lived in during January '67. I contacted him, and he gave me permission to use them on my Web site.

At about that same time, John Cathy (now editor of the *Annals of Saudi Medicine*, Riyadh, Saudi Arabia) was employed as a technical writer for several pharmaceutical companies. John and I used to frequent a local pub. One evening, I told him about contacting LBJ after thirty-two years and the flood of memories of Vietnam it had triggered. John had recently completed a Web site he had collaborated on called Plaguescape.com (no longer on the Web), which offered modern explanations of the biblical twelve plagues of Egypt. He encouraged me to write about my Vietnam experiences. I put together some simple Web pages, and he posted them on his site. After receiving favorable feedback on those few pages, I decided to start a more complete accounting of the time spent in Vietnam.

In 1999, I created my Web site http://www.gruntfixer.net, where over a period of months, I assembled 180 photos and created 70 pages of text summarizing my combat experience.

Until I published my Web site, I had no communications with any of the Marines or corpsmen who had shared the experiences of combat in Vietnam in 1967. As word got out about my site, names of old friends began to appear as entries on my guest book.

In 2003, after four years procrastinating going to a reunion, I attended my first with the veterans and their families of Lima Company Third Battalion Third Marines held in Branson, Missouri. The reunion included Lima Company members from 1965 to 1969.

Dave "Tiger" Schwirian, Francis McGowin, and Doc Paul Churchill were the only attendees that I knew, but it was great to see all those guys again. It was as if we had just seen each other a week ago, except the room was now filled with middle-aged men and their wives. I vowed that from then on, I would make a concerted effort to attend and to encourage others to attend reunions of their military units.

In 2005, I made contact with Louise Johnson Ebling, whom I had known in high school and with whom I communicated with after joining the navy. I asked her if she still had the photos I sent to her while I was in Vietnam. Her response was not only had she kept all the pictures, but also still had all the original letters I had written to her from 1964 through 1967. A few months later, she and her husband came to visit her father in Fort Bragg, California, and brought her collection, which she left with me for several months so I could scan them onto a CD.

On March 2, 2007, I attended a relatively impromptu muster in Washington DC of the members of Ripley's Raiders. We met to commemorate the fortieth anniversary of a major battle we fought in Cam Lo and to honor our members who did not make it off the battlefield that day. Over sixty of us spent the weekend together looking at photos, drinking beer, and talking.

Our company commander, Colonel John W. Ripley, USMC (retired), an icon for the Marine Corps for his heroism on his second tour of Vietnam in 1972, made arrangements for an exclusive tour of the new National Museum of the Marine Corps in Triangle, Virginia, and acted as our tour guide.

The next day, we attended a ceremony held at the Wall. When the memorial park staff tried to keep the general public away, we insisted that they be allowed to stand with us and hear the presentation. In front of the panel that listed the dead from that day forty years previous, Colonel Ripley presented details about that battle that I had not previously known about.

It was after returning from that event that I decided to write this book. I had the need to get the thoughts out of my head and in the form of something more substantial to share with others. I found the process very therapeutic, and having done this has helped me to live with my ghosts.

Chapter 1

How It Began: Family History

GEOGRAPHICALLY ISOLATED BY poor roads and limited access, the small Northern California coastal community of Fort Bragg on the Mendocino Coast was an ideal place to raise children. Everyone in town knew everyone else, and strangers were scrutinized to determine if they should remain in town or be encouraged to move on.

Fort Bragg was a safe place to live. Neighbors kept an eye on each other's property. The streets were lit at night. The police force mainly issued traffic tickets and kept the nightlife under control. Drunks were asked to park their cars and given a ride home. No one locked their doors at night, and it was safe for children to play outside until bedtime. The adults of the community had no problem reprimanding each other's children when they observed them doing something that was not approved by the community.

Though the community had less than five thousand residents, it had its ethnic neighborhoods. The Catholic sections of town consisted of the Portuguese living west of Main Street, and the Italians lived on the south side of town. The Protestants included the Finns and Scandinavians in the center and southeast. These communities for the most part stayed within themselves establishing their own churches and lodges. At one time, *Ripley's Believe It or Not* listed Fort Bragg as having more churches and saloons per capita than any other city in the United States. Some residents boasted having a five-generation history of living on the coast.

Growing up in a small community has its advantages and disadvantages. Although the advantages far outnumber the disadvantages, living in a small isolated community doesn't adequately prepare its children to survive in the rest of the world.

My family arrived in New England fifteen years after the pilgrims. My paternal great-grandfather George Orrington Jewett grew up back east. After the Civil War, it was popular to become a missionary and to travel to the Pacific Islands to convert the inhabitants to Christianity. He met his wife, Emma Ava Nella Jones, at a school sponsored by the Methodist Church, preparing graduates to go overseas. George learned all the trades, which would enable him and the mission to survive. Just before they were to get their first assignment, the sponsor of the mission died, and the mission lost its funding when the surviving family members decided to keep the money for themselves. He had to be satisfied traveling around America's frontier building churches employed as a circuit rider. My grandfather Edward Fletcher Jewett was born in the Oklahoma Indian Territory in 1898. The family worked its way west through Wyoming, Montana, Oregon, and Nevada.

In 1918, the family was living in Anderson Valley in Mendocino County, California. Their children attended Anderson Valley High School. Grandpa graduated in June. His girlfriend asked him to accompany her to the county seat of Ukiah where she was taking the test to become a schoolteacher. He agreed to go, and when they arrived at the courthouse, the examiner convinced him to also take the test. When the results were in, he passed, but she did not.

Teaching was not a lucrative endeavor, and Grandpa had more interest in making money than enriching the minds of the youth. He went to work for a logging company owned by Port Lawson. Because of his mechanical ability, he soon became an engineer on a steam yarder known as the Greenwood Flyer. When he was given a small donkey engine to run on his own, a miscalculation caused the steam engine to end up on its side; Grandpa was fired.

The need to work and lack of available jobs caused him to seek employment in a teaching position. He was hired, and his first job as a teacher was up on the Covelo Rancheria Indian Reservation in the northeast corner of the county. When he arrived in Round Valley for work, there was no schoolhouse, so he set about and converted a large chicken coop into a classroom for his students. After he fulfilled his contract, he accepted a more civilized position at Cloverdale High School in northern Sonoma County.

Charles Hulbert and his wife, Lola, left Missouri to manage a thousand-acre sheep ranch for San Francisco businessman Austin Wickersham located in Yorkville, California. In 1907, my paternal grandmother Lola Belle was born on the ranch. When it came time for my grandmother to attend school, she was sent to live with her maternal grandparents in Cloverdale, located just over the Mendocino-Sonoma county line. She met my grandfather when she was returning home on the stage from Cloverdale to Yorkville. He was traveling home to Boonville, which took him through Yorkville. They soon became good friends; when she was seventeen, they got married.

My dad, Norman, was born in Cloverdale in 1925 when my grandmother was a senior. She missed her graduation ceremony because she was in labor. When Dad was one year old, his parents moved from Cloverdale to Fort Bragg when Grandpa accepted a job teaching industrial arts at Fort Bragg High School. They lived in a section of town known as Nob Hill, which was occupied by teachers, doctors, and other professionals. Their social life revolved around the school system, the Masonic Lodge, and the Presbyterian Church.

August Alexander Rantala came from Finland. When the Russians came into Helsinki to conscript young Finns into the Russian army, Great-grandpa Rantala fled and booked passage on a ship bound for California. The ship traveled around the horn and arrived in San Francisco in 1889. Eventually he settled in the California coastal town of Navarro in 1892 and managed a hotel on the Navarro Ridge. He married Sophia Jokilehto and in 1894. In 1899, their second son, August "Kig" A. Rantala Jr. was born. They moved to Fort Bragg when Grandpa Kig was five years old, and worked for Union Lumber Company in the automobile shop. Grandpa did not speak English until he started public school. Growing up, he was very athletic and excelled at playing baseball for the high school and city league.

After graduation, he joined the army. While at basic training in Oakland during 1918, he came down with swine flu, and his training was delayed until he recovered. When he recovered, WWI had ended, and he was discharged without any further service. He returned to Fort Bragg.

William Dexter Cleveland left the family farm in Cape Cod, Massachusetts, leaving it to his brother and went west. He met Nellie May Nickerson, twenty years his junior. Nellie was very athletic and loved riding horses. In 1899 while living in the town of Atlantic City, near Lewiston, Wyoming, they had a daughter they named Nettie. The family traveled west, and William died in San Rafael, California. Nellie married Otto Poe in Tuolumne, California. They moved to Healdsburg and then settled in Fort Bragg. Since high school was not a requirement in those days, Grandma Nettie finished school after graduating the ninth grade. She then went to work to help support the family. She worked as a switchboard operator for Union Lumber Company. Grandpa Kig worked at Bishops market. They were married in 1922, had a son, Dexter, born in 1923. My mom, Carol Louise, was their second child born in 1926.

My parents were a year apart in age and were acquainted throughout their school years. Dad played trombone, and Mom played clarinet in the school band. As teenagers, they both hung out with their friends at the Green Parrot, a popular malt shop near the town's recreation center. The only time either of them traveled outside Mendocino or Sonoma County was in 1940 while on a school band trip when the band played at the Sacramento State Fair.

Dad graduated from high school in June of 1943 and joined the navy under the V-12 Program. The V-12 Program utilized universities around the country as training facilities for reserve officers training programs. He traveled by train back to the Midwest where he was stationed in Madison, Wisconsin, for basic training. From there he was transferred to Valley City, North Dakota. An urgent need for radiomen caused a shift in his training, and he was put into the enlisted ranks as a radioman third class. After radio school, he was assigned duty aboard the aircraft carrier USS *Essex* located in dry dock in San Francisco receiving a retrofit. He traveled from Valley City to San Francisco on a train so full of servicemen that he had to stand the majority of the trip across country.

When Mom found out about his transfer, she was still a senior in high school. She convinced her parents to allow her to travel by bus to her aunt's house in San Francisco for a short visit. She met him when he arrived at the Ferry Building, and they traveled back to Fort Bragg by bus. Dad stayed in Fort Bragg for a two-week leave before returning to San Francisco. Mom accompanied Dad and his parents and sister back to the Ferry Building to say their good-byes. The *Essex* sailed on April 16, 1944, and joined Task Force 58 and 38 under Admiral Bull Halsey. On November 15, the *Essex* was hit by a kamikaze, causing extensive damage, killing fifteen, and wounding forty-four. On April 11, 1945, a Japanese plane tried to hit the *Essex* with a one-thousand-pound bomb. It missed, and the bomb went off in the water next to the ship. The explosion shook the ship badly, causing some damage to the hull. Dad was slammed against the bulkhead by the impact and explosion, slightly injuring his shoulder.

On August 15, 1945, the *Essex* was preparing to hit the Tokyo area when the Japanese surrendered. On September 3, after surviving over thirty air attacks since leaving San Francisco, the *Essex* was ordered to Bremerton, Washington, for deactivation. They anchored in Puget Sound on September 13 after being at sea for seventeen months. Dad returned to Fort Bragg with the intention of never leaving home again. He and Mom were married on September 30, 1945, and I was born on July 1, 1946.

Chapter 2

How It Began: Growing Up

IN ADDITION TO teaching, Grandpa Jewett had several small businesses that he operated out of his home. He purchased a dairy farm at the edge of town while Dad was out at sea. He set up a typewriter repair business, a print shop, a dog kennel, a rabbit farm; he raised roses and African violets as well as several other small businesses. When Dad returned home, he began working in Grandpa's print shop, doing business as Redwood Coast Printers. Prior to my brother being born in 1948, Dad often took me to the print shop. He entertained me by teaching me to sort the type. He showed me the typeface and said the letter and placed it in the appropriate bin. In no time, I learned to recite the alphabet and place the appropriate type in its designated area. It was great fun putting the lead letters in the large divided wooden drawers. Mom did her part by reading to me almost every day. By age four, I was able to read.

Until I started school, my world consisted of my relatives on both sides of the family. However, the only times my grandparents socialized with each other was on birthdays of grandkids held at our home. Other than that, the families did not get together. The only thing that my grandfathers had in common is that they were both members of the Freemasons and the Eastern Star. Thanksgivings and Christmases were usually at my mom's parents.

When I started kindergarten, I was forced outside the insulated cocoon of my family, exposing me to the other kids in the community for essentially the first time. Kindergarten consisted of four large classes (we were the first of the baby boomers).

Though community children were integrated, the school administration still took steps to maintain the social order of the community. Our classes were made up to essentially keep the Protestants and Catholics separated in the classroom, as well as socioeconomically; but on the playground, fights still occasionally occurred, usually within the less civilized student groups. My friends and I grew up never getting into a fight at school or on the streets.

At the beginning of the second grade, the Knights of Columbus sponsored Cub Scout Pack 85. Most of the boys in my class joined because it was the only scout organization for our age group. Though it was sponsored by a Catholic organization, members were accepted from both Protestant and Catholic families. The dens within the pack were created by address so that transportation to the weekly meetings would not be an issue. The monthly pack meetings were held at the Parish Hall next to the Catholic Church. I developed friendships with other kids outside of the classroom. After three years, we became old enough to be Boy Scouts. The Masonic Lodge (possibly fearing the potential of their children coming under the influence of the Catholic Church) sponsored troop 43 for their kids to continue in the scouting program meeting at the Presbyterian Church.

Just before I turned eleven, Dad obtained a permit to camp in the Big River Forest owned by his employer Union Lumber Company. With the arrival of his third child, Dad had taken a second job working at the lumber mill. He was eventually promoted to the electric shop and had enough seniority to lease a campsite from the company for $25 per year. We were allowed to pick out and develop our own campsite. Most of the other campers on the river constructed cabins to live in, but we slept and ate outside under the trees in a grove of redwoods. The highlight for me was swimming in the river where we had our own swimming hole. The camp was located far enough inland that the temperatures were in the 90s during the day. Our swimming hole was deep enough to dive off the rocks. We spent afternoons playing in the water and lying in the sunshine. During the summer, I spent two weeks at Mendocino Woodlands at 4-H camp, which was located several miles downriver from our camp.

When I was eleven years old and halfway through the sixth grade, I joined the 4-H club at the encouragement of some of the girls in my class. Many of my classmates had joined 4-H rather than go into Boy Scouts. The Fort Bragg Eager Beaver 4-H club met upstairs at the Presbyterian Church. I chose the field of forestry as my project. With the help of the older members of the forestry group, I learned a great deal about the field and completed my project by the end of the year along with those who had been in since the beginning of the year. Our group did so well that we went to state convention at UC Davis in the Sacramento Valley. Except for the rare occasions when my family went to neighboring Lake and Sonoma counties, this was my first time out of Mendocino County. The most fascinating thing for me on the entire trip was riding on the straight roads in the valley. I had never seen so many miles of noncurving roads before that.

That summer, I experienced my first extended time away from home when I attended 4-H camp at the Mendocino Woodlands, which was located about four miles downstream from my parents' camp on Big River.

After summer camp was over, we spent the rest of the summer at our camp. Except for Dad's two-week vacation, he spent every weekend at camp.

During the week back in Fort Bragg, we were under the fog most days during the summer. Inland Northern California communities enjoy clear skies and warm days. When the interior of the state heats up, the convection currents bring in the cool air from the ocean. Teens inland take advantage of their summer vacations enjoying the luxury of large outdoor swimming pools or a trek out to a nearby river for a cool dip in their favorite swimming holes. While the inland communities enjoyed temperatures in the 90s and 100s, the fog shrouded us, keeping our temperature around 55 to 60 degrees. Even on sunny days, the prevailing northwest wind kept the temperature below 70. My friends and I had access to the indoor community swimming pool located in the recreation center in the city hall. This small pool was heated and way over chlorinated. Admission cost a quarter to swim from one to four in the afternoons. It was against the rules to wear any goggles, so we had to endure the irritation of the chlorine causing the whites of our eyes to become bloodshot road maps. When it was time to go home, we took a shower to rinse the chlorine off our bodies; but no matter how much soap I used, I still smelled like a bottle of Clorox. After a summer of swimming, my brown bathing trunks bleached out to almost pure white. When I had the funds to afford the rec pool, I would go there; but most of the time, I couldn't afford it. A week at the rec cost a $1.50 of my $2.00 weekly allowance from my parents.

As an alternative, my brother Steve, two years my junior, our friends, and I rode our bikes several miles inland on Sherwood road, taking us out of the fog belt into the sunshine. Out there, a trail – established years ago by fishermen accessing the steelhead and salmon runs during the fall and winter – led from the road down a steep hillside to the Noyo River. The trail was a narrow path traversing back and forth down the hillside through the redwoods and Douglas fir. It ended at the south end of the California Western Railroad tunnel. We walked across the trestle crossing the Noyo River and continued a mile or so along the train tracks until arriving at several holes deep enough to swim in. The air temperature was much warmer on the river than in town, getting up into the 80s. The Noyo River winds its way through the narrow valleys with tree-covered slopes keeping the river in the shadows, and the water temperature doesn't get much over 60 degrees. We spent the afternoons lying in the sun. To cool down, we dove off the rocks along the riverbank and swam.

That's not to say that I never got to go swimming in the warm rivers during the summer. When I was fourteen, I dropped out of 4-H and went back to Scouts. Steve had joined Troop 85 with his friends, and I decided to also join. During the summers, I attended camp at Camp Navarro on the north fork of the Navarro River.

Before camp started each year, the river bottom was bulldozed and shaped into a swimming hole with a sloping beach. Wooden panels were bolted into concrete pilings forming a dam, creating a small lake behind the dam. The deep end near the dam was about ten feet deep, and the upper reaches were shallower, but still deep enough for canoeing and rowing. The shallow north fork of the Navarro runs through wider valleys than the Noyo, giving it more exposure to the sun. The water behind the dam was warm, allowing us to stay in the water for long periods. It was there that I earned my swimming, mile-swim, canoeing, and life-saving merit badges.

Chapter 3

How It Began: Swimming

THE SUMMER BETWEEN my freshman and sophomore years at high school, the American Red Cross sponsored beginner's swimming classes for young children of ages three to five. They contacted our scoutmaster requesting instructors. Being the good scout that I was, I volunteered. Doing this, I also earned my community services merit badge. An added bonus allowed me to use the community swimming pool freely in the afternoon and evening. A series of three one-hour classes started at nine and ended at noon. At noon I went home, ate lunch, and returned to the pool at one to practice diving on the springboard and socialize with my friends.

My brother Steve and I always did things together as we grew up, and teaching swimming was no exception. As a result, Steve also took a job as a lifeguard at the pool and became very popular with the younger junior high girls.

After lessons were over one morning, I was taking a shower washing off the chlorine from the pool. I walked out of the shower just as one of the younger instructors, a girl of junior high school age, walked into the dressing room. Steve and I, as well as the other guys, were in various stages of dress. We quickly covered our exposed genitals and yelled for her to leave. She stood there for several moments looking around before she turned and walked out. After she was out, we all laughed and made macho comments about the incident, finished dressing, and headed out of the dressing room on our way to lunch.

As I walked out of the dressing room door into the main hallway, I spotted the girl who had so boldly intruded, talking with several of her girlfriends (also instructors) near the soft drink machines. All were looking in our direction and giggling. Steve shrugged his shoulders and walked out of the building on his way to lunch. As the oldest of the group, I felt compelled to reprimand this youngster for her rude intrusion into the sanctity of the dressing room clearly labeled MEN at the entry door.

I approached and confronted her, informing her of the immorality of violating our space. As it turned out, she was trying to get Steve's attention, hoping he would take her on a date. Steve was going into his sophomore year at high school and enjoyed the popularity of being in the "in crowd" of his class. He and his buddies were highly lusted after by many of the junior high-aged girls experiencing their newly raging hormones. In the safety of her giggling friends, she told me to mind my own business. Since I considered them all children, using my authority, I warned them about violating the rules of the recreation center and went on my way.

Chapter 4

Navy Reserve

IN AUGUST THAT same summer after returning from two weeks at Camp Navarro, I realized that this would be my last year in high school. I was suddenly faced with what to do with my life after I graduated the following June. With four other kids to support, my parents were not able to afford to send me to college. Even though I was a college prep student, I had not prepared financially for college. My options for the next summer were limited. I could work for the local lumber mills stacking graded lumber into their appropriate pile. I could go to work for one of the local mom-and-pop businesses around town, but they usually hired students returning from college to earn their next year's tuition. As a last resort, I could take a seasonal job in the local harbor cleaning fish. None of my options were particularly appealing.

I mentioned my dilemma to my scoutmaster Bruno Donati at our weekly meeting. Several days later, he introduced me to Ed Alves, who had retired from active duty in the navy. Ed was senior chief petty officer. He was a machinist mate in the navy, but now worked at the mill, as did most of the men in town. He attended naval reserve meetings once a week in the county seat of Ukiah at 7:00 PM every Wednesday. Ukiah was fifty miles away, but it was the closest reserve unit to Fort Bragg. Ed invited me to attend a meeting with him to determine if the Navy Reserve was something that would interest me. I could always go to college after active duty using the GI Bill to defray the costs. I informed my parents of the offer. They agreed it wouldn't hurt for me to go and check it out.

The following Wednesday, I rode with Ed to Ukiah. As he drove, he explained the advantages of going into the service, including the educational opportunities and travel. Arriving at the Reserve Center located below the Coyote Dam at Lake Mendocino, I received a tour of the facility and talked to all the enlisted men and officers. All were very encouraging and reinforced what Al had told me. I liked what I learned. At eleven thirty that night, Ed dropped me off at home with a handful of recruiting brochures and a book listing all the different ratings (job classifications) the navy had to offer. I also had an enlistment contract. I was still only seventeen and still in high school, so I had to obtain my parents' permission before I could enlist. After enlisting, I would still only be attending weekly training meetings in Ukiah. I would not have to decide on a rating until after I completed boot camp and a reserve cruise after graduation from high schools. It would be like being in the Sea Scouts.

My mother was not enthusiastic about the idea. The sudden realization that her first baby was now old enough to serve in the armed forces did not set well with her. I lobbied my dad for support; he had enlisted in the Navy Reserve in the STAR Program right after high school in 1944.

Evidently there was some lengthy discussion between them about the issues over the next few days, but my dad finally came through and signed the recruiting form granting his permission for me to enlist. I joined the Navy Reserve the next week. I found out years later that my mom never forgave my dad for giving his permission without her approval.

Reserve meetings each week at first consisted of taking different aptitude tests and learning some general navigation skills, working with a Teletype and onboard communication equipment. After several weeks, I received a seabag full of uniforms, a peacoat, and *The Bluejackets' Manual* containing basic information all sailors need to know. I had a single diagonal white stripe on the left sleeve of my uniforms, designating me as a seaman recruit.

At the meetings, all the sailors smoked, so I started smoking Kent cigarettes. At home, I hid them in my desk drawer under a bunch of things so Mom wouldn't discover them. Dad smoked a pipe, but was never allowed to smoke at home because Mom said she was allergic to tobacco smoke. That was always curious to me, as she had no problem with her father or brothers smoking or being in their homes where they smoked. Somehow it was only Dad's smoke that bothered her.

One Wednesday, Ed came by to pick me up and informed me that we would have another person riding with us that evening. Bill Mertle had just been released from active duty and was required to attend reserve meetings for a year before he could become inactive. Bill was a second class petty officer with a rating of storekeeper. He had just gotten a job working in supply at the mill. All the way over to Ukiah, he told us about his time in Yokosuka, Japan, his last duty station. According to Bill, a sailor couldn't ask for a more perfect duty station than Yokosuka. The next week, Bill presented me with a pamphlet the navy had given him in preparation to going to Japan. I was grateful and soon digested all the information. It was then that I decided to go to Japan while in the navy.

About the same time that I joined the reserves, our football team started practice for the upcoming football season and the coach had the team working out every day. On one of the first days during one of the drills, I was hit high and low by two tacklers coming at me from two directions. I was hit hard and sustained a lower back injury, which made it painful to get up from the set position for the rest of the practice that day; as a result, I did not make the team.

After Labor Day, the school year started. During gym class, we were playing softball. It was my turn at the plate, and I swung hard at the ball and missed. In the process, I rotated my spine, which aggravated my already injured lower back, putting me in the hospital for two weeks. After I was discharged from the hospital, my doctor told me no more gym class for the remainder of the year to help reduce the chances of reinjuring my back. I was faced with the possibility that if my back did not heal up sufficiently, the navy might end up not being an option. I reconsidered my career. In place of physical education class, I decided to take an English course to complete my college prep work.

Chapter 5

Louise

NEAR THE BEGINNING of the previous year, a young arsonist set fire to the school. The fire was contained in the junior high section of the school building. The extensive damage required demolition of all the classrooms and small auditorium. To accommodate classes for both junior and high school classes, it was necessary to use the remaining high school section of the building. High school was held in the morning starting at seven twenty and running until noon. Junior high classes started at twelve twenty and ran until five in the afternoon.

When track season came around, I still was not able to participate due to my back injury, so I became the team manager. My job was taking care of equipment, rosters, and anything else the coach could think of to keep me busy. The track team practiced after school in the afternoon while the junior high classes were in session.

One afternoon, I sat in the coach's office located at the end of the gymnasium. The office window had privacy shutters, but opened, providing a view of activity in the gym. I opened the shutters and watched the eighth-grade girls playing basketball. As they tossed the ball around the court, one of the girls caught my eye. It was the same girl who had walked into the dressing room at the recreation center pool last summer. She looked pretty good and had filled out her white one-piece gym suit in all the right places. After track practice was over, I hung around until school recessed at five. I waited for her to come out of the building. When I saw her, she was talking to her friends. I walked in front of her, stopped, acted surprised to recognize her, and said, "Don't I know you?"

She replied, "I was the one who walked into the dressing room this summer at the rec center."

Nonchalantly I replied, "Oh, yeah, I remember you." As if she were one of many girls who paraded through the men's dressing room on a regular basis.

I introduced myself. "My name is Russ. What's yours?"

She said, "I already knew who you are. You're Steve's brother and was the one who chewed my butt when I was with my friends, remember?"

"I do remember, but I assume you have a name. What is it?"

"What do you care? You'll probably be just as rude as you were last time."

"I apologize for that, but I had to say something."

"Well, you said it, now leave me alone."

"I said I apologize. I'd like to get to know you."

"Well, if you have to know, it's Louise."

"I'm happy to meet you, Louise. Do you have a last name?"

"Why do you care, you're too old for me. What are you, a junior?"

"Senior."

"See, I told you you're too old."

"Can I walk you home, Louise?"

"I know my way home. I've used the same route the past year. Besides, it is out of your way."

"How do you know it's out of my way?"

"I know where you live, you're Steve's brother. I assume you both live in the same house."

"Yeah, we do. Nice meeting you, Louise." I walked away.

When I was some distance away, one of her friends yelled, "Her name is Johnson. Louise Johnson."

I waved and continued on my way home.

Several days later, I was leaving the gym, and she just happened to be waiting outside on the sidewalk that leads to the street. I again offered to walk her home, and this time, she accepted. She lived nine blocks away from the school and eight blocks in the opposite direction from where I lived. I offered to carry her books, and she handed them to me. We walked and talked about teaching swimming during the last summer. I asked her why she had entered the dressing room, and she stated it was a dare from her cousin. I was impressed that she would do such a thing. I would never have taken a dare to walk into the girls' dressing room, but I was a Boy Scout and would never have considered such an immoral act.

Walking Louise home after school became a routine for me during track season. We went on dates every Friday night. Her mother would drop her off at State Theater. I would meet her in the lobby, and we would find a seat. As soon as the lights went out, we would start kissing. The theater employed usherettes, who would walk through the theater in their maroon uniforms and pillbox hats with flashlights to ensure that the teenagers were minding their p's and q's. No hanky-panky on their watch. It became a challenge to make out without getting caught. We became good at it. After a while, we were groping each other. I would have my hand in her bra, and she would have her hand in my pants. Who knew or even cared what the movie was. After the movie, her mother would pick her up in front of the theater and I would walk home by myself.

Three other guys from Fort Bragg enlisted in the reserves since I had joined. Ordinarily I would not have been associated with any of these guys if it hadn't been for the reserves. All three were from families of a different social status than me. None of them were in scouts or any other youth organization and were more in tune with street life. They were friendly, and I enjoyed their company in small doses. They all smoked and drank on a regular basis.

Charles "Chick" Ash had graduated a year ahead of me and had been working in the mill. Chick joined the reserves much for the same reason that I did, he needed to get out of Fort Bragg. Chick drove a '52 Chevy coupé, so instead of riding to Ukiah with Ed Alves, I decided to hang out with my new friends.

Ed Hall was in my graduating class, but he was not a popular student, slightly overweight and a bit slow mentally. He just barely graduated. Ed smoked cigarettes from the time he was ten. His family lived out in a shack in the woods, and his parents were on welfare.

Steve Kaden was in the class behind me. His father was a self-employed electrician and his mother a bookkeeper. Steve's parents hung out in the bowling alley bar. Steve also was a heavy smoker by the time he was seventeen, consuming two packs of Marlboros a day. Steve was a constant talker; he talked about people and things in the news. He loved to gossip about everyone he knew and had delusions of grandeur. Whether he knew anything about them or not made no difference to Steve.

When school recessed for Easter week, the family went to Yorkville to stay with my great-grandmother while Dad's uncle Austin and his wife, Sylvia, went on a trip to Texas to visit their daughter. Lola Hulbert – or, as we called her, Dala – was eighty-six years old and still was working on the ranch. She was spry and got along in her environment without any problem. I missed seeing Louise and decided to start writing to her while I was at the ranch sixty-five miles away from Fort Bragg.

Sunday March 22nd, 1964
10 O'clock

Dearest Louise,

Man! What weather! It's snowing! It has been since yesterday. My hands are so cold that I can hardly write (you can tell by the writing). So far it has been fun tooling the jeep, motor scooter, and pick-up. My uncle left me in charge of the ranch, so I have to feed the sheep, chickens, a lamb and the dogs and cat. This weather doesn't help it any.

I brought my Bermuda shorts and a lot of summer things and the weather turned out wrong! Oh well, that's life. If it keeps up we'll be snowed in by morning tomorrow.

It has been just a little over one day (it seems like two days since I've seen you and I miss you already. I hope you and your cousin are having a good time. I wish I could be with you.

My great grandmother just brought in an electric heater to heat up my room man does it feel good. Of course I could go out in the other room, but what the heck.

The snow is really coming down now. It is just like someone was up on the roof and dropped feathers off. The snow is getting further and further down the hill. I hope the new lambs aren't freezing. Later I'll have to drive up and see.

I really miss you and wish you were here. We could have a lot of fun. I dream about you every night, which sounds goofy, but I do.

Love always,
Russ

Ps my address is:
Russell Jewett
C/o AB Hulbert Ranch
Yorkville, Calif.

Monday March 23rd, 1964
2 O'clock PM

Dearest Louise,

Well, it stopped snowing at last, but it is still cold. The snow has melted around the house and the lower hills. Yesterday after I finished writing the letter to you I went out in the jeep with all the little kids to get pellets for the sheep, which were hungry. The feed barn is about a half a mile from the house and about half way there the jeep stalled and I couldn't get it started again. We sat there freezing for about 15 minutes and then I tried starting it again and this time it started. When we got back to the house our hands were numb and we could barely move them.

Yesterday it started snowing early in the morning and didn't stop until about 6PM. We had the stove and fireplace going all day and most of the night to keep warm. My brother and I have a heater and a radio in our room and every one else has nothing. Ha, Ha! TV broke down yesterday, too, darn it. Now we just sit around and look at old National Geographic.

Today my little brother and I went way up on the hill to play in the snow. About 6 inches of it was on the ground and it was melting fast so last night there must have been about a foot. We built a snowman (fun and games!) We also about froze our hands off and I could hardly drive the jeep afterwards.

I still miss you, even more than yesterday. It's getting so that when I don't have anything to do I just sit and think about you. Boy, I've got it bad! Oh, well, why fight it?

How are you and Maggie doing? By the time you get this she'll probably be gone. But I hope you are having fun anyhow.

Don't write after Thursday because I will probably be gone by the time it gets here, but I'll keep writing each day.

I wish this week would hurry up so I can see you again!

Love always,
Rus
Xx

Tuesday March 24th, 1964
4 PM

Dearest Louise,

Boy we had fun today! When everybody went into Boonville Steve and I took the jeep up on the hills as far as we could go. In an hours time in the hills we put almost 20 miles on the speedometer. After that we took out the motor scooter and put about fifty miles on it. We ran out of gas though, but we were close to the ranch and so all we had to do was push it there and fill it up and take off again.

There is still a little snow way up in the hills, but we aren't getting any more. It's melting pretty fast.

We painted the living room today. Man what a mess (us, not the living room).

I hope Steve Kaden comes tomorrow, I kind of doubt that he will show up because I've had experience with him showing up late or not at all. But sometimes he comes. I don't want to miss Reserves tomorrow.

If it didn't take so long I'd come home for a couple of hours, but it would take me a little over an hour each way, so that kills that.

My sister and her friend, Diane Devine, sit around talking with their hands like deaf people do and I'm catching on, you should see the things they say!

I miss you more than ever and I can't wait for this week to end so I can see you again. I still dream about you every night.

My great grandmother asked me today, "Russell do you have a girl picked out yet?" and I said with a grin, "Who, me?" and Susie and Di started giggling! Then they started talking with their hands and spelled out your name. Oh, well. I miss you

Love always,
Russ
xxx

One of the reservists was a member of the Ukiah Chamber of Commerce. The chamber was sponsoring an event with a parade. He asked for volunteers to escort a group of young ladies in the parade in convertibles provided by all the local car dealerships. Each car needed a driver and an escort in uniform. On Saturday, Chick, Ed, Steve, and I showed up in Ukiah ready to help. We were delighted to find ten beautiful women in strapless formals as our passengers. We drove them about town before, during, and after the parade. As a token of appreciation for our service during the event, a party was thrown by one of the chamber members for all of us who had participated. He provided four cases of beer and a couple bottles of whiskey. Only several of us were minors, but we were accepted as part of the crew. Since there were no nonalcoholic beverages, I joined in. This was not the first time that I had tasted beer; my dad would occasionally share a beer with me after we split a load of firewood together. This party was the first time that I had no limits to restrain me. I now could drink more than one if I so desired, and did. I kept up with the others can for can. We listened to music and had sandwiches and chips. One of the guys brought his collection of Redd Foxx party records. Redd Foxx was a performer who told risqué jokes in nightclubs long before he became the star of TV's *Sanford and Son* in the 1970s. I had a great time drinking, dancing, and laughing. This was much more fun than the Boy Scouts. After the party ended around midnight, Chick drove us back to Fort Bragg. By the time I reached home, I had sobered up, and it was a fortunate that I did because Mom was still waiting up for me. I hadn't called because to call from Ukiah to Fort Bragg was a long-distance call.

After the conclusion of track season in May, there was no reason for me to be at school when Louise got out of class. Louise and I went our separate ways. Though I enjoyed her company, she was too young to take to the senior ball or the junior prom, so I started dating girls my own age.

Chapter 6

Boot Camp

TWO WEEKS AFTER I graduated, the four of us received orders for naval reserve boot camp at Treasure Island in San Francisco Bay. We decided to all ride down to the Bay Area with Chick a day or so before we had to report to hang out in the city. After boot camp, we planned to take a road trip to Salt Lake City to visit Chick's aunt and uncle. We would all take turns driving and drive straight from Treasure Island to Salt Lake City, stay the night, and drive back home.

We packed some clothes and loaded our seabags into Chick's car and headed for San Francisco. We decided to go to the YMCA near the embarcadero and get rooms to stow our seabags. After checking in, we drove to the boardwalk at sunset beach where there was a large amusement park called Playland at the Beach. We spent all afternoon roaming through the park trying to meet city girls. We rode on all the rides and went through the fun house.

That evening, we returned to the YMCA to eat dinner. Afterward, we ventured out on Market Street on foot visiting the peep shows. The shops had signs posted that no one under twenty-one was allowed, but none of the proprietors checked our identification as long as we were spending money. We found metal machines with ornate cast bodies. By dropping a nickel into the slot and looking through a metal-rimmed viewing window, we watched cards flip at a rapid speed making them appear as a movie. These all had one theme: beautiful women with large breasts stripping and posing in seductive positions, many with full frontal nudity. Due to my younger appearance than my companions, I was carded in one of the establishments. After I produced my navy ID card, they let me in.

After hitting all the sights on Market Street, we headed back for the YMCA. On the way back, Steve (who was the youngest, but looked the oldest) went into a liquor store near the Y and purchased a bottle of apricot schnapps, which we consumed up in one of our rooms in the Y. The next morning, we reported into Treasure Island for duty.

Boot camp in the regular navy lasted twelve weeks, but in the reserves, it was condensed into two weeks of intense training designed to turn us into sailors. We lived in barracks on the west side of Treasure Island. Reveille was at 5:00 AM, and we fell out for inspection. Marine Corps drill instructors with their Smokey Bear hats put us through our physical training and obstacle courses in the morning. We were taught to march in formation and do the manual of arms with old Springfield rifles. My Boy Scout training made this easy for me to master. After lunch, navy personnel taught classes on being a sailor. This included going through a tear gas chamber and removing the gas mask before being allowed to exit. Another class was fighting fires aboard a simulated ship. We had to man hoses and extinguish the fires as hose teams. All meals were eaten in the chow hall and weren't too bad, but we were hungry from all the physical activity, and any food would have tasted good. In the evenings, we would shine our shoes and boots, write letters, and smoke. Most of the recruits were from the Bay Area. There were no black families in Fort Bragg, so this was my first experience with blacks. In the evening, a group of them from Oakland would stand outside the barracks, smoke, and sing a cappella harmony and clap their hands. They were quite entertaining.

After boot camp, the four of us drove to Salt Lake City. We took turns driving across Nevada at night and arrived in Utah the next morning. Chick's teenage cousins got us dates, and we all went to a big outdoor community pool. I had never seen a swimming pool that large. It was hot in Salt Lake City even at night, and we swam and played in the pool with our dates until it closed. After the pool, we said good night to our dates and slept on couches, chairs, and the floor. The next day, we drove back to California and arrived in Fort Bragg the following afternoon.

In August, the four of us went on a two-week reserve cruise. We received orders to a destroyer, the USS *Twining DD 540*, out of Treasure Island. We were all still E-1 (seaman recruits) and were assigned to the deck force berthing in the forecastle just aft of the chain locker with the deck apes. I spent a lot of time swabbing decks, chipping paint, repainting and polishing brass. We spent the entire first week tied up to the pier at Treasure Island.

When not on watch, we went on liberty into San Francisco. We caught the bus from TI to the embarcadero and then transferred to a trolley. We headed up Market Street to catch the cable car to Chinatown. We walked through Chinatown and then over to North Beach. Topless dancers were the headliners at all the clubs. One club, Big Al's, featured Carol Doda, whom I had read about in *Playboy* magazine. The barkers outside the clubs were trying to get anyone who passed by to come in and see the show. We never went into any of them; not that we didn't want to, but because we didn't have the money.

After a week in port, tied to the pier, we were informed that we were to embark on a cruise to San Diego. We all lined up in formation along the rails in our dress blues. The lines were cast off, and the ship proceeded through San Francisco Bay, past Alcatraz, and out under the Golden Gate. Once outside the bridge, we changed back into our dungarees for the trip south to San Diego. All the recruits stood watch at various other stations while underway. I was assigned as starboard lookout on the bridge. I received a pair of binoculars and was told to sweep the ocean with lenses and report everything and anything I saw on my side of the ship from the horizon to the ship. I never realized before that time that there was so much floating garbage on the ocean. Anything I spotted, I reported. Periodically I would be relieved of the watch and told to enter the bridge to steer the ship. It took a while to get the hang of it, but I soon learned to make only subtle adjustments to the course and stopped zigzagging. While under steam, we were on port and starboard duty, which meant we stood watch for four hours and then were off duty for four hours. It was great fun. Many of the recruits were seasick, but I had no problem. Chick also did fairly well, but Ed and Steve were so sick that they found it difficult to get out of their racks when not on duty.

When morning came, we were down the coast of California near Big Sur. The sea was smooth and the water blue. I was enjoying my cruise unlike some of the others. The next morning, we were off the coast of Orange County. While out swabbing the forecastle just after sunrise, I was amazed by the flying fish in our bow wake. Several of the fish landed on the deck. I retrieved them and threw them back overboard. Finally we entered San Diego harbor. As we entered, we again got into our dress uniforms and stood in formation until tied up at a pier.

Steve and Ed couldn't wait to get off the ship. When liberty came, I was on duty on the quarterdeck, so I was unable to accompany Steve, Ed, and Chick ashore. They left the ship, grabbed a taxi, and headed to downtown San Diego with the intention of getting drunk. Later that evening, they returned to ship, mission accomplished.

The next morning, I sought them out to hear about their trip to the beach. I found them all hung over, and all three of them sported fresh tattoos. I was fortunate to not have gone with them or I would probably have been in the same predicament. Steve and Ed got a little round-headed comic strip devil with a pitchfork and the words "Born to Raise Hell" on their forearms. Chick had gotten an anchor and "US Navy" on his.

While in San Diego, President Johnson came on the radio late one afternoon to announce that the United States was escalating their involvement in the conflict in Vietnam. The bridge put the radio on the intercom so that we could hear the speech. After the president concluded his words, a cheer went up from the crews of the ships moored around us.

The next day, we headed back to San Francisco. After leaving San Diego harbor, we had gun practice. My battle station was in one of the 5" 38s gun turrets loading the breech. After loading the projectile and powder, the breech closed. The gun was stationary during loading, but when it was ready to fire, fire control took over, and the guns remained steady as the ship rolled around them. From inside the turret it appeared as if the guns were moving. We were instructed to cover our ears and open our mouths to equalize the pressure on our eardrums. Then came the blast as the guns went off. As soon as the guns fired, they again became stationary relative to the ship, and we reloaded for another volley.

After securing from gun drill, we went back to our normal routine until that afternoon when we rendezvoused with a tanker to refuel underway. The ships came alongside, and lines were passed between the moving ships. Eventually the tanker was able to extend their hoses to us and the fuel was transferred into our fuel bunks. This process is very dangerous for both ships and takes a great deal of coordination between both crews. Finally the hoses were withdrawn and the lines cast off, and we proceeded on our way to Monterey Harbor, where we dropped anchor just before the sun went down. Before it got dark, we did a lifeboat drill and placed the boats in the water. They circled the ship and were retrieved. During the night, we weighed anchor and headed back to San Francisco.

Entering the Golden Gate, we sailed past Alcatraz and past Treasure Island. We continued east to Mare Island. We took on another load of ordinance for our guns. When we cast off, we steamed back through the bay and made a course for the Farallon Islands. The water was choppy, and the fog was thick. I was again on the bridge. It was a challenge to stay standing and looking through the binoculars. We again fired our guns at targets pulled by tugs. The blast of the guns was louder outside than in the turret. After securing from the drill, the ship turned back toward the bay. As we turned, the ship began steep rolls. The bridge watches were called into the bridge, and the incline indicator on the rear bulkhead of the bridge indicated the rolls were in excess of thirty degrees. On the way back to the bay, the sea got rougher, our bow submerged as we plowed through the waves. The entire forecastle was awash back to the weather doors.

After several hours, we reentered San Francisco Bay and steamed to Treasure Island and tied up. Our last day on board was spent scrubbing down the ship and polishing the brass. The captain held a ceremony, and all the seaman recruits were promoted to seaman apprentices.

The day we left the *Twining*, we decided to take one more trip through San Francisco. We parked Chick's car near the YMCA and took off for North Beach. After wandering around all afternoon, we decided to head back to the Y where Chick had his car parked and head back to Fort Bragg. We caught the trolley down Market Street to the bus Y. A sailor from another ship started talking to me. He gave me a sad story about how he was broke and asked if he could borrow $10 for a bus ticket to go home to Reno because his mom had just died. He assured me that if I gave him my address, he would pay me back next payday. I had $15 left, but I was headed home so, trusting him, I gave him the $10. My streetwise friends had a good laugh at me when I told them about it. Needless to say, I never heard from him again, and I was out the ten bucks.

Chapter 7

Going Regular Navy

BASED ON MY GCT/ARI (General Comprehensive Test / Arithmetic Test) score of 132, I qualified to attend either electronics technician or nuclear electronics technician schools. Though my scores showed I could go into either of those fields, I had no interest in either of them. I tried a basic electronics course my last semester in high school to see how I liked it. This only confirmed that I had no interest in that field. I had taken three years of biology and was more inclined to become a medic with the hope of eventually going to medical school after the navy.

I put in a request for Hospital Corps School, but the reserve unit commanding officer, Commander Broaddus (one of the county judges at the time), would not approve my request. I was called into his office and told that my latest request to go to Hospital Corps School had been denied and that I should reconsider my decision. This was very discouraging to me. I only had a short time left before they would send me to the school of their choice or I would end up on the deck force.

The next day, I sought out and asked for the advice of the navy recruiter. He assured me that I could get into Hospital Corps School if I enlisted in the regular navy. This meant that I would be required to serve four years active duty instead of the two required by the reserves. He also stated that I would not be required to repeat boot camp. At that point, I decided to "ship over" and make the navy my career.

Within a month, I was headed for processing at Oakland Induction Center. I was the only one who reported in uniform, everyone else was either committed to a branch of the service or draftees. I went through all the lines and exams with all the rest of the inductees. At one point, they had all the draftees line up. The sergeant in charge had the draftee line count by fours. He told all the ones, twos, and fours that they would be escorted to the army bus waiting outside. He then told the threes that they were destined for the Marines, and they were escorted to the waiting bus outside. After all the processing was completed, I was given orders to report to the US Naval Facility, Treasure Island, and directed to a bus stop where I could catch the bus to the base.

On Treasure Island, I was assigned to the transient unit for the time it took for them to enroll me into Hospital Corps School located in San Diego. Members of the transient unit were all waiting for further orders somewhere; some of the guys were being discharged, some dishonorably, some had washed out of boot camp. It was a strange mix of people. I stayed pretty much to myself. Each morning I checked my work assignment on the duty list posted in front of the master-at-arms. The jobs varied from boring to interesting. I buffed floors in the transient center. I had never used an electric floor buffer before, but soon discovered that to control it took a light touch lifting up or pressing down on the handle to change the direction of the rotating brush on the floor. I bussed and cleaned tables in the gee-dunk (snack bar). At night, I stood fire watch in empty buildings. I worked at the base grocery store stocking shelves. After the store opened, I bagged groceries for the customers. After the store closed, I cleaned scuff marks off the floors before they were mopped and buffed. I worked in the mess hall making pancakes, prepping food for the upcoming meals, and cleaning equipment in the bakery. I filed records in the base commander's office. I worked with public works digging ditches to repair water lines. Finally I landed a job in the base dispensary typing discharge medical exam forms. The corpsman in medical records stated that he was happy to get someone who could type with more than just one finger. I suggested that it would be easier for me to come in on a daily basis rather than having to train a new person each day. He agreed and sent a request to the transient master-at-arms to assign me to his office for the remainder of my stay on Treasure Island. I purchased caduceus patches and sewed them to my uniform above my seaman apprentice stripes to show that I was a Hospital Corpsman striker even though I was not yet officially in Corps School.

In addition to corresponding with my family, I started writing to some of the girls back home, trying to cultivate relationships via the US mail. Three or four of them responded, and I started getting regular letters from Carol Patterson, one of my classmates; Shirley Walters, a lower classman in my chorus class; and Anita Galli, a younger girl who hung out at the recreation center.

One of the guys in the transient barracks had an uncle who taught at Stanford in Palo Alto. We made the trip by bus on several weekends to hang out and watch football on TV. His aunt and uncle drank martinis and manhattans. That was my first exposure to drinking gin.

The first week in October, I received orders to Balboa Naval Hospital in San Diego for inclusion in the next class at Hospital Corps School. I received travel orders assigning me to a group of other sailors headed for San Diego. A petty officer first class was NCOIC (noncommissioned officer in charge). His responsibility was to assure that we all reached our destination on time. We boarded the bus to the San Francisco depot and boarded the train for Los Angles. The NCOIC presented us with two bottles of whiskey from his valise. He told us to stay in our staterooms because we were all under twenty-one. There were four bunks per stateroom as well as a toilet. The four of us did our best to consume the contents of the bottles. We sat and played cards and talked until we all went to sleep. When I awoke the next morning, the train was pulling into Oxnard. An hour or so later, we pulled into the Los Angles depot. It was still early, and we were the only ones out and about. While we were waiting, the NCOIC gave us all a bit of sage advice to remember. If we were ever placed in the position of NCOIC responsible for moving sailors from one location to another, they are much easier to control if given alcohol and confined to quarters. We boarded the train for San Diego several hours later. In San Diego, we split up, and I caught a taxi to the naval hospital located at the southeast side of Balboa Park, several blocks from the San Diego Zoo.

At the gate, the guard checked my orders and directed the taxi driver to the location of barracks. The buildings on the base were predominantly Spanish-style stucco exterior walls and tiled roofs. The base was located on a hillside. There was a narrow street running north and south below the main building. We passed by a tall gray building on the east side with a bridge five stories up that connected into the ground level of the pink building visible from the gate. The Grey Ghost was a twelve- or fourteen-story building with three basements that was painted navy gray. This building housed the new Balboa Naval Hospital wards and chow hall. We proceeded south until we reached my destination – a one-story barracks on a hilltop near the south end of the complex. I paid the cab and checked in and was assigned to company 14-65 scheduled to commence in several days. My weekend off before school started, one of my new buddies, Scott Jarvis from Whidbey Island, Washington, and I went to Mission Beach, rented surfboards, and spent the weekend surfing.

Before starting classes, we received several days of orientation. Chief petty officers lectured us on the Hospital Corps and its history. We viewed a movie that showed the various areas a corpsman could work in the navy. These were hospitals, hospital ships, the larger ships, overseas hospitals, and the Fleet Marine Force. We were also given information on avoiding "queers" downtown. We were also shown movies of battle wounds and the resulting plastic surgeries repairing damaged hands, legs, and faces. Lots of blood and gore, some of the guys got sick just watching the movies, but no one dropped out. After orientation was complete, we moved over to main side to the student barracks.

School started the next day with formation at 0630 on the road on the east side of the school. We marched to breakfast in formation. The entrance to the Gray Ghost mess hall was through a door located on the downhill side at level B2 into a stairwell and up into the serving line of the mess deck, which was on level B1. After eating, we returned individually to the barracks to prepare the berthing space and head for inspection. Once our bunks were made and the squad bay cleaned for inspection, we reported for muster at 0800.

From eight until noon, we attended classes with a smoke break every hour. At noon, we broke for lunch and reconvened at 1300 and attended classes until 1700. After classes were over, we spent an hour cleaning the classrooms and offices of the school before going to dinner at the chow hall. After dinner, we studied, wrote letters, and polished our shoes. This was the daily routine Monday through Saturday noon. The classes consisted of first aid, anatomy and physiology, patient care, pharmacology, and ABC warfare.

Shortly after starting classes, we were required to state our duty station preference after graduation. There was no guarantee, but the navy often tried to grant the request if a billet was available. Most of my fellow students requested duty close to their homes, but I had joined the navy not only for an education, but also to see the world. Yokosuka, Japan, sounded like a good place for me to start. My second and third choices were Europe and the Philippines.

Every Friday morning, we stood inspection. On Thursday after class, we headed for the barbershop for a haircut. The shop had only five chairs. Since we were not the only company standing inspection on Fridays, the shop was always filled with a hundred or so students waiting for a turn in the barber's chair. We had to take a number and wait to be called. When called, the barber would trim our hair and then shave the back of our necks. The process took less than five minutes and cost twenty-five cents. After several weeks wasting time on Thursday afternoon, I decided it would be quicker and easier to go in for a haircut on Wednesday evening after class when the barbershop was not so busy. The next Wednesday, I went in to the shop, and there were only seven or eight men waiting for a haircut. I was in and out in no time. During inspection on Friday, I was gigged for not having a haircut. Evidently, the one day's growth of peach fuzz on the back of my neck stood out like a sore thumb to the inspecting officer. From then on, I endured the Thursday afternoon shearing sessions.

After receiving our haircuts, on Thursday evening, we spent an hour holding field day on the barracks to prepare for Friday morning inspection, which was stricter than the daily inspections. The inspecting officer actually used a white glove to judge the cleanliness of the building.

When Thanksgiving came, we were given the day off from classes, but had to remain on base. We were served a traditional dinner of turkey, mashed potatoes, dressing, peas, salad, and pumpkin pie. It was my first time away from home, and I missed my family, but I enjoyed being with my fellow classmates.

In December, both students and instructors were given two weeks' Christmas leave. The Santa Ana winds stopped, and it began raining. It was still raining when I went to the Greyhound bus station to travel back to Fort Bragg. My only experience up to then with buses was the trip from Fort Bragg to San Francisco. I checked the prices of trips from San Diego to San Francisco. Not knowing the difference between express and regular bus trips, I chose the cheaper of the two. I had no idea when I boarded the bus that it was the "milk route" and stopped at every town on Highway 1 between San Diego and San Francisco. We stopped at every little town along the way, and the trip to San Francisco took a day and a half.

Arriving in San Francisco late in the evening the next day, I discovered at the bus station that there was a YMCA close to the bus station. I checked in for the night and was back at the Greyhound station the next day. The only bus for Fort Bragg left at 1300, but before leaving the terminal, I upgraded my return trip to San Diego to express.

Chapter 8

Graduation

ONCE HOME, I was more interested in hanging out with my friends than staying home visiting with family. I quickly located some of my friends who were still in town. This was an easy task; there were only a few areas to hang out – the recreation center, the show, or the bowling alley. I found most of the action was at the bowling alley and hung out there during the evenings. In addition to bowling, the facility had pool tables and a snack bar. There was also no restriction on smoking. Most of the kids that hung out there were two to three years younger than I, but I felt very comfortable around them. They looked up to me because I was in the navy.

During the day, I went to the beach at Hare Creek (which at that time had the best waves for surfing). A group of teens hung out there calling themselves the Hare Creek Surfers. My brother Steve and our cousins Mark Taubold, Kent and Ray Whited, and Bobby Paoli were part of the group of twenty or so members. Despite the rain, we went to the beach to surf. We stripped and donned pairs of Levi's jeans with the legs cut off, which we left at the beach. We dressed like the surfers we saw in the popular movies of the day. No one bothered to tell us that the weather was much warmer on the beaches of Southern California (only the kids from wealthy families could afford wet suits). We were tough, and basically did not know any different. I told them stories of surfers in the warm water of Southern California wearing wet suits.

We spent mornings and afternoons surfing and hanging out on the beach. When we arrived, the first order of business was to gather driftwood and build a bonfire. We surfed until numbness drove us from the water to stand by the bonfire to thaw out. For the most part, the Hare Creek Surfers purchased their boards with a partner, not only to defray the expense. While one guy was thawing out, the other could use the board. Once the feeling came back into our hands and feet, we were back into the water. So it went, surfing during the day and hanging out at the show and the bowling alley at night.

One evening, I walked into Noyo Bowl, and there was Louise. She was now a freshman in high school. Since she was from a strict First Baptist Church family, I knew she didn't usually hang out at the bowling alley. She informed me that some of her friends had told her that I was back in town. She was happy to see me. She told her parents that she needed to go to the library for a homework assignment. Her mother dropped her off, and she went inside until her mother drove away. When the coast was clear, she walked the four blocks to the bowling alley to see me. We talked briefly and then made a date to meet again at the theater before I had to return to San Diego. She then headed back to the library in time to be there before her mother arrived to retrieve her.

The next evening, we met at the State Theater and picked up where we had left off some seven months earlier. We enjoyed each other's company, made out in the darkened theater. Her mother picked her up after the movie, and I headed back to the bowling alley.

The rain continued to fall for the better part of the two weeks I was at home. It wasn't long after I arrived that the Navarro River rose over its banks flooding Highway 128. The other highways, 20 and 1, had mudslides that prevented travel, as did California Western Railroad. This isolated the town for over a week. I wasn't concerned, my friends and I were having a good time. If I was late getting back to San Diego, it would be due to circumstances beyond my control. All I would have to do is show a map of Mendocino County to explain my tardiness due to lack of transportation.

The day before the date I was scheduled to leave, the Navarro River subsided enough to allow the Greyhound bus through a circuitous route on a county road to Comptche. From there, we took Flynn Creek Road to connect with Highway 128 above the flooded area. The state highway road crews were still scraping the mud off the highway when the bus passed through the area. From then on, it was clear all the way to San Francisco. At the bus station, I located the express to San Diego and, after only fourteen hours, was back in San Diego. I then caught a cab back to Balboa Hospital and reported back into the barracks.

Most of us had returned from leave, and I was amazed at how I had missed all my navy buddies. The feeling seemed unanimous among us. It was a great reunion telling stories of our adventures while on leave. After lights-out, we kept talking and were reprimanded by the duty NCO of the school for keeping the rest of the barracks awake. When he departed, one of the guys passed the word that everyone was to jump out our bunks in unison and then immediately get back into bed. On the count of three, forty pairs of feet hit the deck, causing the building to shake. The duty officer came back again, but no one would confess to causing the commotion. This did not deter us. Someone went to the stairwell and rolled a metal bucket down the stairs. We all lay in our bunks laughing as the bucket crashed from step to step all the way down the stairwell. When the duty officer returned this time, he turned on the lights. He ordered us all outside immediately to stand formation in the cold night air. We were so glad to be back that everyone endured our punishment standing in our Skivvies shivering until 0100 when we were allowed to go back to the barracks to sleep a couple of hours before reveille. It was great to be back with our "real family."

Upon return to San Diego, I started to correspond with Louise on a regular basis.

January 5, 1965
Co.A-14-65
Hospital Corps School
San Diego, Calif.

Dearest Lou,

Well I made it down here again. It's sunny and warm as usual. I hear on the news that it's still raining up there.

The company hasn't changed a bit. Our first night back here we all got in trouble. It seems that we were all causing too much noise. All we did was jump up and down on the floor and woke up the company below us. Then one of my best friends decided to pound on a bucket, but I suggested he throw it down the stairs so he did. This caused the watch to go and get the Officer of the Day and he made everyone get up and go outside and stand at attention for an hour in the cold night. We finally got back to sleep at sometime after 1 AM. We call our company Easy Company because we don't do anything we don't have to in the way of work that is!!

Do you still want me to explain what "Hung like a mule" means? If so, I will.

I got some film for my camera today, so I'll have someone take a picture of me as soon as I can.

Where were you on New Year's Day? I came by to tell you good-bye, but you weren't home. How do you expect me to see you if you don't stay home?

Well I have got to go to the movie now. Don't forget to write.

Love always,
Russ

P.S. LDI 193 (Figure it out)

I took some pictures of the area and myself around the corps school and included them in this letter hoping to get her to reciprocate and send me some pictures of herself.

January 14, 1965

Dearest Lou,

I got your letter today and I was overjoyed to hear from you (cough, cough!)

Yes, I did see those shows, all three "I'd Rather Be Rich", The Lively Set" and "Topkapi". They were all good.

Hey, Hon, how about a picture of yourself so I can recollect your cute face and remember our good times together. (Like "Muscle Beach" and others). No one knows but you and me that's all that counts.

It is not cold at all down here now. Today we had 79 degrees F and its still winter!

Today I gave my first shot. We had to give them in nursing class and everybody had to give one and have one given to you. My arm doesn't hurt at all. Luckily!

Here's the picture I promised you, Doll, I'll have more later.

Boy that sure sounds like something Mike Bianchi would do, he is so dumb it's pitiful.

What do you mean the corner in the show is no good? I'll bet no one would see us, not even the usherettes. We could have all kinds of fun!

School is pretty good down here. We go to school from 7:30 AM to 3:40 PM. We have 7 classes a day. Look at the picture; see the building in back of me, that's the school upstairs. There are offices below; I am standing next to the barracks. Instead of having 2 stripes on my sleeve I have 3 now. How about that? More pay, too!

Well, Love, I got to go now almost time for taps, you know. Bye, Hon.

Love always
Russ xxx

P.S. Try this: LAGNAF

I had not been the least bit discreet in my letter writing. Louise discovered that I was writing to several other girls in town and let me know that she was not happy about that and some of the things I was saying to them in my letters. She also surmised that I was telling stories about our dates at the show, which I wasn't.

January 27, 1965

Dearest Lou,

 I was glad to get your letter, even if you did chew me out. You made me realize that I can't say things like that. The truth of it is, Love, I like you both about the same I mean it!! I think you are both real cool heads. I can't make up my mind on either of you so what can I do? I tried to tell you each individually that I have a great deal of love for both of you, but I never thought you'd read each other's letters, Hon. So forget what I wrote in the past, please, Doll!

 When I come home again we'll have to try out the show and see how things come out. XX

 What do you mean I'm dirty minded? I'm no different than you when it comes to things like that.

 Got to go now, Hon.

Love,
Russ

P.S. I'm not mad xxx

 OK, if you really want to know – Hung like a mule – An expression used to express the abnormal size of that part of the male body used during back seat fun and games.

  Soon I graduated from Corps School on February 18. I discovered I had received orders to the duty station I requested – naval hospital, Yokosuka, Japan. I was the only one in my graduating class to receive orders to a foreign country. I received a week's leave before having to report to Travis Air Force Base for a Military Air Transport Service (MATS) flight to Japan. The guys who drew stateside duty were transferred directly from San Diego to their new assignments without leave.

February 18, 1965

Dear Lou,

 By the time you get this letter I will be home, so, Hon, I'll tell all kinds of goodies then.

Love always,
Russ

  I had learned my lesson about taking the bus, and this time, I caught a Pacific Southwest Airways flight from San Diego to San Francisco costing me $35. Sure it cost three times as much as the bus, but it was faster. The flight took only an hour and a half. I arrived in San Francisco with enough time to take a bus from San Francisco International to the Greyhound bus terminal in time to catch the 1:00 PM bus home to Fort Bragg. By taking the plane, I arrived in Fort Bragg in less than ten hours from the time I left San Diego.

Arriving home, I prepared for my trip to Japan. I was limited to what I could pack in my seabag. I had to decide what civilian clothes I needed to take and what to leave behind. Several of my neighbors wanted to wish me bon voyage. Nello and Ester del Grosso lived across from our house on Oak Street. They had known me since I was very young and asked me over for cake and coffee. I also visited my retired second grade schoolteacher Effie Johnson for her personal insight into Japan. She and her husband, Carl, had been to Japan several years prior. She warned me about the stench in the air that greeted them when they got off the plane in Tokyo, but said they got used to it after a few days.

My last evening, Louise invited me to eat dinner at her house with her parents. Afterward, we went to the movies. Louise's parents, knowing I was about to leave the country, allowed her to go out with me as long as she got home by 10:00 PM. Our last night together I promised to continue writing her when I was in Japan.

Chapter 9

Flight to Japan

THE NEXT MORNING, Mom gave me a ride to the Greyhound bus station. Dad had said his good-byes earlier that morning before he left for work by shaking my hand and wishing me luck. Mom gave me a big hug. I was about to board the bus when Louise's mother's green '58 Chevy pulled up, and Louise jumped out and ran up to me. She hugged me tight and kissed me good-bye again as if she would never see me again. Finally, the bus driver interrupted by saying he was leaving, and I got on the bus. As the bus pulled away for the trip to Santa Rosa, Louise and my mother stood waving after the bus until it was out of sight.

In Santa Rosa, I transferred to a bus to Fairfield, California. Arriving in Fairfield, I got a taxi to the Travis Air Base. The guard at the gate checked my orders and gave the taxi driver directions to the transient barracks where I would spend the night. I checked in and got a bunk and locker to stow my seabag. When suppertime came, I ate in their chow hall and attended a movie before going to bed for the last time in the States until I returned in two years. I retired with both the exhilaration of going on an adventure and the overwhelming loneliness of knowing I would not see my family for the time I was gone.

The next day I went to the assigned area to board the MATS flight to Tachikawa Air Base, Japan. There were not only servicemen from all branches, but families with children of all ages. The plane waiting on the tarmac was a tri-tailed, four-engine, Lockheed Constellation C-121. A stairway led up into the plane as it waited for the passengers to leave the staging area. I walked across the tarmac to the bottom of the stairs and climbed the steps. At the top, I stopped momentarily to look back over the hills surrounding the Fairfield-Vacaville area. Entering the plane, I noticed that all the seats were turned to face the back of the plane, unlike those on the PSA flight from San Diego that faced forward. The section designated for enlisted men and their families was more cramped than that those assigned to the officers and their families. I had a seat on the aisle just forward of the wing. From my seat, I could see two of the four engines that would power the plane across the Pacific. After a short wait, the plane taxied out to the runway while the cabin crew instructed us on the importance of seat belts, oxygen masks, and flotation devices. By the time all the instructions were completed, it was our turn to take off. The plane turned onto the main runway and hesitated a moment. The props became louder as the engines revved up for takeoff. We began picking up speed, and soon we were airborne. It wasn't long until we were over the San Francisco Bay, headed for the Golden Gate. I watched as what I could see of California slipped away from view. Our destination was a short stop in Honolulu for our first refueling stop. The seats were cramped and close together. The back of the seat would only recline about three inches. Most of the young children on the flight soon became bored and cranky. Since my flying experience had been only the one PSA flight from San Diego, I was still fascinated by looking out the window, which I did the best that I could considering that I was on the aisle.

March 7, 1965
Somewhere over the Pacific
Between California and Hawaii

Dearest Lou,

Well, Hon, I'm on my way. We've been flying for 4 hours now and all I can see is water and clouds. We are flying at an elevation of 10,000 feet and are really moving along. It will take 5 more hours to reach Hawaii. (9 hours all together) and this is the short part of the trip. From Hawaii to Japan will take longer.

Last night I stayed at the transit barracks at Travis Air Force Base. Boy, that chow was lousy! This morning I had to wait 8 hours before my plane took off.

Please excuse my handwriting; it's kind of hard to writing in these small seats.

Did your parents say anything about Friday night? I hope not. It was fun reading books wasn't it?

Ah ha! I see that they are getting dinner ready now. I hope it is good. It looks like frozen something right now.

Boy, was that a good meal. We had salad, potatoes, vegetables, beef, bread and milk. It was worth waiting for.

Another couple of hours and we'll be in Hawaii. I think the whole Pacific is covered with clouds because the only way you can see the water is through breaks in the clouds. The clouds look like snow, but more like cotton. It's real neat; I wish you could be here to see them.

I still miss you very much, Love. I'll never forget for a moment that I love you and that you love me.

I'll write you another letter on the way to Japan. Oh, we stop at Wake Island also.

I love you,
Russ

I had watched the bright and colorful lights below in the cities on the islands as we made our landing approach. We landed at the military section of Honolulu International Airport. We were allowed off the plane while it refueled, but not out of the terminal. When the door was opened, a warm, humid breeze met us at the door. This was even warmer than San Diego. I strolled around the open-air gift shop and purchased a book on how to surf. I figured that I could always learn something to improve my techniques. I also purchased a copy of Samuel E. Martin's *Basic Japanese Conversation Dictionary*, 1957.

With the plane full of fuel, we boarded and took off on the next leg to the final refueling stop on Wake Island before heading on the last leg for Japan. Since this was my first long flight, I couldn't sleep. The seats were unyielding. I asked the soldier in the window seat if he would mind trading seats with me. He was agreeable. I occupied my time by reading my books and looking out the window at the cloud tops and stars above and the dark ocean below.

Finally dawn began lightening the sky, and I could see more out the window. There were fewer clouds now, and I could see the ocean far below and the occasional cargo ship with its long wake spreading out behind. Finally we came to Wake Island. Looking at it from the air, it consists of several small islands with a coral atoll in the middle. The larger island had a long airstrip on the southern leg.

We descended down through the clouds and soon were on the ground taxiing to the refueling area. We were allowed to go to the gift shop/snack bar. I ate breakfast and then walked around the island. The weather was overcast with a high ceiling, and the air was warm and humid. The highest portion of the island was only about twenty feet above sea level, but the majority of the island was only ten to fifteen feet above the ocean. I wandered down to the seawall constructed near the edge of the island to keep it from eroding away during storms and checked out the ocean. I then headed back to the snack bar/waiting room to wait for departure.

March 9, 1965
Wake Island

Dearest Louise,

I am now on Wake Island, what a small place! I think if I spit it would drown the whole island.

Hawaii was beautiful. Too bad it was night there, otherwise I would have taken some movies of the place. We landed at Honolulu and had a 3-hour wait there. I bought a book on surfing at the Base Exchange. We took off at 15 after midnight which would be 2: 15 AM Fort Bragg time.

Notice the date at the top of the page. We crossed the International Date Line sometime last night.

Well we just took off again. It was raining at the low levels below 7,000 feet, but now we are above the clouds again in the sunshine.

It is 8 AM on Wake, which is 1 PM Fort Bragg time.

I miss you very much.

I love you,
Russ xxx

Soon after leaving Wake Island, I noticed several of the crew left the cockpit one at a time to look out the side of the plane at one of the engines. I noticed that there was a thin brown mist flowing from the engine back across the wing. Soon the captain came on the PA system and announced that we would be turning back to Wake Island due to a minor mechanical problem that needed to be addressed. Soon the brown mist became thicker as it came from the engine flowing over the wing in steady stream. The pilot then turned the plane around and descended low over the water to dump fuel. Soon there were thick clouds of fuel leaving the plane on both sides. The number 2 engine was shut down, and the prop feathered for less resistance. As we flew back into Wake on three engines, I decided to add a postscript to the letter for dramatic effect.

PS
We've been up a little over an hour and the engine next to me (No. 2) is fouled up some way. There is fuel leaking out. We are going back to Wake to have it repaired, but before we do we have to go low over the ocean and dump fuel. For all we know this thing could crash. I want you to know what ever happens, always remember that I love you.

Russ

Returning to Wake Island, fire trucks waited at the end of the runway. As we crossed over them, they followed us as our plane touched down and continued following along as we taxied. This time, instead of turning into the terminal area, the plane continued to a remote area, where we were instructed to deplane in a "rapid but orderly manner." No stairs were there to greet us, but the pneumatic escape slides had been inflated, which allowed us to slide safely to the ground. The cabin attendants guided us away, and we assembled in a group away from the aircraft. Soon after leaving the plane, several gray busses moved quickly toward us. They pulled up next to the assembled groups. We boarded for the trip back to the terminal. On the way back, we made a stop at the main chow hall where we were invited to partake in an early lunch. This had a calming effect on those passengers who had become mildly upset during the emergency landing. After lunch, we transported back to the snack bar at the terminal. Several hours on the ground and the plane repairs on the plane were completed. It taxied up to the terminal. The announcement came to begin boarding to resume our flight to Japan. The remainder of the flight was uneventful.

It was night when we flew in over the coastline of Japan. I was intrigued by the size of the area covered with city lights from the coastline, extending as far as I could see. Seated backward, I could only see where we had already flown over. The view from the cockpit must have been spectacular. Forty-two hours after leaving Travis, the plane touched down twenty miles east of Tokyo at Tachikawa Air Base.

When the door opened, we were met by cold air. I was surprised that the air smelled like any other airport that we had been in. We deplaned and walked across the dark tarmac to the terminal. I checked in with the navy liaison office where they gave me information about transportation to Yokosuka. I had a three-hour wait before the bus arrived, so I walked around the terminal. I learned that Tachikawa was originally built as an Imperial Japanese Army airfield. It was the site of the first commercial airport for flights to Osaka. During World War II, it was the site of several aircraft-manufacturing plants and was bombed heavily. After the surrender of Japan, it was taken over by the US Air Force. Since there was not much else to do, I sat in one of the wooden theater-style seats to try and rest a bit before the bus arrived.

March 9, 1965
Tachikawa, Japan

Dearest Lou,
We made it to Japan. Right now I am at Tachikawa Air Force Base. Japan doesn't smell as bad as they say it does.
It is 11:45 PM right now, which is 5:45 AM in Fort Bragg. I have to wait until 4 AM until a bus gets here to take us to Yokosuka.
There is a TV here, but I can't understand a word it is saying, all in Japanese, which is natural since I'm in Japan.

Boy, Tokyo sure is big. It took us 30 minutes to fly over it. It looked different than Honolulu. Honolulu was real colorful, but Tokyo was just yellow lights and looked a lot different.

Oh, about the plane engine, we had a 3-hour delay on Wake because the No.2 engine blew out 2 spark plugs. The engine could have caught on fire.

They have a big map of the world on the wall here and guess what, they have Fort Bragg on it! See we are known internationally. Fort Bragg was on the map at the Hawaii terminal also.

I bought a book on surfing in Hawaii and after I read it I found out that I learned through my own experience the correct way of surfing, because the ways it says in there are exactly the way I found was best, so I feel pretty good finding out I do it the right way by learning through my own experience.

Well, Hon, I got to try and get some sleep now.

I love you,
Russ

The bus ride from Tachikawa to Yokosuka took three hours. Boarding the bus, the driver had asked to see my orders so that he knew where he was to deliver me. I went back and took a seat, and soon there were six or seven passengers on board, and we departed on the last part of the journey. We traveled out the gate of the base and into the strange world of Japan. The streets were dimly lit, and all the shops that lined the streets appeared to have garage-type metal doors in front of them with metal roofs over the sidewalks. Most of the writing was in Japanese characters, but occasionally there were letters on the signs of the shops. There were many stoplights along the road to Yokosuka. We traveled through what seemed to be an endless city. There were no gaps between the cities. Eventually I realized we were going through the city of Yokohama. The bus stopped at the naval base there and let off two of the passengers, and then we continued on to Yokosuka. It was just barely light when we came to the main gate of the base. The bus stopped, and a Marine boarded the bus to inspect our orders and check our identification before letting the bus through. Once we were cleared to enter, the bus took the first right turn after entering the gate, traveled down a tree-lined street, turned left, and stopped. The driver announced that I had reached my destination.

Chapter 10

First Day in Yokosuka

AFTER THE BUS drove away, I was standing in front of a walled-in area with trees along the street. A sign above the entryway arched over the street proclaiming that this was the Fleet Activities Hospital. I picked up my seabag and walked into the compound to the entrance with its two large wooden entry doors to the administrative section of the long two-story building.

Immediately inside the door, I found the master-at-arms' office and found a sleepy-looking sailor starting a pot of coffee. He greeted me and looked at my orders. The day crew would not arrive until eight, and so he gave me a temporary chow pass and directed me down the hall to the main hallway where I would find the mess hall. I walked down the hallway toward the dental clinic and made a left into the main hallway. The hallway was concrete, dimly lit, and looked about a quarter mile long. I passed cross hallways leading to various areas such as lab and x-ray, central sterile supply, and some of the doctors' offices. About halfway down the length of the hallway, I finally came to the mess hall. I entered to find a large room full of tables with a chow line. The line was very short, and in no time, I had a hearty breakfast in front of me.

After breakfast, I returned to the master-at-arms' office to check in. The day crew had just arrived, and they gave a chow pass, a liberty card, and a mailbox. I was given directions to the office of the nursing director. I was introduced to Commander Feeny (the head nurse) and assigned to the general medicine ward and was told to check in with the barracks master-at-arms before reporting to ward 3-B.

The Hospital Corps quarters were located at the opposite end of the hospital compound from where I was located. I picked up my seabag and was advised that the easiest way to get there was to go outside the building and follow the street signs. I walked out of the building and to the end of the wing housing the dental clinic and turned left. The street paralleled the hospital. A number of Quonset huts lined the opposite side of the street from the hospital. I passed the hospital's barbershop, small stores, and movie theater. Eventually I came to the Hospital Corps quarters, a two-story H-shaped building. I went to the lobby and found the barracks master-at-arms' office. I checked in with the first class boatswain's mate who had the badge of authority. He greeted me and briefed me on the laundry service that operated in the lobby during the day. A representative of Fuji Laundry welcomed me and presented me with a laundry bag. I was instructed that they had one-day service and asked me my preference on the amount of starch I wanted on my clothes.

I was then shown a berth down in the wing closest to the hospital on the first floor on the lower left leg of the letter *H*. I soon discovered that my room wasn't actually a room with four walls and a locking door, but a cubicle with eight-foot-high walls separating each cube. The wall of the building had a window for every cube. My cube contained a bunk bed, a desk, chair, and locker. A heavy curtain drawn across the front provided privacy. I stowed my gear, showered, and got into the uniform of the day.

I left the barracks and walked to the closest entryway on the main hallway of the hospital. I was between wings 6 and 7, so I headed back toward the mess hall until I found the medical ward located upstairs in the third wing. I found the office and reported for duty. Several corpsmen were sitting talking when I came in.

The ward next to the office consisted of a large open squad bay with hospital beds along each side of the room. There was a head at the back end of the ward and a separate section that had its own air handling system and air-conditioning for asthma patients. I was informed that the Tokyo Bay area was one of the worst places in the world for asthmatics. In addition to my routine duties on the ward, my job was to treat the asthmatics with a new machine called the Puritan Bennett intermittent positive pressure breathing (IPPB) machine. It was mounted on a large oxygen tank attached to a cart. A hose connected the machine to a manifold mounted on an arm. The manifold held a mouthpiece and a medication reservoir. I was shown how to mix the medications (Isuprel and Alevaire) and how to clean the equipment between patients.

There were also several nurses with the ranks of LTJG and Lt working in the office of the ward in case we needed to get medications from the narcotics locker when prescribed. I was shown lab slips and how to fill them out. It was made clear that I was at the bottom of the pecking order, and my work assignments would be those things that no one senior to me wanted to do. At the end of the day, I got off work and returned to my cube.

The barracks was now busy with off-duty corpsmen, and the curtain across the front of the cube provided visual privacy, but not auditory privacy. I overheard several other corpsmen talking about their lack of finances. One of them decided to introduce himself to the "new guy." He stood outside my closed curtain and requested permission to enter. I invited him into my cube. He introduced himself as JC Knight from North Carolina and that he worked in central sterile supply. He explained that he and his friends would be happy to show me the town but they were short on cash. If I gave him a loan until payday, he and his friends would be happy to accompany me and impart their knowledge on surviving the "alley." Having nothing better to do, I took him up on it.

The first item of information was that base personnel never wore their uniform on liberty. Only fleet sailors wore uniforms off the base. I donned my civilian clothes and headed for the main gate. At the gate, we presented our liberty passes and identification to the Marines on duty. They waved us through, and we walked out onto the main street of Yokosuka. Traffic filled the street. Taxis honked and weaved through the cars, motor scooters, bicycles, and pushcarts. Directly across the street from the main gate were souvenir shops, tailor shops, and art galleries. We crossed to the side of the street and walked south several blocks until we came to the Enlisted Men's Club Alliance, a three-story building with a large open patio area. It had originally been constructed as the officers club for the Imperial Japanese Navy. This building had a main gate leading into a large complex of bars, restaurants, movie theater, slot machine casino, and a small store to buy everything from cigarettes to cameras.

Inside the gate, JC then explained that the big bar on street level had happy hour from four until six when all drinks were ten cents each. A Japanese band was playing rock and roll, and Japanese women in short dresses were waiting on the tables. We found an empty table up front and ordered drinks. I ordered a Dutch beer I had never heard of – Heineken. We enjoyed the music and drinks until happy hour ended at 1800.

The next item of wisdom was never to go out after happy hour on an empty stomach. The club had several restaurants, and so we all had an Italian dinner. During dinner, we consumed several baskets full of bread to help soak up what we already had to drink.

After dinner, we proceeded across the patio to the package store where liquor was for sale. JC explained that liquor was cheaper if we bought it in the club and then take out into the Japanese clubs, where for a small "set-up" fee, the bar would serve you your drinks. Outside, the store had a display case of the types of liquor that was available with their prices. A fifth of Smirnoff vodka was only 75¢. A bottle of 151-proof Ron Rico rum was about $3.50. We went in and told the attendant at the counter what we wanted to buy. He sent one of his assistants back to the storeroom to retrieve the requested item while we paid for it. That night, we purchased a case of warm Olympia beer in bottles for $2.15 (9¢ per bottle). With the desired libation now in hand, we walked out of the Club Alliance onto the street and turned left.

JC began my orientation tour of the "alley." Before heading back into the alley behind the Club Alliance, he pointed up to the street that intersected with the main street and headed up the hill. He said there were clubs up there in the area called the Jungle. I was warned never to go up there alone because those clubs were for blacks only, and anyone who was not black got unmercifully beaten if they entered any of the establishments.

We then turned left and walked along the south side of the Club Alliance to another street directly behind. JC brought my attention to the open sewers called "benjo ditches." These were concrete lined on the tops and sides but were not covered except for in high-traffic areas.

We started at the south end of Honcho known as Submarine Alley and walked north. JC advised me that the bars at this end catered exclusively to submariners. We were not welcome in those bars unless we wanted to fight.

We continued to walk along the street past souvenir shops, tailors, and bars. JC explained that each bar had its own personality – some played jazz, some rock and roll, some country and western. The entire area was a mass of bars and gift shops catering to the Seventh Fleet. Several blocks later, we came to a bar called Honky Tonk where JC and his buddies hung out. There was no music, but was set up more for conversation.

The entire bar staff greeted us when we walked through the door. The woman in charge of the floor ushered us to JC's favorite booth. The girls gathered around us and took each of us by the arm and sat with us in the booth. The bar manager came over; JC gave him three hundred yen. He took our case of Olympia in their walk-in refrigerator behind the bar. He came out with four ice-cold Olympias, and a waitress them to our table and handed JC a ticket that had "Olympia" written at the top and the date. Also included on the ticket were numbers from 24 to 1. Numbers 24, 23, 22, and 21 crossed off. JC explained that the ticket was good for three days. Any beer not consumed after three days belonged to the bar. The same rule applied to liquor except the bottle was marked with the date it was received behind the bar.

Now that we had our drinks in front of us, the girls solicited us to buy them a drink. Their drinks were usually tea or watered-down liquor. JC informed the girls that it was my first liberty in Japan. They began teaching me Japanese rules of the bars on the alley. When we paid for their drink, we were actually paying for their company. If we wanted to be alone, just tell them, and they would find someone else who would. The navy regulated all the bars and brothels in Yokosuka. Bars were not brothels. Brothels were separate businesses where all the girls were prostitutes. Bar hostesses were considered higher class than the brothel prostitutes. Not all girls working in bars were prostitutes, but most were working as independents. Bar hostesses could not leave the bar while on duty unless the bar was paid a fee. The amount of the fee was based on the girls earning potential for the evening. The bar manager based the "buyout" price on how busy the bar was that evening. The more the clients and the brisker the business, the more it cost to buy the girl out of the bar. The bar was not going to lose any money because a girl wanted to make a few bucks on the side. On slow nights, the basic buyout fee was a thousand yen; but on a busy night, it could be as much as ten thousand yen. They also said the bars valued base sailors and appreciated them as regulars during the slow times; but when the fleet was in, they were committed to making money for the bar. When the fleet was in, regulars would be treated politely, but generally ignored.

The girls said they liked steady boyfriends that were base sailors. If we had a steady girlfriend, we should wait until closing time and then take the girl home; this would save us money, but usually the girls would also expect presents from the base exchange. These could be anything from jewelry to household appliances.

We had a lively time talking and joking with the girls. They were helpful at teaching me basic Japanese phrases helpful in everyday life.

Several hours passed when the shore patrol entered on routine rounds checking the bars to make sure all military personnel were behaving themselves. The bar was full, but they walked right up to our booth. One of them asked to see my identification. They passed my military ID among them shining their flashlight through it, checking to see if it was altered or forged. Finally satisfied that it was authentic, they handed it back to me and left without a word. To drink legally in Japan, military personnel have to be at least eighteen. They were sure that they had just busted an underage military dependent out on the town. Everyone thought it was a great joke, and the girls started calling me *aka-chan*, which is an endearing Japanese term for *baby*.

Finally at 11:00 PM, the bar announced last call. None of us were petty officers, and the rules of the base were that if you had a rank below E-4, you could not stay off base past midnight. This is known as Cinderella Liberty. We finished off our ticket with one last round before walking back to the barracks.

10 Mar 65
Yokosuka, Japan

Dearest Louise,
    First day is done with. This place is OK. I am working a general medicine ward. There is hardly anything to do. I go to work at 7:00 AM and get off at 3:30 PM this week, next week I go on the PM shift, which is from 3:00 to 11:30 PM.
    Today is warmer than yesterday. It's about 55 degrees out and sunny.
    Last night a bunch of guys and I went out into town. Boy what a hole! The main street is just wide enough for two cars to pass each other. Then we went to one of the back streets, where all the bars and "bad girl" houses are.

The streets are like alleys back there, it would be hard to drive though them, but these "streets" are just as brightly lit as main street if not more. I think I'm going to like Japan.

I miss you very much like I said before. I wish you were with me. I know you'd like it here. Maybe someday you can be with me. And we won't have to be apart again.

Boy you can get things cheap here. There are 360 Yen to a dollar, so you can see why things are so cheap.

Well got to go now always remember I love you.

Sayonara,
Russ
xxoxo

Chapter 11

Daily Life in Japan

TWO DAYS LATER, it was payday. JC, true to his word, paid back the money he owed me. By the weekend, I had met several other guys who were more into Japan for things other than what the alley had to offer. On Saturday, a group of my new friends invited me to travel with them on the train to Kamakura about ten miles from the base. We took a taxi to the train station and bought our tickets and waited on the platform until the train pulled in. This was my first experience with the commuter train travel. The train resembled the pictures of the trains on the subway system in New York, except they had overhead electric wires that powered the train along its route and were not underground. Vendors sold cigarettes, chewing gum and candy, and snacks of roasted nuts, crackers, and dried squid.

When the train arrived, the doors opened; and after the passengers exited, we boarded. This was the end of the line; the train reversed direction and proceeded toward our destination with stops in Taura, Higashi-Zushi, Zushi, and finally Kamakura.

We caught a cab for the *daibutsu* in the Kōtoku-in Temple. Inside the temple was a raised area where an enormous bronze statue of Buddha has sat since the twelfth century. Some of the Japanese visitors were praying to the shrines. They clapped several times, placed their hands together, and bowed several times. Some bought sticks of incense and placed them on the altar, others simply left monetary donations. Around the back of the statue was the entrance to the inside of the statue. For a small fee, we entered the interior of the enormous statue. Inside was another shrine with incense.

After we left the shrine, we caught a train on a spur line to Enoshima, the island where the Olympic yacht races were held in 1964. We walked across the bridge to the island and up a very steep street lined with shops to the top of the island. On our way down, we stopped in a shop and had a drink of green tea and talked to the locals as best we could. By the time we left, it had gotten dark, so we headed back to base by train.

On Sunday, a couple of my new friends and I again caught the train to Kamakura. Leaving the train station, we walked to Tsurugaoka Hachiman-g Shrine where we spent several hours roaming around. Shrines and temples were located in a wooded area on a hillside. There were steep stone steps leading up to one of the larger shrines. It was then that I decided that one of my first major purchases would be a good camera.

After leaving the shrine, we wandered around through the town. In Kamakura, we rarely saw any other Americans. We ate from the street vendor carts and shops. That evening, we went into a restaurant to have a typical Japanese dinner. Entering the restaurant, we were greeted by all the employees bowing low and encouraging us to take off our shoes. We were shown to one of the low tables. We kneeled on opposite sides of the table; a young lady kneeled at the table on the aisle. We were presented with hot towels on a small lacquered tray to wash our hands and face. Then we were served bottles of Kirin Beer and small soy sauce-flavored crackers with an occasional dried green pea covered with wasabi. After several beers, the meal courses were delivered to the table starting with a delicious soup. Next came a variety of delicious foods including prawns, fish, chicken, pork, and beef. Dessert consisted of various baked goods and sweet fruit. Throughout the dinner, we were treated like royalty. Every time we took a sip of beer, we had to give a toast by raising our glass and saying *kampai* and drinking the entire contents of the glass, which was immediately filled. To stop the flow of beer, the glass had to be emptied and immediately set down upside down to keep it from being filled again. After dinner, we were offered hot sake until we could drink no more and it was time to return to the base.

15 Mar 65

Dearest Lou,

Well, today is my 6th day here. The more I'm here, the better I like it, but I still miss you, Hon.

The other day a bunch of us went to see the Great Buddha in Kamakura. What a statue! It is all made of bronze. I guess you've seen pictures of it before. Well, we went there and paid 10 yen to go inside it, which is really an experience. (10 yen is about 4 cents).

It's real cheap to travel around here. You can get on a train and for 40 Yen you can go all over the place.

After we went to the Buddha, we went to Enoshima Island. That place is honey combed with caves. They have at least one stone god in each cave and plenty more big ones on top the ground. This place was where they held the Olympic yacht races this last summer.

Yesterday we went to Kamakura near where the Buddha is and we went to some of the temples and then to a restaurant where they have girls dressed in kimonos and they wait on you hand and foot. To them it is a sin for you to feed yourself, pour your own drink, or anything like that. One of the guys started to light a cigarette and one of the girls got all bent out of shape because she was supposed to light it. We were teaching them English and they were teaching us Japanese. It's real neat because no one in the place spoke English at all. A Japanese man came up to one of the guys and was looking at his lighter and liked it, so he gave it to him along with a pack of American cigarettes. The man immediately left and came back later with a real nice silk scarf he had gone down and bought and gave it to the guy. I think we made some more friends for America last night. When we left the people who owned the place all walked us to the door and as we went out they all bowed to us and said "Sayonara". That's what I call real true Japanese hospitality.

Well, Love; I got to go eat chow now. Remember that I love you very much and miss you greatly.

I love you,
Russ
Xoxoxoxo

Life began to fall into a pattern for me. Working days and going out when I got off duty. I ate in the mess hall to save money. After dinner, I went out to the Club Alliance for happy hour. I would then go to the movie. If I happened to miss one of the movies, I could always see it at one of the other theaters, at the hospital, or at the Benny Decker Theater. The movies made the rounds of each. I was able to see all the new releases. After the movie was out, I would drop by the package store and purchase a case of Olympia and take it to the Honky Tonk bar. The girls told me when I finished the beer to peel off the label. On the back of the Olympia label was a series of dots – as few as one and as many as four. A label with four dots was considered good luck. I saved all my four-dot labels, and after several months, I had a stack of over seventy in my desk drawer before I threw them all in the trash.

I saved enough money to purchase a camera and started taking pictures when I traveled. It wasn't long before I became familiar with the area. When I finished a roll of film, I took it to the gift shop at the hospital, and the film was sent to the photo lab across base where it was developed, and the prints came back to be picked up the next day.

Until the first part of May, I had my cubicle all to myself. One day I got off work to find I had a cube mate. Carl Darsey was from Tallahassee, Florida, and was a couple years older than me. He resembled Marlon Brando, but thinner. We immediately became good friends. Carl had little interest in going off base. His girlfriend Linda was still back in Florida. She was a senior and was due to graduate in June. He devoted much of his spare time working through the red tape of getting her to Japan. He planned to bring her to Japan and marry her upon her arrival.

Carl was madly in love with Linda, and I got caught up in the process and emotions. I was writing to several girls back home, and my letters to them started getting more intimate. Louise was the only one who responded to my loneliness, so I started asking her for photos, and after a while, I asked her to go steady. She agreed, and I sent her my high school class ring, which she wore on a chain around her neck. We became more intimate and began planning for our future after she graduated from high school.

June 10, 1965

Dear Louise,

As it gets more and more toward summer I miss you more and more. I think of all the things we could do together, beaches, dances, or just being together. Oh, well it just can't be this summer. My buddy who sleeps in the same cube as I do is getting married; his fiancé is coming over from Florida.

I got transferred to a different ward again. This one is orthopedics (broken bones, new type) most of our 22 patients are bed patients and we all run ourselves to exhaustion every time we go to work.

I am buying a Honda 50, which costs $80, so I'm spreading the payments over 3 paydays. That leaves me with about $10 for 2 weeks to live on.

On the 20th is the Hospital Corps 67th anniversary, which is going to be a real blast. We're having a picnic with everything anyone could want.

I had some pictures taken of me in Kamakura Sunday, so they will probably be ready soon.

What size clothes do you wear? I ask because I would like to get you some if you want (kimonos, etc.)

My buddy just handed me a picture of me he took last week when he first got his camera. He didn't have the lens open enough, so all you can see is an outline of me, my glasses, lamp, and cluttered desk. Sorry, but it's the best I can do until the other pictures get in. It was about 5PM and was cloudy out, so it didn't expose enough.

Well, I've got to get some sleep now it is 1:05 AM. How 'bout that, I stay up to this time to write a letter, it must be love that keeps me awake.

Love always
Russ

p.s. I dream of you almost every night. I love you very much, more each day. I still miss you.

It was boring to go out and sit in the same bars and listen to the same jokes and antics night after night. I started looking for other things to do. I purchased an electric guitar and amplifier and started honing my guitar skills. I soon was invited to join a band by one of the other corpsmen. After I purchased my Honda 50, I started to broaden my activities, and my trips to the alley decreased.

On the nineteenth of June, the hospital celebrated the Hospital Corps' birthday by throwing a party at one of the parks on base. There was beer on tap and lots of food available. We played touch football all afternoon and generally had a good time.

As Carl's wedding date approached, I got more involved with the preparations. I went with him to look at a house near Hayama beach where the navy had authorized him to live in off-base housing. It was a quaint little place on a hill with a sliding front door. With the exception of the kitchen, it was Japanese style. The floor was covered with tatami mats. It was close to the beach; I could walk from their house to go surfing when I visited them.

June 22, 1965

Dear Louise,

I'm glad that you finally sent me a picture of yourself. It turned me on just to see you again, even if it was just a picture.

I belong to a band now. They needed another guitar player and so I got the job. We are called the "Disciples". There are 3 guys who are still in school, whose fathers are in the Navy, another corpsman, and myself. We play at the teen clubs on base here and in Yokohama, and at a Japanese teen club next weekend. We are also scheduled to play at one of the large hotels here in Yokosuka. Pretty good, huh?

Yes we did have a blast on the 20th. It was one big booze party. It started at noon and lasted until it got dark. Needless to say we finally ran out of beer. Everyone was stoned, the commanding officer (he's a rear admiral) the doctors, nurses corpsmen and the wives. Boy I'll never do that again until next year! You should have seen this one nurse! She got the wrong door and walked into the men's lavatory instead of the women's. We had a band there and were dancing and all kinds of games, football, baseball, tug of war, etc. Boy, was I sore all over the next day!

That size clothes is American size I have to know in inches and convert them into centimeters before buying you anything, because the Japanese just don't go by American sizes, like I wear a size 95 shirt and coat.

I forgot to send my brother my money for a copy of <u>Breath of Ocean</u> before it was too late, so I didn't get one. Sorry 'bought that.

My friend says "thanks" for the congratulations. He said for me to bring you over and we could make it a double wedding, but I had to explain that I would like it to be that way, but you are still in school. He said, "Well, she can finish over here." I said that your parents probably wouldn't let you get married until you were out of school, let alone come to Japan. Oh well, wishful thinking. Some day, though, our day will come.

Every night I dream of you especially of our last couple nights together. To put it frankly, you turn me on so far I can't turn off. I mean it. In fact some of my dreams are of getting married, our honeymoon, and all that good stuff. I wish it were true right now.

Well, I have to go now it is 2 AM and I have to get up tomorrow and go to band practice at 9 AM. Bye for now, Hon, in case you don't know it, I love you so much it hurts to be this far apart. I'll be dreaming of you in a little while.

Love always,
Russ

Chapter 12

Marine Casualties from Vietnam

ON THE FOURTH of July, the base had a fireworks display from a barge on Tokyo Bay. The fireworks show lasted for two hours and was the most spectacular show I have ever seen before or since. That night, I started working the graveyard shift on the ward from 11:00 PM until 7:30 AM.

Working nights gave me the opportunity to hang out at the swimming pool across the street from the Hospital Corps quarters, but prevented my continuing with the band. When I got off work at seven thirty, I ate breakfast and got a couple hours' sleep then spend most of the day at the pool swimming and diving. Around three, I returned to the barracks to nap until dinner, followed by a trip to the movie. Afterward, I took another nap before reporting to work.

In August, we started to get hit by typhoons. The base went on alert. When the wind started blowing, we secured all items that could be blown away. At the next level, windows were covered with storm shutters to prevent them from breaking. At the highest level, we were restricted to quarters with minimum movement between the barracks and the hospital.

On August 17, the Marines in Vietnam launched their first major campaign with Operation Starlite. In the midst of a typhoon alert, we spent several days preparing for the influx of casualties. Additional hospital beds were brought in from storage and assembled. Once assembled, they were delivered to the wards and placed side by side, separated only by a bedside cabinet, providing only about eighteen inches between beds. There ended up being four rows of beds with twenty-five beds in each row, one along each wall the length of the ward, and then a double row down the center of the ward with the heads of the beds together.

Six days after the beginning of Starlite, several hundred casualties from Vietnam arrived by bus from Tachikawa, and soon our wards were filled with wounded Marines. In addition to the wounded that were admitted to the surgical and orthopedic wards, the medical ward filled up with falciparum malaria patients.

23 Aug 65

Dearest Louise,

Things are really jumping now. As you may have read in the paper, we are being hit by typhoon Lucy. It has been raining since Saturday morning. The wind is blowing about 55-65 MPH and to top it all off the temperature is near 90 during the day and near 80 at night. I've never seen anything like this. I was going to go surfing Saturday and stay at the beach all night because that was my night off. I was taking a shower, when they passed the word that liberty was secured. Boy, that made me mad! Everyone was restricted to base. Then later we got the word that we had to be in uniform, so we all got into our uniforms. I went to sleep until evening chow. Later they let us have base liberty. Wow, we got to go to the movie, thrills! The "Glen Miller Story" was playing. Then I went back to the barracks and went to sleep and dreamed of you.

Yesterday we were still restricted to base but for 2 reasons this time: 1) The typhoon and 2) Air evacuation of patients from Viet Nam. They sure were in bad shape all shot up and all it was neat.

There was an article about that 8-year-old kid drowning at Caspar in the newspaper over here. The paper must have been hurting for news if it prints things that happen in the Fort Bragg area.

I found out how much of a pay raise I got. I used to get $109 a month, now I am getting $165 thanks to LBJ. He sure is a good guy!

I sure do love you, dearest one. You are all I live for. It is a great thing to know that you love me too. I can't wait for the day when I get home and hold you in my arms and kiss your sweet lips. I love you so much it hurts to be far away from you. I know our love will last forever. I thought about what you said about my bunk being big enough for the both of us and how you wanted to be in it with me, so now I sleep with your picture under my pillow. I guess that's about the best I can do for now, I wish your picture was you and not just a picture.

I guess that's about it for now. Hope to hear from you soon.

I love you,
Russ

With the arrival of the casualties from Vietnam, I became familiar with the various Marine units like 2/4, 3/3, and 3/7. The Marines passed the time telling war stories that glorified their actions. Many of them encouraged the corpsmen to volunteer to be a combat corpsman. They told us that corpsmen got more respect from the Marines than we could ever receive working in a naval hospital or being on board a ship. I enjoyed working with the Marines as patients. Even those who had been wounded were still full of bravado and confidence. Most couldn't wait to get back into combat with their units. Some of the corpsmen at the hospital started volunteering to go to Vietnam. Though I admired them for being so gung ho, I was not willing to cut my time in Japan short by volunteering to go to Vietnam. However, I did consider it as a possibility when it was time for me to leave Japan in 1967.

30 Aug 65

Dear Louise,

I don't care if you go out with someone else, I don't expect you to stay home and do nothing while I'm over here, but always remember that you belong to me and I belong to you.

I had a dream last night, wishful thinking, I guess. I dreamed you came over all of a sudden and the first I knew of it was when the Barracks Master-at-Arms called me over the loudspeaker and said I had a visitor in the lobby. When I went down there, there you were as big as life standing there. I stood there a moment, then you saw me and rushed to me crying, we kissed and all the good stuff people in love do when they haven't seen each other in a long time. You said you were crying because you couldn't stand living in America without me and that you just had to come to Japan to be with me. Well, my buddy said we could get married with he and his fiancé, which we did. Then we went on our honeymoon way out in the boonies near Mt. Fuji. It was so perfect and lovely that I didn't want to wake up, but I did because my buddy was slapping my leg trying to wake me up. Oh well, I guess all dreams have to come to an end sometime no matter how good they seem. I only hope that it is so in real life.

I found out I goofed when I told you I got extended, it was just the guys who were supposed to get out next month, so I will be home in 18 months if all goes well.

Yes, I got the St. Christopher; I am wearing it right now. Haven't had it off since the day I got it. I wear it as long as we love each other, which I hope will be forever.

My buddy volunteered for Vietnam duty the other day and wants me to go to, I told him that I would like to, but I love you too much to get killed down there, never seeing, holding or being with you again. I won't volunteer, but if they send me I guess there is nothing I can do about it.

I guess school starts again in a couple of weeks. Hope you like High School as well as I did.

Well, I guess that's it for now. I need you more each day. Every time I go to bed I take your picture out from under my pillow and look at you for a few minutes and kiss you goodnight and when I wake up I do the same.

I love you,
Russ

P.S. You are the only person in the world for me. I love you so much; I wish you were here with me right now. From the bottom of my heart, I love you.

Chapter 13

Reunion of Homeboys

ONE MORNING WHEN I got off duty and was walking down the long passageway to the chow hall for breakfast, someone behind me called my name. I turned around and was surprised to see it was Steve Kaden from Fort Bragg. He had been admitted to the hospital the night before and was also headed for the mess hall. Over breakfast, he brought me up to date on what all our friends were doing. I asked him why he was in the hospital, and he gave me one of his usual self-aggrandizing stories, which sounded too far-fetched. He was admitted to the neuropsychiatric ward for evaluation. I visited the ward later in the day and reviewed his chart before going in to visit him. As I suspected, the story he told me was not even close to the truth.

Steve's best friend in Fort Bragg, Ed Hall, was stationed in Yokohama. I called him and told him that Steve was in the hospital, and he came to visit. When Ed arrived the next day, he informed us that his cousin Doug Smith, also from Fort Bragg, was in port on the USS *Maddox*. Since Steve was a patient, he could only leave the hospital if accompanied by a corpsman, and could not leave the base. We arranged a reunion for the four of us at one of the base snack bars on the other side of the base near the ship. Doug gave us a tour of his ship, and then we returned to the hospital, and Ed went back to Yokohama.

17 Sep 65

Dearest Louie,

You'll never guess who is a patient in the hospital here – Steve Kaden! He said he got hit in the head by a block and tackle when they were loading his ship in Okinawa. Unluckily he had a safety hat on and all that happened was he blacked out and doesn't remember what happened for 7 hours after that. I read in his records that he said he threw a marine overboard. They have him on the neuropsychiatric ward examining his brain. Looks like they have a long job ahead of them, they have to find it first. Kaden, Ed Hall and I were all together the other day and we went to one of the ships here to see Doug Smith, Ed's cousin, who is also from Fort Bragg. Chick Ash is on his way over on a ship and will be here next month, then there will be five of us from Fort Bragg here, look out Japan!

Things are about the same around here. It is getting colder now it gets as low as 65 degrees at the lowest. After getting used to the heat, 65 seems cold, we wear jackets on days like this.

Right now we are about to have another typhoon. These things are getting to be routine. This is the 21st one we've had this year. They call it Trix; the last one was typhoon Shirley. Seems like we have one a week.

How do you like being a sophomore? Who are your teachers? Are you in the new school yet?

I sure do miss you. What really made me miss you more was when I was helping my buddy work on his house and yard I could imagine us living there and all the fun we would have together for the rest of our lives.

I have to go now; it's time for me to wake up the patients. I love you.

Love,
Russ

Things were pretty much routine, except for Kaden being in the hospital. In order for him to leave the hospital compound, he had to be accompanied by a corpsman. He was bored and came looking for me on a daily basis. He would wander from the hospital into the corps quarters and wake me up after I only had several hours' sleep, wanting me to go with him so he could wander around the base. I finally had to report him as being a nuisance, and he was confined to the ward.

During this time, his brother Carlton, a corpsman with a Marine unit in Da Nang, Vietnam, got emergency leave to visit his brother in the hospital in Yokosuka. Carlton was two years older than me. After he visited with Steve, he invited me to go out to dinner in a little restaurant he discovered on a previous trip to Yokosuka. We headed out to a suburb of Yokosuka where there were no Americans. When we arrived, the owner and staff was pleased to see him again. During dinner, he told me how great it was to be stationed with the Marines.

After several weeks of evaluation, Steve was determined to be unfit for duty and sent back to the States for a medical discharge.

Back in Fort Bragg, the movie *The Russians Are Coming, the Russians Are Coming* was being filmed, and the locals were invited to the theater to watch the "dailies" where all the day's film was reviewed by the director. Louise attended many of them and actually met some of the stars.

7 Oct 65

Dear Louie,

Sure is good to get a letter once in a while. I guess school has you pretty busy, so I understand.

Steve Kaden finally left (whew)! He sure was a nuisance. I'd work all night and go back and hit the sack and around 10 AM here he came, pounding on my bed and wanting me to go here or take him there just to talk. After he left I got 2 days of 14 hours per day of sleep. I was exhausted. Steve is a real honest medical "nut". He was on the psychiatric ward. No kidding. He had a diagnosis of paranoid reaction, which is a feeling the person has where he thinks everyone is against him. The truth finally came out about him. He was on a ship and wouldn't take a shower and when he got to where he stunk too much for the rest of the crew to stand him they gave him a GI shower and scrubbed him down. After that he just curled up in his bunk in the fetal position and was so withdrawn that he wouldn't get out of his bunk. They transferred him to a shrink and he gave them the story of being hit in the head and going crazy and throwing a Marine overboard. What a weirdo!

Life with me is the same old thing. Go to work at 11 PM work until 7 AM and go back to sleep until about 3 or 4 PM and then goof around until it is time to go to work again. I've been working nights for 3 months and 3 days now, it sure doesn't seem that long ago I started.

The weather is getting cooler we had a temperature of 45 degrees the other morning. Next month it starts to snow, so they say. The seasons sure change fast around here. One day it is warm and then the next is cold and you are headed toward winter.

Sounds like you are having quite a time watching them film the movie. What do they do when they are filming it? I'll bet you really treasure Brian Keith's autograph don't you.

Right now on the radio the first game of the World Series is starting. We are getting it from the states by short wave to the Far East Network, which is run by the Armed Forces. It is just like KDAC. Plays good music for 1 hour a day and rest is junk, like I say, just like KDAC.

Well, that's about it for now, except that I love you. Oh, when are you getting your pictures? I want one you know.

Here is some money from Vietnam. One of my patients took it off a dead Viet Cong and gave it to me and here is some of my hair just to show you how light it is. I sure do love you I love you more than anything in the world. I still sleep with your picture under my pillow and wish it were you with me there. I still wear the St. Chris also, I always will.

I love you,
Russ

Chapter 14

Italian Gardens

WE WERE RECEIVING casualties on a regular basis now from Vietnam. I was assigned to an orthopedic rehab ward. The patients were mostly Marines with bone injuries that were healed enough, allowing them to go on work parties around the hospital compound during the day. As soon as the patient had recovered enough to be up out of bed, they were assigned work to keep them occupied.

After Carl and Linda were married, I acquired a new roommate. He was a nice guy, but did not go off base much, and he and I were not close. I started hanging out with my Marine patients, and when they got well enough to go on liberty, I started showing them the town. Most of the time they had back pay coming to them, and some wanted to do some sightseeing while they were in Japan. I took it on myself to show them Japan.

5 Nov 65

Dearest Louise,
This last weekend we went up to Tokyo. I finally made it up there. It's big! A patient of mine (a Marine who got shot in Vietnam) and I took a train up there. He had all the money so I wasn't arguing about where we went. When we got up there we went to the USO to get oriented. We decided to just wander around the Ginza (a shopping district near by). It was raining and we got

pretty wet but we saw quite a bit. Then we went back to Yokohama to a dance and then back to Yokosuka.

I am growing a mustache now. It looks pretty neat.

We are getting about 200 new patients per week in the hospital now. Most of them are from Vietnam.

One of the other Marines on my ward gave me a jungle hat. It has one brim turned up on one side and is made of camouflage material. I wear it just to goof around with.

I have duty this weekend so it doesn't look like I'll be going any place except for work.

Oh, for the last couple of nights I've helped change dressings on patients who got shot and hit with flying metal. There is one who has a hole in his side, which is about 2 and a half inches in diameter and you can see his intestines. Looks real neat! Smells good too. I dug a piece of metal out of another guy's leg tonight. Oh well, that's business.

The picture of the sub at Noyo looks real neat. Some of the guys thought it was Disneyland.

Hope you do real well in the Jamboree. Who is in it besides you?

Love
Russ

P.S. I love you more than anything in the world. Every day gone by is one more day closer I get to come home to you. I love you so much that if you weren't still in school when I get home I would ask you to marry me the first time I see you. Some day though I will.

Back in the States, Steve Kaden had been discharged from the navy and returned to Fort Bragg. He made a point to look up Louise only because he knew that I was in love with her. Kaden was a pathological liar and would say anything about anyone to get attention. He told her some stories about me that upset her. He also decided he wanted to date her.

The movie *The Birds* was being filmed in Bodega Bay, south of Mendocino County. It seemed that Hollywood had discovered the Mendocino Coast.

I started going to a nightclub called the Italian Gardens in Yokohama where a lot of older Japanese teens hung out. IG was located in a cellar under a business on the main street and owned by an American who had retired from the navy. The facility was small with a bar, jukebox, booths, and a dance floor. It was very popular and always busy. The jukebox had music that was popular in the States. We listened to "Eve of Destruction" by Barry McGuire and some other songs by Bob Dylan, banned from Armed Forces Radio Network for being antiwar. There were also many soul music selections. That was the first time I heard James Brown and Marvin Gaye.

23 Nov 65

Dear Louise,

    Sounds like you got a real good report card this time. How did the Jamboree go?

    So they are going to make an Alfred Hitchcock movie too. I'll be darned. (This pen is no good.) I'll bet that will be a cool movie.

    What did you and Steve Kaden talk about; I mean what did he say about me?

    This last weekend I went to Yokohama to a nightclub called the Italian Gardens. If you can imagine a room about 24' x 12' filled with 300 people then you can get a picture of what the "IG" is like then to have all of them trying to dance the jerk and all these other dances. It's a real swinging place if you like to be a sardine I stayed from 2PM to 4AM the next morning (I guess it was that's about the time it took the crowd to finally dwindle enough so I could push through to get out the door). A lot of college students hang out there. There is a group there who is always there and is considered the "in" crowd. I got in good with them, goofing around, joking and such, so now when I go in they have a place at their booth saved for me since I go up there pretty regularly.

    Tonight when I was at work one of my patients gave me a set of camouflage utilities (the fighting uniform of the Marine guerrilla forces in Vietnam). They are real neat. That means that I now have 2 sets of regular utilities, a set of camouflage, camouflage hat and a regular cap. All I need now are combat boots and a rifle. I'll have to send you a picture of me wearing my Marine uniform.

    It's just my luck! I have to work Thanksgiving. I better get Christmas off! You know I haven't had one holiday off except for Veterans Day!

    It's getting late now (its been the 24th for 20 minutes now) I guess I better get some sleep.

                                                     Love always
                                                          Russ

PS. I love you. I am sending my ring with your Christmas present.

    I was starting to identify myself more with the Marines than I should have and started becoming less restrictive in supervising them on the ward. One evening, one of my Marine patients decided he couldn't wait to go out on the town. He checked out to go the hospital movie theater, but instead of the movie, he jumped the fence and headed for the nearest brothel. It wasn't long before he was picked up by the shore patrol and returned to the hospital. He was confined to the ward required to muster with me every hour. I had to sign each time to verify that he complied. He convinced me to forge the document for him and went over the wall again. This time he made it back without a shore patrol escort.

When his captain's mast for disciplinary action came up, I testified that he had complied with his restriction. There were some accusations from one of the nurses that I was covering for the Marine, as she stated that she had not seen him during her shift. I stuck to my story.

Soon after that, based on my scores of the test I had taken several months earlier, I was promoted to petty officer third class. I was reassigned as the senior corpsman on the Dependent Female ward. The head nurse on the ward informed me that I had been reassigned because the nurse on the other ward had said I could not be trusted working with the Marines. They were right.

22 Dec 65

Dearest Louise

Thank you very much for your picture and your class ring. I hope you have received my package. I will never take off your ring. I wear it on my left little finger. I am really glad you sent it.

Guess what. I am now a Petty Officer Third Class in the USN. They promoted me so now I get more money and have a better job. I now wear an eagle, a corpsman's insignia and a chevron on my arm. I am working on a dependent ward and take care of sick wives here in the hospital, work with 4 nurses and 5 doctors.

Went to Mt. Fuji last weekend. It was cold to say the least. During the warmest part of the day we were walking around with sweaters, coats, and gloves and were still cold. We stayed at a little town called Gotemba and Fuji was to the west of the town about 20 miles. It was real clear and you could see the mountaintop. The only snow was at the top of Fuji. I'll send you a picture of me with Fuji in the background. We didn't get to go up on Fuji because there were no busses running, they don't go up there until ski season opens in January.

Every time I look up I see you smiling at me. Your picture is sitting on my desk. You sure are cute. I love you.

I guess that's it for now I love you more every day. In two months I'll be able to start counting downhill until I see you again. Do you realize it's been almost 10 months since I last saw you? I love you, Hon.

I love you,
Russ

Chapter 15

Busted

LOUISE HAD SENT me her class ring that she had just purchased. It was too small for my ring finger, so I wore it on my little finger of my left hand. I started to realize that my time in Japan was almost half over, and I decided to see as much as I could before I left the country. I also decided that I was going to request to go with the Marines when it came time for me to be reassigned.

One weekend, a couple of my corpsmen buddies and one of our Japanese interns, who was from Thailand, decided to take a trip up to Lake Yamanaka for the weekend. It was quite a trip. I took movies while riding on a steam train to Gotemba, the closest city. We had a great time riding the bus from Gotemba to Lake Yamanaka, where we stayed the night partying in a Japanese-style hotel. We were waited on in the traditional Japanese style. Ladies in kimonos served our meals in our room. Dinner and drinking continued well into the night. The next day, we caught the train back to base.

The base special services division, who handled all the base recreation and entertainment events, sent out flyers announcing that the Beach Boys were scheduled to put on a show on base. I made plans to be there and sent a flyer to Louise.

17 Jan 66

Dear Louise

    I guess I better sit down and write you a letter. I had presents from home for Christmas. I got candy, cookies, two pairs of pants; a turtleneck knit dickey and a couple of other things. The best present was yours though. I still haven't taken off your ring. When I wash I put my two little fingers end to end and slip it to the other finger, to wash under the ring.

    On New Years Eve I spent the day in Tokyo with two of my buddies. We went up into Tokyo Tower.

    This last weekend we went up to Mt. Fuji. We went up to one of the lakes where there was about 10 inches of snow. It was real cool!

    One of the trains we had to take to get there was a steam engine with coal car and everything like the old west style passenger cars and everything. I got some good movies hang ing out the door of the train. I'll send you some snap shots.

    Oh, speaking of snap shots, here are some of me in my cube I took last week. I am going to do a lot more traveling since I only have 1 year and a month until I leave Japan and I want to see all I can.

    Yes, I eat a lot of Japanese food here, when I'm off base, I've eaten rice, raw fish, squid, octopus, sea weed, bamboo and a lot of other stuff I don't even know what it is. I can eat a bowl of rice with chopsticks. It fills you up pretty well.

    The only resolution I made was to love you more and more each day.

    Why do you think I want to know your ring size?

    I don't know what I want you to do to show me you missed me. I guess we'll have to wait and find out.

    You asked me what I want to do when my time over here runs out. Well I'd like to go the rest of my enlistment with the Marines as a Marine Corpsman, wearing the Marine uniform and living like one in the dirt and everything. This will be for a year and a half or so.

    Do you have a picture like the one you sent that is wallet size? If so I'd sure like to have one to carry around with me.

    In the pictures I enclosed, please forgive the pictures on the wall, they are called "memory aids" Note on the picture of me the chain around my neck. That's where the St. Chris is. Oh, they told me to shave off my mustache before I could get a picture of it. Sorry 'bout that, Hon.

    I love you so much, I wish you could have been up at Fuji with me; it was a perfect place for a honeymoon. You would have loved it.

I've gotten into a physical fitness mood, so every night I do push ups, sit-ups and other exercises to build up the muscles a little more.

I miss you so much, like I say we'll wait and see what we do when I come home.

I better go now it is now 15 minutes into 18 Jan. I have to get up in 5 and ¾ hours and go to work.

Love always
Russ

PS. I love you

Enclosure:

Beach Boy Concert Flyer

Special Services Yokosuka
Presents
'The Beach Boys'
At Thew Gym
U.S. Fleet Activities Yokosuka
January 21 at 1730 hours
Tickets on sale at Special
Services Yokosuka Tours Office
$1.50 $1.00 $.50

I thought I'd show you who we are going to see this week. I'll send you pictures!

My life had become pretty much routine working the Dependent Female ward. I also was planning my summer trips. I met and went out with several women whom I met when they were patients. One of them was twenty-two and married with an eighteen-month-old baby. Her husband was a LTJG stationed on a ship home-based in Yokosuka. When he went out to sea, she got lonely and would leave a message for me to come and visit. She had all the Bob Dylan albums. We would sit at her house and play chess while listening to Bob Dylan.

In May, I enrolled in a conversational Japanese course offered by the base Special Services. Classes were held twice a week, and I became fairly fluent in Japanese.

It was getting warmer, and I was spending as much time as I could at the beach. I was hanging out with a bunch of Japanese students. We were all trying to learn each other's language, so we had a deal that I would only talk to them in Japanese and they would only speak to me in English.

One day I made the mistake of giving a friend a ride to the beach on my Honda 50. I thought nothing of it because I saw many Japanese riding Honda 50s loaded down with their family and supplies. It was about a quarter of a mile from Carl and Linda's house headed to the beach. As I neared the beach with my buddy riding behind me, a Japanese motorcycle cop pulled me over and wrote me a ticket for having a passenger. After writing the ticket, he gave me the address of the police station where I was to surrender my bike. I followed the directions and went to the station. I entered the building looking more like an accounting office. It was full of desks covered with stacks of paper and everyone busy at work. I was referred to one of the desks, and the officer behind it went through his stack of papers. Finally he came across the documentation and the ticket written by the motorcycle cop. He indicated that I should follow him outside to identify my cycle. He then took a screwdriver out of his pocket and removed the license plate and had me follow him back in to this desk. After stamping a series of papers, none of which I could read, he produced a manila envelope into which he put the license plate. He gave it to me in an envelope and told me I could go. I rode back to the base on the train. My bike had been shipped to the base and was impounded.

The week I was called to appear at the provost marshal's office in the Marine barracks, my driver's license was revoked. I thought it was a bit harsh, but I was informed that they did not give any second chances with motorcycle traffic violations.

June 27 1966

Dear Louise,

Well summer is here now over night it has become hot and sultry. The nights are not cold, just right for making out under the stars. Wish you were here to share them with me. I love you.

You ask me if I was going to bring my Honda home or sell it or what. Well I got a traffic ticket from a Japanese Motorcycle cop (omawari-san) for riding double. It seems that you have to have a 51cc size engine or over to ride double, according to the Japanese law and I only have a 50, so they sent the ticket to the base and I had to go to traffic court. There they revoked my drivers license and took my bike and locked it up. They told me to ship it home, sell it, or junk it! Since it will cost me too much to send it home and I'd lose all my money if junked it, I have to sell it within 30 days yet! That really makes me mad, because guys who get tickets for drunk driving, speeding, reckless driving, and wrecking their car only get a warning or license taken away for 30 days, but never taken away like what happened to me. I've talked to the legal office and they said that there is nothing I can do to get it back. That really perturbs me!!

This weekend was beautiful. I went to the beach both days. Saturday there weren't very many people on the beach and the surf was down. Sunday I went out there at 10AM and the beach was so crowded you had to watch where you were stepping to keep from stepping into the middle of anyone. The surf was really up and we body surfed and swam all day. One time me and this other kid swam out to this rock the waves were breaking over and when I tried to climb up on it the water came pouring over the top and I got all scraped up on the barnacles that covered the rock. I tried again and this time I got my fingers torn on the barnacles while trying to hang on. Finally I got up and stood up for about 5 minutes to catch my breath and "crash" a big wave hit me and washed me off so I decided to swim in. When I finally reached the shore I looked at my fingers, elbows, knees and stomach and they were a bloody mess, luckily the cuts weren't as bad as they looked, they quit bleeding in 15 minutes or so and I went back out and swam and body surfed. The water was almost as bad as the beach in the number of people that were out there, you couldn't body surf without running into a bunch of kids. Wish you could have been there with me or be with me all summer.

Last week I took an allotment out of my paycheck to buy a $25 savings bond every month for the rest of the time I'm in the Navy. At least that way we will have some money in the future. I am making them out for you and me. How's that to prove I love you and want to marry you?

Right now we are waiting for a typhoon to come it's raining and windy out. We went into a condition called "Typhoon Condition Two" that is when you secure all doors, screens, windows, lawn furniture, mops, garden tools, etc., even bicycles, anything that might blow away. They even moved the ships out to sea. Next we go into "Condition One" where everyone is supposed to stay in unless absolutely necessary.

Well, next week I go on leave. I plan to go to southern Japan. I will go to Tokyo and catch the Bullet Express (which travels at 150 MPH) to Osaka. From there I will go to Sasebo to see "Chick" Ash, then while I'm down there I will go to Nagasaki. After that I will go up to Hiroshima, Kobe, Kyoto, Nara and any place I happen to think of while I'm down there. Then back to Fuji and if it's open for climbing, climb it. Then if I have any time left I am going to lie around on the beach. My leave starts July 4th at 8AM. I wish you could come with me. I want you to be with me so bad Louie. I love you!

Oh, if you can't get a yearbook for me I'd sure like it if you sent me yours to look at and you can keep the money.

What did your Dad say about the money order? Bet he was surprised.

You know, I haven't really thought too much about my birthday. I really don't want to turn 20; I want to stay a teenager all my life.

Oh, guess what happened at the beach the other day. My chain broke and my St. Chris fell off into the ocean someplace. Sorry. I was just heart broken, almost any way, when I found out I lost it being that you gave it to me. I guess the chain I had wasn't strong enough.

Well, I guess I better go now, it's almost midnight and I have to get up at six in the morning. I can't think of anything else to write to you right now except that I love you with all my heart and I want more than anything to have you with me forever as my wife someday. I can't wait to hold you in my arms and kiss your sweet lips and get totally turned on just by being with you. I love you so much. I better close now I'm getting turned on just thinking about it. Bye for now, hon.

Love,
Russ

P.S. I love you

Chapter 16

Nagasaki

IN JULY, I went on two weeks' leave and traveled alone to Nagasaki. Leaving Yokosuka, I took the train to Tokyo where I caught the bullet train to Osaka. After traveling through Nagoya and Kyoto, I arrived at Osaka station after dark and transferred to the train to Sasebo. We traveled all night passing through Kobe and Hiroshima. The next day I passed the time talking to Japanese kids who wanted to practice the English they had learned in school.

When the train came to the end of Honshu, it entered a tunnel that went under the ocean to Kyushu and continued to Sasebo. Sasebo had a large harbor with a large shipbuilding facility.

In Sasebo, I stayed in the Hospital Corps quarters at the naval hospital overnight and ate at the hospital mess hall. The next day, I caught the train to Nagasaki. The trip lasted several hours, but we finally arrived.

In Nagasaki, a cab driver offered to act as my tour guide. He took me to a park where a tall green monument in the form of cylindrical column marked the hypocenter of the nuclear blast. Next to the marker were the remains of a brick wall and statues of a Catholic church. From there we went to the Peace Statue located right next to the atomic park. Next he took me to Glover Garden, which was the home of the woman who was the inspiration for *Madame Butterfly*. Then we went to see the first Catholic church in Japan and a memorial to the martyrs who were executed for practicing their religion in Japan. We also visited a Chinese temple.

The end of the tour, he dropped me back at the park, and I spent the afternoon in the Nagasaki Atomic Bomb Museum viewing the pictures and artifacts of the atomic blast. I then caught the train back to Sasebo.

The next day I headed back north. I wanted to make a stop in Hiroshima, but in Sasebo, they advised against Americans going there due to antinuclear and anti-American demonstrations taking place. I decided to proceed on to Osaka.

July 9, 1966

Dear Louise,

Well here I am in Osaka! I am on leave at present since 4th of July. So far I have been all the way down to Nagasaki on the southern Island of Kyushu.

I left Yokosuka on the 6th and went to Tokyo, where I caught the express train to Osaka, which is the fastest in Japan (130MPH) It took 3 hours to get to Osaka, where I caught another train to Sasebo which took 14 hours. I checked into the hospital corps quarters at the hospital there. Slept all that night and then went to Nagasaki. Saw right where the bomb hit and a bunch of other things. Then went back to Sasebo and went to sleep.

This morning I caught the train for Osaka again at 8:15 AM and arrived here at 7:45 PM. This hotel is real neat. 12 stories high and I am on the 9th floor giving me a good view of the city.

Tomorrow I think I will go to Tokyo and get some more money changed into Yen. The hotel room is costing me 2400 yen ($6.67) a day and I only have 12,000-yen ($33.32) left and I want to see this area it is very beautiful

Oh, thanks for the birthday package it sure was good, I finished it off the first night (with the help of my mooching buddies).

Well, that's about it for now except I love you and wish you could be here with me, only 8 more months until I come home.

Love,
Russ

PS. I love you

The next day I caught the bullet to Tokyo to convert some more of my military script to yen and then headed back to Osaka. Round-trip took me about seven hours. It was nice to be on vacation with no other Americans around. Everyone I met was very friendly. Back in Osaka, I had dinner in the hotel dining room and stayed another night in the hotel.

I visited Osaka Castle, an impressive five-story structure built on a tall stone foundation surrounded by a moat. After touring it for several hours, I decided to walk back to the hotel (which was a distance of several miles) instead of catching a cab. I walked through a section of the city where I observed small factories and watched as several men with sledgehammers fashioned molten steel in a shop no bigger than a garage.

The next day, I took the train to Kyoto, the old capital of Japan. I visited Higashi Honganji, a large Buddhist temple a few blocks from the Kyoto Station, which is the largest wooden structure in Kyoto. Inside, a heavy rope reinforced with human hair used to move the logs was on display. Outside I met three young ladies, and we went to lunch at one of the local restaurants. They suggested that I also go see the Nijo Castle, the shoguns' home; and Kinkakuji Temple, the Golden Pavilion. There were beautiful gardens and exquisite carvings and paintings at both places. I then visited Kyoto Gosho, the old Imperial Palace grounds, and gardens that were very ornate and beautiful. Those working on the grounds all dressed in period costumes.

July 21, 1966

Dear Louise,

Well, I'm off leave and back to the same old work grind. Back on the ward same old boring job working with the women.

My vacation was real good. After I stayed in that hotel in Osaka I decided to stay two more nights, so I had to run up to Tokyo to change more money into yen so I got on the train, which travels at over 130 MPH. It took 3 hours 18 minutes to get to Tokyo and I changed my money and in another 3 hours and 18 minutes I was back in Osaka. The next day I went sight seeing around Osaka and then the next day I went to Kyoto and went on a tour there and then back to Yokosuka. The rest of the time I just bummed around the beach. I wish you could have been with me; we could have had a blast.

A bunch of the guys went up and climbed Fuji last weekend. The first weekend that I have off in August I am going up there and conquer Fuji also.

I am enclosing a couple of pictures of myself that one of the guys took last month while I was on one of my lunch hour sun bathing times. This was before I lost my St. Chris.

It sure is getting hot now days. It was about 95 degrees and humid as heck. It is getting hotter all the time. It is 11:30 PM now and it is about 80 degrees out and still humid.

Oh, I got another St. Chris. This one is oblong and has a heavier chain on it so I hope it won't break as easily.

What about the yearbook, any news on it?

I am still trying to sell my Honda; I think I have a guy on the hook that might buy it. I hope so.

I sure do wish we could be together right now. I love you so much. Only 8 more months until I get home and can be with you once again. Louie, I miss you so much. I want to be with you for the rest of my life.

I guess that's it for now, except I want you always.

Love,
Russ

PS. I love you

Chapter 17

Mount Fuji

THREE WEEKS LATER, I prepared to go and climb Mount Fuji. A friend joined me. We both wore Marine utilities and combat boots to hike up the mountain. After work on Friday, we caught the train to Ofuna and then the steam train to Gotemba near the base of Fuji. It was dark when we reached Gotemba. The buses to the mountain only ran during the day, so we decided to start walking along the road toward the mountain. At around ten, we came to a small restaurant that was still open and decided to get something to eat. After eating, we inquired if there was a place to stay, and the innkeeper told us we could stay there. We spent the night sleeping on futons with a couple of the girls that worked there.

Next morning, we continued on our journey toward the base of the mountain. We passed the entrance to Camp Fuji, a Marine training base. After several hours of walking, a bus came down the road, and we flagged it down. It took us several more miles to the start of the Gotemba trail.

The base of the mountain is scree like very coarse sand. Before starting our ascent, we each purchased a six-sided wooden pole about five feet long called a Fuji Stick. At each way station up the mountain, brands are burned on the stick to document events on the climb and descent of the mountain. We followed the trail as it zigzagged up the mountain. At each station, there was a mountain hut where we purchased food and drink and got our sticks branded. The view became more spectacular the higher we got up the mountain. Weather on the mountain changed very rapidly. While climbing, we had clear, unobstructed views as well as fog, rain, snow, and hail; but most of the time, the sky was clear.

By nightfall, we were well over half the way up the mountain. We stopped at a way station to eat dinner and get some rest. The proprietor served a bowl of hot rice mixed with a raw egg and some dried fish. He informed us that most people found climbing the Gotemba side too strenuous. There was a bus that went up most of the way and was more popular for descending than climbing. After dinner, we turned in so that we could get an early start the next morning. We wanted to be on the trail to observe the sunrise. Our accommodations for the night were a futon on a wooden platform shared with a few other climbers.

After several hours' sleep, we awakened and headed out onto the trail. It was still dark, but we could see just fine by the light of the stars. Just before sunrise, the horizon became a small red line that brightened until the sun finally rose out of the ocean. This occurred at around four and made for some beautiful photos.

As we went higher, the scree disappeared, and the trails entered talus made up of larger rocks as the trail got steeper. Near the summit, there was still a large patch of snow that had not yet melted. Some of the hikers had gone over to it and were playing. Around noon, we arrived at the top of the mountain. We spent an hour taking photos and buying souvenirs at the large way station at the top. Across the crater was a radar weather station.

On our way down, we again took the Gotemba trail. Once we got past the talus rocks and got to the scree, we decided to go off the zigzag trail and go straight down the mountain. We leaned back slightly to keep our balance and step forward as we slipped down the slope and "screed" down the hill, which was like skiing with no skis. We slid about ten feet with each step.

August 13, 1966

Dear Louise,

Here I am 6000 feet up on Mt. Fuji. Climbing this mountain is a real blast. I am wearing my Marine Corps Jungle utilities, combat boots and hat. I look like I am straight from the jungles of Vietnam.

I am at the 4th rest station on the hardest side of the mountain to climb. From here I can look all over the valley because it is pretty clear today. Well, got to get on with the climb I'll write on this letter again at the next station.

Well, I'm at the next station and now that I am rested, we are just about to go again, I wish you could be here with me to see this view, it's beautiful. Well off to the next station.

I am now at the next station. For dinner I had rice, raw egg, raw fish, seaweed and I guess it was onion soup. We are staying here tonight and I am in bed right now and the light is real bad, so I can hardly see what I am writing.

I sure wish you could be here with me, laying here beside me in this Japanese bed. It is real clear tonight and you can see all the way to Yokosuka and all over. Over near Tokyo you can see all kinds of lightning activity, no thunder can be heard here though. I guess I better get some sleep because I have to get up at 1 o'clock to get to the top to watch the sun rise. I love you. Goodnight.

We got up this morning and started out again at 2:30 AM. We watched the sunrise at 4 o'clock. Now we are almost near the top and we had a little snow just now, my hands are so cold I can hardly write, so I will continue at the next station.

Here we are at the top. It took 26 hours to get up here. It was clear for a few minutes, but now it is hailing. The crater is large, but not very deep. Everything is red lava. I wish you could be here to see it. It's really spectacular. It's time to start down, so I'll finish this letter when I get down.

Here I am at the bottom again. It took us 2 ½ hours to come down. We almost ran all the way. It was hard not to. I didn't get sore muscles going up, but coming down I got some good ones.

I am sending you something I got at the top. I hope you like it.

Time to get back to Yokosuka. I sure could use a bath and massage about now.

I wish you could have been with me on my climb, I'm sure we could have enjoyed it more together I love you so much.

Love,
Rus

PS. I love you

Chapter 18

Yokohama Dreamland

PERSONNEL SENT OUT a request for volunteers to go to Antarctica as part of Operation Deep Freeze '67. I saw it as another opportunity to see another part of the world. I was one of the only volunteers from the hospital. No one else saw any reason to go where it was so cold.

I was under a deadline from the provost marshal to dispose of my Honda 50. I had to sell it, send it home, or scrap it. While at work, I met Gunnery Sergeant Jose Maize from the Marine barracks. His fifteen-year-old daughter Rose was a patient on my ward, and he and his wife visited her regularly. We became friends, and I told him of my dilemma. Several days after his daughter was discharged from the hospital, he called and invited me for dinner with his family. I accepted, and he gave me directions to his home. They lived in base housing in a Quonset hut. Inside it was very nice home. After dinner, he told me that he would take the Honda off my hands.

August 26, 1966

Dear Louise,

I just got back from the movie; it was "Viva Maria" starring Bridgette Bardot. It sure was a good one, you should see it if you get a chance.

Right now I am sitting here listening to my stereo tape recorder with earphones on my head. Boy do I look weird.

I guess I didn't tell you, but I got a Sony 260 tape recorder, which cost me $140 and then today I got a set of stereo speakers that you hang on the wall and have a design in the center, that cost me $30 and also I got these earphones. They are real neat. I can sit here with my tape recorder on full blast and not disturb anyone. They cost me $6.00.

I also bought 3 prerecorded tapes. The one I am listening to now is Kai Winding playing the "Theme from Mondo Cane" (More) and other surfing beat type tunes, like "Pipeline", etc. I also have one of the Beatles and the album from "Hard Days Night". The last one I have is by the Ventures and is called "the Ventures play Tel star". On it are "the Lonely Bull", "Tequila", "Apache" and a lot of the others.

We are going to have another typhoon this weekend. Wouldn't you know it, on my weekend off, too!

Well, that tape is over. I have to put on another one. There, I put on the Beatles and they are singing, "I should have known better". This stereo sure is cool on these earphones. You hear bass in one-ear drums in the other and it seems like right in the middle of your head you have the rest of the instruments and singing.

Now they are singing "If I Fell" Just think someday this will belong to both of us.

Oh, I forgot to tell you I volunteered to go to Antarctica for Operation Deep Freeze-'67. I put in my request and it was approved at the command here, now it has to go to Washington DC to the Bureau of Naval Personnel. I hope it gets approved.

Now the Beatles are singing "And I love her". Louie you don't know how much I love you. I wish I had the vocabulary to say what I feel about you, but I guess what I feel can't be put into words in any language.

Now they are playing "This Boy" No words, just music. "Can't buy me love" is on now.

I ran into a buddy of mine from when I was in Hospital Corps School in San Diego. He was down in Vietnam and didn't like the job he was doing so he shot 5 holes in the roof of a building he was in with his .45 pistol, so now they think he is crazy and he is on our "Nut" ward.

The theme from "Hard Days Night" is on now.

I'm getting rid of my Honda finally. I know this Gunnery Sergeant Jose Maize here on base who is a good friend of mine and he says he will trade me an electric guitar and amp for it. The guitar and amp are almost brand new and sound real good. I was over at his house for a Mexican dinner last week. He is half Indian and Mexican and his wife is Mexican. I had 10 tacos, a bunch of beans, watermelon and Spanish rice. Boy was I full.

I sure wish I could be with you right now. Everything I do I think of how much more fun I could have if you were here with me. I know you'd love it over here. I wish you could come over here right now and we could get married. I mean it with all my heart. Honest!

Well, I guess I better go now, I'm getting too turned on and there's nothing I can do about it. It is only 6 more months to go until I'm home again.

Love,
Russ

PS. *I love you*

By September, I had been in Japan for eighteen months and was getting bored with my job at the hospital. Though I enjoyed the staff and patients I was working with, my job consisted mainly of record keeping and administrative functions on the ward.

One day the barracks master-at-arms mustered all personnel to the lobby of the barracks. Once assembled, he read a request for volunteers to go to Field Medical Service School for duty with the Fleet Marine Force. I listened to the information and was interested in becoming a combat corpsman, but I was in the process of being evaluated for duty with Operation Deep Freeze in Antarctica. I went to bed that night and thought about another six months working on the ward. The next morning, I went to personnel and withdrew my application to Deep Freeze and volunteered for Field Medical Service School.

The personnel department ended up with twenty-seven other volunteers, and I was one of the first. Altogether, forty of us received orders to Camp Pendleton in Oceanside, California. Those who had not volunteered were unmarried and had more than two years remaining on their enlistments.

September 7, 1966

Dearest Louise,

Something very unexpected has come up; I know it will be a shock to you too. The other day 40 of us Corpsmen got orders. I will be home next week sometime after the 15th to tell you in person.

I love you even more than ever. I'm sorry I can't tell you anything now, but I don't really know how to tell you, so I'll have to do it in person. I may be home even before this letter gets to you.

I love you with all my heart and want to be with you forever. I have to close now.

Love always,
Russ

PS. *I love you.*

Now I had a deadline to meet. All I was allowed to take on my flight home was my seabag. I had to pack up and ship my stereo equipment, civilian clothes, books, and all the personal items I had collected home. I sold the guitar and amplifier I had just received from Jose Maize and used the money to purchase a set of sixty-one-piece Noritake china for Mom and other items as gifts from Japan. The china was $53 dollars including shipping. The navy exchange shipped all my purchases, so they were not a problem. All my other items had to be packed and shipped.

September 9, 1966

Dearest Louise,

Just a short note to tell you that there has been a change in plans, not as to that I'm coming home, but as to I will be home sometime after the 21st. All the guys that live in California won't be leaving until then. So anytime after then I'll be home. I would appreciate it if you would call my family and tell them.

It's a real weird thing the other day I had 6 months to go over here and now several days later I have 12 days left. It was kind of a shock.

I love you more than anything in the world. I can't wait to be with you again.

My best buddy Paul Barney came in drunk. It is the first time in several months that he has had a drink. He's real broken up about me leaving. I can't blame him. He says he feels guilty about not getting orders along with the rest of us. I kind of know how he feels, I know if it were me and he got orders I'd feel the same way.

See you in less than 2 weeks.

Love
Russ

PS. I love you

The following weekend, two of my buddies who were staying in Yokosuka and I decided to go somewhere that we hadn't visited. We decided on Yokohama Dreamland. This was a theme park located in Totsuka, a ward of Yokohama. There was a monorail near Ofuna Station that transported visitors to Dreamland.

On Sunday, we caught the train to Ofuna. Before going to the monorail, we visited Ofuna Kannon, a seventy-five-foot-tall white concrete statue of a female Buddha. I had spent eighteen months passing this statue on my way to Yokohama, and this was my last chance to visit it. The statue contains stones from ground zero of both Hiroshima and Nagasaki atomic blasts. American bomber pilots used the statue as a landmark to turn north to Tokyo. We spent an hour touring the site. We then walked to the monorail for the ride to Dreamland.

When we arrived in Dreamland, it reminded me of pictures I had seen of Disneyland. It had a large central park area. The most prominent feature was a large Ferris wheel that rotated slowly with passengers in hanging gondolas similar to those on an enclosed ski lift. The central garden was surrounded by buildings that resembled the different theme areas at Disneyland. There was a section that looked like Buckingham Palace, complete with Beefeater guards. There was a storybook castle and an area that housed pinball games. Around the peripheral area was a ride similar to the Jungle River at Disneyland, but it also included dinosaurs and cavemen.

We were walking through the park when a young woman ran up and threw her arms around me only to realize I wasn't whom she thought (all "round eyes" look alike). She was very embarrassed and apologetic. I convinced her to stay with me that afternoon. Her name was Mariko Kobayashi, and she was nineteen years old. She worked in the office for a British shipping firm in Yokohama and spoke very good English.

I left my buddies to fend for themselves. Mariko and I spent the day taking all the rides and looking at the exhibits. We ended up sitting making out on a park bench in the central garden until 2100 when the park closed. I had given her the impression that I was a visiting college student from America, and that every year, my parents sent me to a different country for the summer. I gave her my parents' address before we said good-bye. My buddies and I met back at the monorail station to return to the main train station in Ofuna where we caught the train back to Yokosuka.

Chapter 19

Back to California

FINALLY THE DAY came for me to leave. I packed my seabag and put on my dress blues, which was the uniform of the day for traveling. I stopped by personnel and picked up my records and orders. Frank Zebley and I were the only ones from California who were leaving that day. We caught a bus to Tachikawa Air Base. When we got there, our flight was a chartered Pan Am Boeing 707. I was glad that we were not going to be flying on another MATS flight. We took off around 1800. The plane was scheduled to refuel in Anchorage, Alaska, the next morning and then continue on to Travis Air Base.

Traveling eastward, it was soon dark, and after a short night, the sun began to rise as we approached Alaska. Soon we were on final approach to Elmendorf Air Force Base. Once on the ground, it was 0700, and the outside temperature was thirty degrees. After an hour or so, we boarded the plane for our final leg to Travis Air Force Base in Fairfield, California.

On the way to California, we were flying at forty-two thousand feet. The sky was very clear, and the snow-covered mountains of the Alaskan Panhandle looked very small below us. Several hours later, we landed at Travis. I told Frank I would see him in a couple of weeks and went looking for a taxi to take me to Santa Rosa where I planned to stay with my brother Steve, who was a freshman at Santa Rosa Junior College.

The cab cost me $16 from Fairfield to Santa Rosa. Not having the address of the boardinghouse where Steve lived, I had the cab driver drop me off at the

Greyhound bus station. I called home and got Steve's phone number. When I talked to him, he said he was within walking distance and was soon at the bus station. I put my seabag in a locker and returned to the boardinghouse where he lived. The next afternoon, I caught the bus to Fort Bragg.

I had two weeks before I had to report in at Camp Pendleton on the sixth of October. Louise had just started her junior year of high school. The first weekend, we took a trip to Northspur on the new steam-powered Skunk Train. While Louise was in school, I visited my friends and family. In the evening, Louise and I continued our rendezvous at the movie theater as we had done prior to my going to Japan. When the next weekend rolled around, we planned to attend a dance where a local band called the Living Children were playing. That would be my last weekend in town.

Saturday evening, I was eating dinner at home with my folks. We had just finished eating dinner when my brother Steve arrived for the weekend, home from Santa Rosa. He had ridden his Yamaha 250 motorcycle, and as soon as he pulled up into the yard, I asked if I could take his bike for a run while he ate dinner. When I started up the bike, my younger brother Bruce, who was just thirteen, jumped on the back and away we went. We rode around town and then decided to go out Sherwood road a few miles and then turn around and go back home so that I had time to get cleaned up for the dance.

All went well until we were turning around out on Sherwood road. Bruce asked me if he could drive the bike back to the house. I asked him if he had ever driven it previously, and he assured me that Steve had taught him how to ride. I gave the bike to him and jumped on behind. He did well until he was going up a hill and was going a little fast. He tried to go around the turn, but got into the loose gravel at the edge of the pavement. The rear wheel slipped, and the bike lay over on its side. We slid down the pavement. Bruce got his leg out from underneath and was on top of the bike, but I was thrown off the back onto the pavement. I bodysurfed along with pieces of motorcycle headlight and mirrors tumbling alongside. When we came to a stop, we picked up the bike and got it out of the roadway. The forks were bent, and the front wheel could not turn. The fender was broken, and the gas tank was dented and badly scratched.

Shortly one of the residents living along the Sherwood road, who had heard us crash, came out and helped us. John Dias rode an Indian motorcycle in the 1930s before he entered the army in World War II. We all joked as we loaded what was left of Steve's bike into the back of John's pickup. After we were loaded up, he gave us a ride home and helped us unload. Steve was furious when we pulled up in front of the house and he saw his bike.

I was running late and had to get cleaned up for my date with Louise. It was then that I actually looked at the abrasions on my toes, knees, stomach, chest, and forearms. I had been wearing a T-shirt, jeans, and sandals that offered no protection. I had a major case of road rash. After taking a shower, I put antibiotic ointment and gauze pads taped over the large areas, got dressed for the dance, and went to pick up Louise.

The dance was well attended, and the music was good. As the evening progressed, my abrasions began to smart and my joints began to stiffen up, but I stayed at the dance until it was over and took Louise home. I promised that I would continue to write her.

The remainder of my stay at home went much the same, except that my abrasions had scabbed over so that I did not have to bandage them. On the morning of the fifth of October, I caught the bus to San Francisco, took a shuttle to the airport. Forty-five minutes later, I was in Los Angeles, caught a shuttle to Oceanside, and that afternoon, I reported to Field Medical Service School, Area 21, Camp Del Mar, Marine Corps Base Camp Pendleton. That was the last time I wore my navy dress blues for over a year.

Chapter 20

Field Medical Service School

MY FIRST DAY at Camp Pendleton was spent just settling into the barracks. I got my bedding and locker, unpacked, and spent the day getting all the required paperwork, liberty card, chow pass, and all the other housekeeping that needs to be done when checking into a new duty station. In Japan, I had had my own cubicle, but at Camp Pendleton, we all lived in a large squad bay barracks with bunk beds on each side of the room. In addition to our metal lockers where we stored our clothing, we also were issued wooden footlockers to store our Marine gear.

The next day, we spent the day getting our course materials and books. The barracks was located across the street from an EM (enlisted men's) club that served short-order food, soft drinks, and beer. In Japan, the legal drinking age was eighteen, but in California, the age was twenty-one. I couldn't even have a beer after two years. Mel Overmeyer (a friend from Japan) and I rented a car and went up to Balboa to try and find some friends of his. When we got there, they were not home, so we went to a seafood restaurant and had dinner before returning to base.

Friday October 7 was our first official training day. Our day started at 0500 and ended at 1630. Physical training started at 0530, consisting mostly of running in formation for an hour. From 0630 to 0730, we ate breakfast and cleaned the barracks. At 0730, we marched to the quartermaster and spent the morning receiving personal gear consisting of a steel helmet, a cloth camouflage cover, helmet liner, chin strap, pack, field jacket, cartridge belt, canteen, entrenching tool, sleeping bag, and shelter half. We then marched to the armory and were issued an M14 rifle and two magazines. In the afternoon, we learned how to use and properly pack, store, and carry all the equipment until 1500. We spent the rest of the afternoon determining our level of physical fitness. We spent an hour and a half performing sit-ups, pull-ups, squat-thrusts, and various other calisthenics as well as running to ensure we met the minimum physical fitness level required for the training.

That evening when we got off duty, a bunch of us decided to go down to Tijuana since none of us had ever been there before. Mel and I rented a car and drove down to the Mexican border. On the way down, we had problems with the generator on the car and stopped in a gas station in San Ysidro to see if we could get it repaired. The mechanic on duty happened to be a guy from Fort Bragg, Robbie Forward, who graduated several years ahead of me. I did not know him well, but recognized him and introduced myself. He was happy to see me. I told him of our predicament. He said not to worry, leave the car with him and he would have it repaired when we returned. We left the car with him and walked a few blocks to the border into Tijuana.

Immediately street vendors and young children trying to sell Chiclets gum accosted us. As we got closer to the town, pimps replaced the children. We walked along the main street and checked out some of the nightclubs. Having just come from Japan, we were disgusted with the bar scene in Tijuana and, after several hours, went back into California. Robbie had finished repairing our vehicle, so we headed back to base.

On Saturday, we spent the entire day drawing our Marine uniforms from the quartermaster. We received our clothing issue, which included the entire Marine uniform: three sets of utility shirts and trousers, a pair of blousing garters for the trouser legs, boot socks, boots, short – and long-sleeve khaki shirts, tie, tie clip, and trousers, green wool pants and jacket, caps, belts, buckles, and subdued (flat black) collar devices. After we received our issue, we returned to our barracks, and the tailors came in and decided what alterations were needed to make the dress uniforms fit properly. They recorded our rank so that patches with our navy rank could be properly sewn to the shoulder of the left sleeves (which was the only distinguishing difference between a corpsman and Marine). They issued a claim check and took the shirts, trousers, and jacket back to the tailor shop.

When liberty commenced at 1630, Mel and I headed for La Mesa to the Cinnamon Cinder on El Cajon Boulevard, a popular alcohol-free nightclub for teens located in San Diego where young adults hung out. We were hoping to find us a couple of girls. We rocked until midnight, but were unsuccessful at picking up any women. Mel remembered that he had an old girlfriend attending San Diego State University, so we stayed the night in a motel in El Cajon. The next morning, Mel contacted his old girlfriend, and she invited us to spend the day with her at the beach and attend her sorority's open house that evening. Late in the evening, we headed back to Camp Pendleton.

Monday morning training commenced again at 0500. We donned our utilities and boots for the first time. During physical training, the scabs on my abrasions on my knees and stomach that I received from the motorcycle wreck the week before started to separate from the skin and ooze fluid that stuck to my shirt and pant legs. We spent the remainder of the morning in close order drill. This was the first time since boot camp that most of us had to march in formation. At noon, we picked up our uniforms from the tailor shop located in the laundry building.

The tenth to the twenty-fourth of October was spent turning navy hospital corpsmen into Marines. Each platoon had a Marine Corps instructor assigned whose job was to teach us to look, think, and act like Marines. All students were E-3 through E-6, so the harsh intimidation techniques used in Marine Corps boot camp were not employed as stringently. However, we were held to the same high standards of conduct and performance required of a Marine.

October 10, 1966

Dearest Louise,

I'm sorry I haven't written, but they have us hopping all day and so we leave the base as soon as we get off at 4:30 in the afternoon.

So far since I've been here I haven't stayed in one evening, oh, except the first night I was here. The second night I went to Balboa, which is up north of here. We went there and ate dinner and then came back. The next night 7 of us from Japan went to Tijuana, Mexico. Boy, what a dirty rotten hole! It really stunk. On every corner some guy says "Hey, Señor, you want nice young girl only $5". The floor shows in some of the bars really stunk, some big fat hog (girl) was out there doing 69 with some guy and in another place there was a – now get this – a donkey doing it to some girl. See what I mean by dirty?

Saturday night one of the guys and I went down to San Diego in a 1966 Comet that we rented up here. We stayed in a hotel in El Cajon, we also went to the Cinnamon Cinder and just cruised around all evening after that until 3 AM.

Sunday we went to one of the girl's dorms at San Diego State College to see a girlfriend of Mel's (my buddy from Yokosuka). After that we went to a dance at the Sorority. Would you believe that I was in every room of the sorority house? Guess what I was doing? I was in every bedroom and bathroom and everything there. Really they had open house and we were on a tour by Mel's girlfriend.

This school is real neat. You get up at 5 am and go to chow then start school until 11am at 12:45pm back to school and then at 4pm we do physical training until 4:30pm then we go on liberty.

You should see me. I have combat boots, utilities, helmet, pack, M-14 rifle, canteen, field jacket, the whole bit. I look like GI Joe.

We have a lot of marching. If we want to go to chow we have to march 1 mile to the chow hall. Real fun. My feet are real sore, but I don't really care it's making me tougher.

I love you more than anything in the world. I can't wait to be with you again. I want to be with you forever and ever. I love you so much. Only 22 months 20 days left until we can be together always again.

Well its about time for taps. So I better sign off for now.

Love always
Russ

PS. I love you
PPS. My address is
Russell J. Jewett HM3 # 682-54-74
Field Medical Service School Class D-2
Marine Corps Base
Camp Pendleton, CA 92055

On the tenth day of training, we finally got to go to the firing range. We first went to the rifle range and practiced with our M14s. I scored fairly well for the first time using the weapon. After the rifle range, we went to the pistol range and fired the M1914, a .45-caliber pistol, the weapon we would be issued when we joined our units in Vietnam. Again I scored well.

On the eleventh day of training through the fourteenth, we saddled up with our packs and all our gear for a four-hour hike to training area 6577, a valley out in the hills of Camp Pendleton, where we set up our bivouac. After camp was established, we spent the remainder of the day in classes pertaining to living and operating in the field. Classes did not end at 1630 on these days, but continued until 2300, ending with a one-hour night tactical march.

At 0500 on the thirteenth day, we were told to strike (take down) our tents and pack up and move out to another area where we learned offensive and defensive tactics. We ran patrols and set up ambushes for the Marines, training with Infantry Training Regiment.

That evening, we were digging our fighting holes around the perimeter of a hilltop. One of the corpsmen dug into a rabbit hole and flushed out a scared bunny. He immediately killed the beast and held its carcass up on his entrenching tool as a gesture of triumph. Another "Doc" had unearthed and killed a rattlesnake and did the same. The entire platoon of corpsmen circling the hilltop started chanting, "Kill! Kill! Kill!" It was a primal bonding of the warrior spirit. In a mere two weeks, thanks to our training, we had mentally prepared to kill the enemy as well as provide life-saving medical aid.

That night, we slept in our fighting holes. One man slept while the other stood watch. Every hour we would switch. Between 0400 and 0500, members of the

ITR attacked our position, and we shot blanks at each other. After the battle was over, we had breakfast, struck our camp by filling in all the holes dug the previous evening. Trucks arrived and transported us back to Camp Del Mar. By 1000, we had cleaned and stowed our gear and were given weekend liberty.

Monday morning, we were given a written examination covering all aspects of our Marine training. After the test, we were introduced to field medicine. The next two weeks would be spent learning field medical command structure, advanced first aid, mass casualty handling and evacuation techniques, and camp sanitation.

During the middle of Field Medical Service School, we all got orders to Vietnam, which was no surprise to any of us. I called Louise and informed that I would be leaving soon. She convinced her mother that she needed to see me again before I shipped out. On Saturday the twenty-ninth of October, Louise and her mother, Francis, showed up on base to pick me up for a weekend visit. We went out to dinner, and then I spent the night with them in their hotel room. We all went to Disneyland for the day on Sunday. That evening, we went to a drive-in movie located in Escondido (with her mom) to see the newly released film *The Russians Are Coming, the Russians Are Coming*, which had been filmed in Fort Bragg while I was in Japan. Louise had seen much of the filming sessions and watched most of the "dailies" in the theater each evening with the director and staff. Her side comments about each scene were interesting. After the movie, we returned to base and said good-bye, and then she and her mother drove home. She missed two days of school (Friday and Monday) due to the trip.

On November 1, the twenty-second training day, we again bivouacked in the hills in training area 6577 to learn more about medicine in the field. As before, while on bivouac, training did not end at 1630, but continued well after dark each night.

During this exercise, we were supposed to be transferred to a ship anchored off the coast to practice loading into landing craft, but this exercise was cancelled because it was unlikely that we would have to hit the beach in landing craft in Vietnam because helicopters were now being used to transfer personnel from ship to shore.

Mid morning on our twenty-fifth training day, we struck camp and returned to Area 21 to clean our gear. After our gear was cleaned and stowed, we marched to the dispensary where we received our deployment immunizations. We got shots for plague, tetanus, typhus, typhoid, yellow fever, and influenza. To help reduce the chances of getting hepatitis, we received five milliliters of gamma globulin. That evening, I went to bed early because I was feeling a bit ill like many of the rest of the class.

November 2, 1966

Dearest Louise

Here I am out in the boonies again, living in the same old tent in the same old dust as last time.

We got out here yesterday and set up camp. Then we went to classes and then to chow. In the afternoon we went to more classes in the hot, sweltering sun until 5pm. After dinner we could do anything we wanted, so I went to bed to make up for the lost sleep over the weekend. I slept for about 11 hours, but I was disappointed after dreaming of you all night I was awakened by someone yelling "reveille" instead of you climbing on my bed and laying a big kiss on me and all that which you did down in the Motel. Too bad your mother was there too. It sure was nice of your mother to bring you down here and take us to Disneyland and to finally see "The Russians are coming, the Russians are coming".

Right now I am sitting out front of my tent on a box that once held a shell for a Howitzer cannon and the sun is again unbearable. We had classes today on bandages and splints and put some on the other guys. Time to go to lunch so I'll continue when I get time. I love you.

Well, that was a long time. It is now Thursday morning and is so cold I can hardly hold my pen. Last night we set up some large house-size tents in the dark. After that we went to bed at about 8:30pm

We went to chow a little while ago, same old rotten scrambled eggs, bacon, milk, but today we had a little something extra, fruit! WOW! We had Bananas, apples, oranges and grapes. We were only supposed to take one kind, but somehow I managed to get an apple, 2 oranges, and 2 bananas.

Everyone here is just standing around; some are brushing their teeth, shaving, washing and like that. I finished early so I could write a little more to you.

The Chief just walked into our camp and area and said to get our rifles, helmets and cartridge belt and be ready to go in 10 minutes so I guess I better get ready. I love you so much. It sure gets lonely without you. I want to be with you forever. Time to go now.

Someone borrowed my other pen and lost it, so I have to write with this one. We went out and played war (ha-ha) what a joke, we didn't have ammunition again, and someone goofed up again! They didn't order it. So we just went out and got shot at and played like we were wounded and got patched up. Later we got to play Corpsman on the same type of deal. Really fun! At night we did the same thing. I got your post card today.

Time to break camp and get back to the barracks.

Here I am back at the barracks and everyone has gone on liberty. Here I sit nothing to do. All my buddies didn't want me to go with them tonight because they all have dates and don't have any room for a tag-along.

I received your letter this afternoon. I wish you were here this weekend. I sure am lonely without you. Each time we have to part it tears me up. I know it will be harder than ever this time. I love you so much if there was a way I could get out of leaving you this time I would.

I want to be with you as your husband. I wish I didn't have to go and that we were married already, then we wouldn't ever have to part again. I love you. I can't wait until I get home and can hold you tight, kiss you, feel the warmth of you against me. I'm getting so bad I can hardly think or should I say write what I think.

I guess I better go now I'm starting to feel real bad. I think I'll go see a show or something like that. Bye for now.

Love always,
Russ

P.S. I love you

On November 7, we turned in all our training gear and weapons during the morning and sat our final exam in the afternoon. Some of the guys joked about possibly failing their exam. "What are they going to do? Send me to Vietnam?"

Tuesday November 8 was our final day at Camp Pendleton. We stood personnel inspection by the school commanding officer, Commander Donovan, MSC, USN. At 1000, our class was graduated and received orders to report to Travis Air Force Base for a flight to Okinawa on Friday November 11.

Most of the guys lived outside California and were going directly to Travis and stay in the transient center and party in Fairfield until flight time. I was not going to waste my three days, so I caught a bus to San Diego and got a flight on Pacific Southwest Airways back to San Francisco. The Greyhound bus to Fort Bragg had already left. I caught the first one out going up 101 through Willits, which was a bus to Portland. I called Mom when it stopped at the Santa Rosa depot and asked her to drive over and pick me up in Willits. I arrived home around dinnertime.

Louise had started her senior year, and we met every day after school. On one of our dates it was raining, and I had my parents' car. We drove out of town and parked near the ocean. We came closer to having sex that afternoon than we had ever before, but didn't. After all, we weren't married yet.

Friday morning, I had to depart from Travis. On Thursday evening, the family had a dinner with both sets of grandparents and my great-grandmother present to see me off. They all took turns having their picture with me in my uniform. Louise and my mother wanted to see me off. Louise called her mother and convinced her to drive us all to the air base, which was four hours away.

At 0400, Mom and I were ready to travel. Louise and her mother came by to pick us up. Her mother drove, and Mom sat in the front seat. Louise and I sat in the backseat. With a blanket over our laps pretending to sleep, we held hands and fondled each other in the dark until we arrived at Travis.

At the gate, the guard directed us to the proper terminal for my flight. Last time I had flown MATS overseas, it was in a four-prop transport plane and took over forty hours. This time, my flight was on a Pan Am Boeing 707 waiting on the tarmac in front of the terminal. They estimated the flight time to take only thirteen hours.

When flight time arrived, I hugged her mom, my mom and kissed Louise. I confidently reassured them that I would most likely get some safe duty in the rear. I told them not to worry and I would write often and my thirteen-month tour would fly by and I would be headed home. Leaving the terminal, I walked across the tarmac and quickly climbed up the stairs. At the top, I turned and waved at the terminal before entering the plane.

Chapter 21

Okinawa

ON THIS FLIGHT, there were no dependents or other branches present. The plane was full of navy hospital corpsmen. The seats were more comfortable than my previous flight from Travis, and we weren't as crowded. Once we were airborne, most of the passengers slept, but I was too apprehensive and spent most of my time looking down at the clouds and the occasional patch of ocean. It took four boring hours to reach Honolulu. On the ground at Honolulu International, the plane taxied not to the terminal, but to a refueling area where we sat for an hour. We were let off the airplane and sent to a room in the terminal with a TV. There were guards in the hallway to keep anyone from going AWOL. When the plane was refueled, we were ushered back on board. Soon we were airborne again for another nine boring sleepless hours before landing in Okinawa in the early hours of the morning.

It was still dark when we collected our seabags from baggage and loaded them on a waiting truck and were ordered to board the military buses. Roll call was held to ensure that everyone was on board for the trip across the island to Camp Smedley D. Butler. The trip took about an hour, and the sky was just starting to get light when we arrived. Inside Camp Butler, the staff began preparing us for our trip to Da Nang. First we were assigned to a barracks where we would sleep that night. The sergeant instructed us to change into our utilities and muster in front of the barracks. After muster, we marched to the chow hall for breakfast.

After breakfast, we were marched back to the barracks to retrieve our seabags. With our seabags on our shoulder, we marched in formation to another building where we lined up outside. Inside this building were long tables set up with many individual three-sided bins with the front open. On the tables inside each bin was another canvas bag. The corporal in charge of this building then gave us instructions to dump the contents of our seabags onto the table, pack our boots, socks, utilities, skivvy shirts, and Skivvies, and any personal items that we would need, such as shaving kit, towels, toothbrush, razor, and writing gear, and finally the last item to go into the bag was our orders and service record packet, which would be the first thing we would take out when reaching Vietnam. All other uniforms were put back in our seabags, to remain on Okinawa. A seal was placed on that bag to prevent theft. This entire procedure was completed within several minutes. We carried both bags out and marched back to the barracks with a bag over each shoulder. The bag going with us to Vietnam was left in the barracks by our bunks. We then carried our other bag to a storage building where we stacked them floor to ceiling to await our return for retrieval.

The rest of the day was spent completing our immunization series started back at Camp Pendleton. In all, we received shots for plague, typhus, tetanus, yellow fever, influenza, cholera, typhoid fever, and (to cover anything else) gamma globulin. The only pill given was chloroquine primaquine for prevention of malaria that would become a weekly ritual while we were in Nam. After dinner, it was suggested that we hit the rack early. Our wake-up call would be at "0 dark 30." Since there were no mattresses or blankets on the bunks, we slept on the metal springs in our utilities. I decided it was too early for me to sleep and went to the base movie. After the movie, I went back to the barracks and slept a few hours.

The barracks master-at-arms awakened us at 0300 by turning on the lights and rattling a nightstick around the inside of a metal trashcan. We fell in formation for muster. After placing our seabags on a waiting truck, we were marched to the chow hall. When we went through the chow line, they gave us brown paper bags with several bacon-and-egg sandwiches to eat on the busses that were waiting outside for us. The busses made a trip back across the island to the Marine air base.

As it was getting light around 0700, we arrived at the air base and pulled up next to a C-130 Hercules. We filed off the bus and into the plane. The interior of the plane had no padded seats. International orange woven nylon mesh cargo straps on an aluminum frame made up the long benches that ran the length of the plane's cargo space. These benches were spaced just far enough apart so that when sitting down, my knees touched the knees of the man sitting directly across the aisle from me. The same woven nylon cargo straps that were mounted vertically made up the backrests. Our seabags were taken off the truck by forklift and placed on the open rear cargo door. The crew then placed a cargo net over the pile to hold them in place. The cargo door closed, and the bags were now sitting in a pile at about forty-five degrees. By the time we were airborne at 0800, we were already cramped and uncomfortable. Our next stop was the airstrip at Da Nang.

The noise from the four turboprop engines during the flight was so loud it was difficult to carry on a conversation with the person sitting next to you. The only toilet facilities were located near the cargo ramp at the rear of the plane. When you felt the need to relieve yourself, the first thing you had to do was unbuckle your lap strap that had to be worn at all times during the flight. Then everyone between you and the facility had to shift their position so that you could step on the frame of the bench and make your way from person to person until you reached the end. Once back there, the urinal consisted of a funnel and tube that allowed the urine to be flushed directly to the outside of the plane for disposal in the air. The commode was simply a container bolted to the side of the aircraft that retained the feces with no enclosure for privacy. The crew had hearing protection in the form of Dave Thomas headsets, which dampened the ambient noise. The passengers were not even issued simple compressible earplugs. Most everyone tried their best to cope, but the noise and anxiety caused tempers to flare.

After several hours aboard, I decided to go sit on the pile of seabags on the cargo door. This allowed me to stretch my legs. Those of us who were sitting in the rear section of the plane took turns going back and sitting there to uncramp our legs and back muscles. After four hours of flight time, the plane started descending through the layers of clouds. It was now raining outside. Soon those of us sitting near the window of the rear door could see land below. Word quickly passed among us that we were soon to be landing. We all had heard war stories of planes landing at airstrips in Nam that had taken enemy fire during landing. Tension rose as we anticipated the plane coming in under fire. Many of us imagined that we would have to run from the rear doors on the sides of the plane and do a low crawl to the closest sandbagged trenches along the airstrip.

When the plane touched down and taxied along the runway, we readied ourselves for the sprint. The plane taxied and finally came to a halt and shut down its engines. This did not make any sense, now we were sitting ducks.

Chapter 22

Da Nang

EVENTUALLY THE CARGO door lowered, allowing a view of the outside. Surprisingly what I saw was not trenches but normal airport activity. A small vehicle pulling baggage trailers pulled up, and the ground crew started unloading our seabags. As that was occurring, the crew opened the doors, and we finally were able to stand to relieve our cramped muscles and deplaned. The weather was cloudy, muggy, and raining lightly. Stepping out on the tarmac, the ground crew directed us to waiting cattle cars (covered trailers with no seats, requiring the rider to stand) pulled by a diesel tractor. We soon arrived at the Marine transient center, about a quarter-mile ride. When we arrived, the baggage trailers waited for us to retrieve our seabags, and then we were directed to go inside.

The Marine transient center was a large tin-roofed building. The waiting area consisted of long flat wooden benches with no backs. The facility was open on the end and one side with a solid wall on the other side and end. We formed a line in front of the New Arrivals window. At the window, a clerk took my orders and service record packets. Another window issued a blanket and a chow pass permitting us to eat in the chow hall located on their compound. The clerk then directed me to the next window to draw a blanket. The blanket clerk gave me a blanket and directed me to one of the barracks buildings behind the terminal building to spend the nights until I received my assignment.

The barracks consisted of a dozen or so cabins that sat on foundations that raised the floor thirty inches off the sandy ground. The floors and halfway up the walls were covered with plywood. Above the plywood on the walls was a fine mesh to allow ventilation but keep out the bugs. The roof consisted of corrugated metal with a center ridge and pitched on both sides to shed water. They reminded me of a cabin at a summer camp. These buildings are referred to as a "strong back," but the Marines called it (or any other dwelling) a hooch. On the outside of the hooch, up near the eves, were bamboo mats that could be lowered to keep the wind from blowing through.

Inside were about twenty folding canvas and wood cots, ten along each wall. The cots were bare canvas with no mattresses and no pillows. After choosing a cot in the middle (away from the doors in case the Vietcong happened to attack us in our sleep), I dumped my seabag and went looking for food.

The chow hall consisted of a screened-in building. The diner walked up to a table outside the building where there were stacks of stainless steel cafeteria trays with a wire handle attached and eating utensils. A screen door was opened when chow was being served. Inside was a field kitchen with a serving line. Walking through the serving line, the cooks placed the food on the tray. Just before leaving, there was a choice of beverage, either Kool-Aid or coffee. The exit was out through another screen door. A group of picnic tables and benches under a metal-roofed building (similar to those at county fairs) made up the dining area. After finishing the meal, any food scraps were disposed of in a trashcan and the utensils placed on the wire handle of the tray. Cleaning the chow gear was the responsibility of the diner. This process entailed dipping them in a series of three thirty-gallon trashcans filled with water heated by an immersion burner (a stove that burned kerosene or other fuel with the burners located under the water near the bottom in a watertight ring that heated the water). The first can had detergent in the water. Holding the wire handle to keep hands out of the scalding water, the tray and utensils were dipped into the water. Using the provided scrub brush, the grease was scrubbed from the gear. After the wash, the items were submersed in a rinse in the next can to remove the detergent, and the last can was a boiling sanitizing rinse. The items were stacked up again on a table provided at the end of the line.

The head consisted of a screened-in "four-holer" with burn barrels filled up halfway with diesel fuel to contain the feces and keep away the flies. The sinks and showers were located out in the open with no roof over them. The showers ran only when a spring-loaded lever was pulled down. When released, the water would turn off. The water was not heated, but was lukewarm, heated only by the ambient air temperature. The water was supplied from a large barrel on top of a short water tower. A large water truck filled the barrel each day.

After eating, I got the uneasy feeling that I was now in a combat zone and I didn't even have a weapon to defend myself if we were attacked. Before retiring for the night, I scrounged around in the trashcan at the sinks and found a used double-edged Gillette razorblade. This was the start of constructing a knife. I then found a stick near the fence by the road and then found some twine. Taking care not to cut myself, I carefully split the stick halfway down and placed the razorblade so that the edges were on the outside on either side of the handle. I then wrapped the twine around the stick to hold it in place. Now I had a makeshift knife and felt a little better.

Back at the barracks, the cots were hard and not conducive to getting a good night's sleep. I placed the blade into the stud of the wall at the head of my cot. If the VC attacked us, at least now I had something other than my bare hands to fight with. The night did not provide for restful sleep. The airstrip was several hundred yards away, and jets, big prop planes, and helicopters were taking off all night. On the other side of the hooch about ten yards away was one of the main roads on the base. Vehicles traveling by added to the noise level.

November 15, 1966

Dear Louise,

Guess where I am! I'm in Da Nang already! Pretty fast, huh? It took us 4 hours to get to Hawaii. We had a 1hour stop there and then 9 hours later we landed in Okinawa. We stayed on Okinawa until 7 this morning. We got on a cargo plane. The same type as they use for paratroopers. No seats, just nets along the walls. After 5 hours of flying we landed in wet, rainy, muddy, humid DaNang.

It's real neat walking around in this reddish-brown sticky mud. Ek! They gave us a blanket apiece and put us up in a cabin type affair with a tin roof and a screen around to keep out the bugs. About half of the way up the wall on the outside they have bamboo mats. We sleep on cots, which are hard as rocks. To top it all off we are only about 100 yards from the main airstrip and all the planes are always taking off. Oh, and on the other side of the cabin about 10 yards we have the main road on the base and all the diesel-type trucks are going by all the time. Other than that everything is just fine. I sure do miss you.

I hope the time goes by fast so I can come home to you again. I sure hated to leave you again.

Oh, my sore throat, swollen neck, blocked up ear and all that junk is gone and I feel fine again.

I guess that's it for now. I miss you. I want to be with you again soon and stay with you forever and ever.

Love,
Russ

PS I love you
PPS I don't know my address yet. Sorry

To my surprise, the night was uneventful though I didn't get much rest. The next day there was no word on any assignments for our group. To break the boredom of waiting, several of us decided to leave the transient center to see what else there was on this base. When we got to the road, we stuck out our thumbs, and the first vehicle to come along stopped and picked us up. I asked the driver of the jeep where the nearest PX was located. The driver gave me directions and said he would drop us at the road that led up to Freedom Hill. We traveled parallel to the airstrip until around the middle where another road intersected. The driver stopped and told us to catch a ride up to Freedom Hill. We thanked him and got out. Within a few minutes, a troop transporter with wooden rails on the back with a bench inside the truck bed came along and stopped for us. We got in, and the truck proceeded on its way. This road soon ran through a Vietnamese village with a crossroad where a Vietnamese policeman directed the traffic. This village was referred to as Dog Patch. Leaving Dog Patch, we were back in US military-controlled area and proceeded past the Freedom Hill PX. We decided to see where the road went, and so we rode on farther past an area that was being used to mine gravel and then up around the other side of the hill to a small base with a barbed wire fence surrounding it. Outside the base was a small wooden shack that was acting as a bus stop. The truck stopped, and we got out, and it continued inside the base. Since there was not much to see, we waited at the shack until another vehicle came out, and we rode back to the PX. As our ride approached the PX, we noticed that bleachers and a stage were being erected.

We got off at the Freedom Hill PX, a very large all-steel building on a concrete slab. Located outside the door, there was a fifty five gallon oil drum with a round hole cut in its top sitting at an angle, allowing access to the interior. Inside was filled about three quarters of the way with sand. I had never seen these before, but after watching for a few moments, I noticed that they were used to make sure that those who had weapons could clear them before entering the building. This required the cartridges to be removed from the breech, and then to assure there were no bullets left in the chamber, the muzzle of the weapon was placed inside the container and the trigger pulled. If by chance there were a round in the chamber, it would discharge harmlessly into the sand. This was to prevent any accidental discharges inside the PX.

Entering the PX, I noticed a snack bar with café tables. Since it was near noon, we each purchased a hamburger, fries, and a milk shake. After lunch, we wandered around and checked out all the merchandise available for sale. There was everything from cigarettes to household appliances. There were TV sets, radios, cameras, shotguns, refrigerators, washing machines, air conditioners, and an assortment of civilian clothes. After checking out what they had to offer and not having any money to make any major purchases, buying a carton of cigarettes satisfied us. Outside there was another wooden bus stop. It seemed that anyone desiring transportation simply had to wait under the roof, and almost any vehicle would stop to provide a lift. While waiting, I inquired about the bleachers and stage and was informed they were for the *Bob Hope Christmas Show*, which would be coming in December. We then headed back to the transient center to find there were still no orders.

Chapter 23

Third Shore Party

AFTER SEVERAL DAYS, there were only a few of our class from Camp Pendleton who had not been assigned to a unit. Most went to infantry and recon units. Finally my name was called, and I went to the window and received orders to a unit called Third Shore Party. I had never heard of Shore Party prior to this. Those who knew about the unit told me that it was a service and supply battalion and congratulated me for being so lucky as to draw choice duty. I was told that these guys were usually in the rear with the gear.

After a few hours, a jeep arrived from Shore Party to transport me back to their compound. I noticed the driver had small rectangular red patches sewn to the outside of his trouser legs near his knees as well as one on the front of his utility cap. He told me that it was a designation for Third Shore Party members. As he drove, I noticed that the route we were taking was the same one that had taken us to Freedom Hill. To my delight, we turned into the barbed wire-enclosed compound directly across the road from Freedom Hill PX. This looked like my kind of duty station.

I presented my orders to the clerk in the H&S Company office and gave him my service record packet. The clerk told me that the first thing I had to do was take my utilities to the tailor and have the small red patches sewn on them. I asked him to elaborate on the meaning of the red patches. He explained that the patches distinguished Shore Party members from other Marines moving around in chaotic situations. It identified supply personnel from infantry, who had no patches.

I proceeded to the tailor shop where a Vietnamese woman was sitting behind a sewing machine. She took my utility trousers and caps and told me to come back in twenty minutes. Then I went across the street to supply and drew my combat gear, consisting of a helmet, a flak jacket, a cartridge belt, and a canteen; then to the armory, where I received and signed for a .45-caliber pistol and two clips with fourteen rounds of ammo. I then returned to the H&S Company clerk and was assigned one of the hooches where I was to sleep. On my way, I stopped by the tailor and picked up my utilities that now sported the hat and knee patches. I then removed the set I had on and donned the ones with the red patches. I waited as she quickly sewed the patches on my other set of gear.

I took my gear to the barracks and found my rack. After that, I went to chow. They had a large enclosed chow hall with kitchen and mess tables all inside the same building. There were several television sets, one in each corner where programs like *I Love Lucy* and *Twelve O'clock High* played on the local armed forces television network.

After dinner, I met up with some of the other corpsmen, and they showed me the club, another large building with a bar that served mixed drinks, beer, and soda. It also included a snack bar, tables, and television. A small stage for live bands was in one corner. This duty station was looking better and better. When the club closed at 2200, we returned to our barracks, and I got my first restful sleep since leaving the States.

In the morning at 0600, I was awakened by explosions nearby. Assuming we were being attacked, I jumped up out of my bed, grabbed my trousers and boots, and was ready to head for a bunker outside. I looked around and saw that no one else was reacting and felt a bit foolish. One of the other corpsmen that had observed me laughed and informed me that a Seabee unit set off explosives every morning in the gravel pit on the side of Freedom Hill. They loosened the gravel with the charges and loaded it into trucks to be transported to other areas of the base for use as road base and filling low areas. He also said that all new personnel had the same reaction.

I got dressed and was about to make my bunk but was told that it was not necessary. The unit employed a "house mouse" (a Vietnamese housekeeper) to make up the bunks and clean the barracks. In Japan, the barracks had *papa-sans* who performed the same services. I was starting to see why everyone had said this was a great assignment. We headed for the chow hall for breakfast.

After finishing a hearty breakfast, we reported to the sick bay to start the day's work. We started out with the usual minor items – headaches, diarrhea, gonorrhea, etc. After sick call ended, we performed preemployment physical examinations on civilian Vietnamese applying for jobs in our compound. These people were hired to work at the various menial jobs that the Marines of Shore Party felt were beneath their dignity. These jobs included housekeepers for the barracks, groundskeepers, laborers, and scullery workers. They also hired good-looking young girls to wait on the tables in the club. After the physicals were completed, we went to lunch. After lunch, we had free time, so I wandered around the compound. There was a big barbecue outside the mess hall, volleyball nets, and a basketball court. There was also a baseball field and a football field. It was like I was living at a country club.

The next day was Saturday, and we were on holiday routine. Except for sick call, there were no other tasks scheduled for the weekend. At noon, the barbecue was sizzling with steaks. In addition to steak, we had chili, salad, garlic toast, ice cream, and beer. All the sports areas were enthusiastically being used. "War? Is there a war?" This was even better than working at the hospital in Yokosuka. On the PA system, someone was playing a James Brown album, and he was singing, "I feel good!"

Sunday, the senior corpsman found me in the barracks and informed me that I was being transferred from H&S Company in Da Nang to Alpha Company up at Dong Ha. I had never heard of that area and inquired as to the location. He explained that it was up north in Quang Tri Province just six miles south of the DMZ and was not going to be as much fun as Da Nang. I knew this place had been too good to be true.

November 19, 1966

Dear Louise,

I am still in Da Nang, but now I have a unit. I am with 3rd Shore Party, which is way back in the rear and the only blasts we hear are across the street, only there they are taking out a hill for gravel and fill for other places on base. We live in a wooden hut much like the one I described before. I have been working in Sick Call and we hardly do anything but sit around all day.

They gave us our pistols when we checked in here the other day; we only wear them when we go off the compound.

Right across the street from here is the PX and USO. The food, believe it or not, is some of the best I've had in the service. We have hot showers, too.

But, as all good things go, it must end Monday. I have to go to a sub-unit of ours up at Dong Ha, which is about 6 miles from North Viet Nam, but I talked to a guy who just came back from there and he said that Shore Party is way back and I'd be doing the same thing I do here, except I'll be going out on patrols every once in a while.

Last night I went to the movie, which was "The Face of Fu Manchu". I saw it before.

Oh, we have TV here too. We get combat, and a lot of other shows in the evening.

I sure do miss you. I think about you all the time. At least I'll be home next December for Christmas or New Year and we can announce our engagement officially. I want to be with you forever.

I better go now, work to do or at least that's what they say.

Love,
Russ

P.S. I love you

On Monday, our driver delivered me with all my gear back to the Marine transient center where I waited to catch a flight to Dong Ha. I presented my transfer orders and was added to the flight manifest. After a short wait, the PA announced that all personnel destined for Phu Bai and Dong Ha proceed to the cattle car that delivered us to the aircraft, another C-130. Boarding the aircraft, I noticed that the cargo area was full of pallets of C rations and other supplies destined for the area. The same nylon web seats were available as my incoming flight, but this time they were only located along one side of the cargo area.

Soon the plane taxied out to the runway and waited for its turn to take off. Finally we were airborne. A short time later, we landed at Phu Bai for a short stop to unload some of the passengers and supplies. I noticed that it was raining harder and the air was cooler than in Da Nang. More passengers came on board, and we were again airborne.

The approach and landing at Dong Ha was a bit different than the smooth landings thus far. As we approached, the descent was more steep and rapid. When the wheels of the plane hit the runway, the props were reversed to assist in a more sudden stop. It was the first time flying that I had felt the necessity for the seat belt and was glad I had it buckled. Once the aircraft had slowed sufficiently, it made a short taxi and stopped, but did not shut down the engines. We quickly left the aircraft as the ground crew nimbly unloaded the supplies with forklifts. Simultaneously the outgoing personnel were loaded in. As soon as the forklifts were clear with their last load, the plane began taxiing toward the run-up area at the end of the runway before the cargo door had even been shut. When it reached the run-up area, it did a quick turn onto the runway and was off, on its way to the safety of the dense rain clouds above.

Chapter 24

Dong Ha

THE FIRST THING I noticed when I stepped off the plane was the air was much cooler and less humid than Da Nang. No one at Camp Pendleton had even hinted that there would be anything but hot tropical weather. It actually felt chilly, and I had no jacket. This felt more like Mendocino County winter weather. The rain was also more intense, not like the tropical showers I had experienced while in Da Nang. The only building was a small shack located near the middle of the runway. I also noticed an F-4 Phantom that had crash-landed and ended up off the west end of the runway.

I checked in with the clerk inside the shack, told him I was going to Third Shore Party. He got on a landline and made a call. He informed me that a driver would be arriving to take me over to the unit. I waited under the roof of the modest waiting area out of the rain.

As I was waiting, another plane landed. It was a DC-3 with "Air America" written on the side. The plane taxied up to the shack. The crew on the plane were dressed in baseball caps and Hawaiian print shirts, no two the same. They sported pistols in shoulder holsters and carbines. Someone told me they were CIA; Air America was their company. He also said that they pretty much could do and act as they pleased.

Finally a jeep from Third Shore Party showed up, and we left the airstrip from the north side and drove parallel to the strip until we hit the eastern end, then turned south. On the way, we passed by a work party of Marines operating road equipment improving the road. A dump truck was spreading gravel on the red clay while graders spread the rock, and rollers packed it into the surface. I noticed that the guy operating the grader had the red patch on his trouser leg.

A couple of hundred yards later, we turned into a muddy area that had a couple of strong-back hooches and numerous tents of various sizes. This was Alpha Company, Third Shore Party's compound. I walked up to the company office and reported in. They sent a runner down to sick bay, and the senior corpsman (an HM2 named Vinney) came up to greet me. The first thing I noticed about Vinney was that he had no strength in his hands and resembled the Pillsbury doughboy.

Outside, the surface of ground was saturated with rainwater. Out away from the strong backs, I noticed that empty shipping pallets had been placed on the ground in rows acting as sidewalks between the tents. Walking on the pallets kept the mud level in the compound to a minimum.

We walked to sick bay, and I met another corpsman and was given a cot in the sick bay tent where I stowed my gear. The tent was small, and one side was rolled up to allow access to the interior. The open wall was held up on tent poles providing a roof over the pallets at the entryway. It reminded me of a covered patio. The floor of the tent was also made of shipping pallets.

At noon we grabbed our canteen cups and went to the chow tent. Inside the tent was a big pot on a burner, a big coffeepot and big metal cans with lids. Lunch consisted of soup that reminded me of Lipton's chicken noodle soup. It was basically chicken broth with small cube-shaped chunks of chicken and lots of thin, one-inch noodles. The mess cook filled my canteen cup with the soup, and I drank off the broth, leaving the noodles and chicken in the bottom of the cup. After going back for more several times, I had enough noodles in the bottom of my cup to eat them with a spoon. While consuming the soup, I observed that the big cans held potato chips; I filled my canteen cup with them, and when I was through with them, I filled it with coffee. Taking my coffee, I went back to sick bay and played cards and became acquainted with the other corpsmen.

On the edge of our compound was a helicopter landing zone. The helicopters coming and going were very loud. They were the big double rotor CH-47 Chinooks, but there were also the smaller UH1Es and the older CH-34s. They landed, were loaded with supplies and cans of water, and then took off, some with a cargo net suspended from the underside. They were delivering needed supplies to the infantry troops out in the hills to the west. All the supplies were being assembled by the Marines of Shore Party. Trucks would come in and be unloaded by forklifts. The loads were assembled and placed in cargo nets or stacked to the side to wait for pickup. It was a well-orchestrated operation with everyone looking like they knew their job.

That night for dinner, we returned to the mess tent and were served ham, sweet potatoes, cabbage, beans, and coffee. I really couldn't complain. It was hot and filling. After dinner, I went to the club tent where there was a makeshift wooden bar with a Marine serving beer. Most of the Marines and some of the corpsmen were playing poker. Our senior corpsman was an avid poker player. He had some sort of nerve damage in his arms and his hands had little muscle tone, but he managed to hold on to his cards and smoke at the same time. When he took the cigarette out of his mouth, he had to hold his arm up so that his hand dangled above the cigarette and then lower his arm until his fingers were straddling it before he could grasp it with his fingers They were playing for payday stakes and kept track of who was winning on a notepad placed in a large Sir Walter Raleigh tobacco can with the poker chips. After a while, I decided to go back to sick bay and write a few letters. After that, I went to sleep. The only noise that night was the rain falling on the tent.

November 21, 1966

Dear Louise,

Here I am at Dong Ha, six miles from North Viet Nam. We flew up here from Da Nang in a plane, which took a little over an hour because we had to let some guys off at Phu Bai.

This place isn't as good as Da Nang. We live in tents and it is cooler, weather-wise that is. For lunch we had chicken noodle soup and potato chips, that was it, but it was good. For dinner we had ham, sweet potatoes, cabbage, beans and coffee. I really can't complain.

Tomorrow I get to go out on a helicopter run for a couple of days; they are breaking me in fast here.

This paper is getting sort of wrinkled. It's the tablet you gave me at Oceanside. It got wet in my sea bag at Da Nang. It was raining real good here for a while there.

We are supposed to get a typhoon or something like that tonight or tomorrow, so we had to make sure that our tents were tied down real good.

Oh, I also got my haircut short again, no use in having long hair over here.

I sure do miss you. I keep thinking of when I was home with you the last time and that one afternoon – remember? I can't wait until we are married and be together all the time. I love you so much. Some how I know I have to make it through to come back to you.

Well that's it for now. I'll write as soon as I can.

Love,
Russ

P.S. I love you

The next day, there was still not much to do but read and play cards. Sick call consisted of minor cuts and scrapes from moving equipment and supplies. Vinney came to me and said that he had scheduled me to go out with the helicopter support team in a few days; the weather was preventing any deliveries today. I learned that in addition to loading supplies on the helicopters, our unit was also responsible for helping get them on the ground where they were needed. This required that a support team go out to the receiving unit's area and direct the landing and supervise the unloading of the supplies. The team required a corpsman in case any accidents occurred during the process. It sounded more interesting than playing cards and reading, so I was looking forward to the trip if for no other reason than just the helicopter ride.

The next day, the weather broke, so I gathered up a few things to take with me. At noon, I met up with three Marines who were radiomen, and we boarded a CH-47 Chinook helicopter for the trip up into the mountains located to the west of Dong Ha. We entered the aircraft through the back cargo ramp and sat along the sides of the internal cargo area on the fold-down nylon seats. The entire deck of the cargo area was filled with five-gallon jerricans of water.

Within a few minutes, the helicopter started rising slowly up off the ground until the cargo net was finally off the ground, then its ascent quickened. The sides of the helicopter had ports to look out. As we passed by the airstrip, I again saw the crashed Phantom at the end of the runway. The land was flat, and much of it was flooded. Soon we were flying fairly high, up through the clouds. Occasionally I could see the ground. There were several other helicopters bringing in supplies on this flight, so our pilot flew around the area at a high altitude until it was our turn to land, and then we descended rapidly. As we came in, I could see the landing zone was just a patch of mud on the top of a grassy knoll. The Chinook came in and hovered as it gently lowered the sling load beneath it to the ground next to the LZ and released the hook and then moved over slightly so that when it set down, it cleared the cargo on the ground.

We had landed on a ridge defended by an infantry unit designated Three-Three, written 3/3. Immediately Marines from the LZ jumped in and started passing out the water cans, loading them on motorized platforms called Mules, which had wide mud tires, four-wheel drive, and four-wheel steering so that they could operate in mud and tight spaces. I followed the team members and stepped off into mud that reached the top of my boots. We slogged our way off the LZ and out of the thick mud over to an area on the adjacent hillside where several small tents made of shelter halves were located. Shelter halves are two-man tents that are designed so that each occupant carries half of the tent. The halves are snapped together at the ridge. This is where the outgoing team lived. This was to be our shelter while we were here. The team leader got report from the outgoing team, and they were on their way to the LZ to head back to Dong Ha.

I had a hard time getting around in the mud. My garrison boots with their relatively flat soles designed for walking on hard surfaces didn't give much traction. I had not been issued jungle boots, which have soles that are designed to give more traction in mud, worn by the other team members. Most of the time, this was not much of a problem because the lower part of the hill where the LZ and our tent were located was fairly flat. The worst part was the closest head; a four-holer located up another muddy hill with a fairly steep slope was fairly troublesome. To get there, I found myself taking two steps forward and sliding back one. It was a struggle, but when you got to go, you got to go. If we had to urinate, we had a piss tube located nearer to the tent.

That afternoon, I heard the sound of mortars hitting down in the valley to the south of our position. Curious because I had never seen mortars or any other form of incoming rounds hitting before, I made my way over to the far side of the LZ where I saw a little fireplug of a Marine in a salty utility cap with his sleeves rolled up around his large biceps. He was standing on the crest of the hill and was apparently trying to determine where the mortars were coming from. He reminded me of a big bulldog riding in the back of a pickup truck with his nose in the wind. I walked up to him and asked him what he was doing. He turned to me, and it was then that I noticed that he was a major and had a stub of an unlit cigar between his teeth. He confirmed that he was trying to locate the shooters. He then glared at me and said, "Don't you think with this incoming, you should be in a hole, Doc?" I told him, "I'll find one, sir!" and headed back to the tent. When I got back, I told the radioman about my conversation with the major, and he told me that the major's name was Stanley J. Wawrzyniak, who was rumored to be the toughest and best Marine since Chesty Puller. He had at one time been with Shore Party but now was with 3/3.

Thanksgiving Day, the rain stopped. It was sunny and a little warmer. The helicopters brought out Thanksgiving dinner in insulated cans full of hot turkey, dressing, mashed potatoes, cranberry sauce, and pumpkin pie. CBS news was on board and spent their day filming and interviewing Marines on the ridge. While I was waiting in the chow line for my dinner, the film crew took some shots of us being served our holiday meal.

The day after Thanksgiving, it started raining hard and steadily. All flights were cancelled until the weather broke. We spent three full days in our tents reading, eating C rations, and sleeping. On the fourth day, the heavy rain lightened up; and during a break in the showers, we got out of our tents and started a bonfire and made an attempt to dry out some of our wet gear.

The next day we were sitting around heating our C rations when the sound of small arms fire erupted on the other side of the ridge to the north. Our tent was located up the hill from the 81 mm mortars, and the larger guns on the tanks were just above us. I got used to the big guns and mortars, but whenever I heard small arms fire, I was ready to jump into my fighting hole. A firefight had broken out when one of the patrols ran into the enemy. It ended fairly quickly, and the report on the radio said that two Marines were wounded and three of the enemy killed. Already attended to by the corpsman attached to the unit, the casualties eventually arrived back at the LZ. Their wounds looked fairly minor, but out in the field, the risk of infection was great. A medevac (medical evacuation) was called in, and soon a helicopter showed up, and they were flown back to Dong Ha for further treatment.

Around the first of December, the weather cleared up enough for the Chinooks to resume the supply runs, and another helicopter support team came out to relieve us. We boarded a returning helicopter, and when we took off, it was clear enough see across the valley to the south. There were several tall rock formations around the valley that were spectacular. As we headed back to the coast, I could see that this country was in fact very beautiful.

December 2, 1966

Dearest Louise

I made it out of the field this morning. We were way out in the boonies somewhere near the Laotian boarder. It was nothing but mud and rain most of the time, but we got out O.K.

Our job out there was directing the landing of helicopters bringing in re-supply for the unit out there.

Thanksgiving day was sunny and warm and CBS news was out there. I guess I was on TV in the states because they took some shots of us standing in line for thanksgiving dinner.

The day after thanksgiving it started raining and we got soaked and didn't dry out for 2 days. We spent the 2 days actually we stayed 3 days in our pup tents. Talk about a closed in feeling! After 3 days we got out and started a bonfire and dried out some of our things that were still wet.

The next day we were sitting around heating our c-rations when we heard a fire fight on the other side of the hill. One of our patrols ran into some VC. They killed 3 VC and they wounded 2 of our guys.

All the time out there the mortars were going off. We were in a real good spot. The mortars were just down the hill from us and the larger guns were just above us, so we were in a spot where there was noise all the time. I got used to the big guns and mortars, but whenever I heard rifle fire I was ready to jump into my foxhole. Luckily the VC didn't attack.

So we got back today and I stink! I haven't had a shower for 2 weeks; I'm still wearing the same clothes I went out in.

When I got back here I found 3 letters waiting for me, 2 from you and 1 from Bruce.

About your engagement ring: I was planning on getting you one when I go to Japan in about 3 months on Rest and Recreation, but your idea sounds good. I mean us going together to pick one out.

I think we should have a church wedding by all means. One thing I always thought would be good is to have Mrs. Harlow as organist; she was for my mom and dad. We have always been good friends. Just a thought, what do you think?

This pen is hard to write with so I guess I better end.

I miss you so much I wish we could be together right now. I love you.

Oh, you wanted to know what Viet Nam is like. It's beautiful, especially from a helicopter. I want to get some pictures of it to send home. I am going to take my camera with me from now on.

Another thing I could use that "Space Blanket", its cold out in those hills with just a poncho over you.

I love you so much I can't wait until we're married.

Bye for now. I love you and never want to be without you.

Love,

Russ

P.S. I love you. By the way my address is 3rd Shore BN (not BR). I love you anyway.

Back at Dong Ha, I again spent most of my time reading and writing letters. After dinner, we went to our club tent and drank a beer and played cards. There was not much for me to do. Mel Overmeyer, whom I had been stationed with in Yokosuka and Camp Pendleton, had been transferred up to Dong Ha from Da Nang, and he was sent out in the hills on the helicopter support team.

By this time, the card games would start in the day and last most of the night. It was still very boring. Around the middle of December, the sun came out and the clouds totally disappeared. The temperature got up into the 90s during the day. I looked for other projects to keep busy. I went through and inventoried all the medical supplies that were stored in the waterproof metal "mount out" boxes. There must have been a dozen or so each containing a unique grouping of supplies stacked in the end of the tent. Some had medications; others had surgical instruments or battle dressings. I also started constructing lounge chairs out of scrap wood.

After a few days, Vinney came by the tent. (It always remained a mystery to me where he hung out because we never saw him on a regular basis except in the evening at the club tent.) He announced that in a few days, Alpha Company was being transferred farther south to an island in the delta of the Perfume River near the old Vietnamese imperial capital of Hue. He informed us that we would be leaving by truck to a ship located on the Qua Viet River and cruising down the coast. The island known as Thuan An was rumored to be another great duty station. Those stationed there could go swimming and surfing on the beach located next to the compound. It sounded like a surfer's dream. This could be almost as good as being stationed in Da Nang. We all looked forward to leaving our mud hole.

December 7, 1966

Dear Louise,

I received the two packages you sent. The first I received day before yesterday and the other one last night.

I have a confession to make: I opened my present already. I couldn't wait. Right now I am writing with the pen you sent me. It sure is handy not only for writing at night, but for seeing also. At night it gets so dark you can't even see your hand in front of your face and its kind of hard to walk around.

The gumdrop cake was real good. I say was because it isn't anymore because whenever anyone gets a package everyone gathers around until you open it and then they want to sample the goodies in it. That candy sure was sticky, like you said. I am trying to pull my rotten tooth out with it. I have it half out and I ate 2 pieces so far.

Also I read "Candy". I started it last night and just finished it a little while ago. That book sure was comical. Did you read it?

You ask if I'm getting your letters OK. I sure am, the last letter I received was written on the 29th and I got it on the 4th. 5 days to get my mail up here isn't bad.

There is one guy up here that was stationed in Japan with me. He is the one that relieved me out in the field, he took my place and I came back here.

We got word yesterday that we may be moving to PhuBai, where our houses are on an island in the middle of a river, so they say.

I wish I had something to send you for Christmas. There just isn't anything up here that I can send. The PX doesn't have anything except soap, shaving cream, etc. and we aren't allowed to go into town. I haven't even seen any Christmas cards. I guess I'll just have to send my love.

It's still raining here. I wonder if it will ever stop.

The mail was just brought in and I got the package from my parents. More goodies.

Just think, next year at this time I should be getting ready to come home to you. Then we can be together again for a while. That will be longer than I've been home before, probably 30 days. I can't wait until I see you again. I love you more than I can say and I want your more than anything in the world. "Louise Jewett", yep! I guess that sounds OK to me in fact it sounds great. I wish we were already married. I love you so much.

Well I guess I better get this letter in the mail.

Oh, you asked me if I wanted anything. I sure would like more things to read. I finished "Candy" in less than a day and now there's nothing to do, if you could, could you slip in a Playboy every month or so. I don't really have any preference on books, just so they aren't westerns or murder mysteries, those don't interest me at all. It's just a thought, you can if you want, if not OK.

I'll sign out now. Be good and remember I love you.

Love,
Russ

P.S. I love you

Chapter 25

Boat Trip to Thuan An

AS THINGS GO in the military, it was another situation of "hurry up and wait." We had packed up all our gear and were ready to go to Phu Bai when we got the word to "stand down." We would not be leaving as planned, but would be delayed for an indefinite period.

When the rain stopped, it was actually warm; the temperature was up in the eighties. With the sunny days, we opened up both sides of the tent and let everything dry out. We strung up ropes between tents to act as clotheslines, and wet gear was hung out in the sunshine to dry. We took this opportunity to inventory our medical supplies. All our supplies were contained in large metal cases known as "mount-out boxes." We spent the better part of the day opening each box and ensuring that all the equipment and supplies listed were accounted for. Anything that was missing had to be replaced. A list was made and forwarded to Da Nang, and we received the items in a day or so when it was flown up and delivered.

December 16, 1966

Dearest Louise,
Here it is nine days before Christmas and boy is it hot. I received two letters from you yesterday. Like always I was glad. I also received a letter from my mom and Steve.

Yesterday for lack of anything better to do we re-arranged our tent, moved all the shelves, desks and my bed. Then we closed up the side that was open and opened the end so not so many flies can get in here. I built a table out of old scrap lumber and use a blanket for a tablecloth.

Last night me and two guys (who were stationed in Yokosuka with me) decided to play cards, so we started playing rummy at about 6:30 and when it was time for lights out we zipped down the tent flaps and windows and door and continued playing until 3am. My bed was cluttered with all my gear, so I slept on a stretcher.

You asked what my address meant well here goes; my name, rank, and serial number are on the top line. Next H&S Co. is Headquarters and Support Company. Then comes 3rd Shore Party BN, which is the Battalion. FMF PAC means Fleet Marine Force, Pacific. The rest is the Fleet Post office address.

No, I don't mind you telling my mom that we are engaged, in fact I was going to tell her myself in the next letter I write to her, but I guess I don't have to tell her now. I told you she was pretty smart.

Oh, my tooth came out thanks to your candy. It sure was sticky, the candy, not my tooth.

I've decided to not get your rings in Japan, but to wait and let you pick one out. I am going to get a bunch of other things while I'm there though.

We found out today that we aren't going to Phu Bai after all, at least not yet anyway. So no telling how long we'll be here.

My next project is going to be to build us some lounge chairs out of wood and canvas, I mean, there is nothing else to do around here.

I just finished reading "Masterstroke" which was about the "I Spy" series on TV. I think Bill Cosby is too cool for words. You know, he used to be a Navy Corpsman, too.

Right now there are six guys in our tent here counting myself. Three of them are reading books and magazines, one is asleep on the stretcher, one is playing solitaire, and I am writing this letter, so you can see we are really busy around here.

I also took a course in Spanish to brush up on that, just to have something to do.

I sure do miss you. I just sit around thinking about us and the future. I can't wait until we are married. I love you so much.

I better go and eat now so bye for now.

Love
Russ

PS I love you (Oh, I just found out I'm now in B Company instead of H&S so I thought I should tell you so you can get the right address.)

Finally on the twenty-third of December, our orders to relocate came in. I got my gear together, and we loaded up on trucks. I climbed aboard the back of a 6-by, and after the usual delay in getting started, our convoy headed out. We left the compound and drove over to an area on the river where several landing craft were waiting. The ships sat with their bow doors open and ramps down. Our truck just drove on board. Inside, the ship was like a cargo hold with no deck above. When we parked, we were told to get off the vehicles and climb up to the main deck, which required climbing a ten-foot vertical ladder out of the cargo deck. Up on deck, we waited to get underway as they continued to load our vehicles (including a road grader) on board. When the cargo deck was filled, the remaining vehicles were directed to the other ships. After our entire unit was loaded aboard, the bow doors were closed for the journey and the ships readied to depart.

Some of the Marines retrieved their folding chairs from the vehicles and placed them on the main deck surrounding the cargo deck below. The weather was sunny and warm. As the ship turned and headed downriver through the delta, it had the atmosphere of a lazy summer river cruise; all that was missing were drinks and ladies. Since I didn't have a chair, I took the seat in the cab of the road grader as my lounge. I had my 35 mm camera and was taking pictures of our trip. Eventually the ship approached the mouth of the river. The chief of the boat ordered all the folding chairs stowed. Crossing the bar at the river mouth could be tricky, and for safety, all hands reported to the mess deck; we were to remain inside during the crossing. I climbed up the ladder to the bridge and stayed inside the wheelhouse. I was still considered a sailor by the ship's crew and was allowed up there as a courtesy while the Marines had to remain on the mess deck where there were no portholes and little ventilation.

As the ship left the river, the coxswain picked up speed to meet the oncoming waves. The water got rougher as the outflow of the river met the ocean waves. As we crossed over the sandbar outside the river mouth, a big wave hit the large square bow of the ship, and the ship broached, putting it almost parallel to the waves. The next wave rolled the ship to the port side so that the starboard side was considerably higher, causing all the vehicles in the cargo bay to shift against the port side. The road grader was closest to the bulkhead, and the other unrestrained vehicles slid over against it. The next wave broke over the starboard side and drenched everything on the cargo deck, including my camera. The coxswain got the ship back on course. The sea was a bit rough, but we at least were back on course.

Out on the open ocean, the chief announced that we could go out on the main deck in front of the wheelhouse, but not back out on the narrow decks on either side or into the cargo bay. They installed safety lines around the deck. Unfortunately, I left my camera out of its case, hanging by its strap on the control levers of the grader. I had expected to return to my seat again once we cleared the bar.

The remainder of the trip down the coast was fairly rough. Sitting out on deck, I got wet a couple more times as waves broke on the bow and the resulting spray showered those of us who were on deck. As the day went by, the wind picked up, the waves got steeper, and white caps developed. As the day progressed, the seas got rougher. The deck was cleared, and all hands advised to stay inside. I went back up to the bridge. As it got rougher, I was summoned below deck. Many of the Marines were seasick. I sympathized with them, but had nothing to treat their nausea. Below deck, the smell of vomit was starting to get to me, so I again took advantage of my status and returned to the bridge for the remainder of the cruise. Up there, I could see the horizon and was able to step out of the wheelhouse for fresh air.

Around 1700, our ship approached the entrance to the Perfume River at Hue. Once it crossed the bar, the water became smooth, and the ship went back to a stable condition. The Marines recovered from their seasickness. I retrieved my camera and found it was drenched and water had gotten into it. The saltwater had corroded it beyond repair. The film was also ruined. I gave it a burial at sea.

Inside the estuary, the ships turned south, traveling parallel to the sandbar in the river's delta. We finally reached our destination, a large flat spit of sand covered with pine trees. Our ship headed into a beach that had a road leading off into the trees. The announcement was made to prepare for landing, and the ship revved its engine, and the bow slid nicely up onto the sand. After the crew was satisfied that the ship was secure, the doors were opened and the bow ramp lowered. Under normal circumstances, the vehicles simply start up their engines and disembark. The next task was to separate the vehicles because they had shifted and now were all crowded together. The crew had to pull each one sideways with a hand winch to allow each vehicle clear of the others before it was backed out onto the beach. Finally all the vehicles were on shore, and we proceeded to the Shore Party compound located farther south on the island.

We traveled along the road through the pine forest. The road ran through several small fishing villages. When we approached a village, the citizens came out and waved to us as we passed. We then passed by several fuel storage areas on the island. These consisted of large black rubber bladders sitting in shallow holes in the sand. Each bladder contained several thousands of gallons of fuel in each.

After traveling several miles, we reached the Shore Party compound. This camp was much different than the previous ones. It consisted of tents erected on wooden platforms two feet up off the sand. It had the same shipping pallet type of sidewalks as the Dong Ha compound, but here the pallets were covered with solid planking and were intended to keep the sand levels in the hooches down to a minimum. No mud here.

After settling into our tents, I went to chow and found the food to be much better here than up north. I guessed because we were closer to the main supply line at Phu Bai, better quality supplies were available. After chow, I wandered down to the beach on the seaward side of the island, which was just outside the chow tent. I noticed there were several surfboards stored in a rack on the beach. This duty was looking better. On the trip down, I heard stories from several Shore Party members about being stationed here previously, but I hadn't imagined it would be a paradise island. I retired that evening very pleased with my current situation. I was looking forward to hitting the beach and getting into the surf again. The weekend parties here on the beach were said to be better than those in Da Nang.

Chapter 26

A Shau Valley

THE NEXT MORNING, we were awakened at 0600 and told to get our gear on and get ready to move out. Bravo Company was the permanent resident on the island, and we were only here as transients. We left our seabags in the tents, which at least meant that we would be returning. After a quick breakfast, we loaded up in the backs of our trucks again and drove to the river where we had arrived the evening before.

This time, we were met by a much smaller landing craft. It was only large enough to hold two trucks at a time and had a ramp at each end. We drove on board; the bow ramp was brought up, and the boat backed out away from the beach and headed for the other side of the wide estuary. When it reached the other side, it slid up onto the sand, the stern ramp was lowered, and we drove off onto another beach.

Once all our vehicles were on land, we took the road and headed east. As we approached the city of Hue, the buildings became more ornate. Instead of grass and sticks (as they were in the outskirts and on the island), these were made of concrete with a textured layer of stucco on the exterior. Trees lined the streets. Stucco-covered walls separated the houses from the streets. Some of these walls had ornate ironwork gates and the gardens behind the walls. They contained what looked like banana and coconut trees as well as a variety of tropical flowers.

As we got nearer to the center of the city, the architecture looked more European. One of the Marines informed me that most of the residents in Hue spoke

French and the culture was more like that of France than Vietnam. The women on the street were very beautiful Eurasians, having both French and Vietnamese ancestry. This was the first time I saw the long white *ao dai* dresses. These women were dressed impeccably and had class, even in the rain. They were nothing like the peasants I had seen thus far in Da Nang and Dong Ha. The men on the streets were not in military uniform but were dressed in European-style suits and ties with jaunty hats and berets.

Our convoy traveled through marketplaces with shops instead of an open market. We passed by an ornate large old Catholic church and hospital. As our convoy continued through the city streets, the neighborhoods started looking like the ones we had passed entering the city, but the architecture styles were in the reverse order as we entered. It wasn't long until we were again passing by grass and stick houses with bamboo fences.

Along the road in some of the flooded areas were large nets hanging on a long pole attached to a fulcrum. Fishermen lowered the big net into the flooded areas near the estuaries, periodically raising the nets out of the water to harvest crawfish, eels, and fish that got trapped in the rising net. We continued traveling on this road until it took us away from the river and farther inland. We soon arrived at the Marine base at Phu Bai.

We passed a convoy forming on the road, continuing until we reached the end where we turned around and joined in at the end. As we waited, vehicles from other units arrived and took their places in the line until there were fifty or more vehicles assembled. By noon, we were getting restless just sitting and waiting for something to happen. Finally the vehicles at the head of the convoy started moving, and as the line started stretching out, we began moving again.

We returned to Hue along the same route we had taken into Phu Bai. The route was the same until we got to the Perfume River. Instead of turning east, we went west. We proceeded past several bridges that had been damaged and their spans were in the water. Eventually we arrived at the only bridge left standing and crossed to the other side. We passed by the old imperial palace known as the Citadel and continued north on Highway 1 until we were out of the city again. Our convoy was now traveling at about fifty miles per hour, and the highway was in poor repair, and the ride was very rough.

After half an hour or so, the convoy slowed down and turned west on a dirt road, but still traveling fairly fast. Twenty minutes later, our vehicles pulled out of the convoy into a large open area and proceeded to an area at the top of a small knoll. There we stopped. The rest of the convoy continued down the road and out of sight.

The weather was still overcast with the occasional shower. We spent the remainder of the afternoon digging fighting holes around the perimeter of the hill. As dusk arrived, it started to pour down rain. After a dinner of C rations, I had nothing else to do, so I tried to get some sleep while sitting on the ground with a poncho to protect me from the pouring rain. This was one hell of a way to spend Christmas Eve.

That was the coldest and wettest night I had spent thus far since I arrived in Vietnam. At least on the HST (helicopter support team) in November, I was able to sleep in a sleeping bag in a shelter half tent. I was cold and miserable. I didn't know why we couldn't sleep under the canvas-covered back of the trucks. The next day, I learned that our officers were using them as their sleeping quarters. It was Christmas Day, and this place was so remote that Santa hadn't even bothered to stop during the night.

Our new senior corpsman came back from a meeting and informed us we were on operation Chinook supporting combat units farther up in A Shau Valley. He informed us that they estimated we could be here as long as six to eight weeks. Truckloads of supplies, pallets of C rations, and ammunition started arriving and were unloaded by hand. Our area was becoming a staging ground. We started setting up camp. A large plastic camouflage tarp was provided, and we erected it as a makeshift shelter tall enough to stand up in, but shed the water on all sides, resembling a short tepee. Once we were out of the weather, the ground underneath was leveled, and we had enough room to set up some cots. I dug a small ditch around the edge of the tent to collect the water running off the plastic and made sure that it drained away from the tent so that our dirt floor would remain relatively dry and mud free as possible. Then the corpsmen thought we'd give everyone a real special Christmas present, so we dug a hole and set up a four-holer; at least now we did not have to squat to defecate in a cat hole.

The next day, the noise of helicopters landing and taking off dominated the area. This time it was the smaller ones, *Huey*s and 34s. They would land, and the Marines would throw cases of supplies on board, and they would fly off into the valley off to the southwest. It rained constantly. We corpsmen had nothing constructive to occupy our time. We hung out in our tent, drank a lot of C ration coffee, wrote letters, read, and played cards. When we needed water for coffee, we would place our canteen cup in the space between the edge of the tarp and the ditch to catch the water running off the tarp. Then all we had to do was heat it up and add the instant coffee.

For seven days, I was wet and cold. None of us even had a blanket, only ponchos without the fabric liners (that were supplied with liners in cool climates). Evidently this went along with the misconception that Vietnam was a hot tropical country. I learned that the reason the weather was so different here than in Da Nang was a high mountain range runs from Laos to the sea just north of Da Nang. The weather south of the mountains is always more tropical than the north side. For a supply unit, we sure didn't have any supplies for our own comfort, but I doubt if Third Shore Party was the problem. Up to this time, most of the US involvement in Vietnam was from Da Nang southward. At least we got our mail. I received a package from back home with books, candy, and cookies. This was shared among all of us, as was the protocol whenever anyone got goodies from home.

December 28, 1966

Dear Louise,

Many things have happened since I've last written to you. I am now out in the boonies somewhere 20 or so miles north or northwest of Hue (way).

We left Dong Ha on the 23rd of December and went by boat to Phu Bai. On the way as we were coming out of the mouth of the Dong Ha river we hit rough water and somehow got crossway in the waves and we almost cap sized and we got soaked. The trip was pretty rough al the way and we got wet a couple other times also. All the Marines were getting sick.

Finally we got to Phu Bai and got to "Paradise Island" which is just what it was. We thought we really had it made. They told us they had swimming every day and they had a couple of surfboards, a real good chow hall, a club and wooden sidewalks. The whole bit.

We went to sleep thinking how we had it made. When we woke up in the morning the Sergeant told us to get our packs, helmets, and weapons and get ready to move out. We hadn't even been there 12 hours and we had to leave.

We went by convoy through Hue and on through. It was raining all the time. Christmas eve I slept in a foxhole full of water. The next morning we woke to find Santa hadn't even stopped to see us. Some wise guy hollered out "Merry Christmas" and we all told him what he could do and where he could go.

Christmas day we started setting up camp. We thought we'd give a real special Christmas Present, so we dug an outhouse hole and were about to put a seat on it when the Lieutenant came up to us and said that he moved the command post and it would be down wind from our hole so we called him a few unmentionable names under our breath and started making the hole longer, thinking it would make a good foxhole, which it did, so we put up a tent right next to it. The next day we had barely gotten up when up came the Lieutenant again and told us to dig the hole for the outhouse. We started digging the ground was so hard it took us 6 hours to dig a hole 4 feet square and 5 feet deep. Now that it's raining again and everything is flooded we're thinking about making it a wishing well.

No sooner had we gotten finished digging the hole than the Lieutenant came up to us again and told us we would have to move our tent the next morning because he wanted the space to store all our stockpile of C-rations. So yesterday morning we got up and it was raining harder than ever, so you see the corpsman's tent nonchalantly moving across the field to its new location. After we got the tent to where we wanted it we got soaked again putting it up and securing it. So far since I've been out here I've forgotten what it's like to be warm and dry. I have in my possession at this moment, one pair of wet socks, one pair of wet boots, a pair of partially dry utility trousers, a dry sweatshirt and shirt. (The splotches on this paper are dirty water from my socks, I just wrung them out and accidentally got some on the paper.) I have no blanket, no underwear, no clean clothes at all and nothing else I need. Even this paper I'm writing on is damp. War is hell! We are supposed to be out here for 6 to 8 weeks. I sure hope we get some more supplies. Oh, the operation we are on is called "Chinook".

I was thinking last night about how much money I'll make over here. It comes to over $3,900 dollars in 13 months. I was wondering what kind of car we will have. Plus all the money I make until I get out of the Navy and the savings bonds I figure over $6,000. I sure do love you. I wish I was with you right now instead of being out here in the middle of nowhere. I want to be with you forever.

Well, it's getting dark here and it's hard to see so I guess I better go now.

Love always
Russ

PS I love you

Chapter 27

MACV-I

THE DAY BEFORE New Year's Eve, with no explanation, we were told to load up, and our trucks headed back out to Highway 1. Coming back from out of the field, we again rode at 50 mph back south to Hue. On the way back, we saw kids lining the highway with their hands out begging for food. We all threw individual meal boxes of C rations to them as we passed. Most of the boxes would break apart when they hit the ground. Every time this occurred, the kids scrambled and fought each other for the loose cans.

Back on Thuan An island, I went to work in the sick bay. We held sick call twice a day. Master Chief Pinchon was the senior corpsman at Third Shore Party, but preferred to live on Thuan An island rather than Da Nang. He was a retread, retired from the reserves, but he had volunteered to return to active duty when Vietnam began to escalate. He wanted to be a veteran of WWII, Korea, and Vietnam. The master chief was from New Orleans. He was good friends with trumpet player Al Hirt, and both owned restaurants in the French Quarter. Though Chief Pinchon was the senior corpsman, he spent most of his time at the officers' mess tent, preparing their meals and tending bar at their club. Our battalion surgeon was a young guy who had just gotten out of his residency in the States.

New Year's Eve, the cooks prepared and served a big barbecue. Chief Pinchon presided over the preparation and was teaching his craft to the mess cooks. There was more food than we could eat. The master chief provided us with a never-ending supply of hot buttered rums. By the time I stopped eating, I had consumed three steak sandwiches, various types of vegetable dishes, several cans of orange soda, and an unknown quantity of hot buttered rums. Even though my knowledge of hot buttered rum was not much, I have never tasted any better before or since.

December 31, 1966

Dear Louie,

Yesterday they brought us back from the field. For 7 days I was wet and cold no blanket or anything. I got the books and candy and cookies. Yesterday was the only sunny day we've had since we left Dong Ha

Now I am on the island at Phu Bai Here we have no mud, just sand. Which is a real relief after being out in knee-deep mud for the last week.

I received your New Years package today. The penlight was real good. Thanks. I got a kick out of that bottle of scotch.

Tonight is New Years Eve. We just had a big barbecue under a shelter. I had 3 steak sandwiches and 2 cans of orange soda.

It's still raining, I wonder if it will ever stop.

The mail just came in. Guess what! I got your Christmas Eve letter. Sounds like you had a real nice Christmas.

So you got a cedar chest, huh? Pretty good, shows future planning.

Coming back from out in the field was quite an experience. We rode in a two and a half tone truck and flew down the road at about 50 MPH, which on these roads is pretty fast. All along the way the people, especially the little kids, wave and holler "OK" and "Number one" and "hello". It's real neat. Like you are a big hero or something.

Oh, when we first came here to the island on the 23rd the little kids came up to us and said "Hey, Doc" and point to their scratches and cuts and sores, by the time we had finished I think every kid had methiolate and Band-Aids on them. We used up all our Band-Aids, a bottle of methiolate and then had to satisfy them by putting on adhesive tape (which is all they really wanted).

Next week sometime I will probably have to go into Hue, where we run a helicopter loading zone, this is right across the street from the University of Hue.

I had some real good snap shots of the trip up here, but my film got all wet on the boat, so they won't turn out so I threw them away.

I miss you and wish you and I could be together right now on this New Years Eve, I love you so much. All I think about is you and I being together forever. I hope the time goes by fast, it is doing pretty good as it is, but I wish it would go by faster.

Thanks again for the Care Packages. The tangerines are all eaten up already.

Well I guess that's it for now

Love,

Russ

PS I love you. Only 49 weeks until I come home to you.

The next day, it was my turn to go out with a work party to Hue. Shore Party had a small compound on the Perfume River across the river from the Citadel and near Hue University. My job was to provide first aid if any of the Marines injured themselves while running their forklifts unloading pallets of C rations and other supplies. I rode into the city, this time in a small pickup-style truck known as a PC (personnel carrier). Once I arrived, I went into the tent and checked in with the Marine in charge to let him know I was on board. He said I was free to do what I wanted and I could walk around Hue if I desired, as long as I checked with him before leaving the compound.

Once again, there was nothing for me to do. I killed time watching the Marines hard at work unloading landing craft, with forklifts bringing in pallets of supplies. These larger LSU crafts brought C rations and munitions up from Da Nang. They were removed from the ships and placed on trucks and hauled to Phu Bai and other military bases in the area. The only area out of the weather was the large tent with a stove where the Marines would take their breaks between ships. The tent contained several cots where they slept at night while standing security on the equipment.

Shortly after I arrived, a sleazy-looking Vietnamese officer and his two bodyguards came into the compound and asked me who was in charge. The officer was a slimy little guy and smoked cigarettes in a long holder. I called the sergeant, who was the noncommissioned officer in charge, into the tent. The Vietnamese officer asked if he could talk in private, so I stepped out of the tent. After several minutes, I heard a commotion and went back into the tent. The sergeant called a couple of his guys in off their forklifts and had all three Vietnamese escorted off the compound. After they were gone, I inquired as to what had happened. He told me that the officer was trying to purchase supplies for the black market, which was one of the things supply units had to deal with all the time. At night, he doubled the guard to help reduce the chances of raid on the supplies by the officer and his men.

Everyone went back to work, and I eventually got bored. I checked out with the sergeant and went for a walk on the street that paralleled the river. To the east from our compound was Hue University, so I spent some time walking around their campus. It was between semesters, so there were no students around; they were all home for the Christmas holidays. To the west, I came across a group of buildings with a sign designating it as Headquarters, I Corps, Military Assistance Command, Vietnam, or simply called MACV-I. I walked in and asked for their medic. This was a US Army compound where the troops lived in a converted hotel built by the French during the colonial days. He was paged, and when he came out, I introduced myself. He was a friendly guy and was probably as bored as I was. He asked me if I wanted to take a tour of their little compound, and I accepted.

The chow hall was a restaurant. The tables were covered with white linen tablecloths; each place setting had a cloth napkin and silver service. In the center of each table was a vase of fresh flowers. These tables seated no more than eight persons per table. The living quarters were individual apartments with a private bath, kept clean by a maid assigned to that section of the floor. All the maids wore outfits that were all the same, like in a fine hotel.

After the tour, he invited me to have lunch. A Vietnamese dining room staff waited on us. There was a maître d' in a tuxedo, waitresses, and bus staff all in clean starched uniforms. According to the medic, to be stationed at MACV-I was like being sent to Siberia compared to the living conditions at MACV headquarters in Saigon.

After lunch, I walked around Hue and admired the architecture and the beautiful women in their long dresses. I purchased food from the street vendors and found it to be delicious. In the evening, I returned to our humble tent, had some C rations for dinner, and slept the night. The next morning, another corpsman came in for his shift, and I returned to the island.

Chapter 28

Hue Hospital

BACK IN MY world, I was working as an assistant to our doctor. After sick call, he and I went out into one of the villages on the island and treated some of the civilians whom he had been seeing as patients in his spare time. We bought hot fresh-baked bread from one of the little shops. The kids would all come around and beg us to give them Band-Aids. They would come in and, with a pitiful face and the eyes of a puppy dog with a small tear in the corner of their eye, would point to a scratch or sore. I would dress it with some Neosporin and the much-sought-after Band-Aid. As soon as the dressing was applied, the puppy dog face with the crocodile tears would instantly change into a big smile, and then they would ask with their hand out, "You give me money?" Some of them would distract you while others attempted to pick your pockets.

While out in the villages, we occasionally would come across real emergencies. There was an old man about eighty years old who had urinary retention. The doctor had me slip a Foley catheter into his bladder and drain off the urine to reduce the pressure causing him excruciating pain. We left the catheter in place and clamped it off and left instructions for the family to unclamp it every two hours to allow the urine to drain. While we were there, one of the shop owners came and asked us to come quick, one of his employees had been thrown from the back of a vehicle as it sped down the road. We went to where the victim was located at one of the small huts on the beach. She had abrasions and contusions, but after the doctor examined her, he determined she had no broken bones.

The next day, the doctor determined that the old man needed to be seen by a urologist at the Catholic hospital in Hue. Since I was familiar with the case, the chief came to me and asked if I could accompany the old man on the transfer. A personnel carrier showed up, and the doctor and I rode out to the old man's house. The doctor explained to the family that the urologist in Hue was expecting the old man at the hospital for admission to treat his bladder problem. We loaded him on a stretcher onto the back of the PC and took him into Hue. The doctor returned to the compound.

When we reached the hospital, I had the driver take us to the receiving area. I walked in and informed the staff that the urologist was expecting this patient. They brought him into their facility. I was struck by how cold it was inside the hospital. Evidently they had no heating system, or for some reason, it was not working. I also looked around their area and found dried blood on their gurneys and pointed out to them that maybe they should improve the sanitation in their receiving area. The person in charge barked some orders, and a few moments later, the housekeeping crew came in with their pails of soap and water and sheepishly cleaned off all the blood that I had pointed out. A while later, the urologist came out and told me he would be keeping the old man for a week or so and that I should relay this message to his family back at the village. I thanked him and returned to the island.

January 4, 1967

Dear Louie,

I got back from the loading ramp in Hue yesterday; I only stayed out there one night. We went out Monday morning and it was raining as usual. The whole day was spent (at least by me) in the tent. It was real cold also.

Later in the afternoon, though, I did get up enough nerve to walk down the street to an Army base where they have it as easy as back in the states, they live in a house type barracks with about 8 guys to a building, their mess hall is like a cafeteria, with waitresses, no less, but I think the thing that impressed me most was – Flush Toilets!! Wow! I went and flushed one several times just to see if I still remembered how to do it.

After spending a cold wet night and eating several boxes of C-rations I came back to the island.

When I got back the Doctor and I had to go out into the village just outside the gate to treat an 80 year old Vietnamese man who had bladder trouble and hadn't gone for 4 days. We slipped a tube into his bladder and you could see the relief on his face.

After doing that we came back and no sooner had we sat down when Mr. Sum, the Vietnamese man who owns a little shop here on base came running in and asked me to come quick because one of the girls that works in his store had fallen off a truck and cut her legs pretty bad. So I grabbed up some bandages, methiolate and other goodies and made it down to the store. She had some pretty bad cuts, but nothing serious. Just to be sure I checked her over for broken bones and gave her a shot of Penicillin just to make sure she didn't get any infection you understand.

Today I had to take the old man with the bladder into the hospital. I sure wouldn't want to be in that hospital. It was dirty and grubby and cold. I thought Japanese hospitals were bad! Then we went into Phu Bai and then back here again.

Oops. I just opened a can of root beer and it sprayed all over the paper as well.

Nothing much else doing here.

I sure do miss you very much. All I think about is us. I want to be with you forever and ever and never be without you or your love. Next year at this time we will have only 9 months to go and then you know what! I can't wait.

Hey, how did your aunt get two pictures of me to put in that charm deal?

I guess I better go now it's about time to get some sleep. Bye for now.

Love
Russ

PS I love you

The next day when I reported to work, I noticed a praying mantis in the window of our sick bay. I watched as it caught other bugs and ate their heads off and dropped their bodies to the windowsill below. We decided to leave it there as it was helping to control the flies that entered into the room from outside, better than spraying them with DDT. Things were going well for me. I was the doctor's assistant, the duty was easy, and I got to go into Hue and Phu Bai, what more could I ask for except possibly a sunny day on the beach. This was soon to end abruptly.

The next day, I came into the sick bay, and the chief looked like someone had just died. He informed me that he had bad news. He took me aside like a grandfather and apologized for what he was about to tell me. Third Medical Battalion, who I found out controlled the distribution of corpsmen in the Third Marine Division, sent orders that I was to be transferred to an infantry unit that was short on medical personnel. I was being transferred back to Dong Ha to 3/3, the unit that was living on the muddy ridgetop, out where I was on the HST at Thanksgiving. I was to leave immediately for Da Nang to process out of Shore Party and then report as soon as possible to 3/3.

I traveled back to Phu Bai again by truck and caught a flight back to Da Nang. I went to the Shore Party compound and picked up my records and turned in my gear and pistol. The next day, I was back in the Marine transient terminal waiting for a flight back to Dong Ha. After waiting all day, I was informed that there would be no more flights to Dong Ha, and so I went back to Shore Party to spend the night.

January 8, 1967

Dear Louise,

Well I moved again. I have been transferred out of Shore Party because they need Corpsmen out in the field.

Right now I am in Da Nang waiting for a plane to Dong Ha I am supposed to be stationed with 3rd Battalion, 3rd Marines. That is the place where I was when I first went on the Helicopter Support Team that time.

I wish I could stay with Shore Party, but I guess that's the way it goes sometimes.

So far since I've been here seems like the only thing I've done is move around. From DaNang to Dong Ha, down to Thuan An Island for 12 hours, back to some different boonies for a week back to Thuan An Island again, to Hue, to Phu Bai, to Da Nang and tomorrow back to Dong Ha, but that will be only for about a month, because 3/3 is going on a ship in February for 3 months. After we get back the guy I worked for on the island told me that he is going to try to get me back into shore party. They had transferred me without him knowing about it until it was too late, but like I said he's going to try to get me back. Besides for that everything is the same old thing.

Being here, not knowing anybody sure is lonely; I wish I could be with you right now. I miss you so much. It seems that at this moment I have only one friend in the world and I also know I love her. When I get home I know I'll never be lonely again because I have you waiting there for me. I love you so much. I better get off that subject before I break up.

I did get all of your packages. I don't remember if I told you that in my last letter or not. I wish it would stop raining. It gets to be depressing when all it does is rain all day and all night. Makes you wonder if it will ever stop.

I haven't eaten since yesterday noon, not because I didn't want to, but there is nothing. I arrived here in DaNang too late for dinner and slept in the transient barracks where I stayed the first nights I was in Viet Nam. I saw my first movie in 2 months; it was "The Plague of the Zombies" which was pretty good.

Today I went to Shore Party to check out and was too late for brunch and next meal wasn't until 4 pm.

It's still raining and they just announced that there won't be any more flights to Dong Ha today, so I guess I'll go back to the Shore Party and spend the night.

Here I am back in the Shore Party area. I managed to miss dinner, but I talked one of the cooks out of two turkey sandwiches, wasn't much, but it tasted good.

Now there's nothing to do so I think I'll go to the club and watch TV or something since I can't think of anything else to write.

Always remember I love you. I want to be your husband and forever be with you. I love you more than anything else in the world I wish I could be with you instead of over here. Bye for now.

Love always
Russ

PS I love you

The next morning, I proceeded back to the Marine transient terminal. Finally in the afternoon, the weather in Dong Ha cleared enough to allow flights in and out. I again boarded a C-130 for the flight to Phu Bai and Dong Ha to begin my life as a grunt.

Chapter 29

3/3 Dong Ha

I ARRIVED BACK in Dong Ha on a C-130 flight from Da Nang via Phu Bai on another rainy day. As in November, the plane made a steep decent to the airstrip, and as it touched down, the props were reversed for the short field landing. With the plane reduced to taxi speed, the pilot brought his craft up to the shack located midfield. This time, the pilot was in no hurry to turn about and take off. The plane stopped in front of the terminal, the engines shut down. The rear cargo door lowered, and I exited the plane. I reported into the terminal, and the clerk made a call to 3/3 to request transportation. While waiting, I noticed that the base at Dong Ha had increased in size in the past several weeks.

After waiting an hour, a jeep with the 3/3 logo painted on its fender finally arrived, and I jumped in. Leaving the airstrip, we traveled a short distance west and turned north toward the air force radar facility, with its metal buildings, radar screens, and tall radio antennas. Directly across the road, we turned off into a muddy field where a tent city was erected. This was Third Battalion Third Marines rear area. The trip from the airstrip took no more than two minutes. If I had known it was so close, I would have walked instead of waiting in the rain.

I stepped out of the jeep into the ankle-deep mud and sloshed to a tent that had a sign outside that designated it as H&S (headquarters and support) Company. I entered and I reported in. The company clerk took my personnel record then directed me to the Battalion Aid Station (BAS) tent.

I sloshed my way to the BAS where the corpsmen welcomed me and took my health record. Since I was still wearing my leather garrison boots and heavy cotton garrison utilities, my next stop was the supply tent. It seems that the supply lines didn't quite make it to Dong Ha and the all the gear I was issued was not new. All the uniforms and boots had been recovered from casualties, laundered, repaired to make them serviceable, and reissued. Jungle utilities have little in the way of insulating ability, made of a light material suitable for the tropics that dry fairly quickly. They differ from garrison utilities in that the shirt is worn outside the trousers and both shirt and trousers have large cargo pockets in addition to the regular pockets. The pair given to me was a size or two too big, but as close to my size that they had available. Next I received a pair of jungle boots. These boots were a half size too small, but it was as close to a 9 that they had in stock. Any of the others would have been way too large. I also received a couple pairs of quick-drying boot socks. Next they gave me a fiberglass helmet liner, steel helmet, and camouflage helmet cover. I then was given a Korean war vintage flak jacket, a poncho (again without the warm fabric liner), pack, E-tool, pistol belt, two quart-sized steel canteens with pouches, KA-BAR knife, a personal medical kit containing a battle dressing, water purification tablets, and foot powder. Lastly I received another M1911A1 .45-caliber Colt pistol, leather holster, and two ammunition clips holding seven rounds each and a pouch for the belt to store the two clips.

Returning to the BAS, I received a Unit One field medical kit containing a surgical instrument kit, battle dressings, arm slings, suture material, antibiotic ointment, a unit of plasma, and morphine syrettes. I was then shown the bunk where I would be spending the night. At 1700, we went to eat supper at the chow hall located in one of the other tents. The corpsman that accompanied me asked if I had a waterproof case for my cigarettes. When I told him I didn't, he took out a small two-piece aluminum case that would hold one pack of cigarettes. He was short and going back to the world and didn't need it anymore. He explained to me that other than the occasional smoke and mail call, there would be very few pleasures out in the jungle. The metal case would keep my smokes dry, safe from being crushed. After chow was over, there was a movie shown in the same tent. It was some B-rated monster movie. Though it was stupid, I watched it because it would probably be the last one I saw for a while. After the movie, I returned to the BAS and turned in for the night.

The next morning, the chief corpsman informed me that I was assigned to Lima Company, located out Highway 9 near the Rockpile. To get out there, I had to catch a ride on one of the two-and-a-half-ton trucks going out on a convoy to the area. I gathered up my gear again, and at 1000, I climbed into the back of a truck, and the convoy proceeded west on Highway 9. After Cam Lo, the highway became worse, filled with potholes and slip outs. We continued out of the flatland into the mountains to Camp Carroll, an artillery base located south of Highway 9 on a plateau. This convoy only moved at 30 mph at the most. Even though it was only a distance of about fourteen and a half miles from Dong Ha, it took a while to get there.

Proceeding west shortly after leaving Camp Carroll, Highway 9 entered a large valley with several prominent granite formations rising from the floor. I recognized this picturesque area from my return helicopter flight out of the hills in November when I was on the HST with Third Shore Party.

The first formation is the Little Rockpile, or – as it was referred to by the Marines – the Witch's Tit or Nellie's Tit due to its 430 feet craggy conical shape. The second large rock formation was the Rockpile and was located a little farther west, roughly in the center of the valley. It towered 720 feet with almost vertical sides. The antennas of a radio relay station could be seen on the top of the Rockpile, which was only accessible by helicopter.

The Razorback was located on the northwest side of the valley. It consisted of another large vertical rock formation several miles long running north and south. The Razorback was made up of several tall mountains. The shorter southern end is only about 660 feet. The next peak to the north is about 1,080 feet, and the tallest one on the north end is about 1,140 feet. It hooked to the west at the north end. Mutter's Ridge bordered the northeast side of the valley. It was pronounced "Mudders Ridge" due to the muddy living conditions the Marines lived in while up there.

Located between the Witch's Tit and the Rockpile, a gravel road turns north from Highway 9. The truck I was riding in and one other left the convoy at this point turning onto that road. The remaining trucks proceeded along Highway 9 toward 3/3's forward battalion area known by its radio call sign "Payable."

After leaving the convoy, the road took us past several abandoned concrete buildings and came to the river just north of the base of the Rockpile. We crossed a bridge several hundred feet long made with fifteen-foot lengths of three-foot-diameter steel culverts positioned so that the river ran through them. It appeared to have been recently constructed. These pipes supported a roadway. Recent heavy rains had swollen the river, and the roadway was under several inches of water. We slowly crossed with the water reaching the trucks' axles and followed a very muddy road up to a hill on the north side of the river, traveling a short distance parallel to the river and heading east toward the Razorback. The drivers then shifted their trucks into all-wheel drive and, even with all six wheels, struggled to get their vehicles to make the climb up the last slippery incline. As we approached this hillcrest, I noticed it had bunkers and trenches around its perimeter. This was my destination – Lima Hill, also referred to as the Fish Bowl, the Punch Bowl, or Alamo Hill. None of these ominous names made me feel any less apprehensive about my new home.

Chapter 30

Lima Hill

AS THE 6-BY entered the perimeter, all six of its tires spun as it labored to climb the muddy road, but finally arrived at our destination, the supply area just inside their perimeter. I jumped off the truck and sank down in the mud. I walked across the road and reported into the company command post where I met the company clerks.

After the formalities were finished, I was introduced to the company commander. Captain John W. Ripley had the air of command, but upon meeting him, he was a friendly guy, and I could tell he cared for his troops. He was from Virginia and had started as an enlisted Marine in 1957. Shortly, he received an appointment to Annapolis where he graduated in 1962. After graduation, he had attended ranger school at Fort Benning, Georgia. He had assumed command of Lima Company only several days before and arrived on the hill on January 8. Ripley was neat and clean and squared away in spite of the living conditions. When he arrived, he noticed his troops were living in filth and mud. His first mission was to get his men out of the terrible living conditions. He was unlike any of the Marine officers I had encountered up until then. His staff showed him a great deal of respect.

Captain Ripley welcomed me to the hill and invited me to have a meal at the newly constructed company mess, a camouflage plastic tarp on a wooden frame near the command bunker. One of the clerks told me that the cook had just come out three days prior. The captain had called to the rear and had his cook and two burners sent out to the hill to provide hot chow to supplement the C rations. The cook heated water and made hot coffee He also heated water for shaving. It did wonders for the morale, and soon he was making sheet cakes and soup.

Inside the mess were a couple of burners with large pots over the gas burners. One pot held hot water and the other held chicken noodle soup. There were also pots of hot coffee. I was invited to help myself to the soup and coffee. I filled my canteen cup with chicken noodle soup and sat down and drank the hot broth leaving the noodles in the cup. I refilled several times until I had a cup full of noodles, which I ate with a spoon. I then had a canteen cup full of hot coffee. I was advised that I could come for a hot meal anytime. After they were sure that I had eaten my fill, I returned to the command post where I was informed that I was assigned to Third Platoon. I was directed across the mud to the far southwest end on the other side of the hilltop where the Third Platoon command bunker was located.

To get to Third Platoon required that I slog through knee-deep mud. It was thick and sticky, making it difficult to walk through. After about five minutes, I was able to leave the mud and find the bunker located a third of the way down the hillside. I walked down to the bunker and requested permission to enter.

Inside I met HM2 John Kelsey. He was Lima Company's senior corpsman and had been covering the night ambushes for Third Platoon until a replacement arrived. He introduced me to Platoon Commander Lieutenant Hansel Osborne. Lieutenant Osborne was a mustang (a Marine who before becoming an officer had worked his way up through the enlisted ranks, usually a battlefield promotion). He welcomed me and introduced me to his radiomen Ron Hebert (which he pronounced "A-bear" but everyone called him "Hee-bert") and Richard Banks.

When joining a new unit, one of the first questions asked is "Where you from?" Banks was from the city of Redding in Shasta County. He was delighted to have another Northern California boy in the outfit. Back home, Banks was a photographer and spelunker. While in high school, he had helped to map the Lake Shasta Caverns. After high school, he was attending Shasta Junior College when he was drafted and ended up as a Marine. When he got orders to Vietnam, his hometown paper, the *Record Searchlight*, provided him with a 35 mm camera and kept him supplied with film. He took pictures and sent the film back to the paper where they were published.

Soon after I arrived, incoming mortars coming off the Razorback ridge hit to the north end of the hill near where I had been when I first arrived. The tanks and mortars on our hill opened up on a cave on the side of the Razorback. After the shooting stopped, I heard that a Marine from the tank crew was killed.

After everything settled down, I was assigned a bunker, which I shared with the other corpsman, HM3 Denver Gray, who was out on patrol. Since we would be working opposite each other, only one of us would be occupying the bunker except for between patrols and ambushes. The bunker was a hole in the side of the hill with a sandbagged roof. Inside was dugout deep enough to stand. A raised area had been carved out, and an air mattress and blanket provided the only bed. There was a wooden ammunition box setting on its end serving as a crude table. On the table was a short candle in a C ration can. I tossed my gear in the corner next to Gray's.

January 12, 1967

Dear Louise,

Here I am out in the boonies again. If you get a hold of the Life magazine from the first part of October you can see what kind of area I'm in. Over to my left is the "Rockpile" which is shown in the magazine. I am almost at the base of it about 100 meters away.

I wasn't here one and a half hours when we had to jump into our foxholes because the place where I was at before got mortared real bad and usually after the mortar up there they swing around and mortar our area. I was in a hole with another corpsman, a couple of Marines and a Lieutenant. The Lieutenant turned to me and said "Doc, do you think you can make it around the other side of the hill to the other hole before we get hit?" I told him I'd try. I don't think I ever ran so fast on a muddy hill in my life. Luckily the VC didn't mortar our position.

Right now I am sitting in my bunker and it's "Razorback Hour". That's usually the time of day this area gets hit from an area which is a long rock mountain which is narrow on the top and the VC live up there. So far nothing has happened.

I was in Dong Ha for a day and couldn't get a helicopter out here because the weather was so bad. This morning I got on a convoy and now, like I said, I'm out here.

Tomorrow I'm going on a patrol and the next night I go on an ambush. Sounds exciting, huh?

Being out here makes me really realize how much I love you. When things start happening I think of you waiting for me and I know I have to make it back OK. I love you so much I just can't think of the words to express myself about how I feel. I sure do miss you.

It sure is cold out here. I only have one blanket to my name, but I guess it will do until I can latch onto another. I'll bet I wouldn't be cold if you were with me, even with one blanket!

What have you added to your cedar chest lately? I guess by the time we're married we'll have all kinds of useful things.

There are some large artillery shells (ours) flying over right now. Sounds real weird, kind of like on the beginning of the TV program "Combat".

That's about it for now, I can't think of anything else and it's starting to get dark. Bye for now.

Love,
Russ

PS I love you.
My new address is:
Russell J. Jewett HM3 6825474
H&S Co. BAS
3rd Battalion 3rd Marines
FPO
San Francisco, California 96602

Later in the afternoon, Gray came in off patrol. He was skinny, wet, and dirty and needed a shave, but had a good sense of humor. He was a friendly guy from Pennsylvania. He had been the only corpsman for Third Platoon for a while, and now that I had arrived, we would share the same bunker. He explained that we would seldom be there at the same time except for an hour or two a day when we were both in between activities. Gray proceeded to shave and told me that Captain Ripley wanted all the members of Lima Company to be clean shaven at all times. This is one thing I didn't have to worry about as my beard had not yet gotten heavy enough to be noticed by anyone other than me.

Kelsey came by and informed me that I would be going out on night ambush after dark. Ambush, I thought, what the hell is an ambush?

Gray briefed me on what I was to do on night ambush and a day patrol. Basically I was to accompany a squad of Marines outside the wire. We would head out through the perimeter and move to a predetermined area where the enemy was known to travel. We would set up along the trail to ambush anyone coming down it. This required us to pair up; I would stand radio watch with the radioman. Each shift would be two hours, and I should sleep while not on watch. He also informed me to take my poncho to sleep under, but it could not be worn while walking to or from the ambush site (to reduce the noise of our movement through the dark).

As it got dark, a single short candle was the only light inside the bunker. Gray showed me how to "black out" the bunker. This was something that I had not yet had to deal with even in the A Shau Valley. When the bunker was constructed, a blackout curtain was installed over the door. Blackout curtains were simply a door made out of shelter halves, tarps, or other opaque material that were rolled up out of the way during the day and then rolled down at night. The purpose was to contain any light from within the bunker, concealing it from the outside. It is made of two layers so that when you enter or exit, you step behind the first and close it behind you. Once between the layers, you go through the second layer trapping the light inside.

When the time came to go out on ambush, someone outside the bunker said, "Saddle up, Doc." I grabbed my gear, exited the bunker, and joined the invisible squad. The squad leader gave us the password for the night and then explained what we would be doing and how we would get out to the ambush site outside the compound's perimeter wire. It was very dark and raining. I could not see what any of the squad looked like as we formed up and walked single file through the mud to the perimeter. At the gate, the squad leader told us to lock and load. We put our magazines into our weapons, put a round in the chamber, and put the safety on. We then proceeded through the gate and the "tangle foot" just outside the perimeter. A tangle foot is a maze of barbed wire staked to the ground designed to discourage "sappers" (Vietcong personnel who try to sneak in and blow a hole in the perimeter wire, making it easier to gain entry into the position during attack) from entering the perimeter wire. There were also C ration cans with a stone inside, suspended from the wires, acting as an alarm if anyone got caught in the tangle foot or perimeter wire. As we walked, I had to reach out and touch the back of the man in front of me so that we didn't get separated. The Marines instructed and guided me with a great deal of patience; they knew I was "the new Doc." After a half hour or so of making our way along a trail, we finally came to the area designated by the squad leader as our ambush site. Everyone took their positions in the tall grass along a road that was seldom used. The squad leader set up the ambush. The radioman and I got out our ponchos and settled in next to each other. He instructed me as to what I was to do and then went to sleep.

Radio watch consisted of listening to the receiver of the handset of the PRC-25 radio. Radio silence was observed while on ambush, requiring a very low setting on the volume, just barely audible when the handset was held to the ear. This meant that while on ambush, we were not to talk on the radio unless contact was made with the enemy. The handset was a combination speaker and microphone, much like a telephone receiver. It was enclosed in a plastic bag to keep it dry. Every fifteen minutes, the radioman on duty in the Third Platoon command bunker back on the hill would call our call sign, Lima Alpha Three (*Alpha* stood for ambush, *Three* for Third Platoon of Lima Company). He would request verification that his transmission was heard and we had not been captured. The correct response was to squeeze the key on the handset, which switched the radio from receiving to transmitting. Releasing the key produced a short static signal. This would be done twice. Upon hearing the response, he would acknowledge the transmission and announce the time. This was done every fifteen minutes. It went like this:

Radio: "Lima Alpha Three, Lima Alpha Three, this is Lima Three. If you hear this transmission, key your handset twice, over."

Handset sound when keyed: "Chhht! – Chhht!"

Radio: "Ah, roger, Lima Alpha Three, the time is 2330. Out."

When my watch ended, I woke the radioman for his watch; he advised me to get some sleep while not on watch. There was no way I could go to sleep. I stayed awake all night. Every time the wind blew or there would be some noise, I was sure that it was the enemy getting ready to attack us. Finally the squad leader terminated the ambush and we returned to the hill before morning light. Coming up to the perimeter, a sentry called out telling us to halt. He then asked for the password. The point man gave the password, and the gate was opened, and we were told to advance. We walked back through the tangle foot and into the muddy compound.

Back at the bunker, I was informed that I would be going out with a patrol. We left around 0800. On patrol that day, the Marines taught me patrol protocol. A patrol usually consisted of twelve men. The order of the patrol consisted of a point man, two riflemen, a grenadier with an M79, squad leader, radioman, corpsman, machine gunner, assistant gunner, two riflemen, and rear security. Chuck Percherke was the radioman that day. He took me under his wing and showed me survival skills consisting of walking quietly with no conversation, no smoking, and spacing out in single file along the trail by keeping fifteen feet between the next guy and yourself. Watch out for booby traps and trip wires especially if it looks like a good place to sit or lean against. I learned how to use water purification tablets when we filled our canteen from a swampy area with an oily scum on the surface. During the day, radio traffic was expected, and he instructed me on the radio brevity code used in communicating over the air. Some that I remember are the following:

    Alpha – ambush
    Papa – patrol
    Any beer name – a patrol checkpoint (We have 3 Budweiser, Michelob, Miller, etc., meant that we were at our third predesignated checkpoint on the patrol route.)
    Housefly – enemy
    Swat – kill an enemy
    Payable – battalion area on Highway 9
    Lima 3 – Third Platoon
    Lima 3 actual – Lieutenant Osborne
    Lima 6 – company command center
    Lima 6 actual – Captain Ripley
    Whiskey – wounded
    Kilo – killed

Walking around all day in the rain, we became thoroughly soaked. (We did not wear our poncho on patrol.) The squad and I returned to our hilltop position with its knee-deep mud. I was still too wired to get any sleep. When I was not on ambush, I shared radio watch at night in the Third Platoon bunker. This was the pattern for the next several days, and after having no sleep for seventy-two hours, I finally was so exhausted I slept for several hours before my next activity. After that, I was able to catnap on ambush, but still never slept for more than an hour or so at any time. This is a sleeping pattern that stayed with me over the next forty years.

The area around Lima Hill was beautiful. There were grassy knolls, banana trees, palms, and other exotic plants and flowers. The riverbanks were lined with shrubs and had established trails, which passed by deep pools, which would have been nice fishing holes or swimming holes (though we never got to partake). Higher on the base of the Razorback were dense jungles with vines and bamboo – where we followed established trails. I observed many types of birds and insects with the occasional monkey or deer.

Every hour or so, we would stop for a ten-minute break to smoke a cigarette or eat a snack of C rations, usually eaten cold. I frequently noticed a highway of ants and observed how long their line was. Occasionally we would hastily heat some coffee or chocolate to wash down the dry fruitcake or peanut butter and crackers. Before starting out again, all trash would be buried and all cigarette butts fieldstripped so that we did not leave any trace of our being there.

The routine of patrol and ambush became the way of life. Since there were only two corpsmen and three squads per platoon, the corpsmen rarely had a day off. Individual Marines would venture out beyond the wire every third activity, but corpsmen were out every other activity. I would go out on a patrol during the day, and Gray would go out on the ambush at night. Every few days we would switch; I would go out during the day on a patrol and then out on the ambush at night for another few days until we switched again. I soon lost any excess body fat that I may have had. To keep warm, I wore several T-shirts, two sweatshirts, and a jungle utility shirt. I received the sweatshirts from home in a care package after informing my family about the cold.

January 17, 1967

Dear Louise,

Things aren't the greatest out here, but they aren't bad at all really. All I do is go on patrols and ambushes. So far we haven't seen any "Gooks" (VC), but we're ready for them.

Last night they told us that there are 3 battalions of gooks coming our way. That shook me a little, what bothered me even more was that last night I had to go on a night ambush.

When you are out there it is so dark you can't see more than two feet in front of you and whenever the wind blows you swear that it sounds like you are surrounded. Last night was the only time since I've been out here that I've been scared. I kept thinking of you and my mind was screaming your name. To calm down a little I thought of all the things we've done together and of our future plans, but that worried me even more. Oh well, that's over with, but there are more to come and the gooks are even closer tonight.

I haven't yet received a letter from you since I left Thuan An Island. I hope it's just that the mail is slow and not that you haven't written or something happened to you. It's most likely the mail is slow, because I haven't received any mail from anyone in 2 weeks.

The sun was out all day today, sure felt good, so good, in fact, I washed and shaved for the first time since I've been out here. Other than that everything is just the same.

Well, looks like it's raining again. Darn it!

Now it's 9 pm and I am standing radio watch in our platoon command post. Seems that over here a Corpsman is the Jack-of-all-trades. The Lieutenant asked me if I wanted to come up from my cold hole that I live in to the command post and have some canned strawberries, they sure were good.

Tomorrow I have to go on another patrol, this one is during the day, so it shouldn't be so bad.

I sure do miss you. I think of you all the time, especially on our night ambushes. I love you and want to be your husband for the rest of my life. I can't wait until we're married and can be together forever. I know I could never go on living if I didn't have you waiting for me to come home to you. I love you so much I can't even express in words what I feel I hope you know what I mean, I'm sure you do.

I still don't know where we'll go on our honeymoon, where do you want to go? I was thinking maybe we could live in the Monterrey area after we're married. What do you think of that? Actually I don't care where we live as long as we're together. Just think only 20 more months and we'll be together as husband and wife forever.

Well I better close now. Write soon please. Bye for now

Love always,
Russ

PS *I love you*

After a while, I became oblivious to the rain. Since we never dried out, undershorts were not worn. Those who insisted on doing so developed a fungus in their crotch, which just made them more miserable because it was not considered serious enough to send them back to the rear area for treatment. Changing our socks frequently prevented the fungus of immersion foot. Carrying them under our poncho on night ambush or, if it wasn't raining, tied to the outside of the pack allowed them to dry somewhat. Any bathing was done out of our helmet, usually confined to just washing hands and face, brushing teeth, and shaving. It was too cold to strip down and wash. Laundering clothes was not an option at that time since the only clothes I had were on my back.

Finally the day came for us to move up onto the Razorback. I was instructed to take everything that I would need for a couple of weeks. Other than my writing paper, pen, and C rations, I did not have much else to take along except for a blanket and an air mattress to sleep on.

January 19, 1967

Dear Louie,

Just a quick letter to let you know that I won't be able to send off any mail for at least a week to two weeks. Our platoon is moving up on top of Razorback mountain and the mail won't be able to go out from there.

I received your letter today. Sure was good to hear from you. It's been over 2 weeks since I last got a letter from you. It was written on the 7th, so that means it took 11 days to get to me due to the mail being shuffled around trying to find me.

We haven't gotten hit by the gooks yet, but we're still waiting! I hope they never come because that means we'll have a big fight on our hands.

Sounds like you are having a blast at the Rec. What does Susie think about us getting married, or does she know?

I never saw your dishes, but like you said they will be our company dishes, they're too old and good to use for everyday use. As for silverware and glasses, I'll add those to my list of things I have to get when I go to Japan.

I wish we could get married when I come home, because I'm going to try to get stationed back there when I leave Viet Nam and that way you could go too. But you have to graduate that year, so it doesn't look possible. It was just a thought.

Everything you have sent so far has gotten here all right. You don't have to send any more books any more, not that I don't appreciate them, but I just don't have time anymore to read. But please keep sending Playboy after I finish with it I lend it out to the other guys since they haven't seen one in a long time.

I ran out of the other paper I was using so I had to break out some of this, it's not the same size, but at least it's writable.

You said that you would keep me warm, how would you manage that? I sure wish I could be with you and not be cold. It's freezing here. I also got a blanket from my parents, which will help a little, but I would be even warmer with you. I love you so much.

You wanted to know what I do at a Helicopter Loading Zone, well all I did was stand around in the tent because it was raining, but the Marines were out loading and unloading supplies.

I dream about us all the time. My dreams always stare out just before we're married on our wedding day and go on through . . . You know what I mean? What do you dream about?

It should be only 40 weeks until I come home because they've cut the time down from 13 months to 11 months 2 weeks, so that makes it 6 weeks less I have to stay over here. I have the weeks on a piece of paper and am marking off each Saturday.

Well, I better start to close now; I have to get some sleep, the other night when I was in the Command Post I only had 3 hours sleep and last night only about 4.

I love you more than anything in the world. I want to be with you always and forever. Even now just thinking about you seems to give me a warm feeling especially thinking about that afternoon. In fact just thinking about you turns me on something terrible. I need you so much it makes me almost want to cry because you're so far away from me. I wish time would hurry up and go so we can be together again.

Bye for now and write soon. Oh, and tell my mom to write once in a while, when she gets time. I'll dream of you again tonight I always do. Always remember I love you

Love Always,
Russ

PS *I love you*
(*Looks like I wrote more than a short letter, doesn't it!*)
I love you and want you always

Chapter 31

The Razorback

ON THE TWENTIETH of January, Third Platoon relieved Second Platoon on the top of the Razorback. This rock formation with its sheer sides rises up out of the valley just to the northwest of the Rockpile. Since the entire platoon was going up, Lieutenant Osborne and his command group came with us. Though it was said to be rough living among the rocks, it at least got us out of the mud for a while. Three days of C rations (nine meals) were handed out to each man. Our packs did not hold them while in their boxes, so all the cans were removed from the boxes and stacked inside the pack. Water on the Razorback was scarce, so we hydrated by drinking several canteens of water before leaving. The last thing we did before leaving was refill our canteens.

Walking in single file, we left the Punch Bowl through the gate in the south end of the barbed concertina wire perimeter and headed out along the main trail. The trail descended down Lima Hill, arriving at the steeply inclined base. We followed the trail up the base until it arrived at the near vertical sides of the Razorback. The point men climbed up and secured ropes. Using the ropes, we climbed slowly up the face, finally reaching the top and arriving at our bivouac area.

Each squad took a position so that we had a defendable perimeter. The command group set up under the trees in a small patch of jungle. Toward the north end of our perimeter was a small opening large enough for a helicopter to lower a cargo net with supplies, or at least that was the plan. I set up my shelter on the south end of our perimeter. I used my poncho as a tarp to sleep under. I pulled the drawstring on the hood closed and tied each corner to bushes and rocks. I then inflated my air mattress. Sitting under my poncho, I had a view of the whole valley. Turning around in the other direction, I could see the valley and mountains to the west. The view was breathtaking.

On the south end, our head (toilet facility) consisted of a board lashed at one end to the trunk of a stout bush that inclined out over the edge and secured by rocks at the other. This allowed us to sit with our butt suspended over the edge, allowing feces to drop to a small ledge twenty or so feet below. Prior to the construction of the seat, a knotted rope tied around a rock provided the necessary handhold to allow defecation over the side.

I was the only corpsman now with the platoon. Due to the shortage of corpsmen, Den Gray remained below with the company on the hill to cover the other platoons. This meant that I participated in every activity, spending very little time in camp. I was outside our perimeter more than each individual Marine. It all became a routine; I would go out with one squad on a patrol during the day, come back, and a few hours later, go out with another squad on an ambush at night. I carried a pad of writing paper in one of the cargo pockets on the leg of my trousers. While on breaks, I would write home. When I finally went back down to Lima Hill twelve days later, I had written forty pages and sent them off in four envelopes with ten pages per envelope.

January 21, 1966

Dear Louise,

Here we are up on the Razorback. Right now we are sitting here on an ambush and there's nothing to do so I decided to write you a letter.

We hiked up here yesterday with enough food in our packs for 3 days. We're supposed to get supplied by helicopter.

This morning we started out on this patrol and just a few minutes ago set up our ambush.

From up here you can see the whole valley. It sure looks beautiful.

Right now some of the guys are cooking C-rations and other things.

Well, we got back from our ambush, we also checked out a couple of caves, but didn't find anything. So we walked back to our area on the hill.

We have only enough food for about 2 more days, because the helicopter didn't re-supply us today. That is we'll have enough for 2 days if we only eat 2 meals a day and we are out of water also. We're going to try and catch some in our ponchos, if it rains tonight.

Right now I'm sitting here on a rock on top of the Razorback looking out over the land below, sure looks neat. Hill all around with the Rockpile sticking up over to my right.

(Page 3 is missing)

I get down and send it off you will have a real long letter coming to you. Bye for today. I'll continue maybe tomorrow if I get a moment or so to sit down.

Patrolling the Razorback was quite an experience. Leaving our perimeter, we passed through a defensive position where an M60 machine gun was posted. It was constructed of rocks piled up for cover with a dip near the middle to allow passage in and out of the perimeter. Outside, the jagged uneven terrain made it slow going. The top of the Razorback between our perimeter and the next hill narrowed, requiring us to walk straddling the ridge with one foot on either side until it widened out several hundred yards later. Once past this obstacle, others presented themselves: stepping across large fissures, climbing rock faces, and traversing narrow ledges along the sheer face. After a time or two out on the trails, we learned where the hand – and footholds were located and were able to move faster on the trails. The rough granite was harsh on our jungle boots, and the short hardy vegetation tore at our utility trousers. For days, the Razorback was shrouded in clouds creating a thick fog, limiting visibility of our surroundings. It had stopped raining except for the occasional shower.

The continuous strenuous activities required consumption of large amounts of water. Each man carried two canteens, and we were constantly in need of quenching our thirst while on patrol. We found we could get by on less food, but water was our main need. On patrol, we took advantage of any water source we could find. When our patrols took us lower on the side of the ridge, we located small streams; occasionally we would run into a patch of bamboo where we could cut into the segments with our knives to harvest the water that they contained, which we drank directly from the bamboo.

January 23, 1966

Hi again, Louise,

Well here I sit on the same rock looking out over the same valley, thinking of the same person, you.

Yesterday we went on a patrol again, as usual, and found nothing.

When I got back I had a bunch of mail that one of the guys that just came up here brought up for me. I got three letters from you, one from my mother and one from Bruce. The ones I got from you were dated the 1st, 11th, and 15th. Sure was good to hear from you.

We're out of food up here now. The helicopters didn't bring us anything for the last two days like they were supposed to. I just ate an extra meal that one of the guys had. (Boy, this pen has to go), They said that there is a package waiting for me down the hill, but I have to wait until I go down because they didn't want to pack it up.

Yesterday on our patrol we didn't have any water so since we were in a bamboo forest, we cut out a few sections of bamboo and drank the water that was in the sections. Then we got to a stream and filled up our canteens.

Today I haven't done a thing but sit around up here in my shelter. We've been trying to catch water in our poncho to drink, but it has just been sprinkling.

I don't know where I can get a map of Viet Nam, but I'll keep my eyes open the next time I get back to a PX, whenever that will be.

You don't have to worry about me drinking like that guy you were talking about, I really don't like to drink that much, the only time I drink is whenever we get anything to drink, but over here you drink only to break the monotony and that is so little it's hardly worth mentioning. When I'm with you I have so much more on my mind that I don't even want the stuff.

Thanks a lot for the pictures, your looking real good these days. I sure do love you.

That sure sounds good, next year we'll be married, yes, it sure sounds real good.

So your mom is saving the TV for us. Do you think we'll find time to watch it?

It's starting to get dark again so I better go. I love you more than anything in the world. All I want out of life is to be married to you. I can't wait until I can kiss you and hold you again. I remember all the things we've done together and I want to come back and do them again, just you and me. I want to be with you always.

Bye for now.

There were basically two patrol routes. One followed the sheer face on the east side of the Razorback and the other went to the less vertical side on the west. On the west side, we often stopped for a break on a large area of jumbled rock. Sometime during the formation of this mountain, part of the cliff face had sheered off and fell into a narrow ravine where it broke up and remained stuck. Many of the rocks were balanced on the others and would teeter as we walked over them. There were spaces almost large enough for a man to go down between the rocks. Richard Banks said that it smelled like there was a cave below the jumble, and he was always looking for a way under them, but we never located a large-enough opening to crawl into.

January 24, 1967

Hi,

Well today so far has been just like yesterday, no food, no water, no VC. At least it's a little clearer today than yesterday. This morning we thought the sun would come out, but no such luck. But it is a little bit warmer and the bugs are starting to come out.

The hill "downstairs" as we say, where the rest of the company is located, is now called "Alamo Hill" because it's almost like in the story of the Alamo in Texas with just a few men ready to stand off a whole bunch of enemy soldiers. Sure hope it doesn't end up like the Alamo though.

You asked me if there is anything I want. I sure could use a big box of powdered milk and maybe some Nestlé's Quick, any food seasoning, like mustard, ketchup, pepper, etc. Some dried or packaged fruits would also be nice. I'll eat anything, so just use your imagination. I'm not choosy.

I sure do stink; I haven't had a shower since I left Thuan An Island. Some of the guys haven't had one in over 100 days. We are so used to being dirty that it doesn't even really bother us any more.

Tonight I go on an all night ambush. We'll go out and sit in the grass or bushes or some appropriate place for an ambush and hope that some VC come along.

I sure am hungry! What I wouldn't do for a nice big steak, with mashed potatoes and gravy, fresh peas, a nice tossed green salad with French dressing, dinner rolls, nice and hot so that the butter melts, apple pie a-la-mode and a nice cup of hot coffee and you sitting across the table from me as we gaze at each other through the candle light. That is really my idea of paradise. Then after dinner, sitting around relaxing and watching TV or something like that, then off to bed for a good nights sleep. Wow!

I love you more and more each day. I can't wait until we're married and we can do that all the time.

Being out here sure makes you think a lot. There isn't much else to do at times like this. You just lay here and think of things you've done or things you should have done, but didn't, things you want to do in the future, etc.

Well, that's all I can think of to write right now. I love you with all my heart, body and soul. I can't wait until we're together again.

Bye for now.

I had never seen a leech until I was in the jungle around the base of the north end of the Razorback. I had always had the notion that leeches were exclusively in the water. I never knew they lived up in the mountains and waited on the vegetation for a warm-blooded meal to come walking down the trail. These little guys were very stealthy; most times I was not aware one was on me until it was gorged with blood and released its suction, and I would feel the fat sucker fall heavily into the bottom of my trouser leg bloused above my boot top. By this time, they would have resembled a large brown marble. This is quite extraordinary: They started out about the size of an inchworm and traveled with the same motion. They would extend their head out and attach and then flex and bring up the back end and attach and then repeat the process. Once I was aware of their habitats, I would be watching for them. They would be sitting on the leaves of plants that resembled bamboo. As we entered the habitat, they would extend their front ends into the air and wiggle around trying to home in on their next meal. When we got in range, they would release from their perch and attach their front end to the passerby. From there, they would seek out their dining site.

On patrol, we traveled in single file, and it was the procedure that when we entered leech territory, we would pass the word to watch out for them. This required that you watch the man in front of you to see that no leech attacked him from behind as they usually would land on the clothing first. One day, some observant individual pointed out that the leeches seemed to never travel down once on its intended victim. It was relatively easy for a leech to find a way under your clothing. If it started near the boot, the first entry area was the bloused trouser leg at the top of the boot. The second was where the bottom of the jungle utility jacket hung over the top of the trousers. Next, and usually of most concern to most, was the fly in the trousers. No one wanted a leech to end up in there. We had all heard stories of a leech getting into the urethra and swelling up and becoming stuck. The next place was between the buttons on the front of the shirt. Finally was the neck and under the helmet. We solved most of the problems by tucking the cuffs of our trousers into the top of our boots and lacing them up so that a leech would simply pass over the seam, as he would have to crawl down to get in. We would also tuck the shirttails into the trousers. This actually reduced the number of successful leech attacks.

One of the problems we had associated with leeches was second-degree burns caused by Marines attempting to remove the leech by using a lit cigarette. Though it worked, they usually would inflict further injury on themselves – when the hot end of the cigarette was placed on the leech, it also got close enough to the skin; by the time the leech let go, the heat had also raised a blister. I found that the best way was to simply remove the leech with the fingers. As far as I can determine, the use of cigarette burns to remove the leech originated decades ago and probably was developed to remove the larger water leeches, who attach to their victim with small hooks in their mouth. The land leech, however, attaches by creating suction and using hirudin (similar to heparin), an anticoagulant to keep the blood flowing freely. Regardless of which way the leech is removed, the lesion usually continues to ooze blood, sometimes for several days before it coagulates. This creates the additional problem of a secondary infection in the wound.

Our biggest problem became lack of resupply. We were isolated at the top of the ridge with the ever-present clouds and fog, preventing helicopters from coming in. Even on a clear day, the wind blowing over the narrow ridge presented a problem when trying to hover and lower a cargo net. Just before Christmas, a CH-34 helicopter had been hit by a gust of wind while trying to lower its suspended cargo net and crashed onto the saddle LZ. Thanks to the quick action of the Marines, the crew had been rescued and injuries were minimized. Our food and water were rationed in hopes that the weather would soon clear up enough to fly in supplies (we did get one delivery while I was up there).

Our alternative was to send a work party "down the hill" to Lima Hill and carry the supplies up. This required the squad of Marines who were not on patrol to pack up the needed supplies on pack frames holding two cases (twenty-four meals), each weighing about seventy pounds. Cargo pockets were also stuffed with cans of food. Jerricans of water were hauled one per pack frame (weighing over fifty pounds).

January 26, 1967

Here I am again.

A lot of things have happened since the other day. We went on an ambush the other night and while we were out there we heard all kinds of movement in this little swamp area out in front of us. Me and this other guy from Northern California, Redding to be exact, wanted to toss down a grenade, but our team leader said we had to wait until we saw something. So we waited. We heard more footsteps going through the mud, but couldn't see anything, mainly because we were too far away (about 200 feet). I even heard someone walking along and it sounded like he dropped a box of cans, stopped, tossed the cans back into the box and continued walking through the mud. Nothing else happened on that ambush.

That same day we finally got in some chow. About 14 guys went down the hill and each brought back 2 cases (24 meals) apiece. No sooner had they gotten up the hill than a helicopter brought a whole bunch of C-rations and a bunch of water. Just as the "chopper" was pulling away, we heard a bunch of gunfire. At the time I was standing up on top of the hill taking pictures of the helicopter. Everyone hit the ground and then scrambled for their weapons. I made a mad dash across an area about 30 feet wide to get my helmet and medical bag. At that time everyone realized that the shooting was just cover fire, form the company across to cover the landing of our supplies to keep the VC from shooting down the helicopter. Se we all got out our cameras and took pictures.

Yesterday was real slack and I didn't have to go out, so I laid on my air mattress all day.

Guess what! The sun finally came out yesterday. We were throwing rocks at the light places on the ground, some of the guys wanted to shoot them, but then we realized that it was the sun and not a VC trick.

Today we went on a patrol searching caves. We had fun tossing grenades in the cave before we'd go in. All we found were some VC rain pants. During the whole thing the sun was shining and it was hot. I drank over a quart and a half of water just by myself.

All this that I've written so far today has been on an ambush. There is a full moon out and I can see to write. This is the first time I've seen a full moon since I've been over here. The rest of the times it has been too cloudy to see it.

And, I have some little bugs biting me. I must have picked them up off these rocks. I don't see how thy can stand to be on me. I smell like, well the closest thing I've smelled like this was my old sweaty gym clothes after a week of gym and track practice and sitting in the warm locker every night rotting. Whew!

You know something. The same moon shines over you as it does me and you see the same stars I do, when you think of it that way, it doesn't seem like we're to terribly far apart, but we are. Right now I wish we could be sitting together maybe on a beach, some secluded spot, or even in our home-to-be, gazing at this full moon, talking, looking at each other, loving each other, just being together. It sure would be nice. I sure do miss you at times like this. I don't know why, but when the moon is out and it's all peaceful like it is right now I miss you more than any other time. But still the same time I feel closer to you because as I think of you, I look at the moon and know that you, too, are probably looking at the moon and thinking of me. I love you so much, Louie, I don't know what I'd do without you. I just can't wait until we are married. I know I've said this in every letter and it's probably sounding old, but I can't wait. I want to be with you so much I just can't help it. You know it's funny when I look back and think that this all started because of a mix up in your cousin's school paper when they LJ+RJ instead of LJ+SJ. It's funny how on just a little mistake like that a whole lifetime of love started. I'm sure neither of us realized what was to happen in the future, but some how it did and we fell in love with each other.

To tell you the truth, I was just trying to see how many girls I could have that year, I don't even know why, but I picked you to love while I was in Japan. I guess our love for each other grew due to absence from each other and after about 6-8 month over there I decided that I wanted to marry you, I can't really think of a better reason, except that I love you and love being with you so much that I want you all for myself. I know this sounds silly rambling along like this, but I'm just writing down my thoughts. I better get off that subject before I get turned on too much and over here there's nothing you can do when you get that turned on.

I got my first leech on me today. I was walking along on the patrol when I felt something like a mosquito biting on my let just above the top of my boot. I rolled up my pants leg and there he was, sucking blood out of my leg, so I just flicked him off on the ground and calmly smashed the hell out of him.

I haven't gotten your package yet, because they wouldn't let the guy who was going to bring it up to me have it. They wouldn't even let him have his own package until we come down off this stupid Razorback on February 1st.

Well, I guess that's all for now I love you more than anything in the world. Time to wake up my buddy so he can go on watch.

Bye.

Hiking the trails on the Razorback stressed the fabric on the legs of my trousers. By this time, my clothes were starting to rot and the fabric of my trousers became very friable, causing it to tear out through the inseam, the legs, and up the crotch. I used silk suture material from my medical kit to stitch them together as best I could. The fabric was so weak that many of the stitches tore out on the next venture out onto the ridge.

January 28 1967

Hi again,

Here I am out on another ambush writing in the light of the moon again. Right now it's 1 am and I just went on watch.

It sure was hot yesterday. We started out on our patrol at 10 am and we didn't have any water because the command post people have control over our water and they give each man 1 canteen full a day ant the only time you can get more water is at 4 in the afternoon. Day before yesterday my buddy and I sneaked down the side of the mountain to a small cave where there is a small pool of water. We used gauze to filter out the worms and mosquito larvae and put some water purification tablets in it to kill what was small enough to get through the filter and we had some pretty good water. The CP group only gives us 1 canteen a day, yet they use 10 gallons of water a day for washing, shaving, coffee, etc. It kind of makes you mad, but what can you do!?

Anyhow, we started out on our patrol and were only out a couple hours when we ran into a patch of bamboo, so we drank bamboo water but that wasn't really quenching our thirst and cutting the bamboo just made you thirstier. So later on we ran our patrol down the hill to a little stream, boy I thought I was going to drop before we got there. We finally got down and filled our canteens and them we took water in our helmets and poured in over our heads and down the front and back of us to cool off. It sure felt good. Then we started back up the hill and set up our ambush.

It sure got hot all of a sudden around here, looks like the monsoon season is finally over at last. All day the sky is sunny and as long as you don't have too much moving around you're all right, but any walking around or work you might as well forget about being comfortable.

I swear if I don't get a shower or something here pretty soon my poor body is going to rot away. Just sitting here I can smell my BO coming out the top of my shirt. I think I'll pass out from the smell here pretty soon.

The moon is still full, well at least most of the way, one piece of it is starting to blacken out, but it's still light enough to write. I know that you think of me just as I think of you at times when the nights are so calm and peaceful.

I hope you don't mind this paper. It's been in my pocket ever since I've been up here and it's getting kind of wrinkled and worn but at least its writable, that's all that counts.

It seems that I am always thinking of you. Like now, when we're walking on patrol or when I get the day off and just sit around. I guess all the guys around here are the same way. They are always thinking of their wives, fiancés or girlfriends. It helps time to pass and makes everyone remember how good they had it and how it will be when they get home again. I know I'm looking forward to coming home to you and being with you. That's all I ever think about.

I love you more than anything in the world. I want to be with you always and forever. I was thinking what we'll do when we are married, I think we'll do a little traveling and just live it up for a while, just be together, do things together, and love each other. If we get an idea to go somewhere or do something, we'll do it without having to worry about anything. I think the only way we can do this is not to have any kids for a while anyway. They also limit you in where you can go and what you can do. Yes I think of this all the time. We'll get a car and do some traveling for a while. What do you think of my idea?

Well my watch is about over, so I'll say bye for now. I love you and always will. I want to be with you always and forever.

Bye.

One evening, we formed up on the drop zone preparing to go out on ambush. The command group was in the trees behind us. We were passing the time until sunset telling jokes, smoking, and writing letters. Suddenly small arms fire broke out on one of the rocky formations above us to the north. Bullets began hitting all around as we all dove for cover and returned fire. I was somewhat exposed, and bullets were hitting around, so I ran to a more protective area near the perimeter. I watched as the machine gunner stood and fired his M60 from his shoulder at the hill above. Every fifth round on the belted ammunition was a tracer, special bullets modified to accept a small pyrotechnic charge in their base. When the bullet is fired, it ignites the charge, the composition burns very brightly, making the projectile visible to the naked eye. This enables the shooter to follow the bullet trajectory relative to the target, allowing him to see where the bullets are hitting. I watched as his bullets arched up and hit on the rocks above in a steady stream of red streaks. Simultaneously he was holding his air mattress on its edge out of harm's way behind a rock with his foot. He was cussing at the enemy and threatening them a fate worse than death if they punctured his "rubber lady." The firefight lasted less than thirty minutes.

After the shooting stopped, I checked, and we had only a few minor wounds and no one needed any medical attention requiring evacuation. Most cared for their own scrapes and wounds caused from fragments of rocks kicked up by bullets hitting in close proximity. Wounded were the following:

Cpl. Belmore, Michael W. 0311
LCpl. Brune, Albert R. 0331
Cpl. Detora, Ernest F. Jr. 0311
Sgt. Jarvis, Lee B. 0311
Cpl. Laferriere, Phillip J. 0351
Cpl. Larson, Jerome C. 0311
Sgt. Marlin, Steven M. 0351
LCpl. Marx, John E. 0311
Sgt. McGowin, Francis A. Jr. 0311

After dark, we proceeded out to our ambush site, and the night progressed with no other incidents.

January 31, 1967

Dear Louise,

Well, I finally got time to sit down and write again. Lots of things have happened since the other night.

To start off with in chronological order, day before yesterday it was the hottest it has been since I've been over here. I got back from the ambush at about 7:30 am and it was getting warm. About 10 o'clock almost everyone was out of water. We were so hot we were all sitting around in our underwear with no shirts on. I took my air mattress and went out and laid in the sun for about half an hour. About 12 o'clock the guys were complaining because we didn't have any water on the hill, so I went and told the Lieutenant that we wouldn't last out the day without water and asked him to send down a patrol to the stream for water, so finally he let some guys go down and we had water.

Yesterday I had to go on a security patrol to take the Lieutenant down to Alamo Hill. We were down there for a couple hours and came back up here and sat around for the rest of the day.

Last night was the most thrilling of the whole time I've been here. We were getting ready to go out on ambush and four of us were sitting around waiting for the other guys to get ready. We were sitting there talking when shots started firing from the next hill. We dove behind a rock. One of the guys dove on top of me. The shots hit right where we were sitting so our whole hill opened up on the other hill and we had a firefight, which lasted approximately 30 minutes. After it was all over we ended up with 9 guys with scratches from flying rocks. This morning I took out my pistol and found that a fragmentation from a VC bullet had hit the handgrip of my pistol in my holster. That's coming a little too close if you ask me. After all the shooting stopped we still had to go out on ambush. Needless to say I was alert all night.

This paper is getting pretty bad off. I carry it around with me all the time and sometimes I have other things in the same pocket, such as grenades.

I sure do love you. I can't wait to be with you again. All I ever think about is you and me being together forever.

Oh, when we went down to the Alamo the other day I had your letter waiting for me. It sounds like we'll be real set for when we're married. You wanted to know what BAS stands for, well it means Battalion Aid Station, but I'm not there anymore, I'm with Lima Company, 3rd Platoon.

Well, bye for now.

The next morning, I accompanied a squad up to the area where the gunfire had come from. After examining the entire area, we found evidence of the enemy being there; some of the rocks had fresh blood, but they had policed up all their shell casings, and there was no further evidence of them being there.

Hi again,

Right now I'm sitting up at one of the spots that we were getting shot at from. I don't see how they could miss from up here. I'm glad they did, though.

We are getting new weapons one of these days. They are the AR-15, which is what you see the Army using in all the pictures in the magazines. You can recognize it real easy because it has a handle on top of it. I am going to try and get one too. They are real light and fire faster and further than the M-14, which is what the Marines use now.

From up here you can even look down on our hill that we are on. It sure is beautiful up here. I will try to show you how it is by a rough map. Very rough is more the word for it.

Like I said it would be a rough sketch.

Tomorrow is our last day up here. We go down to hot food, mail, packages, and beer (2 cans per man). Wow! That's what I call living. But as all things go around here good things last only a couple of days because on the 4th we are going on an operation to go look for the VC instead of just sitting here waiting for them to come to us, so that should be fun. No rest for the weary, I guess.

Just after we left on this patrol a 'copter came in with more food and water for us, so it looks like we get all we can eat our last night up her. It's about time.

I just can't get over how beautiful this place is. If only I could be here under different circumstances.

Well, we're getting ready to move on so I better get going. I love you.

Bye for now.

After several more days, we finally received orders for the platoon to leave the top of the Razorback and went back into the muddy area at the top of Lima Hill.

The lack of rainfall the past week or so had allowed the mud to dry up considerably. Upon arrival, clean utilities were supplied. I now had two sets, so I could put on a dry set every day. My old ones were beyond repair, so I burned them.

The battalion armory brought in some M16s for "fam fire" (familiarizing firing) of the weapon. The M14 was designed for long range and too powerful for the short-range fighting that most of the battles in Vietnam entailed. Compared to the M14, the M16 looked and felt like a toy rifle that could have been made by Mattel toy company. We would not be issued the M16 until much later in April, but we got a chance to fire a couple magazines of ammunition through it.

February 2, 1967

Dear Louise,

We made it! I am now down on Alamo Hill again and was sure glad to see 6 packages from your family and mine. I sure like all the goodies. The cookies and candy were real good. I got more packages than anyone else, so everyone was mooching from me today.

They haven't got enough corpsmen to go around down here, so tonight I go on ambush with 2nd platoon and tomorrow I go and patrol with 3rd platoon. I wish I could stay with 3rd platoon, because they are a great bunch of guys.

I fired the AR-15 today and it's just like shooting a 22, even on full automatic. The corpsmen are even getting them so I'm glad.

Everything seems to have gone perfect today. Morale is high and it was payday and I got a $292.00 check which I have to change into a money order and send home to the bank for our future.

I hope you like this long letter. I can't promise that they will all be this long, but when ever I can't mail my letters I'll do it this way.

I sure do miss you and I love you more than anything. When we're married I'll show you how much I love you in everything I do or say.

Well, I have to go on ambush, so bye for now.

Love always,
Russ

PS I love you

While out on the patrols and ambushes, I had become concerned that even though I had learned to use all the weapons the Marines carried (M14, M60, and M79), I wanted something with more firepower than my 1911A1 .45 semiautomatic Colt pistol when we got into the inevitable firefight. One of the Marines told me of a Marine in the 81 mm mortar unit who had an M3A1 .45-caliber "grease gun" that he would sell for sixty dollars. He had acquired it by playing cards with a guy from tanks. The tanker had given the weapon to him as collateral until he could pay his $60 debt.

I went to his bunker and talked to him about it. He agreed to sell it to me and was willing to wait until payday before I paid him. The weapon is fairly heavy, weighing eight pounds. With a thirty-round magazine, it weighed about eleven pounds. I had three extra magazines, and when fully loaded, each weigh about three pounds apiece. I now had my own automatic weapon and was feeling like John Wayne. I was willing to carry an extra twenty pounds.

Chapter 32

Payable

WHEN THE TIME came for us to move off Lima Hill, I saddled up with all my gear, joined the platoon, and walked off the hill via the muddy road that I had arrived on the month before. We walked along in single file down the hill. After crossing the bridge, the road became wider, and we changed to a staggered double-file formation along each side of the road. When we arrived at Highway 9, we continued west and soon arrived at the two small hills on either side of the road guarding the entrance to a small valley. A concertina wire gate blocked the highway between the hills. Inside the gate straddling Highway 9 was Third Battalion Third Marines forward base of operations, code-named Payable. After passing through the entrance, the valley contained many bunkers, tents, and self-propelled artillery.

Lima Company took up position in the bunkers along the trench line on the south side of Highway 9. First Platoon took the entrance hill to the south, and Second and Third Platoon took up the valley next to the artillery units and around to a bridge crossing a small stream. After settling in, I met a couple of other corpsmen in Lima Company. Dan Fuss and Wayne Knabe had both joined 3/3 while in Okinawa in October. Since I was the new guy and had never been to the BAS, Kelsey (the senior corpsman) asked me to accompany him to the Battalion Aid Station to pick up medical supplies and to introduce me to the other corpsmen and battalion surgeon.

The BAS was a large bunker located in the center of the compound on the north side of the highway. Engineers excavated a hole in the hillside and built the structure in the hole with huge wooden bridge timbers. Once completed, they backfilled the hole with earth on three sides to protect the structure. The exposed west side and roof were layered with sandbags, protecting it from any direct hits. The battalion surgeon and higher-ranked corpsmen worked there and lived in smaller bunkers located near the BAS. After that, I seldom had any need to go over there. Our senior corpsman went over each week and picked up our malaria pills and any needed supplies. Inside the BAS, I was able to weigh myself on their scales and discovered that my weight had dropped from 155 to 125 pounds since joining Lima Company less than a month ago.

Adjacent to the BAS was a large open area of packed dirt. On the south side was battalion supply. On the western edge of the clearing was the fuel dump. The battalion mess hall area consisted of tents where food was stored and prepared. This was located to the west of the fuel dump. The dining area adjacent to the tents was a group of tables constructed of half-inch-thick sheets of plywood supported on empty fifty-five-gallon oil barrels. This allowed personnel to stand while eating their hot meal from a chow tray placed on the table. The cooks provided three hot meals a day.

Where the bridge crossed the stream at the western side of the compound, the engineers had constructed a concrete slab with a framework of pipes on the west side of the stream. A large mobile water-heating unit on a trailer pumped water out of the stream to a pressure tank that forced the water through the pipes to the showerheads. The spring-loaded valve to the shower had a cord attached. When the bather pulled and held on to the cord, warm water flowed from the showerhead. After being dirty and cold, nothing felt better than having a hot shower. When we arrived at Payable, the Marines had not had a shower since five months previously in September while they were in Okinawa. Downstream from the uptake for the showers, we were able to launder our utilities. Having no laundry soap, we used bar soap to attempt to clean them; however, it was difficult to rinse all the soap out of the fabric, so most of us just did the best we could with water only.

In addition to the M108 and M109 self-propelled howitzers, the Marines had a number of M48A3 tanks and several M50 Ontos with six recoilless cannons attached to the outside. There were also several army units that had M42A1 Dusters with navy twin 40 mm antiaircraft guns and several 6-by trucks with M55 .50-caliber antiaircraft machine guns mounted on the back (known as Whispering Death). All of these units fired missions day and night. The night missions of the twin forties were especially interesting. Each round they fired had a tracer that created a red streak in the night as it arched out over the valley on its way to the target. The M48A3 tanks were equipped with infrared searchlights allowing them to "illuminate" the area and used special scopes to observe enemy movement. They then directed their guns on them.

The patrols and ambushes continued, but one day, the senior corpsman told me to catch the convoy back to Dong Ha. The exam for hospital corpsman second class was being given, and I had met all the requirements to sit for the exam. I loaded up that afternoon and rode back to 3/3's rear area. That evening, I happened to run into a guy from Fort Bragg who was a year behind me in high school. Warren Main and I sang in our high school chorus, singing at school functions and entertaining the community. He and I were in the cast of an operetta; he sang tenor, and I sang bass. He joined the Marines after graduation and now worked as a radioman for 3/3's rear area command group. We went to the mess tent and ate dinner and caught up on the hometown gossip. After dinner, we went to the movie. It was great to visit with someone from home.

The next day, all the corpsmen slated to take the exam were instructed to meet at the air force radar station compound across the road. They had the only buildings large enough to accommodate the group taking the exam. Arriving at the compound, I saw a couple of my buddies from Japan, and we wandered over together to the designated assembly location, the air force's club building. Inside the building, we saw slot machines, tables, and a bar with padded swivel barstools. Someone had put out several pans of freshly baked cinnamon rolls and sheet cakes on the tables with pots of fresh coffee. We helped ourselves, and as other corpsmen arrived, we invited them to partake also. After we had consumed most of the food and were finishing our second cup of coffee, a navy chief arrived and announced that we would be taking our exam in the building next door. We walked over as a group and entered the large metal building, which turned out to be their movie theater equipped with seats with fold-up desks. The test booklets, answer sheets, and number 2 pencils were passed out, and the testing began.

At around 1000, during the middle of the exam, a very angry air force sergeant barged into the theater and demanded to see the chief outside. When the chief came back inside, he couldn't contain his joy. He interrupted the exam stating that he was very proud of all of us. The sergeant was upset because the air force guys were extremely upset with us for consuming their morning break refreshments. Since the navy and Marines consider the air force as a bit on the sissy side (the "chair" force), we enjoyed a good laugh at their expense. Those poor airmen had to wait until the next morning for their little tea party. After the exam, I said good-bye to my buddies and caught a convoy back to the Rockpile and returned to my hole in the ground.

The next day out on patrol, we were headed back to our position walking along Highway 9 when our point man signaled that he heard voices up ahead. We immediately took cover in the elephant grass along both sides of the road, setting up an ambush. As the voices got louder and louder, we heard women and children's voices, and everyone was told to hold their fire. The group rounded the bend in the road and revealed that the voices were a large group of Montagnards on their way to trade their wares at the market in Cam Lo. These people were dark-skinned and dressed in a completely different style of clothing than the Vietnamese. Radioing in our situation, we learned that the group had just come through Payable's position and had been cleared. We stopped them and checked their baskets and papers again just to make sure nothing was amiss. They spoke a completely different language from Vietnamese. The older women had brownish red teeth from the betel nut they chewed to relieve dental pain. The entire group seemed to be unconcerned by our presence and submitted again to our search. When we finished, the squad leader apologized for the inconvenience, and they went on their way and we went ours.

Arriving back at our bunkers, the platoon sergeant told us that Lima Company was on standby for an operation out into the hills to the southwest of the Razorback.

February 11, 1967

Dear Louise,

The other day I had to go back to Dong Ha to take the test for HM2. We went by jeep from here to there, which was quite a ride.

We got back there and I found Warren Main, who is from Fort Bragg, we sat around and talked and then went to a movie, a real flick the first one I've seen in a long time. "The Collector" was the name of the movie. The next day I took the test, I think I passed. We had to go onto the Air Force base to find a place large enough for 45 of us to take the test, so we were going to use their club, but they were going to have coffee hour, so we had to go to their theater. After the test we went to coffee hour and had coffee, coke, and cake. Their club has a bar, slot machines, tables and chairs, jukebox and a whole bunch of other things, just like back in the states. What gets me is that they are getting paid "Inconvenience" pay as well as combat pay. I wish I could be as inconvenienced as much as them.

I now carry a "Grease Gun" which is a sub machine gun like you see in the movies. The magazine holds 31 shots and as long as you keep your finger on the trigger it keeps shooting. It cost me $60.

Tomorrow or the next day we go on operation for 5-8 days hunting VC. Please don't worry so much; you're too young to have an ulcer. Anyhow, nothing is going to happen to me.

You asked me where I'll be stationed when I leave here, I really want to go back to Japan, but I want to stay with the Marines so I really don't know where I'll be going. I would like to get married when I get home, but it wouldn't be practical, being that you still have to graduate. But I do think that the date you were thinking of sounds good because I get out on the 2nd of September so that date sounds good. I leave here in November as far as I know. At least that's the closest I figure.

Right now I'm sitting in my bunker with a couple of other guys. We just got finished with some hot chocolate, Nestle's Quick to be exact, sure was good.

Today we were on patrol when we heard gook voices along the road, we immediately jumped down and everyone was ready to fire. Then we saw them they were "friendlies" so we didn't shoot, but if they weren't we sure could have slaughtered them. They were civilians, men, women and children walking to Dong Ha. We stopped them and searched their baskets and then let them continue on their way.

I won't be able to write while I'm on operation, I should say that I can't mail any letters, but I'll do like I did when I was on the Razorback so you will know what's going on.

I love you more than anything in the world. I can't wait until we can be together forever. Every time I think of you I get turned on. If I think real hard I really have to control myself. The longer I'm over here the more I miss you. You better watch out when I get home! But, I'll try not to act like a horny toad who hasn't seen a girl for a long time (at least a little).

Well, I better get some sleep, just don't worry about me, please, and take your antacid tablets and get well. Bye for now

Love always
Russ

PS I love you

When we were not out on patrol or ambush, we began preparing for the upcoming Operation Prairie. We received supplies for three days and loaded up our packs. I rechecked my Unit One and stuffed in a couple more battle dressings. I made sure my grease gun and pistol were well oiled and clean. We were scheduled to leave the next morning. Lima Company didn't send out a night ambush, and all the bunks inside were occupied. That night, I slept on the roof of my bunker rather than inside.

Chapter 33

Friendly Fire

THE NEXT MORNING, February 17, we prepared to "saddle up." Third Battalion Third Marines was flying out into the mountains by helicopter for a search-and-destroy operation. India Company and the command group were also going with us on this one. We loaded up with all our gear, preparing to move to the staging area to board helicopters. After an hour or so, the word was to "stand down." We returned to our bunkers and took off our packs and other gear and waited. The helicopters came in and picked up the leading elements of India to take them to their assigned LZ. Then the command group and the remainder of India were flown out. Finally at about 1440, we again were told to saddle up and, this time, moved to the staging area. A half hour later, several CH-47 helicopters came in and landed in the flat area between our perimeter and the river. They lowered their tail ramps, and we loaded in, and away we went. The afternoon was clear, and the area was beautiful from the air.

Flying southwest out into the mountains, we were soon near a hill designated as 492, a grassy knoll surrounded by jungle. The helicopters, with their tail ramps lowered, landed just long enough for us to exit. We charged out the back and set up a defensive perimeter around the LZ as the next one came in. Each successive helicopter did the same until all of our troops were on the ground. When we all got on the ground, we picked up fifteen-foot intervals between us and started moving uphill toward the jungle.

We followed a trail that led higher up on the hill. It wasn't long before we were hiking through an area of the jungle with broken tree trunks surrounded by bare muddy ground. Either bombs or artillery had devastated the vegetation. Passing through, we again entered thick jungle. At sunset, we stopped and set up a defensive perimeter for the night. Those of us not needed on the line went to sleep where we could. The hillside was steep, but I found a small hollow at the base of a tree and curled up in my poncho on the uphill side and tried to get some sleep.

The next day, February 18, at first light, we hiked up and down trails in the area. Except for patches devastated by bombing and artillery, the jungle was beautiful and the trails well established. Some areas had stairways constructed of logs and earth so that anyone carrying a large heavy load could more easily climb or descend the inclines. All along the trail, we were on constant lookout for booby traps and *punji* pits, and several were discovered before they could do any harm.

After humping higher into the hills at 0900, we came across a base camp that looked fairly fresh. In the process of destroying the camp, a hundred pounds of rice were discovered. An intensified search turned up a lone NVA soldier up in a tree. He was quickly killed and his body and weapon retrieved. His pockets and rucksack were searched, and he had a great deal of money and a record book with him. The rumor was that he was a paymaster.

At around eleven thirty, we discovered another base camp with ten fighting bunkers. Footprints in the mud indicated that the area might have been occupied in the past few days. We set about demolishing all the bunkers. At about twelve forty-five while in the process of tearing down the bunkers, we captured a Vietcong who was not carrying any weapon. His rucksack was full of chow, and he was dressed in black clothing.

At around 1700, a man and a woman carrying a baby ran out of the brush and down the hill. A couple of our Marines pursued her, but she eluded them, and they were unable to locate her. The old man was captured and held as a VC suspect. A few minutes later, an NVA soldier with bandoliers crossed on his bare chest wielding a submachine gun Rambo-style shot our point man in the neck. The point man's squad leader with his .45 pistol in hand charged the NVA, and after a brief exchange, the body of the NVA was lying on the trail. Shortly thereafter, a woman with a baby, and an old man were captured in the same area.

We commenced a search of this area, and at 1835, we found a complex of three base camps within one hundred meters of each other. We also found two new NVA uniforms and assorted pieces of uniforms, a pack with foreign-made map enclosed in plastic, and a notebook with writing. We also discovered a fresh dead body dressed in a gray NVA uniform who had apparently been killed by small arms.

We continued farther up the ridge and dug in for the night. Radioman LCpl. Richard Lynn and I shared an improvised tent made out of his poncho staked out over a sapling that we bent to form the ridge. We made it low to the ground to help keep the heat inside closer to our bodies. After dark, the clouds quickly enveloped the mountain, and we spent one of the coldest nights I could remember. Inside the tent, we used my poncho as a blanket. It got so cold that night that Lynn and I decided to sleep with our backs together to try and decrease our shivering. It helped, but it was still miserably cold.

The next morning, February 19, we awoke at first light and had a breakfast of C rations. The mountain was still shrouded in clouds. During the night, the woman with the baby escaped. The Marine guarding her looked away from her to give her some privacy to breastfeed her baby, and she took advantage by dashing away from him and down the hill. The old man was still in custody.

One of the platoons started down the small ravine and, at around 0800, discovered the entrance to what appeared to be a weapons cache. After checking for booby traps, one of the Marines entered and came out indicating that we had hit the jackpot. The cache was built into a narrow area of the ravine. Long logs were placed over the V to form the roof between the sides of the ravine. These logs were then covered with a plastic tarp, and the plastic tarp was covered with leaves and other vegetation to hide it. It measured about twenty-five feet long and was loaded with a large quantity of rifles, mortars, rockets, and other supplies. First Platoon was given the task of digging up the cache, and Second Platoon was assigned to climb the adjacent hillside and set up security. Inside the cache, they found two new 82 mm mortars complete with baseplates and sights and tripods. As they dug deeper, they came out with a large number of 82 mm mortar and rocket rounds, about five pounds of explosives for demolition, and six antitank rounds. The old man was brought down to the scene and interrogated about other caches that might be in the area. He was shaking and pleading for his life when I passed by him

A trail led from the cache up the other side of the ravine. A squad of Second Platoon was directed to follow the trail up the hill, and I accompanied them. As we crept up the hill, our point men startled a group of NVA soldiers in the process of cooking rice for their breakfast. The startled group shot at us and fled up the hill leaving a pot of not-yet-cooked rice on the fire along with all their gear except for their rifles. The squad called to inform the platoon commander of the situation – they had found some hooches dug into the side of the mountain with a bunch of rucksacks and supplies. At some point, the artillery forward observer was directed to call in a mission. Spotter rounds of white phosphorus started exploding higher on the hill, causing more NVA to run out of their hooches farther up on the steep hillside and hastily follow their comrades. This time, the Marines took off after them, pursuing them up the hill. I charged up the hill with them. One of the Marines in front of me decided to check out one of the hooches as the others continued up the hill. I stopped and covered him as he entered the side of the hill through the door.

Unfortunately, the next adjusted barrage from the artillery was on its way. I had on previous days noticed the sounds of incoming fire missions. The farther away I was from the target, the longer the time between the sound of the report of the distant guns and the sound of the approaching shells. This time there was no gap; I heard the report and instantly the sound of the shells coming in. Instinctively I dove straight down the hill away from the where the shells had landed previously. Time seemed to stop as I floated through the air. I saw leaves and twigs on the ground and even bugs crawling along. I could smell the dirt and decaying leaves as well as the rice cooking in the pot. After what seemed like an eternity, I landed and rolled down behind a berm and curled up into the fetal position. Dirt and shrapnel flew through the air just above me through the tree branches as three rounds of high explosive hit right on top of the pursuing Marines just up the trail from me. Numerous voices yelled frantically to cease fire. Evidently the forward observer down the hill must have heard this and relayed "check fire" to the artillery. No further rounds came in after that.

    The next thing I heard were numerous calls for "corpsman up" filling the air. I scrambled up the hill and came across the squad. One member of our team, Lance Corporal Pete Liberati's body was sitting with his back against a tree with his bandoliers of ammunition crossing his chest and his grenades attached to his flak jacket. He looked as if he were lounging, except for the skin on his face was hanging loose on his skull like a rubber mask. Corporal Bill Branock was also dead, as was PFC Johnnie Mason. Mason's hand was also missing. I began treating the other wounded and requested the help of the others to assist them down the hill away from the impact area. After everyone had been attended, I picked up one of the wounded and packed him on my back down the hill, placing him near the entrance of the hooch where I had been prior to the explosion. I left him there and returned up the hill. By this time, all the wounded had been cleared. I then assisted in finding all the body parts, placing them with the appropriate bodies. I found Johnnie Mason's hand several yards away and returned it to his body. After the bodies were wrapped in ponchos and carried down, I returned to where I had left the wounded man outside the entrance to the hooch. He had been moved, and it was then I noticed I had placed him on top of a partially buried basket full of Chi Com grenades. It was fortunate that none of them went off. I moved down the hill to the ravine to assist with further care. Our casualties numbered fourteen. Some minor wounds and some major. Cpl. Richard MacKenzie had shrapnel near his spinal cord and was numb from his wound down. After ensuring that our area was secure, a medevac was requested.

    The jungle canopy was so thick that our engineers had to use C4 to blow down several trees. They molded the plastic explosive around the tree trunk at the level they wanted it cut and electrically detonated the charge. The tree trunk severed, but foliage at the canopy was still hanging it in the vertical position. Two or three Marines grabbed the trunk of the tree and wrestled with it until the foliage let go from the tangle, and they pulled the trunk down the hill until it was laid on the ground. This task was repeated several times until there was enough room for a helicopter to lower a basketlike Stokes stretcher. The clouds were still thick, but one helicopter made it in and hovered over the hole in the canopy. Our most critically wounded man was placed in the basket and hauled up to the chopper. The clouds were closing in, and we were only able to get one other of our wounded out before the clouds closed in on the mountain and the pilots lost visibility, making further evacuation attempts impossible. As the day progressed, conditions did not improve for medevac.

In the meantime, all the hooches and gear left behind by the NVA were searched along with rifles, ammunition, mortars, rockets, mines, explosives, and other munitions. We also had packs with freshly laundered clothes, about one thousand pounds of rice, knives, digging tools, uniforms, helmets, and bags of mail. We had run into a way station for North Vietnamese coming down to South Vietnam. Pictures of Ho Chi Minh were found on the walls. Many of the packs contained pictures and letters from home.

We continued to search the area, and around twelve fifteen, two more complete mortars, four boxes of antitank rounds totaling twenty-four rounds, twenty-six cases of Chi Com grenades with ten in each case, three cases of 82 mm mortar ammunition with six rounds per case, five cases of explosives containing one-hundred-two-and-a-half-pound blocks per case, twelve packs with assorted food, letters, and personal gear.

At 1440, another cache was located, and we found four boxes of antitank rockets, twenty cases of Chi Com grenades, three cases of 82 mm mortar rounds, and five cases of half-pound blocks of demolitions.

Weather conditions were not getting any better. We kept hoping for a break in the clouds. The weather in the valleys was clear, but at our level on the mountain, the bottom edge of the cloud was several hundred feet below us. All the corpsmen gathered together the morphine in our Unit Ones to help our wounded deal with their pain.

The search for weapons' caches continued, and at 1515, another twenty-five Chi Com grenades, one claymore mine, and twenty-five sets of Marine utilities were uncovered. At 1930, we discovered one Chinese carbine, one hundred fifty pounds of rice in bags, and a thousand pounds of rice in a bin in a tunnel complex. Samples of all weapons, munitions, and gear were saved, and all the rest were placed in a large pile to be destroyed.

We had to get our casualties out, their pain was becoming excruciating. We were advised to begin moving our wounded and dead down the mountain. If we could get them below the cloud cover by morning, another medevac would be attempted.

After we moved down the hill, a safe distance away, our engineers detonated C4, destroying the entire pile of captured gear. Even at a safe distance around the hillside, the explosion was deafening.

Most of our wounded were able to walk, but several of them required assistance. A makeshift litter was fashioned from material found around the NVA compound. After a while, the numbness caused by his spinal cord injury started to subside, and despite shots of morphine, Corporal Mackenzie was now in agonizing pain. Weapons Platoon Sergeant Gallegos donated his air mattress to provide a cushion for Mackenzie's litter, which provided him with some relief from the jarring ride. Even with the air mattress, the trip down the steep trail was torture for Mackenzie.

The Marines have a policy of "no man left behind." Our dead wrapped up in their ponchos were also transported down the mountain. This trail was more primitive and steeper than the one we had come in on. Moving down the trail was slow and tedious. The head of the column would go forward and set up security. When we caught up with them, another squad would go forward and do the same. Eventually we ran out of morphine for our wounded. We became concerned that they (and especially Mackenzie) would go into irreversible shock. At night, Mackenzie's buddies sat and talked to him to try and keep him quiet.

We continued to leapfrog down the hill, and finally more than twenty-four hours after being hit, we descended below the clouds. On February 20 at twelve thirty-five, a CH-46 came into our position to pick up our wounded and dead. The prisoner was also flown out. Some brass from the army flew in to consult with our commander about the caches we had uncovered.

Later that day, we hiked farther down the hill, and the next morning, we uncovered another cache. This time it contained one hundred canisters containing vitamin pills. Labels identified them as vitamin C and B. They were destroyed.

We proceeded down the hill and entered a large valley with elephant grass twelve to fifteen feet tall. The CH-46s had to land to pick us up, so the grass had to be burned for an LZ. The Chinooks finally arrived around twelve fifteen. We scrambled on board, and they lifted out. On the way back, I was sleepily looking out the port at the ground below. Suddenly the ground appeared as if it was rising up toward us. The helicopter then shuttered, and we started rising again. Evidently we had hit some turbulence or warm air mass that momentarily interfered with the craft's ability to fly. I looked over at the crew chief standing at the .50 caliber in the side door. He seemed unaffected by the event, so I didn't worry about it. Finally we landed back in the field outside the wire at Payable, exited the helicopter, and walked back to our bunkers. Time to decompress a bit with a hot shower, hot food, and mail call.

It was bad enough when our troops were killed and wounded by the enemy, but our own artillery? Casualties are casualties regardless of how they occur, but "friendly" fire had hit us. Back in the safety of our perimeter, we had time to think about what had happened, and morale was very low. Needing someone to blame, some of the friends of the wounded and dead were angry with artillery's forward observer. It was little consolation that the squad had pursued the enemy into the kill zone of the fire mission. That action was not evident to the forward observer lower down on the hill or to the artillery shooting the mission back at Payable. The forward observer did immediately radio a cease-fire when he realized what had happened. If the artillery had been allowed to fire for effect, we would have sustained more casualties than we had. The official record of those Marines' deaths lists the cause of death simply as "misfortune," giving no indication that those brave Marines were in hot pursuit of the enemy at the time of their death.

Our casualties that day consisted of the following:
Killed
    Cpl. Branock, William M. 0311
    LCpl. Liberati, Peter J. 0311
    PFC Mason, Johnnie 0311

Wounded
    LCpl. Abraham, Joseph H. 0331
    LCpl. Ames, Arthur S. 0311
    LCpl. Anderson, Jennings R. 0331
    LCpl. Beardsley, Gordon E. 0311
    Cpl. Bigelow, Alphonso R. C. 0311
    LCpl. Camacho, Patricio 0311
    Sgt. Disch, Willis F. 0311
    Cpl. Mackenzie, Richard A. 0311
    PFC Marshall, Robert 0351
    Cpl. Richardson, Herbert 0351
    Cpl. Zwiefelhofer, Joseph F. 0311

After my first experience with real casualties, I realized that the grease gun I had previously thought so important was just an encumbrance when performing my job. I went back to the mortars and gave it back to its owner. I decided that if I ever got into a position where I needed to defend myself in a firefight, there would be plenty of spare weapons from our own casualties available for me to pick up.

February 21, 1967

Dear Louie,

Well we're back from the operation already. We started out on the 17th and as usual with the Marine Corps we were late getting out of here. We were supposed to leave at 9 am, but didn't get out until 4 pm. We flew out to a hill called 492, which is west of here. When we got there we formed up and marched out and stayed on a wet slippery hillside that night. The next morning we started out hiking again. We hiked about 10 miles along a jungle trail; well actually it wasn't jungle, but a rain forest, when a woman carrying a baby ran out in front of the column. The marines who were up there took off after her, but she got away. Then we went along the trail about 20 meters when a gook stepped out from behind a tree and started shooting at the front man. He was a bad shot and even with his machine gin he missed the guy and hit the second man in the shoulder. The first man shot the gook 7 times with his .45 pistol. Then we found a VC complex. It seems the woman ran and warned the people in the complex and everyone took off, but an old man that couldn't run fast enough and we captured him. Then we found the complex. There we found foxholes, maps, rice, money, uniforms, and all kinds of other goodies. Later we spotted some more VC and shot at them, but they got away. We spent the night there. The gook we killed had a Russian made rifle.

The next morning we started out and right away we ran into an ammo dump with brand new mortars and all the goods that go with it, plus demolitions and rockets for a bazooka. We brought the old man down and showed him what we found and he started shaking. Then someone down the trail started shooting so we all ran down there and found two houses that people had just left, the food was still warm.

I was covering a guy who was going to check out one of the houses when the artillery forward observers started calling in artillery in to try to get the gooks that got away. Someone goofed up and the next thing I knew I heard a shell coming in and I hit the dirt. It hit about 100 feet from where I was. I started to get up when I heard another one coming in, so I flattened out again. The first one had hit right up the hill right where some of our troops were, so I ran up there and started treating the wounded guys. All together we had 10 wounded and 3 killed. We started chopping trees so we could get a chopper in to evacuate the wounded and the bodies. We had to move them down the hill when they were going to blast one of the trees that was too big to chop. I grabbed one of the wounded and carried all 180 lbs of him down the slick hill to the outside of one of the houses and set him in a hole the gooks had dug in the bank. Then they decided to move them up to the top of the hill where we had spent the night so we made stretchers and finally got them all to the top of the hill after a couple of hours work. When we were moving the guy out of the hole, I found 8 Chinese Communist grenades under him that had a thin layer of dirt over them.

After we got all that done we went down and searched all the houses and found guns, ammunition, packs with freshly laundered clothes, pictures on the walls of Ho Chi Minh, the leader of North Viet Nam, about 1000 pounds of rice, knives, digging tools, uniforms, hats and all kinds of other stuff like that. We had run into a way station for North Vietnamese coming down to South Viet Nam. We even found a bag of mail. Most of the stuff we blew up, but I found a pencil made in Czechoslovakia in one of the guys' packs and a clean, brand new wash cloth, which I kept. Then we moved out a platoon to find a way down to where we were to meet up with India Company. The trip was made during the dark and we made good time.

Yesterday they finally had weather good enough to fly out the bodies and wounded and we linked up with India Company and kind of took it easy. This morning we started out to where the helicopters were to pick us up. We got back here this afternoon about 3 pm.

Yesterday when we were loafing around General Westmoreland came out all the way from Saigon to see what we had and he was real pleased.

When we got back we had some hot chow and 2 beers per man waiting for us. Then they passed out the mail. I got two packages from you and one from my parents, two letters from you and one from Steve.

We were told today that we're going on another operation Saturday, either back in the same area we were in or west of the Razorback. So this may be all that I'll have time to write, but I'll try to get at least one more letter off before then.

You asked if the tapes in the Playboy were the type for our tape recorder, yes, they are.

You know I've been thinking that we should have a joint bank account. Could you see what I have to do to start one? Oh, could you also check to see if I am getting my savings bonds at home all right?

Another thing I want to do is after we're married let's take a trip to Japan. What do you think? You always said that you would like to go there, maybe that could be our honeymoon spot.

All during the operation I thought of you and planned and remembered things we did together. I carried all the pictures of you that you sent me and every night I look at them.

I wasn't really scared during that thing, but I know this now. A firefight doesn't really bother me, but you can't shoot back at mortars, bombs, or artillery shells, those three things just scare me to pieces. When we go out I hate for them to call this stuff in because it has no eyes to guide where it's going to hit, just measurements and figures back in the rear where they are shooting this stuff. Well enough of that.

I love you more than anything. All I want to do is come home to you, to get out of this god-forsaken country. Only 8 months to go and I will be on my way home to you.

Well got to get some sleep now. Oh, how 'bout sending some more pictures? The little book is only half full. Bye for now.

Love always,
Russ

PS I love you
PS (again) Keep an eye out in the paper for any time after today, because we had news correspondents with us. Look for anything on captured equipment for "L" company 3rd battalion 3rd Marine Regiment. If you find anything, could you please send it? Thanks a lot.

Chapter 34

Lima Company to the Rescue

ON FEBRUARY 27, we were sent out again to the west of the Razorback near the DMZ to rescue a battalion from the Ninth Marines that had been overrun by the NVA. We fought our way in and secured the area. We found their command group had been captured, tied to trees with communication wire, and were dead. The most horrifying thing was that several of them had their skin removed as torture before they were executed. We provided security so that the survivors could leave the area and then dug in and stayed the night. During the night, we set out our security and ambushes. All night, artillery shells were called in to help keep the enemy away from our perimeter. Many of the shells were hitting fairly close. Due to our experience a few days before, the explosions and showers of dirt were very unnerving.

Early the next morning, we started hiking out. There were some short firefights. In one area, we were walking through an abandoned farm area along a path when we started taking incoming small arms fire. I was in the open, so I hit the dirt. While lying there, bullets were flying close enough to me that they sounded like angry bees as they passed just above me. The Marines in front of me and I slowly inched our way forward and to get behind some more substantial cover. Air support was called in, and soon jets were flying over our position. Because of the enemies' proximity to us, we did not want to "pop smoke" (mark our position with a smoke grenade), so the air controller had us place colored panels on the ground in between our line and the enemy. The jets were then instructed to drop their ordinance beyond the panels on any movement they observed. Soon the ground in front of us was washed in napalm and high explosives. The heat from the napalm was intense even lying flat on the ground. Eventually the incoming small arms fire stopped, and we continued on our way.

We continued our sweep through the area. As we got closer to the Razorback, we heard tanks from Payable coming out our way. Slowly they were coming up through the hills and crushing all the smaller vegetation in front of them. This terrain made it very difficult for them and was not really conducive to their type of operation, but they continued toward us. Finally they passed us in the direction that we had just come from. After they passed, we followed their newly cleared swath through the brush back down the hill.

We stopped to take a break. I pulled out my copy of John Steinbeck's Travels with Charlie I was carrying in my trousers cargo pocket to help pass the time and escape from my reality. I was sitting there reading when a Marine sitting across the trail from me raised his rifle and fired a round with the muzzle of his M14 not more than a few inches from my right ear. It startled me, and I immediately dove in the opposite direction. He apologized to me and told me that he had seen an NVA soldier come out of the tree line and immediately duck back in and didn't have time to warn me. I couldn't hear anything out of my right ear for several hours, and when I did regain my hearing, it was very diminished.

As we continued back toward Payable, we had to cross several deep narrow streams. I saw that the water was chest deep by watching the Marines in front of me go through. I pulled my book out of my cargo pocket on my trousers and made sure that anything that could be ruined by water was held over my head. I waded in, and when I reached the other side, the man in front of me reached down to help me up the slick bank. I did the same for the man behind me. There were no further notable incidents, and we eventually reached Payable that day.

On March 1 we were sent out to the area north of Cam Lo on a search-and-destroy operation. We loaded into the backs of trucks, and they transported us by noon to our jumping-off location where we dismounted and began walking. By 1415, we made contact with the enemy. We received incoming small arms, automatic weapons, and grenades. The firefight lasted about ten minutes, and then the enemy broke contact. When we went into the area where they had been, all we found were spent rounds and a few M79 grenade casings.

At 1515, Lima Company made contact with large group of NVA. After twenty minutes of fighting, the enemy withdrew again. This time they left behind a .50-caliber machine gun. There were three Marines wounded, and they were medevaced by 1700. We had no further contact with the enemy that night.

Wounded 3/1
    Private First Class Blackburn, Charles R. 0311
    Corporal Holcombe, Richard W. Jr. 0311
    Corporal Howard, James E. 0311

Chapter 35

Ripley's Raiders

THE NEXT DAY March 2, we headed south to connect up with the headquarters group. We were sweeping down through an area with a well-established trail. At around eleven, we discovered two Chi Com grenades. Evidently they had been dropped because they had not been set up with a trip wire or any other method to detonate them. There was also rice scattered on the trail that was mixed with blood, indicating that whoever dropped the grenades was carrying a bandolier of rice and had been wounded. Following the trail of bloody rice, we came across bloody bandages that had been discarded. We continued following the trail.

At a juncture in the trail, Captain Ripley had First Platoon snooping around in a brushy area. At around 1300, the point man was silently walking down the path, and through the bushes, he saw two NVA sitting on top of bunkers wearing radio headsets with their backs toward him. One was busy tapping out code with a telegraph key strapped to his leg. The point man signaled his squad leader, and they decided to take advantage of the radiomen's inattention and capture them.

They stealthily crept up on their unsuspecting prey, and in a moment, they were overpowered, gagged, and their wrists tied. The captors were hurried out of the area, and the Marines grabbed all their gear including their radios and code and log books. As the two of radiomen were brought back through our column, they didn't look very happy. Captain Ripley examined the captured equipment and determined by the complexity of the radio equipment and an antenna mounted in a tree that this was a regimental headquarters for an NVA unit.

We withdrew slightly to keep from being discovered. Battalion radioed Captain Ripley to avoid contact, so we advanced and tried to go around the enemy, but they discovered that their radiomen were missing and came looking for us. At around 1440, they found us and attacked. We started getting small arms fire and mortars. They were so close that we could not call in artillery or mortar support.

We fixed bayonets and charged in shooting and yelling, which surprised the NVA. They abandoned their gear and retreated away from us to a distant area to regroup. Now we were inside the area that they had just occupied and had all their supplies. It wasn't long before that they realized that we were a small unit and decided that they might be able to retrieve their gear. They came at us again with small arms and automatic weapons fire. They also sent in mortars to further harass us. Soon we were experiencing casualties. The enemy units were still to close to us to call for artillery or air support.

The first wounded Marine I encountered was Private First Class Jack Harris. He was lying in a trench that had formerly been occupied by the NVA. He had been shot as he apparently had been exiting the trench. He had been shot in the chest and had no respirations or heartbeat. I started doing cardiopulmonary resuscitation (CPR) on him, but quickly abandoned my efforts as there was nothing I could do for him. There were too many more wounded who needed my immediate attention. As we progressed, I remember thinking how the bullets passing just above me again sounded like angry bees. I wished I could get flatter on the ground. I was crawling around the area putting battle dressings on the wounded and pulling them back into a trench or a hole to keep them out of harm's way.

I crawled out into a more exposed area and was attending to one of the wounded when fifteen or twenty feet away to the left, an NVA stood up from behind some brush where he had been hiding and was preparing to throw a grenade. I had been crawling with my pistol in my hand and quickly fired off two or three shots, which hit him in the midsection. The impact of the .45-caliber bullets doubled him over, and the grenade went off in his hand before he could lob it. Later when I examined his body, I could not determine if I had killed him or his grenade had done the job. I was just glad he was dead. I continued treating our casualties. Sometime during the battle, I was hit in the upper left arm by small pieces of shrapnel.

Eventually the NVA withdrew, and the firefight died down. I checked my wound and found that it was small and not bleeding much due to the adrenaline that was pumping through my body. I put a small battle dressing on my arm wound and rolled down my sleeve enough to cover it. Compared to most of the other wounds I had just treated, mine seemed so minor, and I couldn't justify leaving the field. We were already short on corpsmen before we began this operation.

We assessed our damages. One of the Marines approached me and said he had found a fighting hole with two NVA who were severely wounded in it and asked me what to do with them. I walked over to the hole and looked in. Down in the shallow hole, I saw two bloody bodies that were still alive, but not conscious and bleeding profusely. I then looked around at our dead and wounded and replied, "Let them die." We counted fifteen NVA bodies in our immediate area.

We still couldn't get in a medevac because the area was still considered too hot for choppers to come in, so we cared for our wounded the best we could. At 1530, we were again attacked by mortar fire raining into our area, but no small arms. This time we were able to utilize artillery and mortar support, and at around 1545, the incoming ceased.

As things calmed down, helicopters standing by on station came in for our casualties, covered by other helicopter gunships. They brought in more battle dressings, ammunition, and supplies. A CH-46 landed, and several cameramen and reporters from ABC and CBS News jumped off. They had heard about the action while they were in Dong Ha and couldn't wait to get to our position and document it.

We loaded up our casualties as the reporters started running around filming and interviewing the Marines. A *Huey* came in and hovered momentarily while a Marine general jumped out. His *Huey* took off to wait for him to call them back when he was ready to leave. He talked to Captain Ripley for a while.

When he was ready to leave at about 1720, he called his helicopter back in to take him out. Just as the general's *Huey* was taking off, we were attacked again, this time by mortars. The general's ride narrowly made it off the LZ and headed out. A mortar hit right where the helicopter had been sitting. Captain Ripley and his radioman were thrown through the air by the blast of the mortar striking the LZ. I was out in the open when the mortars started to rain in on us again and ran and jumped into a hole inside the tree line until the barrage was over. This attack only lasted about five minutes, but was very intense. As soon as it ended, I ran back out into the open area summoned by the calls of "corpsman up" and began treating our new casualties.

The first casualty I came across was a Marine who had the right half of his lower jaw blown away. I seem to remember he was one of our mortarmen. He was gurgling blood, and I couldn't establish an airway by normal means. I removed my scalpel from my minor surgery kit and performed a chricothyroidotomy, which is done by cutting a hole through the membrane just below his Adam's apple. I then took my pen apart and used my KA-BAR to cut off the narrow end, which allowed more air to pass through it. I then inserted it through the incision into his trachea so that he could breathe through it and secured it with adhesive tape. This bypassed his damaged upper airway and allowed the air to enter his lungs.

Again the reporters and cameramen were swarming all over, documenting our actions during the aftermath of the mortar attack. During the filming, one of the other corpsmen, Dan Fuss, was doing CPR on a wounded Marine adjacent to where

I was working. He was getting frustrated at the inability to get the victim's heart started again, and he yelled over to me, "Hey, Jewett, you have any epinephrine?" to which I yelled my reply, "No!" The news team recorded this. We were finally able to get out our dead and wounded. My patient was still alive when I put him on the next medevac helicopter. I learned later that he had died after he reached Delta Med in Dong Ha.

Back at home several days later, my sister (who had just turned ten) and my mom were driving to visit my grandmother in the hospital. They had the car radio on and heard something on the news about 3/3. My sister turned up the volume. They heard a firefight going on, and in the middle of it, she heard Fuss hollering to me. When Mom heard my voice, she almost ran her car up on a sidewalk.

Less than a week later, the edited footage showed up on the ABC Evening News, and my family and friends wrote me about seeing me on TV. Louise and her family saw it while they were eating dinner watching the evening news.

At 1820, the NVA attacked us again. We still had their gear and were stacking it up to destroy as much as we could. The Marines gathered up all the enemy's abandoned gear and ammunition and placed it in individual piles to inventory it. We had rucksacks, bags of rice, cans of ammunition, radios, and a machine gun on a trailer with a seat for the shooter to sit in. It was much more enemy gear than we anticipated.

At around 1900, India Company linked up with us, and we received ten rounds of mortar fire and some sniper fire. We fired back, and after ten minutes, the firing ceased, and we had three more wounded.

At 2100, they tried again with another mortar attack. In the dark, I took this opportunity to go into my backpack for some nourishment. Opening my pack, I found the inside covered with a sticky liquid. I tasted it and found it to be peach juice. Exploring farther, I found that my can of peaches was also a casualty of the firefight. This was a big disappointment to me because I always saved my peaches for last, and now I had nothing left to eat.

To our surprise, Captain Ripley was told by the command group to withdraw with India Company from our position back to the battalion command group's position. This didn't make much sense to us because we spent the better part of the day capturing and holding the area and gear. There was no time to go through the gear for intelligence gathering and no way that we could carry it out to examine it later, so our engineers made a feeble attempt to blow it up. All the gear was stacked in a large pile, but they simply did not have enough explosives to destroy all of it, so they set the charges they had. As we left the hill, accompanied by India Company, and headed back to the battalion command group's area, our engineers set off the charges and joined us for the walk back. On our way out, we passed a large number of NVA bodies still lying where they had fallen.

Casualties 03/02
  Killed
    PFC Barker, John W. 0311
    Cpl. Blinder, Richard B. 0311
    1st Lt. Goodwin, Forrest 0302
    Cpl. Graham, Richard S. 0311
    PFC Hanscom, John W. 0311
    PFC Harris, Jackie L. 0311
    2nd Lt. Heekin, Terry G. 0301
    PFC Martin, Robert E. 0351
    PFC Odonnell, John P. 0351
    Cpl. Strahl, Richard W. 0311

  Wounded
    PFC Barker, John W. 0311
    PFC Barry, John A. 0331
    Cpl. Belmore, Michael W. 0311
    PFC Berry, Don M. 0311
    PFC Bodzash, James D. Jim 0311
    LCpl. Clark, Charles W. 0311
    Cpl. Crosser, Jackson H. 0331
    Cpl. Crow, Roger W. 0331
    Cpl. Derosier, Joseph A. 0311
    LCpl. Devine, Freddie T. 0331
    LCpl. Franch, Bruno F. 0311
    PFC Garrison, Norman C. 0331
    Cpl. Glover, Randall J. 0351
    HM3 Jewett, Russell J. 8404
    HM2 Kelsey, John F. 8404
    HM2 Knabe, Wayne L. 8404
    Cpl. Larson, Jerome C. 0311
    LCpl. Lothringer, Floyd C. 0341
    LCpl. Martin, Morris G. 0351
    LCpl. McClary, Donald 0311
    Sgt. McGowin, Francis A. Jr. 0311
    Cpl. Nowak, Peter J. 0341
    GySgt. Peroutka, Frank Jr. 0369
    Sgt. Price, Alfred E. 0311
    Capt. Ripley, John W. 0302
    Cpl. Rizley, Billy W. 0351
    SSgt. Witkoski, Gerald L. 0369

During the night, the NVA continued to harass us. At 0445, we received incoming mortars on our position. Our mortars returned fire, and they soon ended. At 0520, one of the platoon ambush units made contact with the NVA and killed two of them as they tried to advance on our position. At 0800, we again had small arms contact resulting in the capture of an AK-47, several packs, and twenty-five pounds of rice, which were abandoned by the NVA in their retreat from the firefight.

We linked up with the command group, and at around 1240, we started sweeping north with India Company and Mike Company from 3/9.

At around 1330, we were sweeping an area and found fifteen cans of Chi Com 7.62 ammunition with four hundred rounds per can that had been abandoned along the trail. Something must have happened for that amount of ammunition to be left just thrown into the bushes.

We began searching the area, and at 1355, we discovered eleven shallow graves. Two of the graves were opened, and the bodies appeared to have died from wounds and about a month old. We also discovered more gear in the area, and by 1430, we collected the following from within a two-hundred-meter radius: 1 antitank mine, one 82 mm mortar baseplate with aiming stake, three land mines, two US M72 LAWS, two AK-47s, a Chi Com submachine gun, one Chi Com carbine, seventy-five 82 mm mortar rounds, assorted small arms ammunition, fifty packs with contents, ten gas masks, two hundred Chi Com grenades, assorted communication equipment with code book and shackles.

At 1615, we received small arms fire and grenades. We advanced returning fire, and the enemy broke contact. We continued to track them by their blood on the trail. At 1630, we again must have been getting too close for them because we received fire again. Again, we returned fire and advanced, and again they broke contact and ran.

At 1730, we observed and fired on eight NVA trying to infiltrate our position. After the firefight, they left behind three bodies and two AK-47 rifles. At 1745 while searching the area, we received a short burst of small arms fire. Again we countered, and afterward we found five more bodies, rifle magazines, a pack and twenty-five pounds of rice. Evidently they had made it back to their comrades who had removed their weapons and ammunition and hastily left the bodies firing at us as we approached to cover their retreat.

At around 1900, we received some more mortar and sniper fire. PFC Freed was shot and killed. Ten minutes later, the contact ceased, and we had another three men wounded. When we started back down the hill, a wounded NVA lying in the grass shot PFC George Webb. HM2 John Kelsey, our senior corpsman, went up to treat him. There were a few more shots, and again they called for a corpsman. I responded this time. I was behind a group of our 60 mm mortarmen and had to pass through them on my way up. Just as I got up there, another NVA tossed a Chi Com grenade out of the grass. I saw it hit the ground several yards away between Kelsey and me. When we checked the area, we found another eight NVA bodies.

We had no further contact that evening and were able to get a bit of rest by taking catnaps.

Casualties 03/03/67
    Killed
        PFC Freed, Robert T. 0331

    Wounded
        HM2 Kelsey, John F. 8404
        PFC Webb, George E. 0311

In the morning, we set out again sweeping north. We had no further contact, but some of the other units, especially Mike Company 3/9, continued to experience sporadic firefights.

At 1500, we were moving north and came near Thon Bai An, a village just south of the DMZ. We saw some enemy troops on a hill ahead. This time we had several tanks with us, so instead of trying to take the hill like we did the day before, the tanks fired as they advanced up the hill, and we followed behind them. We killed at least ten with no casualties on our side. The tank continued north toward the village where it hit a mine and was also hit by rocket propelled grenades causing it to burst into flames killing one crewman and wounding three others. The tank was destroyed. We continued north sweeping through the village. As we swept back through the village, we took ten rounds of mortar fire resulting in seven Marines wounded.

At 1745 heading back toward south, we observed and killed an NVA in a green uniform in the vicinity of the destroyed tank. He was carrying five mortar rounds, a two-hundred-round belt of machine gun rounds, and five Chi Com grenades

We put all wounded and dead on one of the tanks to get them out to another area where it was safe. We then walked out with the tanks following us. We rejoined the command group and India Company. No further action occurred again that night.

Casualties 03/04/67
    Wounded
        Sgt. Bennett, Joseph M. 0141
        PFC Bennett, Larry C. 0311
        PFC Bolevich, Michael J. 0311
        HM3 Hamilton, Hance T. 8404
        Sgt. Meredith, Gary 0311
        LCpl. Palmier, Vincent 0311
        Cpl. Schwirian, David A. 0311
        Cpl. Wardell, Edward H. 0311

The next day, the command group India and Lima moved south to link up with Mike 3/4 who was coming in to the area to relieve us, and at about 1000, we met them and they relieved us. The NVA were still in small groups trying to make it back across the DMZ. We had a few casualties. Third Battalion Third Marines stayed in the area for another day acting as a blocking force in case some of the enemy tried to flee south.

On March 6, we received word that we would be linking up with 1/9 and sweeping to the east where we were to link up with 3/4 and then were told to head back in the opposite direction. We moved to a road and waited for transportation back to the Rockpile. Transportation did not arrive until after dark. We loaded up on the trucks and proceeded back to Highway 9 under blackout conditions with no lights on the trucks. When we reached Highway 9, they turned on their "blackout lights" to give minimal illumination to the road ahead. At 2130, all of 3/3 was finally back at Payable.

Colonel Wilder, our battalion commander, was very pleased with our action. From that time on, we were known as Ripley's Raiders. Soon a sign was erected outside the Lima's Command bunker. It read as follows:

The Home of Lethal Lima
Wilder's Wildest
Ripley's Raiders
When the going gets tough . . .
The tough get going!

When we got back to Payable, Mike Company was leaving the hill in the Punch Bowl, and Lima was sent in to man the position while they were gone. There were very few of us left. We spent the days just watching the perimeter. A journalist from *Stars and Stripes* came out and interviewed us and took photographs. He had me stand in a trench and pretend that I was folding up a battle dressing. I guess that's all he could think of to make it look like he had caught me in the act of working. This picture ended up a month or so later in my hometown newspapers with a small caption stating that I was with 3/3. We stayed there for another day, and then India or Kilo Company came to relieve us, and we went back to Payable.

March 9, 1967

Dear Louie,

Things have been jumping around here. We went on another operation behind the Razorback and were out there for two days with no results.

We no sooner got back and didn't even have a chance to sit down when they loaded us on trucks and took us out to Cam Lo where 3rd Battalion 4th Marines got the heck kicked out of them and we had to go and help them out.

We walked all night after they let us off the trucks and at 4:30 am we got to where we were going.

The next day we were still walking when we got in a firefight with the North Vietnamese Army, commonly known as the NVA. That lasted for about 20 minutes. Finally they ran and we came out with 2 wounded. We stayed the night there.

Morning of the next day we were walking again. We reached a place where everyone was to meet and they sent us out from there. One of the groups (1st Platoon) ran into some NVA and killed 2 and captured one. They called 2nd platoon (us) down to help them search the area. Then the battle began. You probably heard of it on TV because ABC and CBS both had newsmen and cameras out there. It lasted about one and a half hours and we got hit real hard by a regiment of NVA. When everything was over we had 7 dead and 27 wounded and most of them were from our platoon. I guess I was just lucky. I sure was busy though. After the battle we were sitting around when some General flew in and was talking to our Captain. The General no sooner got back in his helicopter and it just got in the air when a mortar hit right where the 'copter was. About 10-20 more hit in our area and I ran and got in a ditch until they stopped and then rushed out to help the wounded. We got 2 dead and 5 wounded out of that deal. Oh, on the battle earlier, I was up on the front lines and we were so close that you could see them. One NVA stood up to throw a grenade and I pulled out my pistol and shot him and the grenade went off in his hand. I got a couple pieces of shrapnel in my arm. We lost some good guys that day, our Lieutenant, a Corporal who was to leave Viet Nam 3 days ago for duty in the states, another guy who planned on being in the 68 Olympics in gymnastics, and other guys all of whom I was good friends with.

That night artillery and planes killed over 150 NVA (they stopped counting bodies at 136, but estimated over 150 bodies in one area.)

We walked north the next day and came near a village, I don't know the name of it, but it is north of Cam Lo and is large. We saw some gooks on a hill, so instead of trying to take them the way we took the other place we had tanks with us and they fired and went up the hill and we followed them up. We killed at least 10 with no casualties on our side.

When we started down the hill one of the wounded NVA was lying in the grass and shot one of our guys. They hollered for a corpsman and I started to go up but the other corpsman, who was in the hole with me held me back and said that there was someone already up there, so I got back in the hole. No sooner had I gotten back in when more shots went off and the hollered for another corpsman, so this time I ran up. Just as I got up there the NVA tossed a grenade out of the grass and I hit the dirt. It went off right in front of me; I didn't get a scratch, but the corpsman that was already up there had his foot shattered. Another close call.

After that we only ran into NVA in groups of 1 to 4 men and easily killed them and finally got back here.

They say the corpsmen might get medals along with the others, but I don't know for sure.

Enough of war! I got your letters and packages. They sure are good.

On those tapes, it sounds like a good idea, the only other one on that list that I like besides the ones you marked are the Supremes. Go ahead and order them if you want.

You asked when I'm going on R&R, I don't know probably in July or August.

If on any of the newscast you saw casualties being taken care of, I was probably in it, because one of the newsmen was taking pictures of me working on one of our guys.

Well here I am back at our old position on Alamo Hill, they moved us over here this morning in case you are wondering it is the 10^h. We came over here to take over Mike Company's position while they go on operation out where we were near Dong Ha Mountain.

I sure do miss you, I think of you always. The other night I had a real neat dream, I don't know where we were, but it was snowing and we were in a ski lodge type house, I was sitting in front of a nice warm fire and could smell food cooking in the kitchen. I turned around and you were coming out with some hot buttered rum or something like that, you had on a pull over mohair sweater and real tight ski pants, you came over and sat down on my lap and we sat and talked, watched the fire and made out. Eventually we ended up in the bedroom and you had changed into a real thin negligee and we were going to bed, I could see through what you had on. The bed was the canopy type and boy did we have fun we did everything and afterwards we took a shower together and both got all hot and bothered again and did it in the shower of all places. I'll tell you I'm really stuck on you. We sure were having fun!

Well I guess that's it for now. I miss you and can't wait until I get home and we can be together again. Bye for now.

Love always/
Russ

PS I love you

Four generations of the Hulbert Family at the ranch in Yorkville, CA 1952. Includes Jewett and Taubold families. Rus Jewett is standing on the left holding on to baseball cap. – *from the Rus Jewett collection*

The Jewett Family in 1959 (l to r) Back Row: Russell, Susan, Steven, Middle row: Carol, Norman, Front row: Mary and Bruce. – *from the Rus Jewett collection*

Rus and Steve Jewett 2nd class scouts during summer of 1959. – *from the Rus Jewett collection*

Rus Jewett's yearbook photo from senior year at Fort Bragg High School. – *from the Rus Jewett collection*

Hospital Corps School graduation photo February 1965, Rus Jewett is on the right end of row 3. – *from the Rus Jewett collection*

Rus Jewett with newly acquired 3rd class petty officer stripe, Yokosuka, Japan 1965. – *from the Rus Jewett collection*

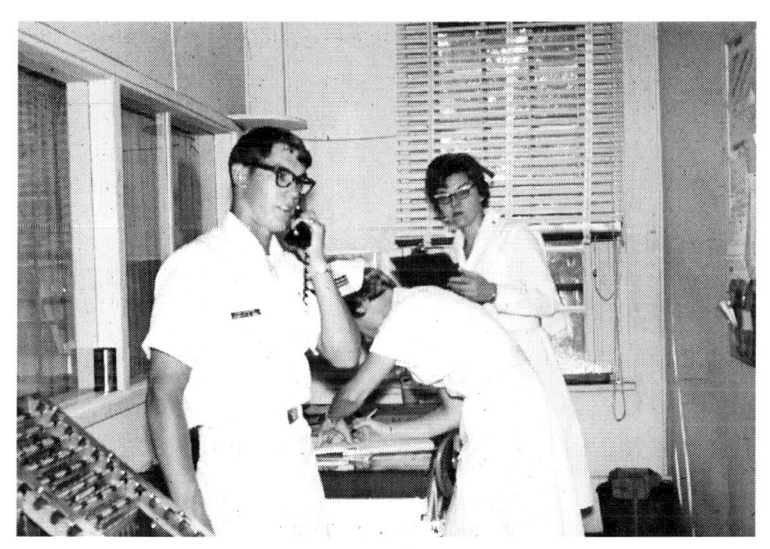

Rus Jewett working as Senior Corpsman on a ward at Yokosuka Naval Hospital, Japan 1966. – *from the Rus Jewett collection*

Rus Jewett at the crater on top of Mount Fuji, Japan August 1966. – *from the Rus Jewett collection*

Rus Jewett with Louise Johnson while on leave back in Fort Bragg, California September 1966. – *from the Rus Jewett collection*

Dry net training on the eighth day of Field Medical Service School, Camp Pendleton October 1966. *Photo by Rus Jewett*

Rus Jewett on liberty at Disneyland while attending Field Medical Service School, Camp Pendleton November 1966. *Photo by Louise Johnson.*

Company D Field Medical Service School graduation Photo. Rus Jewett is in the left side of third row 6th from the left. *– from the Rus Jewett collection*

3rd Shore Party boat ramp near Hue University on the Perfume River December 1966. – *from the Rus Jewett collection*

Lima Company Corpsmen Dan Fuss and Rus Jewett at the Fishbowl January 1967. *Photo by Richard Banks.*

Sgt. Francis "Buddy" McGowin at the Fishbowl January 1967. *Photo by Richard Banks.*

The Fishbowl (also known as Punch Bowl, Lima Hill) as seen from the south end of Razorback Ridge January 1967. *Photo by Richard Banks.*

Rus Jewett at "the saddle" camp on the top of the south end of Razorback Ridge talking to Frank Ludwig. *Photo by Richard Banks.*

Radioman Ron Hebert and 3d Platoon Leader Lt. Hansel Osborne *Photo by Richard Banks.*

Rus Jewett during combat operation near the DMZ with captured AK-47. – *from the Rus Jewett collection*

RPGs and other gear abandoned by the NVA was captured while in transit out of the DMZ. *Photo by Richard Banks.*

F4 Phantom delivering a load of High Explosive bombs on enemy site. Marines from 3d Platoon in foreground. *Photo by Richard Banks.*

Marines deploying from a CH-46 near the DMZ. Marine to at the right is Lt. Marquis Wingard commander of 2nd Platoon. *Photo by Rus Jewett*

Bomb crater providing a reservoir for filling canteens near the DMZ. Marines in foreground are Robert Peugh and Jennings Anderson. *Photo by Rus Jewett*

Rus Jewett at Ca Lu Rough Rider staging area. – *from the Rus Jewett collection*

Non serviceable bridges at the Hairpin Turn crossing the Ruo Quan River on Highway 9. Lima Marines crossing the Bailey bridge. *Photo by Rus Jewett*

Up stream at the Hairpin curve on the Ruo Quan River. Rough Rider convoy to Khe Sanh crossing on the portable bridge upstream from the non serviceable bridges. 11th Engineers cut the road to install the portable bridge to cross the river. *Photo by Richard Banks*

Ripley's Raiders calling card left along Highway 9 between Ca Lu and Khe Sanh. *Photo by Rus Jewett*

Ernest Detora and Rus Jewett on six by at Rough Rider staging area at Khe Sanh. *– from the Rus Jewett collection*

2nd Platoon squad and ARVN regional force personnel crossing the Quang Tri River by dugout canoe returning to Ca Lu. Radioman is Gerald Baryo. *Photo by Rus Jewett*

Cpl. Anthony Williams on patrol near Ca Lu on the south side of the Quang Tri River. *Photo by Rus Jewett*

Squad from 3d Platoon crossing the Quang Tri River by foot. *Photo by Richard Banks*

Lima Company Commander Capt. John W. Ripley with a young python captured in bunker at Ca Lu. *Photo by Rus Jewett*

Radiomen Richard Banks and Ron Hebert at 3d Platoon command bunker at Ca Lu. *Photo from Richard Banks collection*

Rus Jewett tending to Montagnards in the village of Ba Tanh in the Ca Lu Valley. *– from the Rus Jewett collection*

Bomb crater swimming hole at the Bailey bridge between Ca Lu and Rockpile on Highway 9 *Photo by Rus Jewett*

Cpl. LBJ (Les Johnson) preparing to take a dive from the rail of the bridge at the swimming hole on highway 9 north of Ca Lu. *Photo by Rus Jewett*

Rus Jewett during visit to friends at Naval Hospital, Yokosuka while on R&R May 1967. Uniform was borrowed from Jacques J Ayd. – *from the Rus Jewett collection*

Capt. John W. Ripley at dedication ceremony of the J.J. Ayd aid station at Ca Lu June 1967. *Photo from Rus Jewett*

Battalion Aid Station Forward at 3/3's combat base at the Rockpile *Photo by Rus Jewett*

HM2 Mike Horner at the Battalion Aid Station at the Rockpile June 1967. *Photo by Rus Jewett*

Battalion Surgeon John P. Miller with completed carving of Playboy centerfold Miss December '66 at the Rockpile Battalion Aid Station *Photo from John Miller*

Nick Longo at the Battalion Aid Station at the Rockpile. *Photo by Rus Jewett*

Dr. John P. Miller on Med Cap to one of the Montagnard villages along Highway 9 going toward Ca Lu from the Rockpile. *Photo from John Miller*

ARVN Dai Uy (Capt.) Quan, Captain John Ripley, and Doctor John Miller at Ca Lu presentation of Ripley's Raiders plaque carved by Dr. Miller July 1967. *Photo from John Miller*

Nick Longo, Michael Brown and Ron Pittler at the stream near the shower unit. The Bridge on Highway 9 provided shade when malaria patients were placed in the stream to reduce fever while awaiting med-evac from the Rockpile. *Photo by Rus Jewett*

Corpsmen at Rockpile Battalion Aid station August 1967 (Left to right): Don Beam, Rus Jewett, Russell King, Chuck Klimansky, and Jim Banks. – *from the Rus Jewett collection*

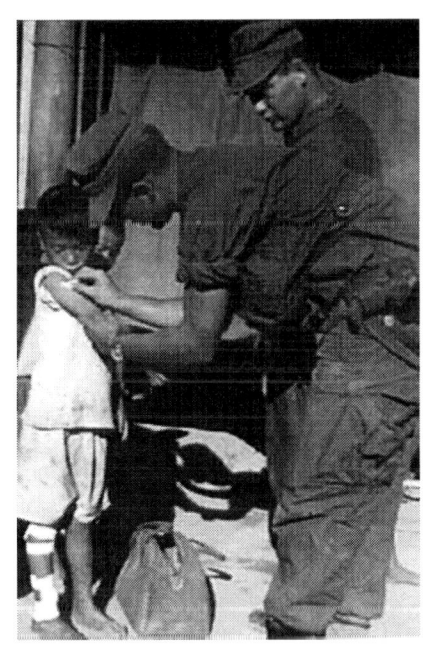

Rus Jewett tending to a patient on Med Cap in the city of Cam Lo. SSgt. Ed Cheever from battalion intelligence looking on. – *from the Rus Jewett collection*

Battalion Aid Station Corpsmen preparing to receive casualties from ambushed convoy on August 21, 1967 unloading litters from CH36 helicopter at the Rockpile. *Photo by Rus Jewett*

Battalion Aid Station Rear at battalion administrative base near Dong Ha airstrip with Motor Transport tent in the background. *Photo by Rus Jewett*

Rus Jewett at China Beach in Da Nang October 1967 – *from the Rus Jewett collection*

Chapter 36

Seeing Old Friends

AFTER RETURNING TO Payable, we spent time with the routine patrols and ambushes around the area.

It turned out that my favorite C ration meal was the one that very few people liked – ham and lima beans. Marines were always avoiding choosing that meal, and if they got them, they would try to trade or end up just giving them away. It wasn't long before they were just giving them to me. Ham and lima meals included a can containing four crackers with a smaller can of cheese. The older rations contained some really unpalatable ham and limas, but a company called Blue Star made the ham and limas for the newer rations. I could eat them cold if necessary, but usually heated the ham and limas and stirred in the can of cheese. After all the cheese melted, I crumbled the crackers into the mixture and stirred them in. This added a bit of flavor and texture to the otherwise greasy, salty meal. Hot meals supplemented the C rations we ate on patrol. Except for the occasional snack of pound cake or peaches, I ate at the chow hall area when I was in the perimeter.

Mike Company was sent out to Hills 881 and 861 and was sustaining numerous casualties with their clashes with the NVA. The battalion surgeon and corpsmen assigned to the BAS were transferred up to Khe Sanh to provide support. Lima's corpsmen were assigned to cover the BAS. We got word that Mike was having trouble with the recently issued M16. The rifle's extractor's inability to remove shell casings from the chamber was causing the weapon to jam. The Marines had to use their cleaning rods to remove the spent shell casing from the chamber after several rounds were fired. When they were doing so, snipers were shooting them as they raised their shoulder up off the ground.

After returning to the line, I lived in a bunker adjacent to the 155s and the 105s. Periodically during the day and night, they would scramble to provide a fire mission. After the fire mission was complete, they went back to whatever they were doing before they had been interrupted. These occurred both day and night. After a while, I didn't pay much attention to them. We received a new platoon commander, another mustanger to replace Lieutenant Goodwin by the name of First Lieutenant Wingard.

March 10, 1967

Dear Louise,

I can't sleep, so I thought I'd write to you. I'm sitting here in a big safe hole in the ground that we call our hospital, but if you look at it you would think it was a part of a hotel room in some old fashioned place. They have beds made of wooden ammo boxes, a desk, cupboards, shelves, chairs, night stands, bookshelves, bed boards and all kinds of other things all made of ammo boxes.

All I've been doing since I've been here is sit around and eat. Frankly, I'm full. I also have indigestion from all the spices on my foods, my stomach isn't used to them, but they sure were good. The other night we made pizza using ketchup, spices, salami, cheese, and Parmesan cheese on top of the bread we get in our C-rations. We used the can you sent the cinnamon things in for an oven and they sure turned out good.

I think of us all the time. I sit and think about how it will be when we're married. You know, Fort Bragg is as good a place to live as any. Actually I don't care where we live as long as I can be with you.

What date did you say you wanted to get married? I think you said sometime around the 20th of September. Anyhow that sounds like a good time.

I still don't know what kind of car we'll get. Probably a Camaro by Chevy, but most likely we'll get a Volkswagen. The Volkswagen is easy to drive, easy on gas, and not as expensive as the other. What do you think? It will be good for traveling, too.

The rats are something else around here, actually they aren't rats, but they run around all night on the shelves and around the walls. Sometimes they get in fights with each other and squeak and raise all kinds of commotion.

I can't wait until I get my cameras so I can take some pictures of me and of this area to send back to you.

That reminds me my grandmother sent some of the pictures of us they took while I was home. They turned out pretty good. I put them in with the rest of the pictures I have in that little book you sent me.

I wish you and I were together right now. That way instead of going to bed with my "rubber Lady" (air mattress) I could be going to bed with you. I can't wait until the day when I can feel your warm soft body next to mine. Just the thought makes me all turned on. Just to be able to feel you next to me and do all the things we used to do.

I think these things all the time, but they especially come to me at night. It seems that at night I can almost talk to you. During the day there is too much going on, but at night everything calms down and you have lots of time to think.

Well, I'm getting sleepy now. I guess I'll go to bed and pretend my "Rubber Lady" is you. Bye for now.

Love always
Russ

PS I love you

Hot showers were again available and were a luxury after being out on a trail during the day and sleeping in the jungle during the night. On the morning of 15 March as I walked back from the showers, another Marine unit was walking single file on the road through our area. Hotel Company 2/26 had been transferred to our position by convoy and had dismounted. They were heading into the hills west of our position to start a search-and-destroy mission. I was walking in the opposite direction when an approaching Marine said, "Well, I'll be damned, if it isn't Rus Jewett." I looked up, and it was my former roommate Carl Darsey from the Hospital Corps quarters in Yokosuka, Japan.

I asked Carl if they were stopping so we could visit. He said that his unit would take a break before going out into the hills. I went back to my bunker and put on my utilities and boots then walked up to the area where they had stopped just outside our perimeter.

I headed up the road on the hill just across the road from our shower unit on the west side of our perimeter. Passing by our trash dump where we burned all our garbage, I continued up the hill and, after a short walk, found Carl sitting eating a can of C rations. I asked him how he ended up here. He responded that being married had protected him from the first draft for FMSS, but when the second draft came along, they needed forty more corpsmen, and this time the married guys were no longer exempt. He entered Camp Pendleton in November, the next class after I graduated. He told me that Mel Overmeyer (who was also stationed with us in Yokosuka and graduated in the same class at Pendleton that I did) was also attached to 2/26. We all visited for about thirty minutes. I was able to also talk to Mel briefly just before they moved out.

I did not run into Carl again until I got out of the navy in September of 1968. I had heard that he got stationed at Oak Knoll Naval Hospital in Oakland, California. I somehow tracked him down and went to visit with them. After that, we lost contact with each other. I believe they planned to move back to Panama City, Florida.

I never heard from Mel Overmeyer again until I received an e-mail from him sometime in 2000. Evidently he had been wounded fairly seriously and was still suffering from the effects.

March 16, 1967

Dear Louise

You mean you didn't even recognize me on TV? I thought you would. The day I did that was March 4th, so I know for sure it was me. Remember what I told you about ABC News in my last letter?

Yesterday I was walking along toward the showers down by t he river when I heard one of the guys call my name. I turned around and saw one of the guys I was stationed with in Japan; in fact he was the guy you gave a ride to when we were in downtown Oceanside. He told me that there was a bunch of guys from Yokosuka stationed in his unit, which is out here now with us. So I went up to his area and saw my best friend from Japan. You remember the guy who brought his girl from Florida to Japan and they got married over there, well that's who it was. I was never so happy to see anyone since I've been over here as I was yesterday. His wife had a baby girl in November and somehow he managed to stay in the states until last month. I sure was glad to see him. All together yesterday I saw 5 or 6 guys from Japan and we had a big reunion. It sure is good to see your old friends.

We were supposed to go on another operation the other day but they keep putting it off and now we aren't supposed to go until the night of the 18th. I hope they keep putting it off, because I really don't love operations and getting shot at again.

You said you hoped that I wasn't in a mess like was on TV, well I hate to tell you, but that was our mess, the whole thing.

Sounds like your dreams are like mine. I can't wait until we don't have to dream of those things and can actually be doing them.

You'll have to send me another picture album or what ever you call it, because the other one is full. I sure do like the picture of you sleeping; you look so happy and content. I just sit and look at it whenever I get lonely and think about how in a year and a few months I can wake up and see you looking like that laying beside me.

You ask where I am now, well look at the map on this page where the little black dot is just under the DMZ.

I got your letter today. (By the way it's the 17th now) I really like the picture of you in the shower; too bad the curtain was in the way. I also like your picture of you in your kimono.

Right now I'm feeling quite high. Last night we acquired a bunch of beer. (About a case) and when we found out a little while ago that we are leaving sometime after this afternoon to go on operation we started drinking a little while ago. I thought I better get this letter written while I still am in condition to write. I just got an idea, I'll finish the rest of my beers and write some more.

Here I am, seven beers later. I am feeling pretty good at the moment. I don't want to go on this operation because we heard that 2/9 got 14 killed and 43 wounded out of 68 guys.

I sure do love you, I can't wait until we're married and I can hold you close to me and be with you always. I long to feel your soft body against mine and feel you all over like we used to do. I can't wait until we can continue on from that afternoon out at Ten Mile. Remember I told you I wouldn't do anything until we're married. That is as far as I'll go until we're married, but after we're married I promise I'll rape you.

Well, I guess I better close before I get too involved in details. I love you. Bye for now.

Love always
Russ

PS I Love you

Chapter 37

The Rest of March

ON MARCH 17 we were sent out again to an area out near the DMZ to help get 2/3 out of trouble. We were dropped off in the mountains and hiked northeast down toward the flatter terrain to the east. While still in the mountains, the sun went down, and we dug in for the night. I was located on a hillside that had been hit by artillery sometime in the past, and the ground was snarled with roots making digging difficult. I started digging my fighting hole, which was only deep enough to keep me out of the line of fire if I lay flat on my belly. When I had completed the hole, it had gotten dark, so I wrapped up in my poncho and fell immediately to sleep. I woke from my dreamless sleep by stinging sensations on my arms and chest. It was then I realized that when I was digging my hole, I disturbed an ant colony in the ground, and some of the ants had gotten into my poncho while I was sleeping. I stood up and brushed the ants off and shook out my poncho. I moved away from my hole and wrapped up in my poncho for some more shut-eye.

The next day, the sun came out, and the clouds had disappeared. It got hot early. As we were continuing our way down the hillside, some of the Marines carrying heavy loads of mortars started fainting from heat exhaustion. We tried cooling and hydrating them with water and salt tablets to get them back in condition to march again, but they were pretty bad off. Not wanting to be considered a slacker, they waited until they collapsed before saying anything, as was the way of most Marines. A medevac was called in to take them back to the rear for treatment. We continued on to the flatlands northwest of Cam Lo.

Once we hit the level land, we went on a forced march. Second Battalion Third Marines was being hit again. We walked as fast as we could. Some of the Marines were complaining that they couldn't keep up. I was moving up and down the line encouraging them to keep moving. One Marine was having a particularly hard time, so I began needling him by pointing out that I – a "squid" – was keeping up and not having any trouble. He replied that I was not as encumbered as he because I didn't have to carry a rifle. I told him to give me his rifle. He was in the process of handing it to me when I reminded him that without his rifle, a Marine was nothing. I must have hit a nerve exposed in his boot camp experience because he immediately took back his rifle and seemed to find his second wind. He quit complaining and kept up.

We finally broke through the NVA lines and met up with 2/3. The NVA retreated, and we went into an area near the DMZ that had the ruins of a Catholic church. There were some civilian farmers nearby in the area who were advised to leave the area. After they left and headed toward the refugee center at Cam Lo, we searched and then burned their grass-thatched hooches. In the process of joining up with 2/3, we sustained the following casualties who we were able to medevac out:

03/23/67 Wounded
    LCpl. Beardsley, Gordon E. 0311
    PFC Beck, Martin L. 0311
    SSgt. Chancey, Eugene 0369

We went out by truck to the Cam Lo area. The night before we left (after two cans per man were distributed), there had been extra beer left unclaimed. Somehow I got more than just my two beers. The next day, several of us decided that our extra beer would disappear before we returned and decided to drink it all before we left. The beer was actually consumed over a period of about six hours, but I was still feeling the effects that afternoon as we loaded up onto the trucks and rode east on Highway 9.

At Cam Lo, our trucks turned north and then, a mile or so up the road, turned west again until they stopped and let us off. It was a hot afternoon, and as we swept through the valley, I became very dehydrated. I decided that I should not drink that much beer before going out again. We walked until it got dark before we made camp. After a day or two of walking through the area, we went back to Payable.

We went out by helicopter to an abandoned farming area north of Cam Lo. After we were dropped off, we swept up to Con Thien and ended up about five hundred yards from the DMZ. The next morning, we were going along a path through a wooded area with short vegetation and shrubs. We had twigs and leaves on our helmets and were walking silently through the brush, which was eight to ten feet tall. Our point man, a skinny Native American scout attached to us from another unit whom we called chief (actually I think we called all Native Americans chief), walked into the perimeter of an NVA camp. It took both the chief and the NVA a moment before either realized what had transpired. He hollered "gooks!" as he was diving for cover and was shot through the fleshy portion of his buttocks. The startled enemy pulled back slightly, and a close-in firefight started up with a lot of shooting and grenades. The bullets were tearing through the thick brush just above us like a weed eater as we lay in the trail. It was intense, but we were not making progress.

Word was passed up through the line to pull back. Artillery and close air support were called in on the NVA position, and they wanted us out of the kill zone. Starting to withdraw, I reminded the squad leader that the chief was still up there wounded and that if they would cover me I'd go up and drag him back so we could pack him out with us. Four Marines provided the cover fire, and I crawled up the path to where the chief was lying facedown on the trail. The NVA had drawn back, and the chief was now outside their line, but he was still vulnerable. There were bullets going both ways over our bodies. I identified myself as I approached him crawling on my belly so that he wouldn't think the enemy had him. By this time, his wound had quit bleeding, so I delayed putting a battle dressing him. I informed him that I was getting him out of there. I grabbed him by the ankles and told him to hang tight. I then dragged him back a little at a time until we got back to the other Marines providing cover fire. We improvised a stretcher by placing him on his poncho and rolled up the excess material to help provide a better grip. Four of Marines grabbed the sides and picked him up, and one provided rear security as we hurried back toward the area where the rest of our platoon had gone. Several hundred yards away, we had to cross an old muddy rice paddy. We no sooner got into the paddy than the artillery shells started hitting in the area we had just vacated. We found it easier to drag Chief across the top of the muck and hurried a little faster to get out of the area.

Arriving back with our guys, I put a battle dressing on the chief's wound and wished him luck. That was the third Purple Heart for the chief, so I never saw him again. When a Marine gets three Purple Hearts, he can take the option of going back home if he so chooses. By the time we made it back to our platoon, two Marine A-4 Skyhawks arrived on station and took turns making passes over the area, strafing and dropping napalm and high explosives into the area we occupied just several minutes before. Even at our distance, the heat from the napalm was intense. A medevac helicopter came to pick up our wounded to take them to Dong Ha.

After things settled down, Lieutenant Wingard found me and said that the squad leader had debriefed and told him what I had done. He slapped me several times on the top of the helmet and told me how proud he was of what I had done. He also stated that he was recommending me for the Bronze Star for my action in getting the chief out. Several weeks later, I found out he was true to his word, but someone back in the rear decided that I was just doing my job and shot down the commendation.

 03/24/61 Wounded
   Cpl. Burgess, Edwin A. 0351
   GySgt. Maxwell, Manny 0369
   LCpl. Pierce, Richard L. 0351
   Cpl. Upton, Wade E. 0311
   Cpl. Webb, Roy F. 0351
   Cpl. Westover, Delwin R. 0341
   Sgt. Wright, Darrel D. 0331

After the artillery and planes devastated the NVA area, we went back in and recovered some of their rucksacks and gear. While searching the area, we received occasional sniper, rife even after all the artillery and napalm. We didn't get much out of that area in the way of equipment.

We tracked them and came across an area with hastily dug shallow graves and found quite a few bodies. We continued to pursue them until we reached the DMZ and followed a short distance into it until we were told to return to Cam Lo for trucks back to Payable.

We were flown back out to the Cam Lo area. We walked to an area where there were open fields with very short grass. It appeared as if it were a large field that may have once contained crops. There were hedgerows around these fields that were eight to ten feet tall and twenty feet wide. Word came down to dig in within the protection of the hedgerows. We had no sooner dug our fighting holes than a mortar barrage hit us.

During mortar attacks, I was always sure that every incoming round I heard was going to hit directly on top of me. Today I dug my hole more vertical in the soft soil and was able to get in and get my head below ground level, making a smaller target for the mortar to hit. The mortars were hitting all around on both sides of the hedgerow. After they stopped, I heard the familiar call for "corpsman up" in the next field. I ran through the brush on a narrow path and into the field to where our mortars had set up to find Weapons Platoon SSgt. Eugene Chancey clumsily getting to his feet. Staff Sergeant Chancey, who normally had things together, was dazed and in shock. I had him sit back down and examined him. Not finding any wounds, I asked him what had happened. He babbled something and gestured toward the sky and the ground. One of the mortarmen told me what had happened. After the attack started, Chancey was out in the open trying to determine from what direction the incoming mortars were coming. His intention was to direct a counterattack. He had taken a direct hit from a mortar on top of his helmet. The Marine then produced Chancey's helmet, and it had a large indentation on the top. The explosion knocked him down, but the shrapnel all went up and out from the point of detonation. Chancey became more coherent and complained of his ears ringing. I checked them and didn't see any blood. Finally Chancey was able to speak and babbled, "I knew it was going to hit me, Doc, but I couldn't move fast enough." I informed him that it was a good thing that he couldn't because if he had, the mortar would have hit right next to him and he for sure would have been killed. He thought about it and then nodded causing pain in his neck, and the ringing in his ears was still present, so we called in a medevac and sent him back under protest to Dong Ha for examination. Several days later, Sergeant Chancey returned to Payable and was waiting for us when we got back.

03/25/67 Wounded:
    PFC Bradburn, James G. 0311
    SSgt. Chancey, Eugene 0369
    Cpl. Solbach, John M. III 0311

We then walked through the area just south of the DMZ. Our instructions were to search and destroy all buildings. We came across some small grass huts that had belonged to some poor farmers. No one was supposed to be living in that area. All civilians had been relocated to a refugee camp at Cam Lo. We burned every one that we came across.

We ended up staying out there for more days than we expected and ran out of food and water. We evidently were working as a blocking force because we stayed in the same area for several days. We were lying in wait for the enemy and wanted to maintain the element of surprise, so a resupply mission could not be risked. We could get by without food for several days, but not water. Finally we had to get water. A patrol was sent out to locate a source of water large enough to supply us. The map showed that we were in an area that had once been a fairly large farm. We sent out a squad to investigate, and they found a large concrete cistern twelve feet square and six feet high within a short distance from our position. A small stream fed the cistern through a pipe. One of the Marines went into the cistern and found about two feet of water still inside. Several of the Marines got into the cistern, and the rest set up a security perimeter. All canteens were passed into the cistern for filling. Several runners were sent back to the location where the company waited. A work party gathered up all the empty canteens and returned to the cistern where they were all filled. At least we now had water. After not eating for two days, we finally had C rations flown in to us.

When we got back, we went back to the normal routine of patrols and ambushes, but that didn't last very long because on March 31, we were called to go out and rescue 3/4 who was in trouble up near the DMZ. Again we traveled down the paths and unused roads with our brushy helmets. Our platoon's point squad sneaked up on three NVA sitting at the side of the road. They killed all three and captured their weapons, two AK-47s and a rocket launcher. One of our bullets had hit and split off the wooden stock of one of the rifles, the other was in good condition. I carried one of the AK-47s until we returned. It appeared to be fairly new and well cared for. The AK-47 was actually felt to be the superior weapon to our new M16. It was well made in China and did not jam easily. The two of us who carried them were instructed if we got into a firefight not to use them unless we absolutely had to. In the heat of a firefight, Marines sometimes locate their enemy by the distinct sound made by the AK-47, and they didn't want to accidentally shoot us. Fortunately, we did not have to test the theory. We returned to the Rockpile the next morning. All captured weapons were turned over to Captain Ripley.

April 3, 1967

Dear Louise,

Well, here we are back from another operation. We got back from the last one on the 29th of March and I was so busy I didn't have a chance to write, and then the next day we had to go help out another unit in the same area we had just come out of north of Cam Lo.

During the first operation we swept up to Con Thien and were about 500 yards from the DMZ. Then we came back to Cam Lo and from there back here by truck.

During that time we only had one or two good firefights. The first one was when we ran into a NVA base camp. They didn't even know we were coming. They wounded our point man and had us pinned down. I had to crawl on my stomach up to him and drag him out because they were going to call in artillery on the area and we had to get out of there fast. He was wounded in the hip.

When we got out of there artillery pounded the area and then the jets took over and bombed the area with bombs and Napalm (jellied gasoline bombs) It was real beautiful.

The next fight we got into was up near Con Thien we saw some gooks coming through the bushes and cut them down.

The next night we got mortared, but only took 2 casualties on our side. One of the guys got a 82 mm mortar right on the top of the helmet and lived to talk about it. He was walking around after it happened, but he was a little shook.

The next day was the day we went up by the DMZ and on our way we burnt every house we came to. Just like the Roman days, we swept through a ville and burned it to the ground. We weren't giving anyone any slack.

When we finally got back I had to go on a patrol and then get cleaned up and was just about ready to sit down and write some letters when they told us to "saddle up" and get ready to move out because 3/9 was in trouble.

Our platoon killed 3 gooks and captured all their weapons and came back in this morning. We didn't have any casualties in our company. I was glad because I was the only corpsman in our platoon the other one who is usually with us is on R&R in Bangkok at the moment.

Today I spent most of the day in the river washing my clothes and myself. I even put on some of that smelly stuff you sent me. I sure felt good.

Down at the river you can get a good all over tan because we don't wear any clothes at all, the only ones I have are the ones I washed. While they were drying I just swam and washed myself.

You asked if there was anything I don't need, well being that we are always moving, I'm pretty swamped with milk, so hold off on the milk until I let you know I've run out. Everything else is OK though. I am enclosing that page from Playboy with the tapes on it as you asked me to do.

I should get paid here in a day or so. My check is for $369, pretty good, huh? That will make over $800 I've put in the bank with 3 checks I take that back it will be over $900, if I remember correctly it is $946.

So you don't like the shower bit, huh? How do you know unless we try? Just kidding of course.

You ask how many cans of beer I had, well let's see we split a case, so that made 12 apiece, then we bought two more off one of the Marines, which made 15 apiece we had altogether. To make things worse after we got them all down we started out on the operation, which is really weird. Riding in a truck and jumping off and walking several miles under the influence of beer. Wow, it's the only way to go on an operation.

I haven't had any dreams lately; I guess I've been too exhausted.

I can't wait until we're married. Then we can do anything we want, anything at all. I love you so much. I think of you all the time. When someone asks me why I dig my foxholes so deep I tell them that my fiancé values me too much for me not to. I think that's a real good reason don't you?

Well, got to get some sleep now, no telling what we might do tomorrow. Bye for now. I love you more than any thing in the world.

Love always,
Russ

PS I love you

Chapter 38

Ca Lu Mountain

FOR THE NEXT week, we settled back into the role of maintaining security around the Payable area. This again consisted of day patrols and night ambushes. During my spare time, I occupied myself with the repair and improvement of my living quarters. During the morning and evening, I held sick call and took care of the minor cuts and scratches on the Marines. With the weather improving, so did the rapidity by which infection set in. My job was to ensure that the cuts and scratches did not progress to major infections, requiring that the Marine be put on light duty until the infection cleared. We also took this opportunity to renew the immunizations for the entire unit. The Marines lined up and received their injections.

April 7, 1967

Dear Louise,

 Got your April fools day package today. Boy, that was a dirty trick. That was down right rotten, but I'll let it go this time 'cause I love you.

 I sure would like one of those swinger cameras, I've been thinking about getting one for a long time.

 What did Mario Savio do to cause such a large amount of trouble in Berkley? I never heard of him.

 You know I never heard of "Hippies" or "Diggers" before. They really don't impress me though. I did something the other day I never thought I'd ever do. We had shots the other day and I was giving them to my platoon. I need three of them, Plague, Cholera, and Gamma Globulin (GG). Well I gave myself the first two and by this time I had a crowd watching me. The GG shot is 5cc and has to be given in the behind. So not to disappoint my spectators, I dropped my trousers, turned around the best I could and gave myself the shot. I think I'll do it that way from now on, because I give a real good shot, if I do say so myself.

When I haven't been going on patrols, which isn't often, I've been working on my bunker that I live in. The other day I took the sandbags off the roof and dug the hole larger, put the roof back on and have built a table and a couple of shelves out of old ammunition boxes. Think I'll build bunk beds next.

Hey, that's an idea, when we get married we'll have bunk beds. How's that sound? (ha) It'd never work because there would always be an empty bed, wouldn't there?

I'm sure glad you sent me that sewing kit thing because my trousers are about to fall off. I've patched them several times with needle and thread that you sew up people with, but they still have holes in them. I can't seem to get trousers to fit me. I have a 28 inch or less waist and they always try to give me trousers for 31 to 35 inch waist. I tell them to keep their "tents" and come see me when they get something my size. So I've been sewing for several months now.

You know one thing I've learned over here is how to appreciate things. Until I came over here I took a lot for granted, but now even the common everyday things are like luxuries to me. I have talked to some of the guys about and they feel the same way. I think everyone should have to live like this just after they get out of high school or sometime there about. You sure learn a lot for such a short period of time.

I just thought of something I can use. A mirror! I haven't seen myself for a long time. Just a small one will do, maybe about 3"x5" in size.

Well, this is just a short letter, but it'll have to do for now.

Oh, I did have a dream the other night. I dreamed that we were married and were in Japan. We lived in a Japanese style house, just like the one my friend who lived in one. In fact I think it was the same house. Anyhow I dreamt about us walking along the beach near the house, going to different place around there. But my dreams always end up one way – in bed. This time our bed was Japanese style on the floor. Boy, did we have fun, wow! I love you so much I can't wait until I don't have to dream and can really do the things we dream about.

Well bye for now. I sure do miss you.

Love always
Russ

PS I love you

On April 9, one of our radiomen informed me that we would soon be moving to relieve Kilo Company at Ca Lu located about ten miles south of Payable on Highway 9. We were supposed to move the next day, so I set about packing the few belongings I had and put them in my Willie Peter bag in preparation for the move.

The next day, we were to stand down from the move because we would be flown out into the hills near Ca Lu Mountain to perform a search-and-destroy mission on a major trail through the mountains to the Quang Tri River.

On April 11, helicopters arrived at our position at around 1130 and flew us out to a hill designated as Hill 492 located to the north of Ca Lu Mountain. We followed some major jungle trails that were wide and had log steps to accommodate climbing the grade with a heavy load. Some of the edges of the trail had fences made out of bamboo and other wood. By 1430, we came across a large group of camouflage bunkers and huts made of grass. One of the huts was designed as a kitchen complete with a cooking oven. The camp was designed to accommodate around fifty men. We also discovered two graves with markers that indicated that the bodies were buried two weeks previously. All the bunkers and huts were destroyed along with some equipment and food that we found in the area.

The next day, we followed the trail farther south, and by 1000, we discovered another campsite again large enough to accommodate fifty men. This position not only had a grass hut, but fighting holes. Again we destroyed the campsite.

As we moved on down the trail, we discovered a tunnel around noon. Inside the tunnel was an AK-47 and a barrel for a submachine gun. Again we destroyed what we found and moved on. As we ascended the north side of Ca Lu Mountain, the clouds rolled in and the fog got thick. We could only see thirty to fifty feet. At dusk, we stopped for the night and set up our defenses.

The next morning, we started out, and around 0800, we discovered four graves marked October 1966. The graves were opened, and the bodies appeared to have been killed by shrapnel. The bodies were returned to their graves and reinterred.

The mist condensed on the tree leaves, and it was dripping on us as we continued down the trail. We passed through a leech area, and the vegetation was alive with leeches sensing us as we passed through the area. Then it started raining pretty heavily. It had turned into a very gloomy day. Halfway up the peak, it was so foggy that we could barely see the man in front of us. We continued walking through the mountains and crossed over the peak at an elevation of 760 meters (a thousand feet higher than Hill 492). The trees near the peak were all broken from artillery or bombs. All the trees were dripping, and the leeches were on the prowl. It was very silent and eerie. We kept walking, and on the other side of the peak, we finally descended below the dense clouds, but it was still raining.

At around 1130, our point man, a PFC named Bob Hice, walked around the corner, and across the small stream in front of him sat several NVA sitting at the trailside taking a smoke break. He and the NVA both got off a couple of rounds, which warned those of us in the following column that something was up. After the brief exchange of gunfire, the call for "corpsman up" went out, and several Marines preceded me to set up cover so that I could get to Hice. It took me just a short time to crawl up to his position. He was lying on his back with a gunshot wound to the chest. The bullet had obviously hit one of the major arteries near the heart. Blood was gushing out each time his heart beat. He was still conscious but dazed and going into shock quickly. I stuck my left thumb into the wound, acting as a stopper to slow the flow of blood. Hice told me he was worried he was going to die. I encouraged him to hang in there and kept reminding him of the information he had shared with me the evening before.

Hice was only about five foot six and wore a pair of Government Issue glasses. He and I had been sitting eating and talking about things back in the world. He and his fiancée were planning to get married when he got out of Nam. He told me about his home, parents, car, and many other things as he reminisced about his life back in the States. He was from Pittsburgh and planned to go back.

I opened my Unit One and pulled out a large battle-dressing package. With my free hand and teeth, I tore open the package. After getting the dressing out of its plastic wrapper, I instructed several of the Marines close by to break out some of their battle dressings. When they were ready, I removed my thumb and pressed my dressing to his chest. It immediately soaked through. I had the other Marines hand me their opened dressings and placed each on top as they continued to soak through. Finally they were holding, and I secured the entire pile to his chest with the ties that are included on each one. I kept encouraging Hice to stay awake, but he was getting weaker by the moment, and his skin was getting very pale. Just before he died, Bob opened his eyes, looked at me, and said, "Thanks for trying, Doc." I was stunned; the last words from this dying Marine were to thank me for my unsuccessful efforts.

We removed his gear and ammunition from his body and wrapped it up in his poncho. Due to the thick clouds, we couldn't get in a helicopter to take his body out. At first we tried to carry his body in another poncho, but that was difficult and required four men. An hour or so later, we came across a patch of bamboo with stocks large enough to support the weight. We cut a pole, placed it on him, and wrapped it full length with com wire to keep it from sagging. With a man on each end, it was easier to handle. His fire team took turns on the pole carrying him out of the mountains.

Meanwhile, a platoon from Kilo Company left their position at Ca Lu and followed a trail along the Ba Ngao River, which was the terminus of the major trail we had been sweeping for the past several days. When our units linked up at around 1800 in the evening, one of their guys accidently leaned up against the fence along the trail. The fence gave slightly and triggered a small explosive device, probably a Chi Com grenade set up as a booby trap. The explosion only slightly wounded five of our men and several of theirs. Though the sky was now clear, all the wounds were minor enough that the casualties did not require a medevac, so we continued the hike toward Highway 9.

When night fell, we were still cautiously moving down the trail. Around midnight, we walked off the trail onto Highway 9 next to the Quang Tri River about six kilometers south of Ca Lu. We turned north and continued walking the highway toward Ca Lu over bridges too weak or damaged for vehicle traffic. Finally we crossed the last bridge and were met on the other side by a waiting convoy of trucks to take us back to the Rockpile. We climbed aboard, and the trucks proceeded slowly with their light off. When we arrived at the outpost at Ca Lu, the platoon from Kilo Company was let off, and the trucks continued on. After leaving Ca Lu, the trucks were able to use their blacked-out headlights to illuminate the road a short distance in front of them, and the convoy was able to travel a little faster. We arrived back at our position at Payable at around 0200 for some much-needed sleep.

Casualties on 04/13/67
Killed
PFC Hice, Robert K. 0311

Wounded
Cpl. Dzikowski, Raymond J. 0311
Sgt. Goggin, Charles F. 0311
Cpl. Lewis, David T. 0331
Sgt. Marlin, Stephen M. 0351
LCpl. Petri, George P. 0311
LCpl. Shindelus, Theodore J. 0311

Chapter 39

Ca Lu

ON THE FOURTEENTH of April, we awoke to heavy rain. During the night, the sky clouded up, and a storm hit bringing in extremely heavy warm rain. This time we were wet, but not cold. Lima Company was scheduled to move to Ca Lu on the morning of the fifteenth. Kilo Company had occupied Ca Lu since January, and Lima was assigned to relieve them. That night, I went out on ambush and slept in the pouring rain under my poncho when I was not on radio watch. We returned inside the perimeter at about 0500 and waited to move to Ca Lu. At about 1100, the trucks arrived, and the leading element of our company climbed aboard and headed for Ca Lu. At about 1330, the trucks arrived back with the first load of Kilo Marines, and the remainder of Lima Company climbed aboard, and we rode in the rain to Ca Lu.

Arriving, I noticed an ARVN RF (Regional Forces) unit under the command of Dai Uy (Captain) Quan who had their compound at the top of the next hill overlooking our position in an old concrete French bunker with trenches around it. In later years, this area would be known as Vandergrift/LZ Stud.

When we arrived at Ca Lu, it was still pouring. The torrential rainstorm had not let up all day, and at times, it was so hard that visibility was limited. This was one of the heaviest rains that I had experienced. Command group and Second Platoon were on a hill, and First Platoon and Third Platoon were on the flat across the narrow highway. Upon inspection, we found that the deluge flooded the trenches and most of the bunkers in the area designated for occupation by Second Platoon.

A few bunkers had only a few inches of water on the floor. I shared a bunker with Corporal Tony Williams and his squad. We had a great time joking around and cooking C rations. At least none of us had to go out on ambush that night like Third Platoon. I had a small tape recorder and taped some of our conversation that evening.

During the early morning, the rain let up and the sun was shining at sunrise. We learned that First Platoon ambush had to come back in early because the squad leader, Corporal Dave Schwirian, had been attacked and mauled by a wild animal around midnight. They terminated the ambush to assist him back the six kilometers or so back to Ca Lu. He was able to walk most of the way, but required some assistance the last mile or so. He was medevaced out.

I talked to HM3 Dan Fuss, who was the corpsman out on the ambush, and he told me his version of what had happened. He stated that they had set up the ambush near where the Ba Ngao River runs into the Quang Tri where we had two nights before. Because of the activity on the trail, they were to ambush anyone coming down the trail onto the highway. They set up their ambush on the point between the Quang Tri River and the Ba Ngao with good coverage of the road and bridge over the Ba Ngao. It was still pouring down rain, and everyone was wrapped up in his poncho. Sometime around midnight, he heard a commotion at the other end of the line, and the word came to him that he was needed because someone had been bitten. Fuss said he was suspecting something small, like an insect or scorpion bite. He crawled down the line of Marines until he reached Corporal Schwirian, the squad leader. He asked him what happened, to which the reply came, "Doc, something bit me!" Because of the need to assess the wound, Fuss placed his poncho over Schwirian and himself to contain the light before lighting his cigarette lighter to inspect the bite (they had no flashlights with them). He then saw that it was not a mere bug bite. The bicep muscle from Schwirian's right arm had been ripped out. Schwirian had escaped by punching the animal several times in the head, but before he could free himself, it had ripped out his right bicep before bounding out of the area. Fuss applied a battle dressing and informed the radioman to break radio silence because the severity of the injury required immediate evacuation back to Ca Lu. Captain Ripley granted permission, and the ambush was broken, and the squad began their walk back to Ca Lu in the darkness of the storm. Schwirian was barely conscious when he was put on a truck to transfer him to the BAS at Payable.

I never saw him again until July of 2003 at a Lima Company reunion in Branson, Missouri. His arm had been repaired, and though he no longer had a bicep, the surgeons had attached one of his other muscles, and with a great deal of physical therapy and retraining, he still has some function of his right arm. He now is known as Tiger Dave and lives in Arkansas where he worked as a geologist.

A squad from Second Platoon was assigned to return to the ambush site with an investigating officer. I was assigned to go with them. We took a fire team of RFs with us because they were more familiar with the area. We left Ca Lu at around 0815 and reached the site around 1100. When we reached the location of the attack, we investigated the area and found cat tracks about four and a half inches in diameter. Even with the rain (which had subsided during the night), we could see the cat's tracks around the ambush site. The tiger had evidently come across them and circled around and grabbed Schwirian, who was sleeping.

We talked to some Montagnards from a Lang Ruou village across the river. They told us that there was a tiger in the area that had been snooping around their village recently. They lost one of their older residents and never found her body.

On the way back, we stopped for a break and were lounging along the road when one of the RFs complained he had been bitten by something. We had no interpreters with us, so I finally figured out by having him draw a picture that a centipede had bitten him. I put some bacitracin ointment on the bite and a Band-Aid on him, and he quit his whining.

Ca Lu is located where the highway and the Quang Tri River join and run parallel. There is a gravel beach on the river next to the road. When we first arrived, there were many civilians hanging out on the beach, some on the land and some on small boats. The RFs were utilizing them to wash their clothes and cook. Initially we utilized the beach and river to bathe and swim. The river was very refreshing, but unfortunately was so contaminated with all the humanity living along its banks upstream that it wasn't long before the entire company came down with dysentery. After that, we started getting our drinking water from Dong Ha waterworks via a four-hundred-gallon water trailer called a water buffalo, brought in several times a week by convoy.

We continued our patrols and ambushes as before. The area north of the river was a large floodplain situated between two sets of mountains. One of our patrol routes on the north side consisted of heading north on Highway 9 until we came to a dirt road designated as 556 going east, which on the maps showed it connected with the city of Quang Tri on the coast. We followed it past fields, many growing corn. A large water buffalo bull occupied one of the fields. Whenever we approached, he charged up to the single-strand barbed wire fence and snorted angrily until we all had passed.

Continuing on, we came to a small Vietnamese village called Ba Thanh. It was made up of five or six grass-thatched huts located at the edge of the Quang Tri River. As we walked back toward Ca Lu, there was a larger Montagnard village called Lang Caht built up on stilts, as was their tradition. This design worked well for them whether in the flatland or the mountains. It kept the living space up off the ground, and the house could be constructed level regardless of the steepness of the terrain. Underneath their living space, they had pens to confine their pigs and chickens at night. After leaving this village, the trail cut through the area that they had cultivated in corn and other vegetables. Then we followed their trail back along the river to Ca Lu.

The Montagnard women in the fields worked with their chest bare, but when we started patrolling through the area, they quickly donned their blouses. After several weeks, they got used to us being there and knew we would not bother them, so they ignored us and continued as they were. I never heard of any incidents between the locals and the Marines in our unit.

April 18, 1967

Dear Louise,

Here we are in Ca Lu; this place is almost 10 miles south west of where we were before. We moved here the other day. Moving was such fun, pouring down rain! It rained so hard that all our bunkers are flooded. In some of them or should I say most of them the water is neck deep.

The next day the water is in our bunker was waist deep and we started bailing. We bailed 420 gallons of water before it was empty.

Here we are working with the ARVN, which is the South Vietnamese Army.

We also have civilians here and when you go to the river for a swim you can get the people to wash your clothes for a couple cans of C-rations. I gave some of the kids there some gum today and also put some medicine and band-aids on them. Now when any of them see me they holler "Bak-si (Doctor) Jewett Numba One". So I guess I made some friends today.

Also today one of the guys had his Polaroid camera out and took the picture I enclosed, in the background you can see the ARVN area on the hill.

I don't think I told you about our last operation. Well, We went out into the same area where we went on the first one when those guys got hit by our own artillery. Anyhow, we were out there for 3 days and on the last day we were walking back in when two gooks popped up and shot our point man. I ran up to him and the first thing he said was to me was "Doc, I'm going to die!" I told him that he wasn't, even though I knew he was. I continued to patch him up and he grabbed my arm and said, " It's no use, Doc, I can't hang on, thanks for trying." Then he died. I felt like crying.

That last day we started walking at 7 am and kept walking until midnight, when we finally got back to our area. We did some walking that day. Everyone's feet still hurt.

I sure do miss you. I think of you all the time and what it will be like after we're married. I can't wait until the day when we will never have to be away from each other again. It will be so nice to know that whenever I need you or you need me we will be within arms reach of each other.

Oh, I forgot to tell you. I am in the process of making a tape to send home. I can't think of much to say on it though. One of the guys has a small battery tape recorder and let me borrow it and gave me some tape he had. So all I have to do is think of something to say.

Well, bye for now. Always remember I love you. Only about 7 months to go now.

Love always
Russ

PS I love you

Again – tell my mom not to go spastic if she doesn't receive a letter for a while. I'm trying to tape what's going on and if I write I'll just be saying the same thing that's on the tape.

    The south side of the river rose up steeply and was more difficult to patrol. Going on patrol across the river usually started on the rocky beach. We originally used some of the civilian locals with a dugout canoe to ferry us across. Several weeks later, all the RFs left Ca Lu, and the mob of civilians on the beach did also. We used an inflatable rubber boat after that. Once across the river, we hiked through a leech-infested area that extended several hundred yards from the edge of the river. The trail then headed up through hills covered with short elephant grass and then climbed up into another jungle area at the top. Along the top, the trail split with one turning left back down the backside of the hill and the other continuing along the ridge toward Ta Ri Mountain. The trail forked, and a trail branched off to the west. We followed the trail downhill. About halfway down, we came across a small stream that flowed into a rocky area where it widened suddenly and cascaded over a large stone forming a waterfall and a wide pool. The pool below the waterfall was narrow and deep and looked like it had been carved into a cistern by some earlier culture. The stream was shaded with trees and was cooler than the surrounding jungle. It was a beautiful little area, and we stopped and took a break.

    Below the shaded area, we continued down the cascading stream as it narrowed again until we came out in a flat area where the stream widened and was only knee-deep. Large groves of bamboo grew along the edges until it finally ran into the Quang Tri River. At the confluence, the Quang Tri was shallow enough to ford where the water was only waist deep and several hundred feet wide. On the other side, a trail led upstream to the small Vietnamese village where it connected with the same trail we used when patrolling the north side of the river.

    Shortly after arriving at Ca Lu, a 175 mm cannon came to our position manned by army artillerymen. The big gun was placed on the flat near Third Platoon. The ammunition for the gun was three feet long with a projectile that was about a foot long. It was a bit loud when fired.

Chapter 40

Ambush at the L

ON THE MORNING of April 25 at 0830, the Eleventh Engineers, stationed in the Ca Lu compound, went out on one of their routine work parties. They were systematically repairing Highway 9 and repairing all the bridges that had been blown out or damaged to the extent that it would not support a vehicle. They were working to improve the highway for traffic through to the base at Khe Sanh. They left Ca Lu with several vehicles, including a small personnel carrier, several dump trucks, a 6-by, and an Ontos. A short time after they left, the Ontos, which had been at the rear of the column, came racing back and reported that their convoy had been ambushed seven kilometers south.

Two squads from Second Platoon mounted up on several vehicles and raced out to the ambush site, located at an L-shaped curve in the highway called "the elbow," a perfect spot for an ambush. As we neared the elbow, we got off the vehicles and advanced on foot, prepared to receive opposition. Arriving at the elbow, we saw the vehicles were abandoned in the middle of the road, all were damaged. A mine in the middle of the road had been set off under the lead dump truck, blocking the narrow road and preventing the following vehicles from getting through. We approached cautiously, expecting to take fire. Nothing happened, so we got up to the ambush site and set up security. Searching through the vehicles, we found five bodies. All the rest of the twenty-eight-man team was missing.

We split up into small teams to search the area. I led a team. We followed a fresh trail through the grass and foliage running parallel to the road for a short distance then turned toward the riverbank. Entering the willows and rounding the corner where the trail descended to the river, I saw the muzzle of an M14 aimed at me. A single Marine was visible above the riverbank. He was wearing his helmet and had a battle dressing covering one eye. I jumped back and hollered for him to hold his fire. I then identified myself and let him know we were from Lima Company and were there to get them out. He acknowledged, lowered his rifle, and gave me permission to advance. We headed down to their position.

There were twenty of them. They had abandoned their vehicles and headed down to the river. Near the river, they were out of the killing zone of the ambush and had set up a defensive position in case the enemy pursued them. I examined them, and they all had wounds, but had already applied the required battle dressings. When we got them back up to the road, they said the only vehicle that was not accounted for was the small quarter-ton personnel carrier (PC). It had been in the lead of their convoy and had three passengers. The NVA ambushers had let the lighter PC pass through because it was not a very good barrier to stop the heavier vehicles that made up the rest of the convoy. Once it had passed through, they exploded an electrically detonated mine under the heavier dump truck.

By that time, a tank arrived from Payable with some other vehicles to evacuate the wounded. We loaded them up and sent them back to Ca Lu. One of the squads and I climbed aboard a tank and a dump truck and told the drivers we needed to find the PC. We continued up the highway toward Khe Sanh. The engineers had been preparing for a crossing by installing a portable bridge. We crossed the river at the shallow area on the smaller tributary of the Quang Tri River and continued up the other side toward the plateau leading to Khe Sanh. Around noon, halfway between the river and Khe Sanh, we came to the PC lying on its passenger's side in the road. It had hit a mine. We found two Marines and a corpsman close by. The corpsman was lying in the shade. He had a broken leg and had applied a wooden splint. Both Marines were also injured, but were busy performing a search on a large group of Montagnards that came down from Khe Sanh walking along the road to the Cam Lo market. We relieved them of searching the Montagnards. As the search continued, I checked the injured and helped them into the back of a dump truck.

When the search was complete and no weapons were found, the Montagnards were allowed to continue on their way. We turned around and headed back toward Ca Lu. On the way back, I rode in the back of the dump truck with the injured. The corpsman told me that members of the tribe of Montagnards had put the splint on his leg and helped him dress the wounds on the Marines. As we approached the elbow, we received some more small arms fire from across the river. The metal sides of the dump truck were enough to stop the bullets, and no one was hit as we raced back to Ca Lu.

Arriving at Ca Lu, the last medevac was called. A short time later, a chopper arrived, and by 1515, all the casualties were removed from our position. The rest of our security team returned to Ca Lu by 1600.

The next afternoon, a salvage team from the engineers consisting of six vehicles and twenty engineers went back out to the ambush site. A fire team from Lima accompanied them to provide security. They returned safely in about an hour from when they left. That night, we heard an explosion to the south of our position.

On the morning of the twenty-seventh, the engineers discovered that a bridge about two kilometers from Ca Lu had been blown during the night. They spent the day repairing the bridge and returned to Ca Lu. The next day, they were repairing another bridge just past the one they had worked on the previous day when a sniper fired at them, grazing one of the engineers' forehead.

April 25, 1967

Dear Louise,

Thanks a lot for the Polaroid camera, I'm sending you a few of the pictures I took to you. I need more film. I took pictures of my friends and they asked if they could have them, so being the kind-hearted person I am I gave them the picture. But I told them that from now on if they want pictures they will have to furnish the film. I also sent 2 to my mom. The first one is of me in my bunker. I was going over a list of supplies we needed with my assistant. The next one is writing a letter to you, this one as a matter of fact. The guy who took it didn't pull it out of the camera far enough, so I had to tape to together. Next is me down at the river with a bunch of Vietnamese kids. They do our laundry for us. Last is me at the river. We usually don't run around like that, but I put a towel on for the picture because I didn't think you wanted one of me the way we usually are at the river.

Today we had a real hectic time. This morning I just came in off an ambush and had just finished breakfast when we got word that the 11th Engineers had got ambushed down the road from here. (I got another pen now) So we had to go and get them. The truck that came to get us had 4 wounded in it. When we got out here I found 11 wounded and 5 dead, then after we got those people out I rode on a tank about 3 miles down the road to where a truck had hit a mine and the corpsman with them had a broken leg, but had taken care of all his people. Altogether today I took care of 21 wounded and 5 dead. I sure was tired when I got back this afternoon. I was so tired I could hardly think straight.

I had a dream last night. I guess you could call it a remembrance or something like that. I dreamed about the things we were doing in the backseat of your car when you were taking me to Travis. Where I had my hands and finger and you had yours. It turns me on to remember those things. I sure do love you. I want more than anything to have your warm body next to mine. Anyway! Just sitting talking or like we were at Ten Mile. I love you so much. I can't wait until we're married so we will always be together. I want to make you the happiest girl in the world. I will always love you no matter what happens. Just to be *together forever, you and me, is all I think about (except for what I remember of the things we did before.) Hurry up September 22, 1968, please!*

Well, I guess I got a little carried away there; I get this way when I'm tired. I better get some sleep now, so bye for now. Oh, check on that bank account deal at Bank of America, that's where I have my money, also I need more film for my camera you gave me. Why don't you send me a couple rolls of film with each package and I promise not to give all my pictures away. Well, Bye.

Love always,
Russ

PS I love you

Chapter 41

Indigenous People of the Area

THE MAJORITY OF our company came down with diarrhea from drinking and washing in the water from the Quang Tri River. Patrols and ambushes had to continue despite our malady. We were taking diarrhea pills that contained morphine and atropine. I had taken some diarrhea medication that morning before I went out on patrol. I took a couple of pills because of the severity of my symptoms. We set out across the river and up into the hills on the south side. It wasn't long before I was so thirsty that by the time I got to the ridge trail on the south side of the river, I drank all the water in both canteens. Luckily we found plenty of streams on the trail where I could fill my canteens, but no matter how much I drank, I was still parched until the effects of the medication wore off.

When we reached the top, we traveled along the ridge for several miles toward Ta Ri Mountain and then followed the trail downhill toward the river. Just after leaving the jungle near the top of the ridge, we came across stalks of corn that were eight to ten feet tall growing on a terraced hillside. Some of the Marines from the Midwest found it incredible that corn could grow anywhere other than flat fields. We followed the trail down and finally came out at one of the Montagnard villages Lang Ruou, located on the riverbank. When we approached the village, they came out to meet us. They all carried machetes and crossbows, but one of them had an ancient bolt-action French rifle. They told us that the NVA had been in their area recently, which was the reason for them carrying arms.

While the squad leader was talking with them, one of the Montagnards asked me to look at a member of his family who was very sick. I climbed up the steps carved from a single bamboo trunk set at an angle. The interior of the house was open and clean. Inside, lying on the split bamboo flooring, was an old woman wrapped up in blankets who was obviously dying. She had a high fever and was barely breathing. I examined her and determined that there was nothing I could do. I apologized to them for not being able to help and instructed them to just make her comfortable. They thanked me, and I rejoined the patrol. At the river, they used their dugout canoe to ferry us across the narrow deep river. We climbed the bank and were back on Highway 9 and walked five kilometers back to Ca Lu.

On one of our patrols north on Highway 9 from Ca Lu, we went west up an old overgrown road located near the intersection of Highway 9 and Road 556. It led us up into the hills where the road terminated at an area that had been a logging camp. Large mahogany logs were stacked up waiting to be hauled away, but had been there for at least a year. The hillside was covered with stumps that indicated that someone had felled the trees by hand using axes.

I had observed a Montagnard felling a tree by the side of the Quang Tri River a few days earlier. He had built a platform of poles on which he stood as he wielded his ax, reminding me of pictures of logging in California 1800s where the choppers used springboards to stand on while cutting at the tree.

Another day, we were patrolling north on Highway 9. There was a path that led from Highway 9 over to Road 556 that we followed. Near Road 556, we visited a Vietnamese home located over against the hills on the east side of the valley. We arrived around noon and decided to take a break. The old man who lived there asked us to join in a meal with him. He brought out a big pot of meat he had been cooking in thick brown gravy. We offered him meat from our C rations to add to his pot. He thanked us, and we opened cans containing beef, pork, and chicken, which he stirred into the pot.

After a few minutes, he tasted the concoction and indicated that something was missing. He strolled to his garden and selected several very small green peppers, each about an inch long. Taking great care, he cut up the peppers into very small pieces adding them to the pot. He gave it a stir and let it simmer for a few more minutes. Sampling it again, he was satisfied with the taste. He indicated his pleasure with the food and said that together we all made great cooks. Inside his house, his wife had been preparing a big pot of rice. He told her to bring it out. We each partook of the meal. The pepper he added had made it fiery hot, but it was delicious. We thanked him, gave him some of our cans of C rations, and went on our way.

Medical Civilian Action Program was another of the ways we reached out to the locals. A MedCAP consisted of a squad of Marines and a corpsman visiting the local villages providing medical care. I liked MedCAP in this rural area compared to the more urban area where I had done similar programs where everyone crowded around with their hands out and the kids were always trying to pick your pockets. In Ca Lu, the people came around and waited patiently, approaching me one or two at a time and showing me their cuts and scratches. I carried a Polaroid camera on one of the trips to the Montagnard village of Lang Caht. I gave the camera to Corporal Tony Williams and told him to take pictures of the MedCAP until he had one picture left. When that time came, I had everyone in the village gather around like a family photo. I was sitting with several kids on my lap. After the picture was fixed with the fluid that preserved it, I gave it to the village chief. He showed it to his clan. They had never seen anything like this. All the villagers took turns finding themselves and poking fun at how their friends looked in the photo.

When we returned a couple of days later, I reexamined my patients, and their cuts were mostly healed. These people had never had antibiotics, so they didn't have resistant strains of bacteria. It was amazing how the use of bacitracin acted on the cuts and scrapes on these villagers. I saw some really bad infections almost healed.

During the night, we heard an explosion south of our position. When the engineers went out the next morning, they found that the bridge located two kilometers from our position had been blown out. They were in the process of repairing the bridge, and around 1445, they received one round of sniper fire that grazed the forehead of one of the Marines.

April 29, 1967

Dear Louie,

Here I am out here sitting on top of a hill with nothing to do, so I decided to write you a letter. We came up here on a patrol and we have to sit here until 4:30 this afternoon. What a waste of a day.

At night I have to go out to a bridge that we are guarding about 100 meters from our area.

The other night we were sitting around talking when there was a big explosion down the road. I said that they probably blew up a bridge, everyone laughed. The next morning a convoy of trucks started out, but didn't get over a mile because the bridge was blown out.

Yesterday we ran a MEDCAP (Medical Civilian Action Program) patrol through the villages. It sure was fun treating all the people. The people I like the best are the Montagnards, the Vietnamese mountain people. They are well mannered and aren't as "Give me – give me" as the other Vietnamese people. In the other villages if you give one kid a pill, all of them want one and they aren't satisfied with just one, they want a whole handful, so I tell them to get lost if they aren't sick.

The village people are building us a hospital, so we will have a place to treat them better than going from ville to ville.

Right now I am playing radioman and am about ready to call in a practice fire mission with 81mm mortars. This looks like fun.

There I'm finished with the fire mission. It was easy and on target. Pretty good, huh?

One of the ARVNs just came up to me and borrowed a piece of paper so he could write a letter to his family.

Chapter 42

Rough Rider

IN MAY, HIGHWAY 9 had been repaired sufficiently to start regular convoys to Khe Sanh. It was our job to provide security. The day before the convoy was due to arrive, the Eleventh Engineers had a portable bridge loaded in a couple of dump trucks. With a couple squads of grunts for security, they headed out to where the road crossed the Ruo Quan River up stream from its confluence with the Quang Tri River called the Hairpin. All the bridges on the road up to that point were smaller and crossed the small streams emptying into the Quang Tri. At the Hairpin were old concrete French bunkers and two old bridges that had been blown out previously. The oldest one appeared to be a curved concrete structure that was lying in the riverbed where it landed after the lower supports had been blown out. The other bridge was an old bailey bridge that had its mid span concrete support column blown out, causing it to sag slightly in the center. Except for a single line of planks running along the middle of the bridge, the wooden deck had been removed. It was totally useless for vehicles, but it was still used for foot traffic. This provided sufficient footing for a column to move single file over the failing bridge. The river running through the narrow gorge was deep and shaded most of the day. That bridge was eventually dropped into the river by blowing it in the center so that both halves fell, but still hung from the banks on either side of the river. The water was twenty-five feet deep, cool and crystal clear, making it a perfect swimming hole. When it was possible, I spent most my time in the river.

The engineers extended the road farther up river where it narrowed and was shallow enough to erect their portable bridge. A platoon of Lima Company Marines set up security around the area and was also supported by mortars as well as Dusters and Quad 50s to ensure that the NVA could not tamper with it during the night.

The day after the bridge was erected, a convoy made up of fifty to ninety trucks arrived from Dong Ha and picked up more Marines from Lima Company at Ca Lu. A second bridge loaded on a dump truck, and another team of engineers also joined the convoy; in case the bridge security failed, another could be hastily erected if needed. We rode shotgun on the trucks, providing defensive fire in case of an ambush. Our squads were split up into fire teams and rode on trucks located throughout the length of the convoy. In addition to the grunts, they also had tanks, Ontos, Quad 50s, and Dusters rolling with them.

These convoys, loaded with supplies, traveled at fifty miles per hour and did not stop until reaching their destination, the combat base at Khe Sanh. They left Ca Lu and ran all the way to the Hairpin, across the bridge, up the other side to the plateau, and on to Khe Sanh.

Once we reached Khe Sanh, we waited in the back of our vehicles near the west end of the airstrip until they unloaded all the supplies and loaded up anything or anyone who was going back. Without the breeze created by the moving vehicles and without any shade, waiting in our vehicles was like being in an oven. My main job was making sure that the Marines stayed hydrated. Eventually the time came to return, and the convoy raced back to Ca Lu. After the last vehicle crossed the portable bridge at the Hairpin, the engineers disassembled the bridge, loaded it back on the dump trucks, security was pulled in, loaded up, and everyone returned to Ca Lu. This went on for several months with minimal interference with the convoy.

The weather was getting hotter, and it was a joy when Second Platoon was assigned bridge security on a bailey bridge located about a mile or so north of the Ca Lu gate. The original bridge had been blown out by a bomb and lay in ruins just upstream from the bomb crater. Before the bomb destroyed the bridge, it had crossed the Sui Soi River, a small stream that ran down from the mountains to the west and then meandered south and east through the valley until it ran into the Quang Tri River. The shallow depth of the stream and lack of shading vegetation along the banks caused the water to warm more than would be expected. By the time the water ran into the crater, it was as warm as a swimming pool, but cool enough to still be refreshing. The bailey bridge spanned over the edge of the bomb crater. The bridge became our diving platform, and the fifteen-foot-deep by thirty-foot-diameter crater made a great swimming hole. We jumped off the bridge into the swimming hole twelve feet below. We spent many hours swimming and diving. We used our rubber ladies to float and relax in the sun. Most of us had a fairly good tan from the waist up from working in the sun without our shirts, but we all had pale legs. The biggest problem I had to treat there was sunburned backsides.

May 3, 1967

Dear Louise,

    Sounds like you're really working on the dances, I know you and Sue will do a good job.

    Let me tell you something I don't care what that woman said I don't even think you are flat chested, you're far from it. I like you just the way you are and don't want you to change.

    When is Mary getting married? I wish I could be home too.

    That sounds like a good idea you have. I like it. The only part that bothers me is what do I say when we announce our engagement? But, I guess I'll think of something by then.

    Lately we haven't been doing too much, except going on patrols around here. I started to write a letter on patrol the other day but couldn't think of much to say. I'll send it in with this letter. It's been in my pocket for a couple of days so it may have a worn look to it. I never got a chance to finish this letter.

    Yesterday I got a day off, shock – shock! The senior corpsman told me I was working too hard and he wanted me to go out to the bridge and take it easy for a day. I sure was glad. All I did was float around on the river on a rubber lady and swim. I got a little sunburn on my legs, but it was worth it.

    Last night I had to go back to work and went out on an ambush. Tomorrow I have to go out on a patrol at 6 in the morning until 3:30 in the afternoon.

    Today I made me a pair of swimming trunks out of a pair of skivvies. I sewed them up the front. I then cut a pocket off an old shirt and sewed it to the back. They are perfect for running around the area instead of going nude. When we wear our regular clothes we never wear skivvies anyway.

    I got a letter from my mom today also and she said that they had all kinds of things about me in the Press Democrat, Mendocino Beacon, and on the radio for 2 days. She also said they had pictures of me. I guess the picture of me was one where I was supposed to be checking my gear standing in a trench with the Rockpile in the background. That's the only time I can think of I had my picture taken by a correspondent, except when we were on operation.

    I have to write on both sides of the paper because I'm just about out of it. I also have to borrow a pen because I lost mine on patrol one day.

    I miss you more than anything. I wish we could be together sooner than December. I figured out how may days I've been in Viet Nam and it came out to 169. On May 27th at 12 noon half of my time will be up over here. We have to stay here 12 months and 20 days, which means I should be home sometime right after December 5th. Only 216 days to go! I can't wait to get back to where it is safe, where I can be with you again.

Well my borrowed pen looks like it's starting to run out of ink so I better quit for now. I love you more than anything and can't wait to get back to you. Anyway this is my last piece of paper. Bye for now.

Love always
Russ

PS I love you

Chapter 43

R&R

ON MAY 9, I was offered the chance to go on R&R to Tokyo. I dropped everything and caught the next convoy back to Dong Ha. When I got back to the rear area, I checked into the H&S Company office and received my traveling orders.

According to the orders, I had to wear a Summer Service uniform (khakis). This presented me with a problem. Having left my seabag with all my uniforms other than my utilities on Okinawa, I had no Summer Service uniform to wear. I proceeded over to our Battalion Aid Station and informed Lima Company's Senior Corpsman HM2 Jacques "JJ" J. Ayd of my predicament. JJ offered his uniform, which I gladly accepted. JJ and I were almost the same size, and his uniform fit me perfectly. No one questioned the discrepancy between the rank on my orders and the rank on the sleeve. I then reported to the airstrip for the flight back to Da Nang, where I again reported into the Marine transient center. After a short wait, we got into a cattle car and traveled across the airstrip where we loaded aboard a Pan Am Boeing 707 for the flight to Japan.

After a five-hour flight, our plane arrived at Kadena Marine Corps air station after dark, and I proceeded to the R&R center. I presented my orders at the new arrivals window. The clerk took them and issued me a liberty card allowing me off the base. They then directed me to a room full of civilian clothes on racks to select attire to wear off base. After finding clothing and shoes to my liking, I checked my uniform into the laundry, to be retrieved on my return. Then there was a briefing on the rules and regulations while on R&R in Japan. We were also given a time to be back at the R&R center. We were informed that if we did not meet this deadline, we would be considered AWOL and receive disciplinary action. The response was, "What are they going to do, send me to Nam?" After all the formalities, I left the R&R center and caught a cab to the train station where I boarded a train to Tokyo. I then took another train to the Tokyo suburb that was my destination.

Since my arrival in Vietnam, I had been corresponding with Mariko Kobayashi whom I had met in September just before I left Japan. Arriving back home several weeks later on my way to Camp Pendleton, there was a letter waiting for me from Mariko. After arriving in Vietnam, I wrote her a letter. I told her that when I got home, I was drafted into the navy and was now in Vietnam attached to the Marines as a corpsman. I told her that if I got a chance to go to Tokyo for R&R, I would look her up, and we started corresponding regularly. Unfortunately when I was offered the opportunity to go, I didn't have sufficient time to notify her that I was on my way. All I had were her address and phone number.

Arriving at the train station of the Tokyo suburb where Mariko lived, I went to a corner police station and asked directions to the address. The policeman looked at me suspiciously and made a phone call to Mariko and explained that some young American was asking about her address. He wanted to get her permission before he would give the directions to me. Mariko told the cop about me, and after he hung up the phone, he became very friendly. After chatting several minutes, he called a taxi and gave the driver instructions. The driver took me to one of the smaller train stations where Mariko had told the cop she would meet me. The cop had also told the driver that Mariko had told him that I had just arrived from Vietnam and I was a sailor. During the ride, the driver told me of his World War II experiences when he was a crewmember on a ship sunk by an American plane. He said one minute he was sleeping in his nice warm bunk, and the next thing he knew he was in the ocean. We both laughed about it, and when it came time to pay the fare, he would not accept any money. He wished me good luck from one sailor to another and went on his way.

Mariko arrived and was very pleased to see me. Evidently she lived with her parents and had gathered up a few things and told her parents she was going to stay with some girlfriends for the weekend. She then hailed another cab, and we went to a traditional Japanese hotel near the 1964 Olympic Village located nearby.

After checking into the hotel, I noticed that in addition to the small room with a futon on the tatami mat floor, the room also had a bathroom with a small deep tub and the little wooden stool for a traditional bath. After I got undressed, she had me sit on the little stool and poured buckets of warm water over me. Then she used a washcloth and a bar of soap and scrubbed me from head to foot followed by several more buckets of warm water to rinse the soap off me. She then had me climb into the tub. The hot water came up to my neck. I soaked there until I was so relaxed that I had to get out. While I was soaking, she had set up a folding massage table that was provided with the room. She then massaged me with oil until I was ready to sleep.

The next day, we went to the Olympic swimming pool where the 1964 aquatic events had been held. It had a large pool on one end and a diving pool on the other. While we were inside, some members of the Japanese diving team were practicing. We sat and watched them for a while. I had actually been there before, but I didn't tell Mariko because she was having such a good time playing tour guide. We also went to Tokyo Tower and Meiji Shrine, where I had also been before.

Monday she had to go back to work in Yokohama, so Sunday evening, she accompanied me to Yokohama, and she got a hotel room near the company where she worked just down the street from the navy exchange and housing area. The next day we said good-bye, and I told her I would write when I got back to Vietnam. She went to work, and I caught a cab to the train station and proceeded to Yokosuka.

In Yokosuka, I caught a cab to the naval hospital and met with some of my buddies who still were stationed there. I checked into the Hospital Corps quarters. The barracks master-at-arms gave me a room to stay in for the remaining days of my R&R. I had a great time. We went to the beach at Hayama and went surfing. That evening, we went out to the bars until midnight.

May 17, 1967

Dear Louise,

You'll never guess where I am; I'm back in the good old hospital corps quarters in Yokosuka! How 'bout that?

I left Ca Lu on the 8th and went back to Dong Ha and flew out of there on the 11th for Tokyo. In case you're wondering I am on R&R. I have to go back to Viet Nam tonight. I'm trying to think of a way to stay here, but can't think of anything they might believe.

I've been hanging around the hospital area herd. My best friend has been letting me wear all his clothes and using his room, car and everything. I bought a small tape recorder. Right now I'm taping music to take back with me.

I've really been having fun here seeing some of the old, by old I mean they were here when I was, people around here. I went back to my ward and saw all the nurses and a patient who was there when I was working there.

I went to the beach a couple of times; it sure is cold here next to down south.

I miss you very much and wish you could have been here with me. I love you so much. Only a little over 6 months and I should be home. Well, I have to get ready to go back now. Bye for now.

Love always,
Russ

PS I love you

Chapter 44

Rocket Attack on Dong Ha

AFTER MY FIVE-DAY temporary duty was up, I reported back to the R&R center at Kadena air station just before the allocated deadline arrived. Retrieving my uniform from the laundry, I turned in the civilian clothes and changed back into uniform. Later that night, we boarded the 707 for the return trip to Da Nang.

When I arrived at Da Nang, I decided to spend an extra day before catching the flight to Dong Ha. I went to the PX at Freedom Hill and bought a swimsuit so that I could have something to wear other than my pair of boxer shorts at the swimming hole in Ca Lu. On the eighteenth, I went to the air terminal and found out all nonessential flights to Dong Ha had been cancelled due to an attack that was made by the NVA on the base early that morning.

The next day, I was able to fly back to Dong Ha, and when I reported into the BAS, I discovered that they had been hit by rockets during the early morning of the eighteenth and three corpsmen were killed and six wounded. If I had stayed on schedule, I would have been there to witness the attack firsthand. It was highly probable that I would have been in the same trench as the three that got killed. I was not given a reprimand for tardiness.

I obtained new utilities from supply and caught the convoy back to Payable. The senior corpsman back at Ca Lu was happy when I arrived because up to that point, he did not know whether I had been in the trench that night or not.

Casualties on 05/18/67
Killed
> HM2 Ayd, Jacque J. Lima
> HM2 Cook, Lewis C. Kilo
> HM3 Nelson, Theodore R. Lima

Wounded
> HMC Kelsey, Orville W. H&S
> HM3 Helm, Richard D. India
> HM1 Hubert, Charles E. H&S
> HM2 Palmieri, Salvatore J. Lima
> HM3 Perkins, Byron R. Kilo
> HM1 Riddles, James N. H&S

Byron Perkins was a hospital corpsman that survived the rocket attack on Dong Ha. The following is his account of that night and the day afterward, given to me in 1999 via e-mail:

> On 17 May 1967 my Sr. Corpsman from Kilo Company, HM2 Lew Cook, an HM3 also from Kilo Company (who's name I cannot remember, I think he was called Ski), and I had a couple of beers together at the old mess tent area behind the Battalion Aid Station. Later we went back to the BAS and took some photos. The guy, whose name I cannot remember, left to go somewhere else. At about 0300 the next morning Dong Ha was hit by a heavy rocket attack. There was an L shaped slit trench just outside the south entrance to the Battalion Aid Station. Most of the corpsmen took cover in that trench. Unfortunately one of the rockets hit right in the corner of the "L" sending the blast and shrapnel down both arms of the trench. Three Doc's – HM2 Lewis C. Cook, HM2 Jacques J. Ayd, and HM2 Theodore "Ted" R. Nelson, were KIA and as I recall five more wounded very seriously.
>
> There was another HM2 who was wounded. He was one of the real heroes that morning after the attack on the BAS. I tried to treat his wounds but he refused treatment until everyone else was treated. As best I can recall his name was John Palmeri. Palmeri, Ayd, and Nelson were tight, so he sent me down into the "L" shaped slit trench to confirm if the others were KIA. I think it was just too much for him to get back into that trench once he'd pulled himself out. I finally got him loaded on the truck with the others.
>
> An HMC was wounded in the face and may have lost his eyes in this attack but once again, I just can't come up with a name for him either. As transient as we were (and I guess deep inside not wanting to

get to know everyone so well) I just spaced out the names over time. It wasn't really until this last 3/3 reunion that I was able to put full names with Ayd and Nelson and then looked them up on the wall with Cook and many others I knew.

Lew Cook, I believe, took the full blast of the direct hit of the rocket, as it blew him out of the hole up against the 55 gallon drum atop the shower frame twenty feet away and there was literally nothing left of him from the waist down. I also have to tell you that of the three dead Corpsman I bagged that morning after the attack that Lew Cook was the only one that was recognizable, a real tragedy all the way around.

I was walking wounded with minor shrapnel wounds on my face, hands and arms and was not evacuated. Imagine a 19-year-old HM3 (kid) running the BAS until some help was sent in. Some grunts helped me bag the bodies, fill the rocket crater and slit trench, and get the shower upright but it was mighty lonely there for some time. Have to admit it still haunts me at times. I was the only one left, not medevaced.

I was so emotionally traumatized after that attack on Dong Ha I could hardly function for days. I recall a small but well stocked refrigerator, which was our beer locker. It had a padlock on it, but whoever had the key was now dead or evacuated. I remember so well because after the attack on the BAS I forced the lock and tried my best to dispose of the inventory all by myself. No one there to stop me, I was alone and in charge.

May 23, 1967

Dear Louise,

I'm back in Ca Lu again. I sure wish I could have stayed in Japan. I really had a blast there.

I flew back to Da Nang the same way I left, on a Pan American Boeing 707. We got into Da Nang in the morning and I decided to spend the night there, so I could go to the PX. During the night VC rockets hit it Dong Ha and one of them landed right in the corpsmen's area killing 3 and seriously injuring the rest of the others that were in the hole. My senior corpsman was one of the one dead. That really shook me up. He was a real good guy and he was married.

Oh well! Enough of the gory details of around here. I have enclosed some more pictures I took. Some are of here and the rest are in Japan.

I really had some good dreams about you while I was in Japan. I dreamed we were out on the Beach at Hayama (the one I used to go to all the time) just walking along the road, and then up on a real high grassy hill. We could see all over the place, but no one could see us and it's a good thing they didn't, because you completely raped me. I tried to hold you back, but I had to give in. So here we were on this hill doing it. Like I say, no one could see us the grass was real high. I sure miss you and love you even more. I wish you could have been in Japan with me. We could have had so much fun together.

So you got some of the tapes, good.

You wanted to know when I'm going home. As close as I can figure, it will be sometime in the first part of December.

What is psychedelic music? I like all the people you mentioned and I really like Bob Dylan and Bill Cosby.

I can't wait until we're married. I love you so much. Only 29 more weeks and I should be home.

I am enclosing a couple of dimes I got in Japan for the milk bottle.

Well I guess that's it for now. I sure do love you and I can't wait until you are my wife. It will be so wonderful. Wow! Total ecstasy. Bye for now from your future husband.

Love always,
Russ

PS I love you

Chapter 45

Rat Catcher

ONE MORNING BACK at Ca Lu, a Marine was waiting to catch the convoy back to Dong Ha. His tour of duty was ending, and he decided to catch up on his sleep while he waited in the Third Platoon area. He was startled from his sleep by something moving across his body. He opened his eyes to see what it was and saw a snake's body on his chest. He jumped up and made a grab for its head. It turned out to be a young python about six feet long. He walked out of his bunker carrying the snake and delivered it to his platoon commander's bunker. Several other Marines took the snake into custody. The platoon commander then told them to pack the snake up to the company commander's bunker and present it to Captain Ripley. Word quickly spread around the camp. We gathered around, and those with cameras took pictures of the reptile.

After everyone had taken pictures of their buddies holding the snake, someone suggested killing it. Captain Ripley intervened on the snake's behalf by saying the snake was only hunting the rats in the bunkers and would do no harm and was not poisonous. So instead of killing it, the snake was put into a sandbag and went out with the next patrol where it was released out on the patrol route away from the camp.

June 3, 1967

Dear Louise,

I got your package the other day, thanks a lot. You asked me what I wanted, well, some Fizzies would be good, candy also.

I am now assistant senior corpsman in the company. That means I don't run as many patrols and ambushes. The only time I go out is when we don't have enough corpsmen here. I have moved into the bunker with the senior corpsman and have a lot better living area. The guy I work for is really great. He says I am the only other corpsman he can trust around here to get things done.

We got some new guys in the other day (corpsmen that is). One of them is a complete idiot. He doesn't know a thing and the only way I can describe him is stupid. They say Marines are supposed to be stupid, but this guy makes even the dumbest Marine look like a genius.

We've had quite a bit of malaria going around here lately. There have been over 60 cases in the last 3 months in our battalion and most of them have been in the last few weeks. You don't have worry about me getting malaria though. Mosquitoes won't even bite me. Even when everyone is getting eaten up by them. I don't even get a bite. I don't even have to use mosquito repellent. I guess they don't like me.

I've enclosed some pictures of me and also one of our Captain with our mascot for "Ripley's Raiders" a baby python. That's just a baby, so you can imagine what it will be when it grows up, size-wise that is.

The picture with me in the helmet with the pistol and hypodermic syringe is just goofing off. Do I still look skinny in the pictures?

I was talking to my senior corpsman the other day about us and he says we should get married when I get back and that way we can get started easier because things are cheaper in the service than on the outside. What do you think? I'm still thinking on the idea. I sure do love you.

I always think of you. I wish we were married and were together right now. We could make mad, passionate love to each other. That sure turns me on just thinking about it. I want so much to be with you always, to make you the happiest person in the world. I need you so much I can't even describe it.

You mentioned the shirt I was wearing in that picture of me in my uniform. I borrowed it, but now the guy I got it from is dead, so it's mine. It fits me perfectly, tailored and everything. I've almost been promised 2nd class in August by my senior corpsman, so I wont have to change the stripes on it. On the test I took in February, I passed it, but they had a high cutting score and only a few made it. That's because they gave it to so many guys and they only needed a few more.

My mom knows all about our plans. So don't think she doesn't. She's real happy for us she says.

Well, I guess that's it for now. Bye for now. I'll be thinking of you, as always. I love you more than anything in the world. I can't live without you.

Love always
Russ

PS I love you

One of the civilian interaction projects that we worked on at Ca Lu was to establish a health clinic for the many villages in the valley where they could seek medical attention. The local people provided the labor to build it. The frame was made of poles lashed together with vines. Once the frame was in place, the entire building was thatched with grass. The plan was for corpsmen to screen the patients, and periodically the battalion surgeon would visit to see the more involved cases.

I received several more letters from Mariko after I got back to Ca Lu. Though I liked her very much, I anticipated that our relationship might eventually interfere with the one with my round-eye fiancée back home. Several weeks later, I had one of my buddies write a letter to her. He said in his letter that I had given him instructions that if anything happened to me, I had made him promise to inform Mariko. He told her that I had been killed in a firefight while saving the lives of several Marines.

On the sixth of June, I received orders to report back to the Battalion Aid Station at Payable for reassignment to that facility. My time as a line grunt had come to an end after five months. I would no longer have to go on patrol or ambush. I quickly packed all my gear and the next day caught the convoy back to Payable at the Rockpile.

Chapter 46

Battalion Aid Station Forward

THE CONVOY ARRIVED back at Payable and turned off the highway into the parking area between supply and the BAS. I took my gear and walked over to the BAS and checked in. The path leading up to the entryway to the BAS was now paved with baseball-sized rocks to reduce the mud and dirt tracked into the bunker. Inside the screen door was a Styrofoam ice chest originally used to transport units of blood where the beer and soda were kept cold. I was told that the first beer was free, but after that, beer and soda required ten cents in the coffee can that resided next to the ice chest. The money was used to purchase replacements when we ran low. Ice came in on the convoy from Cam Lo. After finishing my free beer, I was given a bunker fifty feet to the north of the BAS to live in. The bunker was crudely built, and the roof leaked when it rained. It was about seven feet square and had a canvas cot to put my air mattress on. The bunker smelled like something had died, probably a rat rotting somewhere between the sandbags. There was a small gas generator just outside the BAS and a GI can with an immersion burner to heat water. The generator not only provided electricity and lights to the BAS, but also had lines running to the corpsmen's bunkers to run a light bulb.

From the time I joined 3/3, there was always an ever-present rumor that the next month we would be going back afloat. The previous year, 3/3 had been sent to Okinawa from Da Nang and came back to Vietnam via ship several months later. When they arrived off the coast, helicopters flew them from the ship into Dong Ha. It was always rumored that we would soon be relocated back aboard ship. This never happened during my tour or during the remainder of the time until 1969 when 3/3 was transferred out of Vietnam service.

June 7, 1967

Dear Louise,
Just a short letter to let you know about my change of address, my address should now be:
Russell J Jewett HM3 6825474
H&S Co. BAS (Fwd)
3/3
FPO
San Francisco, Calif. 96602
The reason for this is because the other day, yesterday as a matter of fact, the senior corpsman came in with a message that I was to report to battalion aid station with all my gear, my replacement was on his way. So now I just sit around all day in the BAS and take care of the guys who come in sick. I will never go on another patrol or ambush again, but I can still go on operation. As I said before we are probably going to Okinawa next month, so I'm not sweating it.

I sure wish I were going home now. I want to see you so bad. Next time I go to Dong Ha I think I'll call you. They have a radio station that has contact with one in California and the only phone bill you have to pay is from the stateside station to Fort Bragg phone bill. It would cost about as much as calling from San Francisco. I love you so much. You're all I live for. You are my life.

I just glanced on the shelf of medicines sitting here by me and saw a box or two of prepared formula for babies! What the heck are we going to use that for? We don't deal with the local people here, because there is none. Maybe it's for us. It says on the box "closest formula to natural mothers' milk"! I think I'll try some and see what it taste like sometime.

Well bye for now. I miss you more than ever.

Love always
Russ

PS I love you

Life was a bit more relaxed at the Battalion Aid Station. The staff was made up of twelve to fourteen hospital corpsmen and the battalion surgeon. The duty crew would start the generator and immersion burner when they awoke at 0600 so that we had electricity and hot water to wash and shave. After we cleaned up, we walked down to the chow tent for breakfast. After breakfast, we prepared for 0800 sick call. The Marines started showing up outside our door shortly before

0800. They would sit around on the low sandbag wall lining the path into the bunker. Each one was brought in, examined, and logged into the sick bay. The diagnosis and treatment were also recorded. Usually we saw the Marines from the line companies first. They were sicker because all the routine cuts and scratches in the line companies were handled by the line corpsmen. We either treated them or arranged for them to be sent back to the rear BAS in Dong Ha for more care. The doctor examined those who were sick enough to be beyond our expertise. We then saw the cuts and scratches on the H&S Company Marines after the line companies were taken care of.

Some of the corpsmen had the job of supervising camp sanitation work parties burning the containers of waste from the heads. The members of these details were usually lower-ranking Marines chosen by their platoon sergeants for some disciplinary action and sent to us as laborers. They were referred to as shit birds. The corpsman's job was to make sure these guys did their jobs properly and didn't goof off too much in the process.

Other corpsmen did mess tent and kitchen inspections. They usually came back to the BAS with some baked goods or snacks as gratuity from the head cook for pointing out discrepancies without reporting them to his officer in charge. We treated them well, and they treated us well.

After completing the morning duties at around 1000, we took a break to drink coffee, drink soda, eat what had come in from the kitchen, and play a hand or two of poker. At noon, lunch was served at the mess tent. After lunch, we went about miscellaneous tasks such as bunker repairs, filling sandbags to reinforce the bunker, or other tasks around the BAS. Every day, field day was held on the sick bay. The floors were swept every day and the floor oiled once a week. All shelving was cleaned and medications restocked. The generator was also refueled. The Marines in supply delivered several five-gallon cans of fuel each day from the fuel dump. We also got our drinking water on a daily basis. They would load them on a mule and drive it up to us. Any C rations or other nonroutine items we wanted, we would have to call them on the landline and order them. At around 1600, we would knock off work and have cocktail hour, which involved drinking a beer or two. We then headed for the shower and got clean utilities on to prepare for supper. At 1800, we went to the mess tent to eat supper. After supper, we returned and went to our bunkers to write letters or read, or we hung around outside the BAS talking. At dusk, the generator was started and the lights turned on inside the BAS and the light trap tarps lowered inside the door. Then we would enter the BAS and play poker until around 2300. Then, with the exception of those who were on duty, we would retire to our bunkers for the night. The doctor and the duty corpsman slept in the BAS. The HM2s and the HM3s all took turns rotating BAS duty at night.

We got news about the Military Affiliate Radio System (MARS) service in Dong Ha. MARS provided telephone patches to allow overseas servicemen to contact their families at home. The plan was that eventually we would be able to call home right from the BAS at the Rockpile. The only cost was if the call from the MARS station receiving the patch required a toll or long-distance call to the recipient.

One morning, a few days after I arrived, our doctor at the BAS (a fill-in for the regular doctor, who was out on an operation with the battalion at the time I arrived) asked if I wanted to accompany him back to Ca Lu to hold MedCAP at the new clinic that had recently been completed. In mid-June, Captain John Ripley and Dai Uy Quan presided over a ribbon-cutting ceremony held to officially open the clinic for use. It was named the Ayd Station after HM2 Jacques Ayd who had been involved with the project, before he was killed in the rocket attack back in Dong Ha on May 18.

The Ayd Station was a thatched building constructed by the Montagnards of the area next to the perimeter of Ca Lu. We went out and spent the day examining and treating the people who showed up. When we finally finished, it was too late to head back to the Rockpile, so we decided to spend the night. We had supper at the chow tent and then tried to sleep in a bunker in Third Platoon's area down near the 175 mm cannon, which was full of rats that scurried around all night. I remembered that this was the bunker that the young python visited several weeks before. We decided to sleep on the top of the bunker for the night. The next day, we joined the convoy back to the Rockpile.

A week later, several of the corpsmen (Longo was one) who were on operation near the DMZ with the battalion surgeon were evacuated to Dong Ha with heat exhaustion. Longo had put booze in his canteen instead of water and had only one canteen he was using for water. When it got hot and they were short of water supply, he suffered with heat exhaustion. I was told I would be going out the next day to take his place. All replacements were required to carry needed resupply items when going into the operation location. I packed my pack with C rations for three days and filled both my canteens with water. The supply mule drove up with ten mortar rounds, five for each of us going back out. Each round weighed fifteen pounds, and I strapped them to the outside of my pack. That evening, I took a landline call from the radioman in the battalion command post. The battalion surgeon had called and said he did not need us because they were returning soon. I called up supply and had the mortar rounds taken back to the ammo dump.

June 14, 1967

Dear Louise,

Happy Birthday sweet 17. I remember your last couple of birthdays. Your 14th I came to your house then we went to the show. Your 15th I was in Japan. Your 16th I called you from Japan. Now this year I am supposed to go out on an operation. I've been on standby now since yesterday in case they need me out there. Today two of the corpsmen were heat casualties, they had to be medevaced, so I am supposed to go out tomorrow. How's that for a birthday present? But maybe we (me and another guy) won't go we haven't gotten any word from the doctor yet.

I received 5 letters from you yesterday, sure was glad to hear from you. That was the first mail I've received since I've been back here at Battalion Aid Station.

Guess what, I just got a phone call and they said that the Doctor radioed in and said he wouldn't need us out there. So how's that for a birthday present.

June 17, 1967

Dear Louise,

Here it is a couple of days later. I just got a letter from you. I sure would like to see you in your nightgown. I can just imagine what you look like, wow!

Things are pretty slow around here, everyone is out on operation and we aren't doing much. This is the first time I've missed an operation since I've been over here.

Right now it's about 100 degrees and it doesn't even bother me. I guess by this time I'm used to it.

Here are some more pictures for you. They were taken out at Ca Lu

You asked if I am near Camp Carroll, I'm about 3-4 miles down the road from it going west on highway nine. As a matter of fact highway 9 runs right down the center of our area.

These letters have no closing because I was not as lonely at the BAS. There were things to do, and evenings were taken up playing poker and drinking beer. The conclusion of this letter is included in the next chapter.

Chapter 47

Malaria

FROM THE TIME I received orders to Vietnam, I was required to take a pill every Sunday to prevent contracting malaria. Chloroquine primaquine are big orange pills effective only against vivax and ovale, two of the three types of malaria encountered in our area. Falciparum malaria, the one most prevalent in the area near the DMZ, had no prophylaxis, so that is the type of malaria our Marines were contracting. I have a natural immunity to mosquitoes, so I was one of the lucky ones who did not get bitten. Mosquitoes were more of an annoyance to me. I hated them buzzing in swarms around my head. The end of May when the mosquitoes were more prevalent, we were issued head nets, which made it easier on ambush. I could still hear them buzzing, but at least they weren't crawling on my face.

Another way to avoid malaria was to discourage the mosquito from biting. Small plastic bottles of mosquito repellent were issued. Like any other insect repellent, it was not always effective. It also presented a problem while on ambush. Due to the smell, the enemy could detect a squad of Marines wearing mosquito repellent. Needless to say, it often didn't get used.

A protozoan that lives in the anopheles mosquito's salivary glands causes malaria. When the mosquito bites, it injects its saliva into the wound. The protozoa then find their ways to red blood cells and burrow inside. Once inside, they continue to grow and multiply, eventually bursting the cell wall. The protozoa then infest other red blood cells, and the process is repeated every few days. When enough red blood cells are infected and burst simultaneously, the body reacts by running a fever.

Symptoms of malaria include fever, shivering, joint pain, vomiting, and convulsions. There may also be the feeling of tingling in the skin. Malaria is cyclical in occurrence of sudden coldness followed by tremors and then fever and sweating lasting four to six hours, occurring every three days for falciparum and every two days for vivax.

There was a rumor among the Marines that if you came down with malaria, you would be court-martialed for not taking your weekly malaria pill. If you contracted malaria, it was proof that you had not been taking your pill as ordered. No one bothered to tell them that there was no prevention for falciparum malaria. Marines were reluctant to report their symptoms until they were very sick for fear of disciplinary action against them. The results were more advanced, and subsequently more severe cases when they finally had to seek treatment.

During the warmer months of May, June, July, August, and September, Marines were dropping like flies from malaria. At the BAS, we would get them in with fevers so high (105) that it required us to immerse them in the stream to cool them off. The shady area under the bridge became our Malaria Ward. We laid the patients on stretchers and submerged them up to their neck with only their heads above water and put a wet towel over their head to cool the brain. The other forms of malaria can be treated as outpatients, but falciparum malaria requires hospitalization. We called in medevac helicopters to get them back to Delta Med in Dong Ha. From there they usually went out to the hospital ship *Repose*.

Another one of our jobs at the BAS was to fumigate the bunkers with DDT periodically. When most of the battalion was out on operation, we took this opportunity to visit each bunker and dust them with a hand-cranked blower that would distribute the DDT as a fine dust cloud and was able to penetrate the small cracks and crevices between the sandbags. It also stuck to the sweat on your body as you were dusting, requiring a shower immediately after the dusting task was done.

In August, we finally got a microscope for our BAS and could make a definitive diagnosis in the field. Despite our efforts, 296 Marines in 3/3 contracted malaria in 1967.

June 27, 1967

Dear Louise,

Sorry I haven't written in so long, but I just haven't gotten around to it. Thanks for the birthday present in a box, we sure had a good time and the cake was delicious. We ate it in the bunker so, being that I didn't have any flash bulbs I couldn't take any pictures, sorry.

It sounds like you've been having a good time. I sure liked the pictures you sent, especially of you at the wedding. I can't wait until I see you again in those circumstances. My picture book is almost filled up again, so I need another one.

The guys said the same thing about your baby picture as the other time.

I'm really sorry I neglected you in not writing, but I can promise you this. I never neglected you in my mind or my heart. I love you too much to do that. We have had a lot of malaria cases lately.

You ask me what my favorite color is. It's red, but I sure don't want a red bedroom, brown or purple or something like that.

Only 161 days left until I come home. I can't wait. I can hold you and kiss you and be with you. I love you so much.

Well, I can't think of anything else to say so bye for now.

Love always
Russ

PS I love you

Chapter 48

Dr. John Miller

WHEN THE BATTALION came back to the Rockpile from operation, our battalion surgeon returned. Without saying a word to anyone, he entered the BAS, threw his helmet and pack at his bunk from across the room, took off his boots and his shirt, put on his shower shoes, grabbed his towel, and headed for the showers. When he returned, he put on clean utilities. Still not saying a word to anyone in the BAS, he pulled a set of wood chisels and a half-finished wooden carving out from under his bunk and headed out of the BAS. He retired to an area underneath his poncho that he had set up to provide shade. He began furiously carving on his handiwork. After several hours, he came back into the BAS, got a can of beer, and went back out to his shelter. This was my first encounter with Lt. John P. Miller, USN MC.

When Dr. Miller came back into the BAS to get his beer, he interacted with his corpsmen in a surly, sarcastic manner. He did not acknowledge my presence or even inquire as to what had transpired while he was gone.

At about the same time that Dr. Miller came back, several other corpsmen who had been with him out in the field also returned. They were friendlier and joined in a reunion with the guys who had remained back at the BAS. I inquired as to what was going on, and they said not to disturb the doctor as he was trying to decompress from the military operation he had just completed as part of the command group.

As evening approached and it got dark, Dr. Miller came back into the BAS with carving in hand. He had a set of wood carving chisels that he used to work on his carving, a *Playboy* centerfold that he was carving into a statue. He sat down and continued carving. I watched him as he concentrated on his work. His wooden mallet made a tap-tap-tap sound as he worked. He seemed oblivious to all of us as he sculpted his statue. We basically ignored him and continued with our poker game for the next several hours. Finally he stood up and said, "Gentlemen, lights out!" We immediately discontinued our card game and headed for our bunkers.

The next morning, I saw Dr. Miller was sitting under his shelter consisting of a poncho tied to several bushes to shield him from the sun. Under the shelter, he had several chunks of wood that he was working on. I cautiously approached him and introduced myself and then asked him if I could see his handiwork. He was not as surly as the day before and brought out his carving. It was a statue of Miss December, and it was almost complete. He had done an excellent job of recreating the *Playboy* centerfold in mahogany. I suggested that when he had it completed, he allow me to photograph him and his artwork, and he could send it with a letter to *Playboy* magazine with the potential of getting it published in the letters to the editor. He smiled and agreed.

Several days later, he called me over and told me that he had completed the carving. We went outside, and using my Polaroid camera, I took a photo of him with his carving. Several months later, the photo was published along with his letter.

Dr. Miller's motivation for carving the *Playboy* centerfolds was twofold. First it helped him relieve his frustrations with dealing with the Marine Corps officers; and second, when the carving was finished, the project was traded for items he needed at the BAS that were not available through normal supply channels.

Dr. Miller always addressed us as "DOC!" and our last name. He would say, "What do you think about that, DOC! Jewett?" He also insisted that we wear pins signifying our navy petty officer status on our caps instead of the Marine chevrons.

Infections that wouldn't heal were one of the major problems we encountered at sick call. Marines reported presenting scratches and cuts that had become infected. They acquired them by coming in contact with the sawtooth edges of elephant grass as well as an assortment of other lacerations of the skin. Under normal conditions, these would not be a problem, but in the tropical heat and humidity, any scratch tended to get infected. Dr. Miller came up with a plan to cure these infections. He had us mix bacitracin antibacterial ointment with sugar. We would do this in a C ration can and slather it onto the infections with a tongue blade. A sterile dressing would then be applied over it and instructions given to come back the next day for the same treatment. The infections started to heal more rapidly than before. The treatment was working. Dr. Miller referred to his concoction as his magic poultice, which he pronounced "pool-tiss."

We referred to Dr. Miller as Tap-tap or simply Chips when we were talking among ourselves about him. He did occasionally take time out from his carving to give us in-service education on advanced skills we could use in the treatment of casualties such as suturing lacerations or inserting a chest tube to reinflate a collapsed lung.

Dr. Miller and I were never close in the BAS, but in the year of 2002, he and I reconnected on the Internet. We started corresponding via e-mail. He had a medical practice in Alabama and was getting ready to retire. It seems that after coming back to California after Vietnam, he went diving for abalone at Point Arena, California. When he was diving, he and I were only fifty miles apart, and when he realized this, he and I agreed to meet. In May of 2002, he came back to the Mendocino Coast and came by to visit me in the kayak shop where I was working. He brought with him photos of several of his *Playboy* centerfolds and other photos of himself in Vietnam. Dr. John and I have been friends ever since. He visits me at least once a year, usually in September, as the visibility under water is better for harvesting the elusive red abalone.

It was after we started reminiscing about Vietnam that I learned why Dr. Miller was so much of a recluse while in Vietnam. At the time, he was thirty years old, compared to the average age of the corpsmen and Marines of twenty. He grew up in North Idaho and later moved to San Diego, California. He was a graduate of UCLA School of Medicine. He joined the navy shortly afterward. Due to his older age and education, he was more in tune with the reality of the Vietnam War than we were.

Dr. Miller, being naturally outspoken and telling things as they were, found it difficult to interact with the Marine brass. He would frequently let his opinions be known during the battalion staff meetings. He was constantly opposing the unnecessary killing of Marines. At one meeting, he presented a plan suggesting that instead of killing the NVA that we should simply pay them off as they came south across the DMZ. He suggested setting up a tollbooth; but instead of collecting a toll, pay each NVA soldier enough money so that he would go home and raise his family. He felt this plan would be much cheaper than what the United States was spending on the support of all the US troops in Vietnam. The battalion commander let him know that from that point forward, he wanted Dr. Miller to confine his statements to the treatment of the casualties that were anticipated to occur and leave the strategies of winning the war to the Marines and the government. As battalion surgeon, he was at the lower end of the officer's pecking order and was not fond of being told in no certain terms that when they wanted his opinion, they would ask for it.

Chapter 49

Cam Lo MedCAP

MY NEXT JOB at the BAS was going into the city of Cam Lo to perform MedCAP. In June, we treated 565 patients in Cam Lo and Ca Lu. We would get up early and load up the jeep ambulance with the necessary supplies. We would meet up with our security and drive to Camp Carroll to pick up medical supplies from the army to use on the civilians and then head out for Cam Lo

In Cam Lo, we would set up in the marketplace and provide medical assistance to the people living there. Mostly we treated minor cuts and infections. The kids would all crowd around and try to pick your pockets. Several kids tried to distract you, while one of the others would feel your pockets and, from the outside, work the contents up toward the opening of the pocket and then grab it and run. Some were openly hostile toward us. One little boy who was no older than eight or nine kept threatening that he was going to kill us. He would look straight into my eyes and, with a slashing motion across his throat, would sneer, "I *caca-dao* you." The kids loved Band-Aids. They would always want more than the ones you put on their infections. The Marines also would bring care packages of clothes for the village people. Kids were given T-shirts, tennis shoes, and numerous items of clothing. As the day got hotter, we would buy ice-cold Tiger beer from the local merchants. They also had black market Budweiser and Pabst.

One of the functions with MedCAP was intelligence gathering. Marines working with the intelligence section would walk through town and talk to the locals. The things they wanted to know regarded the Vietcong activities as well as any NVA troop movements. Some of the Marines were involved in teaching the kids basic conversation and how to count in English. This made it easier to gather information.

On the outskirts of Cam Lo on the north side of Highway 9 was a fenced refugee relocation camp housing Montagnards. We would visit them also. I felt more at ease with them than with the Vietnamese.

Before we returned to the Rockpile, we stopped by the local icehouse where we purchased blocks of ice that were around six inches by ten inches by three feet long.

On my twenty-first birthday, a bunch of us gathered at Longo's bunker to celebrate my birthday. We had some whiskey to drink that Longo had acquired, and I suggested that we build a club as an alternative to always hanging out in the BAS. It was agreed upon, and over the next several days, we collected empty ammo boxes to salvage the wood.

I built a framework for the walls, and it was starting to shape up. One morning, one of the captains from the command bunker came up and told us that the structure had too high a profile and the colonel sent him up to tell us that it had to be torn down. I asked him if it was the structure or the height that he objected to. He replied that it was the height, as it was taller than the bunker. After he left, we simply dug out the dirt beneath the frame and lowered it into the ground – out of sight, out of mind. It wasn't much, but it was our own space.

One evening, we were sitting in our half-constructed club when the battalion chaplain showed up on his rounds visiting all the bunkers and offering spiritual support to the troops. He was a big man and was a Southern Baptist. He began chatting, and Nick Longo offered him some pineapple juice that we were consuming. No one warned him that it was laced with 180 proof alcohol. The taste was very subtle, so he did not reject the libation. After a cup or so of spirits, the chaplain became jollier, and as he left, he was singing on his way back to his bunker.

July 12, 1967

Dear Louise,

Thanks a lot for all the birthday packages they were sure good.

I've been pretty busy here lately. I've been getting up at 5:30 in the morning and going into Cam Lo on MEDCAP. I really have a blast with people. When we come back we buy ice to keep our soda and beer cold.

Today I was helping the people get water from the well. They really thought that was something, an American helping to get their water. I also was playing a guitar for them.

So far this week I've driven over 500 miles in our jeep between here and Cam Lo and sometimes into Dong Ha.

I've also been working on a club. I got the framework up and the captain came up and said we had to tear it down because the Colonel said it wasn't supposed to be that high above the ground. So to beat that we dug a hole in the ground and put the frame in the hole. When I get finished It will look like a bunker on the outside and a club on the inside.

About now you should be out at camp. I wish I could be with you. We could really have a blast. You and me out in the boonies together. Boy we sure could have fun.

Friday the 14th we are supposed to go out on operation Hickory II up near the DMZ and might even go up into the DMZ. I hope it isn't much.

I was up at Camp JJ Carroll the other day and ran into 4 guys I was stationed with in Japan. They are all with 3rd Battalion 3rd Marines. We had a good reunion talking about the old times. One was one of the guys you met at Camp Pendleton the first day you came there. Remember Frank Zebley. Another was the guy we gave a ride to when we were going to Disneyland. They both said to tell you "hi".

Well I guess that's about it for now. So I guess I better go. Another long day again tomorrow. I sure wish I could come home now. Only 146 days left.

Love always,
Russ

PS I love you

Chapter 50

Nick Longo

HM2 NICOLAS LONGO was from Pennsylvania. He was assigned to BAS 3/3 on June 2 and claimed he was half Italian and half Tunisian. Nick served as an infantryman in the army in Korea. After his army tour was up, Nick joined the navy and became a corpsman. Dr. Miller met Nick when he was with 2/26. When he was transferred to 3/3 on May 5, he requested that Longo be reassigned to 3/3 also.

Nick stood about five foot five and was considerably overweight compared to the rest of us. He was so out of shape that I wondered how he got through FMF training. Nick was a naturally friendly and jolly individual who possessed the rare talent as a "cumshaw artist," which is a term used in the navy to describe someone who does well in negotiating trade. A cumshaw artist is usually appreciated within a unit for the ability to provide items obtained usually outside normal channels through unofficial means (whether deviously or simply ingeniously). His main job was to find and acquire items needed by Dr. Miller for the BAS.

Dr. Miller would periodically send Nick to Da Nang and Phu Bai after items he needed for the BAS. Longo took with him the wooden statues of the *Playboy* centerfolds carved by Dr. Miller. On one such trip to Da Nang, Nick returned with a portable diesel generator and a refrigerator. We then had electricity in not only the BAS, but lines were run to the corpsmen's bunkers as well. The refrigerator was used in the BAS to preserve our antibiotics, but most of the space inside the fridge was filled with beer and sodas.

On Operation Cimarron, Nick took a canteen full of scotch whiskey. Unfortunately that left him with only one canteen of water. He hadn't been out in the mountains for more than two days when he was medevaced back with heat exhaustion.

On a medical supply run up to Camp Carroll, I accompanied Nick. While there, we visited an army medical unit. Longo told the army medic what we needed. He showed us into the supply tent and accompanied us. Longo took his time locating and retrieving the requested items. It was hot in the tent, and the medic got anxious for us to complete our list so he could return to his cooler bunker. After all our supplies were gathered, we took our time loading them into our jeep ambulance. When we were just about to leave, Longo said there was one more item that we needed and asked the medic if he could help. He told the medic that we were about to reimmunize our entire battalion and we were a bit short on isopropyl alcohol. The medic told Longo to go back into the tent and help himself to one of the five-gallon cans. Longo went into the supply tent and grabbed one of the olive drab cans and placed it in the jeep ambulance. He then thanked the medic, and away we went.

After leaving, I questioned Nick about the battalion immunization, as I was not aware that we were going to have to do it. He replied that there were no such plans, but while in the tent, he had noticed that they had both isopropyl and ethyl alcohol sitting next to each other, and unless the label was actually read, they looked identical. He grabbed a can of the ethyl because we could dilute it with water and drink it. He said that if the medic noticed he had taken ethyl rather than isopropyl, he would have claimed that because they both looked identical, he had inadvertently grabbed the wrong can and would have returned it and brought out the isopropyl.

We returned back to the BAS with not only our supplies, but also a bonus. When diluted with three parts water, one part alcohol, it tasted like vodka, but would not produce the hangover effects caused by vodka. He had cumshawed the equivalent of eighty quarts of vodka. That evening, Nick produced a can of pineapple juice that he had received from the cooks the previous day and mixed us each a "mai tai".

Nick traded alcohol in five-ounce cough syrup bottles. The five ounces when mixed with water became twenty ounces of vodka to the cooks or anyone else that was willing to trade. The cooks kept us supplied with cans of pineapple juice. As an added bonus of this trade agreement, we no longer had to go down to the mess tent for food. We simply picked up our landline telephone and get connected to the mess tent to inquire what was on the menu. If it sounded good, we'd ask him to deliver it to the BAS. If it didn't sound good, we put Longo on the phone, and he would ask to talk to the mess sergeant. When he came to the phone, Longo asked him what else they had in stock. The sergeant would run down what else he had in stock, and Longo would order it up; and half an hour our so later, the cooks would deliver the hot meal in vacuum containers. Longo would then give them a ten-ounce bottle of alcohol to give to the mess sergeant. Occasionally we received an unexpected delivery of a tray of Spam-and-cheese sandwiches, freshly baked cake with frosting, and many other culinary delights whipped up and delivered by the grateful cooks.

Chapter 51

The Long Hot Summer

THE DAYS WERE getting hotter. The daytime temperatures were near 100, and the nighttime lows around 80 degrees. In the afternoon, we had sudden downpours of rain. Ordinarily after a rain, it would have been a bit cooler, but not now. With the humidity running 98 to 100 percent, the rain no longer cooled us. It would rain so hard that we took advantage of the shower, strip down, grab our soap, and stand outside our bunkers and wash then head back into the bunker for a towel and a fresh change of clothes. When it quit raining, we went about our duties as before.

On one of my trips back to Dong Ha, I went to the PX. Not only had the base expanded, but so had the number of items carried by the PX. I purchased a portable radio with AM, FM, and several shortwave bands. Now we had music in the evening. Most of the music was Armed Forces Radio-approved flower power music. We listened to the *Chris Noel Show* at 2000. She played the latest music from the States.

Dr. Miller had HM1 Chris West obtain a bunch of brass navy petty officer pins to replace the Marine Corps rank pins we were using on our hats. Because of his ongoing personal conflict with the command group's philosophy, he was trying to remind us that we were really sailors and not Marines. We all secretly hoped that enemy snipers wouldn't mistake our brass eagle and chevrons as an officer's insignia.

One day, HM1 Russell King arrived at the BAS. Russ was a short likeable guy. He claimed that he was a nephew of Martin Luther King. He brought a small acoustic guitar with him, so he and I hit it off right away, and he taught me some chords. Russ told me he had volunteered for Vietnam as a musician for navy special services and had been stationed in Da Nang where his job as a musician and singer was to entertain the troops. King had been reassigned to 3/3 on June 6, and though he was not happy about his new assignment, he was able to tolerate working in Dong Ha in the rear BAS. Russ and the chief corpsman at the BAS did not see eye-to-eye on many things, and he was reassigned to BAS forward. Russ was not at all happy with his new assignment and spent a great deal of time writing letters to his congressman and other influential people he knew back in the States. One day, Russ showed me a letter he received from Sammy Davis Jr. Russ stayed with us about three weeks before he was reassigned back to Da Nang.

One day I was bored and needed something to occupy my time, so I decided to take the top off my bunker and remodel it. There was something rotten smelling in it. When I removed the sandbags, I found that the smell was coming from a decomposing rat. Once I had the roof off, I used my E-tool to dig out and smooth the walls. After deepening the hole slightly, I placed wooden shipping pallets into the hole and improved the drainage so that when it rained, the hole wouldn't fill with water. After I had that done, I took ammo boxes and removed the boards from the bottom, but left the lids and sides intact. Then I installed screens made from wire mesh we used on the heads for insect control to keep the bugs and other critters out. I installed the boxes so that the hinged lid was on the inside. This allowed me to keep the bunker ventilated during the day and easily shut it up at night for light suppression. I then replaced the timbers that supported the roof and replaced the sandbags. I also took this opportunity to add a couple more layers of sandbags for extra protection. I then erected an antenna for my radio made of copper wire on a long bamboo pole and ran the wire back into my bunker where I was able to plug it into an external antenna jack on the side of my radio. I could now pick up stations from Thailand that played more rock and roll than Armed Forces Radio. One of the first songs I heard was the new Beatles tune "All You Need Is Love."

On the fourteenth of July, we participated as a blocking force for Operation Hickory II. Our battalion along with several others went north to Helicopter Valley. Longo and King were among the few corpsmen we left back at the BAS. Again all the corpsmen who went were loaded down with mortar rounds. We spent several days out in the valley just south of the DMZ. We had no contact and then went back to the Rockpile.

A week later on the twenty-first, an NVA battalion had dug in along Highway 9 south of Ca Lu between the rivers. A platoon of Mike Company was making a sweep on Highway 9. As they rounded a bend in the road, they observed an NVA up on the bank relieving his bladder. A firefight ensued producing three dead and forty-three wounded. After securing the area, it was searched, and over five hundred fighting holes were discovered along two thousand meters of the road. The preparation for a major ambush on the Rough Rider to Khe Sanh by a regimental-size force of NVA had been disrupted. They found mines alongside the road, which were to be placed in the roadway. The NVA had also put many trip wire booby traps on the riverside where troops from the convoy would have gone to take cover.

Due to the close proximity of the NVA to our area, a directive came out that we were to destroy all personal correspondences. This was ordered because if the NVA overran us, there would be no personal information for the NVA to use as propaganda. I had all my letters from home in a waterproof bag. I spent the whole day reading each one before I burnt it. It really hurt to see all those letters go up in flames. I sent my collection of photos home. If I had been thinking, I should have sent the letters back home also.

July 24, 1967

Dear Louise,

We got back off the operation OK we went though the valley just this side of the DMZ. We are the first battalion to go through there with making any contact with the enemy.

The other day (the 21st) a platoon from Mike Company was ambushed by an NVA battalion. So far there have been 11 killed and 45 wounded. That is out in Ca Lu where we were. One of the villages out there helped the NVA. One of the villages I used to MEDCAP in. How's that for a shock.

I built me a new hooch. The one I was living in was old and had dead rats in the sandbag roof so I tore it down and rebuilt it. Now it is livable.

The other day I had to do something that really made me feel bad. I had to take every letter I had and burn them. I spent the whole day reading each one before I burnt them. It really hurt to see your letters go up in flames.

I am sending back the pictures of the wedding like you asked me to though I sure would like to keep all the ones of you. I'm sending some pictures of me.

You said that I forgot your birthday, well I didn't I just found the letter I wrote on your birthday. So here it is in this envelope. Like they say better late than never. Sorry, but I never finished it before it got misplaced.

Sometime we'll have to go swimming together in our underwear or if we prefer in nothing that would be fun wouldn't it?

Got your package today. The cookies were as fresh as if they were baked a couple of hours ago. The guys here said you're a great cook. Russ King said he's going to come and visit us when he gets back in the states just to get some of your good food.

You know good and well that if we spent the night together we wouldn't do "nothing". We'd be busy all night doing "something" right?

I sure do love you. I am always planning for our life when we get married next year. You know something? Only 131 more days until I come home. Just a little over 4 months. I want to kiss you, feel you next to me, go places with you, do things with you. My whole life is centered around you. I love you more than I can say in writing or words, only my heart can tell you. What else can I say except you mean everything to me?

Well I guess I better go now. Until the next letter, Bye.

Love always
Your future husband

PS I love you

    The command found it necessary to employ civilian labor from the village of Cam Lo to help out on the work details. These included clearing grass and brush from the fields of fire, filling sandbags for building and reinforcing our bunkers. They also were hired to construct a mess hall and chapel with the materials available in the traditional Vietnamese style with wooden frames lashed together. Once the frame was completed, they used elephant grass to create thatched roof and sides. The workers were paid with salad oil and bulgur as their wages.

    One morning, I was supposed to have the day off. I was sitting in my bunker when West came and told me that I was going out with a work detail that Madfes had originally been assigned to go on. I was not very happy about it. The work party was a bunch of Montagnards who were building the chapel and a chow hall. They needed to harvest elephant grass to thatch the roofs and sides of the building, the same style of buildings as the Ayd Station at Ca Lu. It was already getting hot when I climbed onto the back of a truck with a bunch of Montagnards and the Marines who were providing security for them. There was also a group of Montagnards that had hitched a ride from Cam Lo and were returning to their village. We sat on the crowded truck with their pigs, chickens, and kids. One of the kids had gotten carsick and vomited on the bed of the truck, and it didn't smell too good. The longer we sat, the madder I became. Finally we got underway.

    When we reached the site where the harvest was to occur, the work party left the trucks and continued on their way into the field, and the harvest began. I found a shade tree and sat down under it. I no sooner got settled than the Marines started hollering, "Corpsman up." I jumped up and ran out to where I was being summoned only to find that one of the Montagnards had lacerated his finger. It was then that I realized that I had grabbed Madfes's Unit One, and he had no Band-Aids in it, so I had to improvise one. I was furious that the Marines had called me for such a trivial item. I told them that next time, they bring the patient to me. I returned to my shade tree and looked through the Unit One to inventory what I had to work with in case I was needed again. It was then I found a bottle of assorted pills including green and black capsules I recognized as Librium, a mild tranquilizer. I had never taken one before, but decided that I needed to adjust my attitude, so I took one. It wasn't long before all my anger disappeared, and the rest of the day went very smoothly

During the month of August, a total of 793 Vietnamese were employed, earning a gallon of salad oil or one sack of bulgur for every two persons per day. Medical assistance was rendered to 87 men, 177 women, and 584 children during the same time in the form of MedCAP visits to villages in our territorial area of responsibility (TAOR). We also saw an average of 250 people a day in Cam Lo.

Our supplies also were improving. The mess hall was receiving things like steaks, jumbo prawns, fresh milk, and ice cream. These items were being flown in from supply ships off the coast. We also received several sets of new jungle utilities that actually fit us well. We now also had regular laundry service. Now that we had several sets of utilities, we could send our laundry back to Cam Lo where the locals laundered and pressed them and sent them back the next day. A mobile dental unit came out to our area, and for several days, they worked on our Marines' teeth. A mobile PX from Dong Ha visited our base several times a week and brought many of the items available back in the rear at Dong Ha. The most popular items were radios and cameras. Life was becoming much more civilized and tolerable.

Around the middle of August, Richard Banks was due to go back to the States. I met him at the convoy and said good-bye. I told him if he ever went out to the Mendocino Coast, he should look me up in Fort Bragg. The last I saw of him, he was on the truck headed out taking pictures as he left. That was the last time I saw him until 1986 when I got a phone call from the hospital I was employed by in Fort Bragg saying that someone was trying to locate me. Since it was against hospital policy to give out employees' phone numbers, they took the number of where he could be reached. I called him not remembering who he was, and we made arrangements to meet. He was located in the town of Mendocino and was renting a house for his weekend fishing trip with his family. As soon as I saw him, I recognized who he was. We visited for several hours, and he gave me his address in Truckee, California, where he was working as a fishing guide on Lake Tahoe. Several weeks later, I had an opportunity to visit him. He was in the process of moving to another address, but invited me to sit and look through his pictures. He had copies of all the photos he had taken while in Vietnam. Looking through them, I found two pictures he had taken of me. One was on the top of the Razorback and the other was in Ca Lu. As he rode off on convoy, he shot a photo of me telling him good-bye. When Banks moved, I lost contact with him, and it wasn't until 2006 at a 3/3 reunion in Colorado Springs that we got back together again.

When I had time, I continued improving my bunker. I used boards from disassembled ammo boxes to put down a solid floor over the pallets. I obtained some large pieces of cardboard that were wrapped around some supplies received at supply. I used the cardboard to cover the dirt walls. I simply placed the cardboard against the dirt and drove nails at slight angles to hold it in place. On the twelfth of August, I was promoted to hospital corpsman second class. My new job was to manage our medical supply tent. This entailed making an accurate inventory of what we had on hand and ordering additional supplies as needed from the rear BAS in Dong Ha. The senior corpsmen from the line companies now drew their supplies from me. Other than that, my duties didn't change.

August 12, 1967

Dear Louise,

Well it sure sounds like you're having a good time on your trip. I sure wish I could be with you guys. I just got the letter that you wrote in Chicago. You sure have been moving around lately. I really enjoy the pictures you sent, especially the ones of you. I like the bathing suit you are wearing. You know that is the first full-length shot of you in your bathing suit that you have ever sent me. WOW. You sure are looking good.

Nothing much is happening around here, except that I am working in supply. I am in charge of all the medical supplies in the forward area. All the companies draw their supplies from me.

I made 2nd class so now I am equal in rank to a sergeant.

I've really been working on my hooch lately. I put a good roof on it, a wooden floor; cardboard on the walls to make it look more like a house instead of a hole. Built shelves, cupboards, bunk beds out of stretchers, even electricity. We now have a diesel generator out here that supplies the whole battalion with electricity. We also have a laundry service. The gooks come here every day and pick up our laundry, take it back to Dong Ha where they have washing machines and dryer, plus an iron, so we get clean pressed clothes out here now.

Oh, they cut the tour of duty over here to 12 months so I will leave here not later than 14 Nov, which means I have about 93 more days until I come home! How's that for a surprise? 93 more days!! Yea!! Wow!! I'm getting short.

I got a letter from my mom the other day, which made me a little perturbed. She was hinting around by using my brother as an example. She said "Steve went on a blind date last night to the show. He's getting acquainted with lots of girls – playing the field. Guess he and Joan broke up before going to JC. He can see things in a different light now that he's standing back and looking. Sometimes you can't see from such close quarters." Now if she isn't hinting something there I don't know what she is doing. But I know what I want. Do you? That's right YOU for the rest of my life. I can't wait until I'm back at home again with you, to feel you next to me, so just be with you.

I've enclosed some pictures I had taken plus some I took just now. The old ones are out at Ca Lu and the new ones are of my bunker. The new shots of me are self-portraits, so please excuse the wrinkled neck and cut off chin.

Well I guess that's it for now. Have a good trip. Be good and bye for now.

Love always
Russ

PS I love you

Chapter 52

Ambush on Highway 9

AUGUST 21 STARTED out like any other day. We went about our assignments as usual. Around 1100, a convoy of three trucks was sent from our position on their daily supply run to Ca Lu. At around 1300, we got word that the convoy had been ambushed about nine kilometers down the road. One vehicle made it to Ca Lu about three kilometers away, but the others were pinned down at the ambush site. At 1312, Captain Ripley and a squad from Lima Company with two Dusters were sent out to the ambush site as a reactionary force.

We went to full alert in case the NVA decided to also hit our position. We headed for our bunkers and put on our helmets and flak jackets. The BAS was probably the safest bunker, but since we had no casualties, we went to our individual bunkers so one round wouldn't take out the whole medical team.

We sat in our bunkers and waited listening to the sounds of the distant battle. After about fifteen minutes, we heard explosions. I stepped out of my bunker to see what was going on. Artillery rounds from Camp Carroll were hitting on the hills to the southwest of our position. Twenty minutes later, the artillery stopped firing and the jets came in, and I observed the air strikes out on the hillside overlooking Highway 9. I went back into the bunker and brought out my camera and photographed the napalm exploding on the hillside. I then noticed that several of the other corpsmen were doing the same thing. After the air strikes ceased, the artillery again started up and pounded the area. Shortly afterward, we were informed we needed to start preparing for casualties from the fight. A CH-34 helicopter came in with a load of litters. I had my camera and stood on the top of the BAS and photographed the other corpsmen unloading the thirty stretchers. As soon as it was unloaded, the helicopter flew off. It would be the last one we saw that day.

About four kilometers out, at 1330, the reactionary force came under heavy mortar, automatic weapons, and small arms fire. Captain Ripley and his radioman Corporal Jesse Torres were on the lead Duster and were able to jump off before an RPG hit it. Both Dusters took direct hits from RPGs and were put out of commission, killing most of the army crewmembers. Captain Ripley and Corporal Torres made a run for cover, and Torres was hit in the helmet by a round as they sprinted. The round did not penetrate his helmet, but knocked it off his head and shook him up quite a bit. Being that they had been out ahead on the lead Duster, they were surrounded by NVA and isolated some distance from the rest of Lima Company, who were also pinned down. Hearing that their skipper was surrounded, another platoon from Lima responded, but were taken under fire at 1335. The remaining platoon from Lima, who had been on a patrol when the action started, had been called back in to the command post. At 1400, they went out and linked up with the previous platoon and were immediately engaged also.

Shortly thereafter, a convoy arrived from the rear area. The command group had called for reinforcements from Dong Ha. The transport vehicles arrived carrying the rear area "Pogues" (rear echelon personnel – clerks, cooks, motor transport drivers, and mechanics.) In the Marine Corps, regardless of your job description, every person is first and foremost a rifleman. Arriving with them was HM3 Charles Klemanski, one of our BAS corpsmen previously attached to Kilo Company, who had relocated back to Dong Ha a week or so earlier. While the officers met to discuss strategy, the Marines on the trucks made a head call and then loaded back on the vehicles. At 1536, with two tanks, they departed Payable for the fight. In Ca Lu, a platoon from Mike Company with two Dusters and two tanks were sent to the ambush site from the south. They linked up and evacuated the casualties back to Ca Lu and then returned to help mop up the ambush site.

At 1713, we started receiving casualties via ground transportation from Lima and Kilo. One of the trucks brought back Corporal Les Johnson and his radioman LCpl. Gerry Baryo, both from my former unit Second Platoon. LBJ had been hit in the hand, which was grossly mangled. Baryo was hit in the lower leg. I checked them over, and they seemed to be in no major distress and put them on the convoy returning to Dong Ha. Finally we processed all the casualties and got them on their way to Dong Ha. The final count was KIA 5, WIA 43, DOW 1, and MIA 1.

 Killed
   PFC Romero-De-Jesus, Benjamin 0311 Lima
   PFC Baca, Isidro 0351 Mike

Died of Wounds
    PFC Leyva, Frank M. 0311 Mike

Wounded
    Cpl. Bryant, Raymond C. 2531 H&S
    HN Madfes, Kenneth H. 8404 H&S
    LCpl. Morales, Victor M. 2531 H&S
    1st Lt. Sexton, Merlyn A. 0302 H&S

    HN Eisenhauer, Jackie L. 8404 India

    Cpl. Salmon, Ronald 0141 Kilo
    Cpl. Smith, Noble B. 0311 Kilo
    Cpl. Williams, Frank E. 0311 Kilo

    PFC Anderson, Jerry A. 0311 Lima
    PFC Baryo, Gerald T. 0311 Lima
    Cpl. Hebert, Joseph R. 0311 Lima
    Cpl. Holcombe, Richard W. Jr. 0311 Lima
    GySgt. Holt, Robert N. 0369 Lima
    Cpl. Hunter, Robert I. Jr. 0331 Lima
    Cpl. Johnson, Leslie B. 0311 Lima
    LCpl. Kerlin, Stanley E. 0311 Lima
    Cpl. Langdon, Michael E. 0311 Lima
    PFC Lloyd, Eddie 0311 Lima
    LCpl. Mackey, Clifford E. 2511 Lima
    Cpl. Mohedano, Jack Jr. 0311 Lima
    Cpl. Orloski, Michael E. 0311 Lima
    Sgt. Price, Alfred E. 0311 Lima

    LCpl. Brooks, Edward H. 0311 Mike
    PFC Devivo, Neil 0311 Mike
    LCpl. Hoskie, Raymond R. 0331 Mike
    Cpl. Outlaw, Elliot H. Jr. 0311 Mike
    PFC Rice, Terrance J. 0311 Mike
    PFC Richardson, Charles M. 0311 Mike
    LCpl. Smith, Paul K. Jr. 0311 Mike
    LCpl. Tressa, Edward J. 0311 Mike

Missing/Captured
    LCpl. Budd, Leonard R. Charlie Ninth Motor Transport

The next day, a patrol from 1/9 was sent out to the site and verified not only the bodies, but also found where they had been bivouacked before the ambush. A fresh dug tunnel was discovered adjacent to the highway near where Captain Ripley and Torres had been pinned down. When they entered, they found it to be seventy-five meters long. They counted 109 NVA bodies adjacent to the highway. A spotter plane flew over the area and reported seeing 305 more NVA bodies farther up on the hillside where they had been killed by air strikes and artillery. The NVA were well-equipped and had used a .50-caliber machine gun, 57 mm recoilless rifles, RPG-2 rockets, mortars, automatic and semiautomatic small arms, as well as grenades. The size of the enemy force was estimated at five hundred, and 414 bodies were counted.

August 24, 1967

Dear Louise,

I just got your package of cheese, boy they sure good.

The other day we had a little excitement around here. The truck convoy going to Ca Lu was ambushed between here and Ca Lu. Lima Company went out and got pinned down right away so they sent Mike Company out and they killed over 48 gooks. The air strikes killed at least 40 and artillery got quite a few of them. All together there were 5 killed and 35 wounded on our side. They killed at least 109 gooks and possibly over 300 more. We stayed back here to handle all the casualties. I got some real good action shots with my camera.

Only 81 more days until I go home. It is getting closer everyday. I can't wait.

I got word the other day I will go back to Dong Ha next month. That means I can't go on any more operations (darn). It really breaks my heart. As if I wanted to go on any more.

Right now I'm sitting here listening to a program, which is playing what they call the "mod" sounds, but they are just regular music of the last couple years.

What are the top tunes in the states now and who are they by? You know that I have to get with what's happening. Sort of a pre-states briefing.

I can't wait until I come home. I want to be with you more than anything in the world. I love you with all my heart and soul. Just to hold you and kiss you and be with you is all I want and all I dream of. I love you so much and I always will until the end of time.

Well it's just about chow time so I'll close for now. I love you more than I can say. You mean everything to me. Bye for now.

Love always
Russ

PS I love you

For the next ten days, there were sporadic reports of small groups of enemy activity around our area, but nothing major occurred. More enemy bodies were found. One of the bodies located on a ridgeline above the highway had map cases and field glasses.

On August 31 at around 0200, about one hundred rounds of mortars hit in the vicinity of a Montagnard village between Ca Lu and the Highway 9 ambush site. The village sent a runner to Ca Lu in the morning to assist with the wounded. At 1000, when they arrived, they found seven villagers wounded and three killed. Two of them required additional medical help. Two Dusters, a PC, and our jeep ambulance went out to the village to bring them back to the BAS. HM2 Nick Longo drove the jeep ambulance, and HN Ken Madfes went along to assist. At 1050 on the return trip, the convoy was ambushed at three different locations. The NVA fired a rocket, mortars, and small arms fire. The convoy was not stopped, but two of the Duster's crew, four Marines, and Madfes received minor wounds in the process. We treated all the casualties and medevaced the Montagnards who were in stable condition to Delta Med in Dong Ha for further treatment.

Chapter 53

Another Ambush on Highway 9

THINGS WENT PRETTY much routine for the next several weeks. No major problems with the convoys. We were still fat and happy in the BAS. I was informed that I was to be reassigned to the rear BAS in Dong Ha sometime in September.

Shortly after midnight on September 6, I was awakened to the sound of mortars exploding. I waited in my bunker until the barrage was over and then headed for the BAS. An estimated forty to sixty rounds hit outside our lines just to the south of our position and did not cause any damage or casualties. This was the first time in nine months that the area was shelled. Since there was nothing for me to do, I went back to my bunker and went to sleep.

The next morning, we went about our normal routine until around noon when a squad guarding the first bridge to the south of Payable reported seeing three enemies near their position to the southeast. We were put on full alert again.

On the morning of September 7, a convoy of nine vehicles stopped at our position. They unloaded cargo and continued on their way to Ca Lu. Shortly after leaving our position, they reported receiving small arms fire and automatic weapons fire. The NVA had ambushed the convoy again about five kilometers south. A command group and two platoons from India Company responded from Payable and headed for the ambush site using mortars to help assault the site. HM1 Chris West and a couple of other corpsmen went out with the command group.

Meanwhile, several vehicles from the convoy were able to extricate themselves and were able to proceed. They arrived at Ca Lu with only three casualties on board thirty-five minutes after the ambush started. India Company on their way to the ambush site found sixty fighting holes, some abandoned mortar rounds, mortar fuses, and some cans of rations next to Highway 9 about two kilometers from the ambush site. According to the calculations, this was the mortar site on the sixth. Around 1100, India advanced to one kilometer from the stranded convoy when they received incoming small arms fire from the hillside to the west of Highway 9. The NVA had set up a two-part ambush, one unit to ambush the convoy and another unit to ambush the reactionary force. Back at Payable, we went on full alert and awaited more casualties.

On the thirtieth of August, Lima Company had been assigned to help provide security at Camp Carroll located seven kilometers to the east of Payable. With the need to reinforce India Company, Lima was called back again to provide reinforcements for India Company. They arrived by truck and proceeded to relieve India at the ambush site at 1300. The fighting continued for the next four hours.

At around 1700, a company from 1/9 was brought in to Payable, and they proceeded south on Highway 9 to provide a rear guard. All 3/3 units returned to Payable. When they finally had returned, they discovered that one of their men, Sgt. Lee Jarvis, was unaccounted for. I had been out on many patrols with Jarvis when he was one of the squad leaders in Third Platoon of Lima Company.

The ambush on August 21 resulted in one man missing in action, presumably captured. For several days after the ambush, we sent out search parties into the area where Jarvis was last seen. Several days later, his body was found in a draw back up in the mountains some distance from the ambush site. It appeared as if he had been tortured before being killed. His body was bloated from the heat, but the most significant injury was the finger on which he wore his Marine Corps ring had been chopped off and the ring taken as a prize by his captors. We wrapped his body in a poncho and brought him back to the Rockpile, where he was shipped back to Dong Ha to graves registration. The body count on the enemy on this action was 187 killed.

Casualties on 9/7
   Killed
      Sgt. Jarvis, Lee B. 0311 Lima
      2nd Lt. John, Noel A. 0302 India
      LCpl. Lawson, Albert C. 0311 Lima
      Sgt. Sibilly, John R. 0351 India
      LCpl. White, Tony Lee V. 2511 H&S

Wounded
> H&S Company
> Sgt. Chrisman, Timothy R. 0331
> HM3 Cook, William H. 8404
> Maj. Harrington, Michael H. 0302
> Cpl. Perry, Paul R. 2533
> HM1 West, Pierce C. 8404
>
> India Company
> LCpl. Arpin, Edward E. 0311
> Cpl. Ashbaugh, Jack W. 0311
> LCpl. Baires, Marcial A. 0311
> Cpl. Beach, Tommy W. 0331
> Cpl. Benson, Howard L. 0311
> Cpl. Burgess, Craig M. 0351
> Cpl. Cook, James C. 0311
> HM3 Freeland, Bruce W. 8404
> Cpl. Gent, Robert A. 0311
> Sgt. Gorey, John J. 0311
> Cpl. Green, James B. 0351
> Cpl. Jaqua, Michael D. 0351
> LCpl. Krawczyk, Jerry L. 0311
> Cpl. Lawler, Thomas R. 0351
> Cpl. Leblanc, Ross A. 0311
> LCpl. Mason, Perry G. 0331
> LCpl. McBride, David M. 0311
> PFC Muehlenberg, Clifford J. 0351
> LCpl. Palmer, Roger D. 0331
> PFC Pommier, James R. 0331
> LCpl. Reed, Sylvester 0311
> Cpl. Reiss, Robert A. 2531
> HM3 Remington, Michael L. 8404
> PFC Richardson, Thomas G. 0311
> Cpl. Smith, Rodney O. 0351
> Pvt. Thornton, William P. 3531
> PFC Torres, Jose Jr. 0311
> LCpl. Yobb, Louis N. 0351
>
> Kilo Company
> HM2 Muskett, Thomas J. 8404

Lima Company
PFC Abrew, William B. 0311
PFC Bostick, Norvel D. 0351
PFC Cruz, John 0311
Cpl. Darden, Ronald C. 0351
Cpl. Delong, Stephen J. 0311
Cpl. Detora, Ernest F. 0311
PFC Dorsey, John H. 0311
Sgt. Hanna, James P. 0331
SSgt. Martin, Michael P. 0369
LCpl. McCormick, Kenneth C. 0311
PFC Salazar, Jimmy R. 0311
Cpl. Sexton, Jack K. 3531
Cpl. Swoyer, Richard A. 0311
PFC Wackerly, James T. 0311
PFC Wolfe, Eric H. J. 0311

Mike Company
LCpl. Hudson, John H. 0351

5 Sep 67

Dear Louie,

Not much has been happening around here lately, except our ambulance got shot at between here and Ca Lu the other day. They were coming back from Ca Lu and got ambushed. The "Arab" and a Jewish kid from San Francisco were in it. The Arab was driving and hit the gas pedal and was doing 55 MPH all the way back here, which is the fastest I've ever seen the ambulance go. The Jew was lying on the floor. I don't see how the Arab was driving because he was on the floor also.

Right now I'm listening to "All you need is love" by the Beatles. I think that is a real cool song. It is number 1 on armed forces Viet Nam radio station. We get some good programs of pop music, every night they have the Chris Noel show from 8 to 9 o'clock and one from 9 to 10, then from 9-12 on Saturday and Sunday. Also the station in Bangkok plays good music all Sunday mornings. Right now "Words" by the monkeys is on I like it also.

Only 69 days until I come home, the magic number. I'm getting short! I should leave Viet Nam on the 13th or 14th of November.

I guess school has started already. Just think what we'll be doing next year at this time. Just think only a year to go. Also next year at this time I will have been out of the Navy for 3 days.

They just played "96 tears" that sure brings a lot of memories back. That was number 1 when I left the states.

I got your package the other day, the Playboy, soup and goodies. They sure were good.

Today sure was hot. This morning it was about 120 degrees and humid as heck up to about 11:30 then it poured down rain all the rest of the day until about 5 o'clock.

We had a bar-b-que the other day, we got some steaks from the mess hall and a bunch of other goodies and had charcoal broiled steaks. They were delicious!

Now they are playing "Summer in the City". It seems like just yesterday when that song came out when I was in Japan.

Here's a picture of me yesterday. I was goofing off again. Would you believe I now have a waist measurement of between 26 and 27 inches?

It's 10 o'clock PM now, which should make it about 7 AM where you are at home and you should be getting up about now.

They (or should I say the Arab) are trying to swing it so we can call home right from here at the Rockpile area. He knows the main switchboard operator at Camp JJ Carroll who has a line to a short wave station in Dong Ha, which has contact with stations (short wave) in the states, which can call your home in the states. Since we have connections with JJ Carroll we might be able to swing it. No promises, but you may get a phone call from little old me here at the Rockpile, How 'bout that?

I sure do miss you. I can't wait until we are together again. I love you so much. Just think, in a little more than a year we will be together forever and never have to be apart again. Things will be great then.

I am going to try to get a job at the new medical center across the street from our house. I'm going to write and find out from the California State board of nursing and see if I can get a license to work in the medical field.

Well I guess that's about it for now. Bye. I miss you

Love always,
Russ

PS I love you, 69 more days.

Chapter 54

BAS Rear

WHEN I GOT back to Dong Ha, the combat base had expanded considerably since my last visit. Though they still lived in tents, there were some strong backs. Our BAS was a tent with a wooden floor surrounded with several layers of sandbags stacked about thirty inches tall. The tent was a general-purpose tent about thirty-two feet long and sixteen feet wide. The ridge of the tent was about ten feet high and the sides about five feet. The east side of the tent was open for ventilation, held up by six-foot tent stakes at a forty-five-degree angle. The flap stayed that way even during the night. Light security was not an issue now in Dong Ha. There was an entrance at each end. The tent contained several desks, shelves of medical supplies, medical records of the battalion's personnel, and three beds for sleeping. There were actually mattresses on the beds. At the north end of the tent was sick bay, where the corpsmen sat and examined and treated Marines reporting in to sick call. The senior chief slept in the southeast end of the tent next to his desk, which had a landline telephone. Another corpsman slept on a cot in the southwest corner of the tent. In the center of the tent was a desk with a typewriter. The tent also had a large ice chest that was kept well stocked with soda and beer.

Outside the BAS tent to the south was a massive bunker that had been built after the disastrous attack on May 18. The bunker was about five feet tall, but the interior was ground level and was only tall enough for crawling on your belly. Massive wooden beams supported the many layers of sandbags.

To the south of the bunker was the medical supply tent. Corpsmen also slept in there. Next to the supply tent was a large reinforced wooden box that was kept padlocked at all times. This was the vault that kept the BAS beer and soda supply. The box was large enough to hold over eighty cases of beer and an equal volume of soda.

Behind the supply tent was our shower, consisting of a fifty-five-gallon barrel sitting on top of a wooden frame. The barrel was filled with water daily and warmed by the sun.

I was assigned the bunk in the sick bay end of the tent. I was also put in charge of sick call, which meant that I slept where I worked.

The routine in Dong Ha was more mundane than out at the Rockpile. At 0530, the chief would get up, go take a shower, and then hold reveille at 0630. The job of the corpsman that slept in the south end of the tent was then to go and wake up everyone else. This usually consisted of distributing a can of beer to each corpsman as they were awakened. After arising and having our "eye opener," we would go to the chow hall and get breakfast and bring it back to the BAS.

The galley was in a strong back enclosed in screens with a screen door at each end. The line formed at the west door, and as you walked through the line, the cooks would dish out the food, and you then exited through the east door. There was a chow tent, but I seldom ate there because the BAS was located just to the east of it.

Sick call commenced at 0800 and ran to 1000. During that time, I would see the Marines who had medical complaints. I can never recall a doctor seeing these patients. If the medical problems were serious enough, I would send them over to Delta Medical Battalion, located near the northeast end of the airstrip. At 1000, I would process all incoming and outgoing personnel. Incoming personnel would bring in their medical record and shot card. Required immunizations consisted of plague, yellow fever, typhoid, typhus, flu, hepatitis, and tetanus and were given at six-month intervals, except for hepatitis, which was given every three months. I would ensure that their immunizations were up to date, and if they weren't, I would ensure that they received any that were out-of-date. I would then make the appropriate entry in their medical record. It also required that I make a notation on their shot card and affix the official rubber stamp on the card. I would then file their medical records in our file bins. I did the same for all personnel going on R&R. Processing out was the same thing.

After lunch, I would get a driver from motor transport to take me over to Delta Med to deliver specimens to the lab, collect lab reports, check on any of our personnel in treatment, and check with graves registration. On the way back, we would often stop at the PX and at the post office to pick up sacks of mail for our battalion and return to our area.

After returning, I would give the graves registration reports to one of the other corpsmen, and he would type up the official report for the deceased's medical record.

At 1700, we would secure from the workday and take a shower and get cleaned up before going to supper. After supper, we occupied ourselves until it got dark in activities such as throwing KA-BAR knives at a target, sharing scuttlebutt, writing letters, reading, sleeping, or anything else we could find to do. Playing cards was not as prevalent in the rear as it was out forward.

As twilight fell, we gathered at our theater area that was just to the south of our supply tent near a Vietnamese grave monument. The theater consisted of plywood painted white on which the movie was projected. Benches were constructed to seat around one hundred Marines. All the corpsmen had their own folding lounge chairs made of canvas and metal frames, which we brought with us from the BAS because they were more comfortable. After the movie, we returned to the BAS, and it was lights-out at 2300.

Every day was very similar, but each day, the NVA would fire artillery rounds and rockets into the base. Usually they would hit near the airstrip or the ammo dump. When that happened, we would head for the safety of the bunker. Some of the corpsmen had not yet been in the field, and so they would stay in the bunker the entire time during the attack. Those of us who had been in close combat, after discovering that the rounds were hitting on the other side of the base, would often sit outside the bunker and watch where they were hitting. If the rounds started "walking" our way, then we would seek the shelter of the bunker, as the explosions got close to our position.

One day, the chief came to me and told me that we had received a shipment of GG (gamma globulin), which was going to expire before we could use it. Injections were given every three months in an attempt to temporarily boost immunity against hepatitis A. I and a couple of corpsmen were charged with the task of destroying several thousand doses, in glass vials containing around 20 cc of thick fluid the consistency of honey. After several hours' work with some ball-peen hammers, the task was complete.

15 September 1967

Dear Louise,
Well, as you probably can tell already I am in a better area than before. I am now in Dong Ha working at the Rear Battalion Aid Station. It sure is busy around here, from the time I get up till 4PM I am constantly on the go. I don't mind though, it makes the time go faster and that's something I really like.

I received your letter and packages and letter yesterday. Only two of the apples were half rotten. All the other goodies were in good shape. I really enjoyed the pictures they sure looked good. I sure wish I could have been with you.

Next year at this time we will have less than a week to go before we will be together forever. I can't wait until then.

Only 58 more days to go until I can get out of this stinking country. I can't wait.

We have it pretty good around here considering that the gooks harass us every once in a while by throwing a few artillery rounds inside the base perimeter. When that happens we immediately drop what we are doing and make it for the bunkers. Other than that we live pretty good.

I sure do miss you. Just a little less than two months and I'll be back home again. I can't wait to come home to you again. Then we can be together again for a while. I don't know how long I will be home this time, but I think it will be for about a month this time. I want to keep some leave on my record so if I get stationed in California I can come home to take you to the prom. How would you like that?

Well I guess I better close now the lights are about to go out so bye for now.

Love always
Russ

PS *I love you*

Chapter 55

New Orders

THE NVA BEGAN a major assault on the firebase located at Con Thien (which was northwest of Dong Ha). The base was defended by 3/9. The area consisted of three hills rising about 475 feet above the surrounding flatland. The name meant "hill of the angels," based on the number of lives that were lost defending the hills through Vietnam's history, but the Marines referred to it as the Meat Grinder. The NVA started shelling them ruthlessly with artillery, mortars, and rockets. It was reported that one day there were over 1,200 incoming rounds. They were being hit so hard that units were only spending a month at a time up there. Third Battalion Third Marines was scheduled to go up there, but there was no definite date.

Our life continued with its routine, and we drank a lot of beer. We would start in the morning and continue all day. Though we consumed the beer all day, none of us drank enough to get drunk.

One day, the sky got dark, and it started pouring down rain. There was not much activity, so we just stayed in the BAS except for when we had to venture out for chow or going to Delta Med. When the rain stopped four days later, all the bunkers that had been constructed below ground level were flooded and were pumped out. Our bunker, being at ground level, was fairly dry.

Our tent was another story, it was leaking to the extent that when the rain stopped, we had to replace it with a new one. The last time I had put up a tent this size was at Camp Pendleton. After removing the leaky one, it took us about an hour to erect the new one. We were handicapped by the fact that all the furniture remained inside and we had to work without moving it.

On one of the artillery barrages, the ammo dump over near the airstrip was hit again. It had been hit much worse at the beginning of the month just before I came in from the Rockpile. I was sitting outside our bunker when it was hit and took some photos of the black smoke rising into the air.

It was time to start thinking about where I wanted to go for my next duty station. The chief provided me with the usual form to request three choices of duty station locations. All three of my choices were in Japan.

22 Sep 67

Dear Louise,

I just got your letter today. I also got a letter from my mom saying that she meant only in Steve's case when she made that statement. So there is nothing in it. She said she likes you and your family a lot and there should be no reason for ill feelings. I just thought I'd mention that because she was pretty upset thinking that you didn't like them.

Things are pretty much the same around here. "Charlie" throws a couple of artillery rounds every once in a while, but they all hit on the other side of the base from us.

We just put up a new tent today because when the rain came the other day we got wet inside our old one. It weighed over 250 pounds, but the 6 of us finally got it up.

I mention the rain in the last paragraph well the other day it rained heavy for 4 days and we all thought the monsoons were upon us, but the sun came out and dried everything up again.

I sure do miss you and I look forward to being with you again. I can't wait, only 52 more days. I should be finding out where I'm going in a week or so. I love you more than anything in this world. When I get home we will be one big happy family again, I know.

I dream all kinds of weird dreams now days. The other night I dreamed we were out somewhere and the gooks started mortaring us and things like that. They are really weird! Well I guess that's it for now – See you in 52 days

Love always
Russ

PS *I love you*

One day the chief called me to his desk and handed me my new duty station assignment. I was reassigned to the Naval Air Station Key West, Florida, and was due to report in on December 20. I was somewhat disappointed because it was in the States. My main reason for joining the navy was to travel. I reconciled it by realizing that I would be closer to Cuba than Miami, so it would be like being stationed in the Caribbean. I also received thirty days of leave before I had to report.

3 Oct 67

Dear Louise

I received your letter yesterday, sure was good to hear from you. Sounds like you are having a blast in school.

Things are pretty much the same around here. I am still as busy as heck. I start out the day by trying to get up at reveille at 6:30. Then I shave and brush my teeth and once in a while take a shower. Then I go to breakfast. By this time it is 8 o'clock so I start sick call. When I get finished with sick call I start giving shots and checking people out who are going home. This lasts until approximately 10:30. After this I file all my health records and papers. This takes until about 11 o'clock. At this time I drive over to D Company, 3rd Medical Battalion to get information on patients I sent over the day before for my morning report. I goof around over there for a while and come back and type out my morning report. After that I can go to the PX or what ever I want. Usually about 5 PM I get some patients in from out by the Rockpile and I have to take them to D Med then I come back and eat chow and then sit around and talk or listen to the radio or something like that.

Only 28 days at the least to go and 41 at the most. Most likely it will be closer to 41, but who knows I may get home in time for the homecoming dance. I sure hope so.

I really can't wait to be with you again. It will be everything I dreamed of I know.

I don't know whether I told you or not but I got my orders in the other day and they said that I will be going to Naval Air Station, Key West, Florida. How 'bout that for a good place?

Well, I guess that's it for now. Oh, I received the cookies and pudding the other day they sure were good. I also made spaghetti last night that my mom sent me. Everyone wanted some of it. It was good if I do say so myself. Well bye for now.

Love Always
Russ

PS I love you

One day the chief brought in a catalog from the navy exchange. It was the first time that I had ever seen a mail-order service by the exchange. I spent time browsing through all the items they had for sale and decided to order some stereo equipment. I had purchased a Sony reel-to-reel stereo tape player when I was stationed in Yokosuka. I ordered a Sansui tuner/amplifier and a reverb unit and had them shipped to my parents' house.

I started getting letters from home that were indicating that the two women that were most important to me, my mom and Louise, were in conflict. I received letters from both sides stating their case. The contents of these letters were tearing down the utopia that I imagined my life would be upon returning home after Vietnam. This did not make me happy at all.

6 Oct 67

Dear Louise

I received your letter today and my first impression was to sit right down and chew you and my mom out by letter. But I think I have thought things out enough to look at this sensibly.

You people have got to stop your stupid imaginations and sit down and look at things how they really are. I will try to give you a little background.

You say that my mom hasn't been too friendly lately, well have you stopped to look at yourselves? My mom says she feels the same way you guys are thinking and she mentioned that night at your house. She says things seem "touchy" and she doesn't know what our family has done to make you mad, so the conversation that night was very limited for fear of offending one and other. The same thing when you got to our house.

When your mom went to our house another day Susie had more than a cold, she had a temperature and had possible flu. It has always been a policy at our house that if someone has a communicable disease that no outsiders come in – to protect the visitor form getting sick also. Same thing if the visitor is sick.

As far as inviting people to our house I can never remember when we have ever invited friends (good ones) to our house. As I remember it whenever any dropped in we were glad to see them unless we were doing something special or going someplace.

I really wish you people would stop your trivial worries and suspicions of each other. I am having a hard enough time trying to fight this war over here without having to worry about the "private" war at home, which involves me more than this one.

Your side of the story is exactly like my mom's story, both of you say you want to get along, but the other one hates you. What's with you people anyhow? I'm glad you brought this to my attention, you should have told me sooner.

Another thing! You don't have to invite my family over every weekend or however often you do. I know from experience that they like to stay home a lot. They don't like to go out that much. Another thing, they don't like to be checked-up on.

Why can't you people (by that I mean both our families) get along? Why? This is really bugging me. I am going to write and say the same things to my mom that I said to you.

And another thing you're sure lucky I calmed down before I started writing this letter. I just re-read it and I'd hate to read it if I was mad. Well, enough of that! I hope you aren't mad, but I had to say something.

Things have been pretty quiet around here lately. They still plan to move 3/3 to Con Thien

I just found this picture of me out by the Rockpile. I was washing my clothes at the time.

The other day I ordered some more stuff for my tape recorder. They were an AM-FM stereo tuner-amplifier and a reverberation unit that can be set up to have an echo effect delay of 3 seconds. They cost me almost $200, but I think they are worth it.

Those kids at school don't know how good they have it. We weren't allowed to do half of the things that you guys get to do.

Only 38 more days to go, that's a month and 8 days at the most.

That's about it for now, but I want you to know that whatever happens I will always love you. We have our own future to look forward to and I don't want anything to spoil it and I know nothing will. I just couldn't live without you with me.

Well, bye for now.

Love always,
Russ

PS I love you.

Chapter 56

Smoking Pot

ONE EVENING WHILE killing time throwing knives at a target, one of the corpsmen showed me a marijuana cigarette he had purchased and asked me if I wanted to share it with him. Up to this time, I had not observed or heard of anyone in our unit smoking dope. Since I had never tried pot before and the rumors about all the kids back in California getting high and I would soon be going back and we were in the relative safety of Dong Ha, I agreed to try it. We went into the supply tent, and he lit it up and took a hit, held his breath, and passed the joint to me. I mimicked his actions and immediately responded with a harsh cough, so I took a less-deep hit and held it in. After passing the roach back and forth until it was consumed, we headed back out to join the rest of the guys. It was approaching 2000, and so the *Chris Noel Show* was coming on Armed Forces Radio Network. It was one of the only programs available on AFRN that played current rock music popular in the States, limited to tunes not considered subversive. I retired to my bunk to listen. After lying there for a while, I realized that I was visualizing the music. I was stoned and hallucinating, so I just enjoyed it until I drifted off to sleep.

A week or so later, the same guy offered me again to share a joint with him. I again tried it and went back into my bunk to listen to the radio. To my disappointment, the high that I got that evening was nowhere near what I experienced the time previously, so that was the last time I smoked pot while in

Vietnam. Evidently the first stuff I had tried had been laced with something else that caused the hallucinations.

One day, I was walking through the compound when I saw one of the guys I had been with in Second Platoon out at the Rockpile. I ran up to him and greeted him. He was with several other black Marines and acted as if he barely knew me. Feeling a bit confused about his response, I went on my way. Several hours later, he came looking for me at the BAS and was his usual friendly self. I asked him what was up with the attitude earlier. He apologized for his aloofness. He then explained that the other blacks he was with were advocates of black power and racist. While in Dong Ha, they expected all the other blacks to avoid socializing with anyone other than blacks. He said they would beat those who did not conform. This was the first time I had seen this level of racism, black or white, since I had joined the navy. After that, I avoided any contact with the groups of blacks that were hanging out together.

Shortly thereafter was the first time I heard of "fragging" occurring. In one of the other units in Dong Ha, there was a racial confrontation between a black enlisted man and a white officer. That night while the officer was sleeping, a black Marine pulled the pin on a fragmentation grenade and rolled it into the officer's tent.

Another first I encountered while in Dong Ha was "passing the helmet." Usually this occurred when a higher-ranking individual was consistently making bad decisions that were causing other Marines to be killed unnecessarily. Passing the helmet consisted of taking up a collection of cash among members of the unit until a significant sum existed. An assassin would do the deed during the confusion of battle appearing as if the death was caused by the enemy.

Chapter 57

China Beach

DURING THE FIRST week of October, one of the biggest disasters to hit the BAS was about to occur. We were getting low on beer. The chief went into a panic. He got on the phone and called Da Nang, and after a few hours, he had come up with a plan. He was sending me down to Da Nang after plague vaccine, and HN Steve Rozzi was to accompany me. We were to spend three days at China Beach on "in country R&R." While there, we were to purchase and make arrangements for shipping a pallet (eighty cases) of beer back to Dong Ha. Buying that quantity of beer required the authorization of an officer, so the chief presented me with a document with the appropriate signature giving me authority to buy the beer. He also gave me a set of instructions on whom to contact to make the arrangements to transport the purchase to the docks and ship via boat to Dong Ha. In the BAS, we had a beer fund that we contributed to; each time we took a beer from the fridge, we put twenty cents into the kitty. A pallet of beer would yield $384, so there was more than enough money to purchase another pallet. I never did inquire as to what the extra money was being spent on since the chief was in charge of the fund.

Almost as an afterthought, the plague vaccine was mentioned. The only beer the chief did not like was Ballantine's. Premium beer (Budweiser, Miller, etc.) cost $216.00 per pallet or $2.70 a case or $0.11 per can. Nonpremium beer (Ballantine's, Flagstaff, etc.) was $192.00 per pallet or $2.40 a case or $0.10 per can.

When the day came to go to Da Nang, I received a copy of the following orders authorizing my trip to China Beach as "temporary additional duty."

Headquarters
3d Battalion, 3d Marines
3d Marine Division (Rein) FMF
FPO San Francisco, California 96602

1/JGG/mdg
1710
9 October 1967
From: Commanding Officer
To: Corporal Joseph ABRAMOVICH 2278306 USMC

Subj: Temporary additional duty; group orders to

Ref: (a) MARCORMAN para 1320
(b) MARCORPERMAN para 5153
(c) CG, 3d MarDiv ltr 37/WHD/jat over 1710 of 1Aug67

1. Pursuant to the authority contained in references (a), (b), and (c) you are authorized to take charge of the below listed Marines, proceed to China Beach on or about 9 October 1967 for temporary additional duty for a period of about (3) three days in connection with R&R.

LCPL W.W. ST HILAIRE 2181946   LCPL J.L. HASCUP 2254302
LCPL C.R. COURVILLE 2251872   LCPL M.A. SAYLOR 2278962
HM2 R.J. JEWETT 6825474   HN S.J. ROZZI B103472
PFC J.B. WARRENBURG 2247864   LCPL G.E. GREEN 2271000

2. Upon arrival you will report to the Officer-in-Charge, China Beach.
3. Upon completion of the above temporary duty, you will return with your group to your present station and resume your regular duties.
4. These orders are issued with the understanding that no expense to the government for travel or per diem is authorized in the execution of these orders. If you so not desire to execute these orders without expense to the government for travel and/or per diem, this authorization is revoked and you will return these orders to this Headquarters.
5. You will have sufficient funds in your possession to defray your expenses while at China Beach.

J.G. GILMORE
By direction

On the ninth of October, a motor transport driver gave Rozzi and me a ride to the airstrip, where we met Corporal Abramovich and the others and boarded a C-130 to Da Nang. Once in Da Nang, we proceeded to hitchhike across the base over to the China Beach R&R Center. Upon arrival, we reported to the officer-in-charge. He checked our orders to verify that we were authorized to stay there. He then directed his staff to issue ID cards, which authorized us come and go from the R&R area while assigned there. His staff also issued us each a blanket and sheets and directed us to the barracks. They gave each one of us a copy of the instructions and information defining the rules. We then checked our weapons into the armory.

China Beach was like paradise. It was located on the ocean with a long curving beach of white sand. Pine trees grew along the edge of the beach under which were a number of picnic benches and tables. Behind the trees were the barracks and outdoor movie amphitheater. There was also a large cafeteria substituting for a chow hall. The staff consisted of Vietnamese workers who cooked the meals and waited the tables and bus staff who cleared and cleaned, all supervised by military staff. Meals could be either short-order or off the menu. The menu consisted of many stateside-type meals and desserts and beverages. The facility also had a large PX so that items such as tobacco products, soft drinks, candy, snacks, and cans of beer could be purchased and taken out and consumed while on the beach or in the barracks. There was also a beer hall for those who preferred to drink in a bar setting. There was also an air-conditioned library and lounge containing books, magazines, and other reading material, as well as a television room. On the beach were volleyball nets, a lifeguard station, and surfboard rentals for those who wanted to join the China Beach Surf Club.

The next day, we set out to take care of business before enjoying China Beach. Leaving the base, we picked up our weapons and boarded the military bus line. We traveled first to Naval Support Activity hospital, near Marble Mountains. There we made contact with HMC Horsley with whom we made arrangements for the truck to transport the pallet of beer from the air force PX to the dock. Before leaving, as instructed, we dropped by the optometry lab and made arrangements for the plague vaccine, which we would pick up and hand carry on our way back north.

We then tried to find Lieutenant Commander Miller at the White Elephant in the city of Da Nang, but were unsuccessful. We then headed for Camp Tien Sha and found LCU-1624, a landing craft that was large enough to travel the ocean, but small enough to get up the Cua Viet River at Dong Ha. After making contact with Chief Hall, we went back to NSA hospital and got the truck with a driver. From there it was off to the air force PX to buy the beer. When we reached the PX, the guard at the gate was not going to let us in because our uniforms were faded, not laundered or starched, and our boots were not polished. We informed him we were not from Da Nang, but Dong Ha. His response was, "Where's that?" We explained it was where the real war was being fought. He still was not going to let us in, so

I asked to see the duty officer. When he came, I explained the situation, and the duty officer gave us a pass to allow us inside. We stood out like sore thumbs and received stares from the squared-away air force customers. I purchased a pallet of Budweiser, and then we proceeded to the storage area. I presented the person in charge of the warehouse the receipt from the PX and waited as the beer was loaded on the truck. We then drove to Camp Tien Sha and waited until it was safely loaded aboard the boat. We then released the driver and vehicle and went back to China Beach via the streets of Da Nang where we did a little sightseeing. We took a water taxi across the canal and then a bus back to China Beach.

The next two days we spent bodysurfing; swimming; playing volleyball; sunbathing; playing nickel slot machines; eating hamburgers, fries, milk shakes; and of course, drinking beer. In the evening, we would eat barbecued steaks, salad, pie, and ice cream. At sundown, we would watch movies, eat popcorn, and drink more beer. The ocean water was the warmest I had ever been in. It was like a Caribbean holiday. The people who worked there had it so easy they didn't know there was a war going on.

One morning I was on the beach, and Ken Madfes was there. He was down from Phu Bai. He had been reassigned from the area out at the Rockpile to Alpha Med Battalion. He had been granted TAD to attend Yom Kippur in Da Nang. Jewish personnel were granted special privileges to attend their religious holidays. This created a wave of anti-Semitism among some of the Marines who were from the South. They argued that no one received special leave for being Protestant or Catholic.

One morning I visited the USO. A young Vietnamese artist was carving a desk plaque out of a piece of stone from Marble Mountains. I decided to get one. It started out as a triangular piece of marble eleven and a half inches long that had black enamel paint on all sides. The artist asked me what I wanted carved on it. I told him on the left end I wanted the Marine Corps emblem, on the right end I wanted the Hospital Corps caduceus, and in the center I wanted my name and USN Hospital Corps. On the back, I wanted a Vietnamese dragon. After sectioning off about two-inch areas at each end, he scratched out the outline of the letters in the seven-inch center section of the plaque. He then chipped out the areas between the letters, leaving the black paint raised slightly above the gray marble. After completing the center section, he then freehanded, chipping out the end designs. After that was done, he carved floral and vine designs around the letters in the center section. When he was finished, he turned the marble to the backside and, freehanded, carved out the dragon design. The whole process took him about an hour.

At the end of three days, we had to head back to Dong Ha. After checking out of China Beach, we dropped by the NSA hospital and picked up the plague vaccine before heading for the airport. We then returned to the Marine transient facility by bus and caught a C-130 back to Dong Ha. Flight time was only about half an hour.

October 17, 1967

Dear Louise,

Sorry I haven't written in a while, but I was on R&R again. This time it was in country at Da Nang. I was at a place called "China Beach". We went swimming every day all day, body surfing and all kinds of fun. When we got hungry or thirsty we'd walk across the beach to the cafeteria and get a hamburger and milk shake or coke. At night we would watch a floorshow (there were always live bands) then there was a movie afterwards. I saw movies like "Hotel", "Double Trouble" with Elvis, and a couple of others. All together I was down there for 6 days.

But not all the trip was pleasure part of it was business. I had to buy a pallet (80 cases) of beer to ship back to Dong Ha for the BAS. So I ran all over Da Nang trying to get it. I had arrangements to have a truck to take the bear to the boat. Well as it turned out I couldn't get the beer because the PX was out, so I had to come back empty handed.

Boy, those guys in Da Nang really have it hard, especially the ones at China Beach. They run around in their bathing suits all day, they don't have a chow hall so they have to eat in the cafeteria.

Well that's it for now. Only 27 more days to go.

Love Always,
Russ

PS: I love you

Chapter 58

Getting Short

A WEEK OR so later, we got word that LCU-1624 had landed at a site in the Cua Viet River, and near dusk we went with a jeep and trailer to pick up our beer. They loaded the pallet of beer in the trailer with a forklift, and under cover of darkness and blackout, we headed back to base. When we arrived back in our area after midnight, all the corpsmen formed a line from the trailer to the storage crate and passed the beer case by case to the storage crate. Once it was complete, the locks were placed back on the crate. We had to keep the beer secret because if the Marines knew about it, we would be subject to rip-offs. This was especially important because at that time, we were the only ones with beer in the entire Dong Ha area. Due to the shipment of higher-priority items such as ammunition to restock the ammo dumps and other items needed to supply the battles to the north, Dong Ha had become dry. We had an armed guard posted on our supply box at all times.

We would also keep the BAS forward supplied with beer. To get it out to them, we used the metal boxes designed for shipping medical supplies. They were large enough to accommodate a case of beer each. We sealed the boxes with two metal bands for security and placed them on the convoy going out to the Rockpile. When we had corpsmen up at Con Thien, we used the same technique, included along with a shipment of plasma and other medical supplies.

One morning, the chief called me to his desk and presented me with a Purple Heart. He told me that it was for the time I got hit by shrapnel in my left arm back in March when I was with Lima. He said somehow it got lost in the shuffle, that's why it took so long. Even though I felt good about receiving it, I remembered all the guys who had been killed and received the same reward. It seemed to have very little significance to me.

A day or so later, I called home on the MARS station located near our area. This process required that the person speaking would have to say "over" after each sentence. This would allow the ham radio operators involved to key their handsets to allow the transmission between stations. Evidently Mom could hear me pretty well, but I only heard my mom one time; the rest of the time, the radio operator had to tell me what she was saying.

On the twenty-second, Steve Rozzi and I were up at one of the places across base when the NVA started firing artillery into Dong Ha. Steve, who hadn't yet had any combat experience, jumped into the ditch, and I stood on the jeep to see where the rounds were hitting. Altogether there were about thirty rounds that came in. The same day, we got hit about once each hour, two to three rounds each time.

That evening, we were sitting around when a round landed nearer to us than they had all day. We all made it to the bunker. When no more rounds came in after the first one, I said the heck with it and started walking back to the tent. I was just about in the tent when I heard two more rounds being shot off and crawled back into the bunker. Just as I got there, the rounds hit real close, even closer than before. When we went back into the tent after it was over, I found a piece of shrapnel on the floor that weighed two pounds that had come through the roof of our new tent.

A couple of days later, we drove over to Delta Med in the evening and were watching the movie *Incredible Journey* in their movie theater. Several times they stopped the movie due to incoming artillery fire, and we headed for the bunker. After several events of incoming rounds, we never did see the end of the movie because one of the shells exploded close enough that it threw dirt on the tin roof of the theater. It was time to go back to our own position across the base where it was safer.

I created a short-timer's calendar, a picture divided up into numbered sections that represented the number of days left. Each day I would mark out the number of days that I had remaining.

27 Oct 67

Dear Louie,

How are you doing? I called home the other night, evidently they could hear me pretty well, but I only heard my mom one time, the rest of the time the radio operator had to tell me what she was saying.

The other day the 22nd to be exact, one of the guys and I were up at one of the places across base when the gooks started firing artillery into Dong Ha. The guy I was with jumped into the ditch and I stood on the jeep to see where they were hitting. All together there were about 30 rounds that came in. The same day we got hit about once each hour, 2-3 rounds each time. Then that evening we were sitting around when a round landed nearer to us than they had all day, and we all made it to the bunker. When no more rounds came in after the first one I said the heck with it and started walking back to the tent. I was just about in the tent when I heard two more rounds being shot off and ran back into the bunker. Just as I got there the rounds hit real close, well not real close, but closer than before. When I came back into the tent a few minutes later I found a piece of shrapnel on the floor that had come through the roof, it weighed about 2 lbs. Other than that there hasn't been much going on around here.

Only 17 more days to go. How 'bout that? It doesn't seem like it is just about time for me to go home yet, but again in a way it does. I have what they call a short timers calendar, in other words it is a picture that each day you mark off another day, I'll show it to you when I get home. I should be home in no longer than three weeks from now. Just think, in three weeks at the most we will be with each other again; I love you so much I can hardly wait. I promise I'll be a perfect gentleman when I get home, at least for the first five minutes and then you better watch out, because you're liable to get raped. I mean it! So, as they say, fore warned is fore armed.

Well I guess that's about it for now, bye and I love you more than anything in the world. It will really be great to be back with you again, to hold you, kiss you, and just to be with you again. It will be great to know that whenever I want to be with you I won't have to dream to have you with me. You are all I think of and live for. Well I guess I got a little carried away, but it is all true. Bye for now.

Love always and forever,
Russ

PS *I love you*

Chapter 59

Graves Registration

WE RECEIVED WORD that one of our corpsmen attached to Lima Company was killed in an assault on the 3/3 position at Con Thien. I met HM2 Mike Horner when he arrived in the middle of July when I was assigned to the BAS at the Rockpile. He was a little older than the rest of us, a levelheaded guy from Joseph, Oregon.

In September when 3/3 sent a company out to the hills near Camp Carroll, Mike volunteered to go with them. He had no previous Line Company experience but wanted to get into the action. As an HM2, he was made senior corpsman of Lima and was with the company command group. The end of September, Lima was transferred to Con Thien. The position where he was working had been hit hard by the NVA; and part of the command group, which included Mike, was killed when an enemy grenade was thrown into the command bunker during the attack. Mike's body was transferred to Delta Med, and I had to go identify him. At Graves Registration, there was a thirty-foot refrigerated trailer that was used to preserve the bodies of the dead. The corpsman on duty opened up the door, and I saw body bags lying on the floor. Toward the back of the trailer, a large number of bodies were stacked like cordwood. The most recent arrivals still needing identification and autopsies were on the floor near the front. We climbed up into the trailer, and the attendant found the bag with Horner's name on the tag. He unzipped it for me to verify that it was Mike. When I got back to the BAS and pulled Mike's health record, I discovered that November 1 was his birthday. He had been killed on his twenty-fifth birthday.

Chapter 60

Orders Home

THE DAY FINALLY came. The chief called me to his desk and presented me with orders that were the first steps to getting back to the world. They were orders to Alpha Med in Phu Bai. For some reason, they couldn't give us orders directly to our next duty station, but transferred us from one unit to another, so I was transferred to temporary duty at Alpha Med Battalion in Phu Bai.

In preparation for my transfer home, I visited supply. The supply lines had improved recently, and instead of a tent, they were now kept in a new all-metal building located across the road from the battalion headquarters. Inside the building, I ran into one of the Marines I had been with in the field. He showed me the new building and all the new supplies. I obtained a set of new jungle utilities and a new pair of jungle boots never worn by anyone before. When I told him I was going back to the States, he asked me if I wanted a brand-new KA-BAR knife as a souvenir, which I gladly accepted. Back at the BAS, I packed all my personal effects except for what I needed for traveling. I included my new KA-BAR and sealed up the box for shipment to my parents and took it to the base post office. By using the mail, I would not be subject to search in Da Nang and Okinawa.

My last full day before my flight to Phu Bai, the chief brought me a can of Brasso to clean my collar devices (sergeant stripes and caduceus), which up to this time were painted flat black. Prior to this time, having shiny brass devices would have been hazardous to my health, as the enemy could have mistaken them for officers collar insignias. After a little work, I had removed all the paint so that the brass underneath gleamed. I presented them to the chief for inspection, and he ceremoniously pinned them to my collar. Evidently this was the tradition among the corpsmen when leaving the Marines and returning to the navy where all brass must be polished.

The next day, there was no big farewell; I just said good-bye to all the corpsmen and headed for the airstrip to catch the plane to Phu Bai.

The short flight to Phu Bai was uneventful. I checked in with personnel at Alpha Med and was assigned a bunk in one of the strong-back hooches. The hooches were arranged in long rows to the south of the hospital area. Outside the hooches were sand walls and areas for protection in case of incoming fire. I then wandered around the base until I found the PX. I purchased a new Olympus 35 mm camera for about $65 and went back to my hooch. Some of the corpsmen who worked around Alpha Med were getting off work. It happened that my buddy from Yokosuka and Field Med School, Frank Zebley, also lived in the same hooch. For some reason, he was not scheduled to leave Vietnam for several weeks and had been assigned a job at Alpha Med in the interim.

The next day, I reported to the transient personnel officer to see what job they wanted me to do and find out the status of my transfer orders. They assigned me to medical supply, so I walked across the compound to a steel building that housed the medical supplies and reported in to the chief.

Essentially there was nothing for me to do, but at least my time was accounted for. We prepared shipments of supplies to various medical units in the I Corps area. At lunch, I decided to tour the facility and brought along my camera. I ran into Frank Zebley at his desk in Medical Records; we decided to meet for lunch in the chow hall. I continued on and went by Casualty Receiving and ran into Ken Madfes, who was working there.

Alpha Med was a series of long screened hallways that connected various offices and wards. Outside to the east were several large Quonset buildings, but instead of steel, they were made of inflatable rubber material similar to that used to make Zodiac boats. Walking in through the door, I was hit unexpectedly by a wall of cold air. The building was air-conditioned to 70 degrees, and compared to the near 105-degree temperature outside, it was like walking into a freezer. This was a post-op ward. The temperature was controlled to reduce the occurrence of postsurgical infections. Inside were hospital beds with barely enough room between to allow bedside care. I estimated that there were around sixty beds per building, and most of the beds were filled. The corpsmen and nurses were busy giving medical care, and it was chaotic and noisy.

I left the ward, and outside I noticed that there was a plane on the runway about to unload some casualties who had been shipped out from Delta Med in Dong Ha. I watched as the stretchers were unloaded and carried the distance of several hundred feet from the back of the plane and into Casualty Receiving. I observed Ken Madfes as he stood with his clipboard and logged in each casualty as they came in. Most of these guys had intravenous fluids hung on a pole attached to the stretchers.

After lunch, I walked over to the air terminal across the street. It was an old concrete building with a control tower. There was a large aboveground sandbag bunker located outside on the street side of the terminal. As I approached the bunker in the area near the entry, I noticed a familiar face. It was Chuck Halstead, whom I had last seen several months earlier when I left the Rockpile. He was waiting for his flight to Da Nang on his way home.

Inside the terminal, there were three windows. One was for flights to Da Nang, the second was for flights to Dong Ha and Khe Sanh, and the other was for Vietnamese passengers. This was the first time I viewed the inside of this terminal; prior to this, I was either still on the plane or had traveled in and out of Phu Bai by road. It was much cooler inside the building than outside in the sun. Outside the terminal was some Vietnamese selling food to the Vietnamese passengers. The fare was rice, fish, vegetables, and tea, which was prepared on small fires by the street vendors as they squatted on their mats.

Later that afternoon, I heard rock and roll music and wandered over to an area that had an outdoor theater and benches. A Vietnamese band was entertaining many of the ambulatory patients in their blue pajamas and blue-and-white striped bathrobes. A female singer who sounded somewhat like Nancy Sinatra was singing "These Boots Were Made for Walking." They entertained us for about an hour.

The next day, I again checked in with the transient office and still had no flight. I again spent minimal time at my job and continued my exploration of the compound. This time I stayed close to the supply building and went by motor transport and preventive medicine sections, where they seemed to be doing about as much work as I was.

Alpha Med had Vietnamese personnel who worked on the compound. Each hooch was taken care of by a "house mouse," who was employed to clean the barracks, make the bunks, clean the showers, heads, and outside areas around the hooches.

The next day when I checked into the transient office, they had my orders to Da Nang ready. I was informed that I should report into the air terminal later that day for the flight to Da Nang. I was also given a large manila envelope containing my health and service records with my orders to NAS Key West in a pocket on the outside of the envelope. I was also given another set of TAD orders to the transient center in Da Nang. I returned to the hooch, picked up my belongings, which were now in an AWOL bag that I had purchased at the PX, and headed for the terminal, where I waited for my flight to Da Nang.

When I arrived at the transient center, I turned in my orders. They told me to check back later that afternoon to find out my status. I hung around the area all day. I wandered around and snapped a few pictures. When I returned to the transient center, I was informed that my flight to Okinawa would not be until the next day.

They directed me to a bus, which took me to the new transient hotel out near Dog Patch. After the short bus ride, I arrived at the newly constructed hotel and checked in and was assigned a room. This was a two-story hotel with rooms on all four sides of a large patio. The patio was set up as a theater for movies at night. I found my room, and there were two beds per room, but it was so new that only the beds and metal springs were in place. Evidently they had not received the shipment of mattresses. After eating dinner at Freedom Hill PX cafeteria, I returned to the hotel; and at dusk, they showed several movies. The late movie was *Barefoot in the Park*. I watched the movie from the balcony outside my room, sitting with my legs over the edge and looking through the railing. The movies ran most of the night since most of us could not sleep in anticipation of leaving. I did manage to get an hour or so of sleep on my bedsprings.

The next morning, I returned to the transient center and waited until they called my name and assigned me to a flight. I then waited several more hours until the announcement for the flight was made. Those of us leaving on that flight were directed out to a waiting cattle car. We were transported across the airstrip to a waiting Pan Am Boeing 727 where we boarded for our flight to Okinawa. The plane was staffed with civilian stewardesses who had great senses of humor and handled the passengers in a friendly, professional manner. They were very talented at handling anyone who got too rowdy or flirtatious.

Soon we were airborne and on our way to Kadena Air Base in Okinawa. I took one last snapshot out the window as we passed over China Beach. As soon as we leveled off, meals and beer were served, and I went to sleep until we landed in Okinawa four hours later.

Back in Okinawa, we were loaded on buses and transported to Camp Smedley D. Butler for processing out. After arrival, we were taken to the building where our seabags were stored and located our bags. Returning to the barracks, we were instructed to take our service dress uniforms to the base cleaners, where they were laundered. While the uniforms were being cleaned, we were instructed to go by the base small stores to pick up our ribbons. No longer did we have just the National Defense Ribbon, but now we all had at least a total of three; we earned the Vietnam Campaign Medal and the Vietnamese Service Medal. There was a list posted as to which other medals we had earned. As a navy corpsman attached to the Marines, I earned the miniature eagle, globe, and anchor to add to my Vietnamese Service Medal, a Purple Heart, and because I was a member of 3/3, I earned the Presidential Unit Citation. Unfortunately, they did not have any HM2 patches to replace my HM3 rank, so I would have to travel and report in to Key West without my new rank displayed on my left sleeve. After obtaining all my ribbons and devices, I returned to the barracks to ensure that my shoes were again spit-shined and that all my brass was polished. Then I went to chow at the mess hall.

After dinner, I went back to the cleaners to check on the status of my uniform. They directed me to a gymnasium across the street, so I proceeded there. Inside there were many young Okinawan women with irons and ironing boards quickly and efficiently pressing our uniform shirts, trousers, and blouses. My uniform was not ready, and they told me it would be another thirty minutes, so I hung around and waited and watched them go about their work. I was amazed to watch them process all the uniforms, place them on hangers, and cover them with plastic. After retrieving my uniform, I returned to the barracks.

Back in the barracks, I put my ribbons on the uniform blouse and got dressed in my uniform. Since I was too wired to sleep, I went to the movies. They ran the movies all night to keep us entertained. When morning came, we loaded into buses and were transported back to Kadena Air Base to await our flight.

In the air terminal, we waited again until our flight was announced and again boarded a Pan Am Boeing 727 for the flight to Marine Corps Air Station El Toro in Orange County, California. We took off, and after the plane got to altitude and leveled off, we were served a meal and beer. Again I fell asleep and slept for the full thirteen hours of the flight until we landed at El Toro.

On the ground at El Toro, we had no instructions or any further assistance or directions. We were on our own. I got my seabag from baggage and headed out to catch a bus to Los Angeles International for a flight back to San Francisco. To this day, I do not remember the bus ride to LAX or the flight on PSA to SFO.

In San Francisco, I caught a bus to the Greyhound bus station on Market Street and bought a ticket for the first bus to Santa Rosa. When I arrived in Santa Rosa, I walked from the bus station to the address where my brother Steve was living. I called home and told Mom that I would be catching the bus from Santa Rosa to Willits as the bus directly to Fort Bragg was once a day and didn't leave Santa Rosa until 1300. I spent the night sleeping on the floor in the house where Steve was staying.

After breakfast the next morning, I caught the bus to Willits, and my mom and brother Bruce were there to meet me at the Ridgewood Station in Howard Forest south of Willits. We then drove an hour the rest of the way home over Highway 20. We talked all the way home.

Chapter 61

Home at Last

WHEN I GOT home, I put my gear away, and after school got out at 1500, I went to walk Louise home from school. We arrived at her house, and her mother and brothers greeted me. When her dad came home from work at 1700, he greeted me, and we had dinner.

The next evening, I invited Louise to attend dinner at my parents' house. Upon arrival, my mother's polite disapproving welcome met us. First she told me that I was late for dinner and that the family had to wait until I got there. She then told me that she had not expected me to bring Louise home for dinner. She claimed she had not prepared enough food for company. I looked at what she had on the table and told her that it looked like there was enough food to me. We then all sat down to eat, but my parents were too polite, and very cold to Louise. When we finished dinner, we excused ourselves and went to downtown to the movie.

The friction between my parents and Louise did not diminish, and several weeks later, her parents came home from the movies. Louise and I were sitting in their front room watching TV. Her mother came in and started interrogating me about my parents' attitude toward them and their daughter. I had no logical answers for them, but she kept ragging on me. Her husband, a veteran of WWII, kept trying to get her to stop, but was not effective at deterring his wife's line of questioning and accusing statements.

It was during this tense emotional time I had my only out-of-body experience. I had been through many stressful situations in combat, but had never left my body.

All of a sudden, I was looking at the living room from up near the ceiling. I could see Louise and myself sitting side by side on the couch and her parents sitting in chairs across from us. I remember thinking that this in not where I want to be. I returned to my body, stood up, and said, "You people are all nuts!" and walked out the front door. I walked down to a bar and started drinking beer until midnight when I walked home.

The next several days, I did not go up to the school to walk Louise home or even call her. I went out and hung out in a bar with a couple other Vietnam vets who had also just returned home. We sat and drank and told war stories to each other until the bar closed. Though we had been in different areas and different units, we felt a camaraderie having all been in similar situations where we did not know whether we would live or not.

Two days later, Louise called me from her aunt's house in San Mateo. She was crying on the phone and told me that her mother had insisted that she leave the area. She started begging me to travel to the San Francisco Bay Area to pick her up. I refused and hung up on her. She called back, and I said nothing but hung up the phone. I left the house, and when she called, my mom told her not to ever call or see me again. That ended all communications between us.

I called the officer-in-charge of the personnel office in Key West and requested an extension on my leave so that I could spend Christmas with my family. He granted my request and extended my leave to January 3, which gave me another two weeks before I had to report to duty.

I decided that since Louise and I would never get married, I went to the Volkswagen dealership in Ukiah and purchased a new 1968 VW sedan for $2,800 cash, which was the majority of the money I had saved during Vietnam. I spent much of the rest of it in the bar drinking with my buddies.

The day after Christmas, I loaded up my newly purchased Volkswagen bug, said good-bye to my folks, and headed out to Florida. I spent a week driving from Fort Bragg to Key West, Florida. Driving sixteen hours a day, I had a lot of time to think. I decided it was less painful to simply close my shell and go about my life. I decided that since Louise and I were not ever going to get back together, I would make a career of the navy.

Chapter 62

My Last Duty Station

I REPORTED INTO Boca Chica naval air station and was assigned to the naval air station dispensary. My job was coordinator of the outpatient dependent clinic, making appointments and coordinating the schedules of the doctors.

There was one other Vietnam vet at the dispensary, and we became close friends. Dave Schlerf had been attached to 2/4 and worked with me in the clinic. Working the clinic was a boring routine that was not mentally challenging. After work, Dave, myself, and B. A. Young, who worked in the lab, would head into Key West, go to Burger King for a dinner of Big Mac with cheese, fries, and a shake. After dinner, we headed for the liquor store and bought a case of beer and a fifth of I.W. Harper whiskey and headed for the drive-in to watch a movie. By the end of the movie, we had consumed all our liquor and drove back to the base. At 0800, we would be back in the dispensary, none of us missed muster or took any sick days because of our drinking. On weekends, we would go fishing and include enough beer to last us the day. Florida has blue laws, so we would purchase our weekend supply of liquor all during one trip.

It seemed that in Key West when a girl reached puberty, they shipped her out, and when she reached senility, she returned to the Keys. One of us made the observation that all there was to do in Key West was work, drink, and fish. My stay at Key West consisted of going to work during the day and drinking at night. Working kept me occupied during the day, but I always self-medicated with alcohol during the evening so that I could go to sleep at night. Even with the alcohol, I could sleep only two to four hours a night.

In July, Dave was discharged on the day before his twenty-first birthday. He had joined as a "kiddie cruiser," which meant that he had joined the navy when he was only seventeen, and under the terms of his enlistment, he only was required to serve until his twenty-first birthday.

In August, BA received orders to Field Medical Service School for duty with the Fleet Marine Force.

In September, when my enlistment was ending, I was required to go to a meeting with the personnel department to determine if I wanted to "ship over," stay in the navy for a second enlistment. I was offered a tour in the Spain or the Mediterranean. They could not guarantee me more than six months at a new duty station due to my job description of field medical service technician, but they tried to convince me that the Vietnam War would be over soon and I need not worry about going back. I decided not to pursue a naval career because if I did, I would be sent back to Vietnam, probably as a senior corpsman of another Marine unit. I had made it through once and did not want to press my luck again. I was discharged from active duty on September 21, 1968.

Epilogue

AFTER I WAS discharged in September, I drove up to Daytona Beach and hung out on the beach with the returning college kids celebrating their last free weekend before classes started. After the parties ended, I drove back to California. Dave lived in Torrance, California. I decided to visit with him before heading home to Fort Bragg. We spent a week going to Tony's on the Pier, Dave's favorite bar located in Redondo Beach where we would drink rum mai tais until closing time.

Returning home, I quickly became bored and returned to Torrance where Dave and I shared an apartment for a while. He and I were working the graveyard shift emergency departments of two local hospitals, Dave in Little Company of Mary Hospital in Torrance and I at South Bay Hospital in Redondo Beach. Since we worked nights, much of our day was spent annoying the other tenants by partying around the swimming pool.

The manager of the apartment complex, which catered mainly to flight crews for various airlines, was a bit pushed out of shape about us diving off our second-floor balcony into the swimming pool, but the last straw was when we had a party with several other veterans and were playing pool in the pool house. We had been drinking Red Mountain wine, which we bought by the gallon. I was making a shot and vomited into the corner pocket. The next morning, we were evicted with a vengeance.

After a year, I decided I should do something constructive with my life. I enrolled in El Camino College in the premed program, but soon became bored. I got married to a girl from Louisiana, who was a nurse in the hospital where I worked.

One of the guys who worked in Respiratory Therapy and I became friends. He was a World War II vet who had survived being tortured as a POW on the Aleutian Islands. When the Americans invaded, the Japanese had tortured him and left him for dead. He said that El Camino was starting a program for Respiratory Therapist to prepare graduates for the registry. I then switched from premed to respiratory therapy.

Before graduating from college, I transferred from the emergency department to the respiratory therapy department. When I graduated, I was the only therapist with a degree (all the others had been on-the-job trained). I was immediately promoted to the position of chief of Respiratory Therapy.

My wife and I were divorced after four years of marriage. In 1975, I moved back to Fort Bragg. I had several love affairs when I met my second wife.

In 1976, Louise returned to Fort Bragg to visit her parents. She showed up unannounced at my workplace for a visit. Both of us had recently divorced our spouses, and she wanted to renew our relationship. We had coffee together, and we talked, but I still had no feelings for her, and after twenty minutes, she went on her way, and I never heard from her again.

After only two years, my second wife divorced me. I again had several more love affairs and ended up marrying my third wife. She had two kids, which we raised. That marriage lasted seventeen years, but as soon as the kids left for college, we were divorced. Another ten years passed, and I married again in 2003.

In 2004, I happened to talk with Louise's father when he was visiting a patient in the hospital where I worked. After my third divorce, I was reconstructing my Vietnam experience for my Web site and was interested if she still had the photographs I sent her in 1967. He provided me with her address. I procrastinated contacting her because I was embarrassed for breaking all contact with her. Several months later, she contacted me. She was living in Tacoma, Washington, and had been working as an accountant for Boeing Aircraft. She was married, and her husband had recently retired from Boeing, and they were traveling around the States. Not only did she have all the pictures, but she also had saved every letter I had ever written to her. I asked her for copies. She said that she and her husband were planning to visit her father, and she would bring the photos and letters to me.

In September 2005, she was true to her word and presented me with every letter I had written to her since I was in high school as well as every picture I had given her. She left them with me, and I scanned all the pictures and letters, returning them to her several months later.

Tom Smith showed up at my house unexpectedly one Saturday morning. He seemed very much at ease compared to the previous visits we had had. He volunteered that he had received a rating of 100 percent disability from the Veterans Administration. He sought help from a local psychiatrist who specialized in vets with post-traumatic stress disorder (PTSD) who helped him deal with the process, and now with his compensation, he was able to purchase a piece of property in rural Oregon where he had moved to enjoy his retirement. He encouraged me to seek resolution for my own PTSD, presenting me with the name of the therapist and several documents describing what the VA had to offer. I thanked him for the information, and he was on his way to live in Oregon.

I had always rejected the idea of going to the VA for help. There were so many other Vietnam vets who were more severely affected by their experiences. Those I knew classified with PTSD usually were homeless and/or had severe drug problems. I never really considered that I had PTSD because I was able to go to college and maintain a good career afterward. Other than my evening post-workday pints of beer, I had no substance abuse problems.

After I left the navy, which (had it not been for Vietnam continuing) I had intended to make a career, I developed some lipomas (fatty tumors) in my arms and torso. In the '70s, I contacted the VA because the area around the Rockpile had been sprayed and I had been exposed to Agent Orange. I heard that fatty tumors under the skin could be a symptom of the exposure. The VA instructed me to consult my own physician and request the performance of blood tests to confirm or deny any exposure. Since I had no other medical problems, I had no personal physician and sought the assistance from several physicians in the area. Agent Orange was a hot topic, and none of the physicians contacted wanted to get involved in the controversy. I also had looked into joining the Veterans of Foreign Wars and the American Legion and found them to be WWII elitists who looked down on Vietnam vets because of the outcome of the war. They considered us losers. I quickly became discouraged in participating in the process and had no further contact with the VA or veterans' organizations.

Half a year later, I walked into the pub, and the bartender told me that there had been someone inquiring about me. He was unable to identify the guy and the description did not sound like anyone I knew. Several weeks later, he showed up at the pub and was sitting at the bar when I came in. He introduced himself and stated he was a navy corpsman who had served with the Marines, lived locally, and knew Tom Smith. Tom had informed him about PTSD treatment and compensation. Tom had mentioned my name because we were both corpsmen. He was on his way to a PTSD group meeting and wanted to know if I wanted to go also. I thanked him for the invitation and declined. Finally, after meeting several times and talking, I consented to go with him to the weekly meetings.

The group consisted of local veterans from WWII, Korea, and Vietnam – all of whom still suffered from PTSD. The group was presided over by Guy Grenny, PhD, a veteran of WWII in his late eighties. His assistant, Chris Hoy, MA, also a psychologist, was not a veteran, but was actively counseling vets and assisted with the Monday evening sessions. The number in attendance at the meetings varied from four to ten and consisted of several Marines, army, and air force veterans. One Marine who never missed a meeting had enlisted before WWII and was eighty-seven years old. During WWII, he participated in all the Pacific Islands Campaign involving the Marines. Another Marine grew up locally and was one of the servicemen that my mother had written to in WWII. He was a casualty on Iwo Jima. Both Marines were still suffering from PTSD after sixty years.

After attending several meetings, I decided it was not a stigma to admit to having PTSD and sought counseling. I now receive assistance from the Veterans Administration. I encourage all veterans to do the same. The VA has changed over the years, and they no longer have the same attitude that we encountered in the 1970s.

On March 2, 2007, fifty-eight of Ripley's Raiders met in Washington DC for the fortieth anniversary of the battle in Vietnam, which gave us our moniker. Colonel Ripley attended and acted as our tour guide at the newly opened National Museum of the Marine Corps near Quantico. He presented each of us a red cap with the 3/3 logo embroidered on the front and Ripley's Raiders embroidered on the back. On the third of March, we all met at the Wall to remember the battle and honor the men we lost that day. It was very emotional and healing for all of us.

In July 2008 at the 3/3 reunion in Orlando, Florida, a bunch of Ripley's Raiders decided to go back to Vietnam in 2009. Col. John Ripley had been back several times after his retirement. Once with a tour group and again with Col. Oliver North and his film crew for North's Fox TV program, *American Heroes*. He was excited about going back with those he had actually been with him in combat.

On November 2, 2008, I received a phone call from Doc Hoppy telling me that Col. John W. Ripley had died. I contacted all of Ripley's Raiders by e-mail and gave the information about the funeral that his family had provided. With just two days' notice, twenty-six of us postponed what we were doing in our individual life and gathered in Annapolis, Maryland. We all wore our red caps with the 3/3 logo on the front and Ripley's Raiders on the back given to us by the skipper at the 2007 reunion.

Colonel Ripley was buried at Annapolis with full military honors. Everyone at the funeral knew of Captain Ripley at the Bridge. *The Bridge at Dong Ha* by John Grider Miller is required reading for all Annapolis midshipmen. Very few of those present at the funeral knew anything about his first tour. When we were asked about our red caps, we were more than willing to relate our knowledge of one of the finest Marines before he became an icon for the Marine Corps. After the funeral, several of us went into the building housing the school's commandant to view the diorama of Ripley under the bridge.

In July 2009, five members of Ripley's Raiders returned to Vietnam to visit the areas we had been in forty-two years earlier. None of us knew how we would feel, but vowed to support each other to endure the emotional roller coasters we were likely to experience.

The experience was one of the most healing I have ever had. Thirty-four years after the American War, as they call it, ended, Vietnam is a growing and thriving country. Cell phones, satellite TV, and Internet cafés are common. Sixty percent of the population was born after 1975 and have little knowledge of the war. Even the NVA veterans we met held no animosity toward us. We ran into a group coming out of the museum at the newly restored Quang Tri Citadel. When they saw us, they waved us over, and we chatted. They all had their pith helmets, and we were wearing shirts with the Marine Corps logo embroidered on the front. Our guide interpreted for us. When we parted, we all shook hands, reminding me of two teams congratulating each other after a brutal game.

We were able to experience the cuisine from Saigon to Hanoi, a luxury I had not had the opportunity to try on my last trip to the country. I would highly recommend that everyone who had been in Vietnam return and experience the country now. The economy is growing, the infrastructure is much improved. There are hotels, streetlights, and paved streets in Khe Sanh. Where our bunkers were located in Ca Lu is now an Internet café. Even the Montagnards have satellite dishes on their homes.

Glossary

MANY OF THE definitions included were derived from sources on www.wikipedia.com

0 dark 30 – Pronounced "oh dark thirty" is a reference to any time after midnight and before dawn (i.e., very early in the morning). It is usually used to refer to any time when the sun isn't up. Most operations start at 0 dark 30, much earlier than a normal person would think civilized.

1/9 – First Battalion, Ninth Marine Regiment is an infantry battalion of the Marine Corps. Also known as the Walking Dead. Formed during World War II, it served until the mid-1990s when it was deactivated. During the Vietnam War, 1/9 sustained the highest casualty rate in Marine Corps history.

The battalion endured the longest sustained combat and suffered the highest killed in action (KIA) rate in Marine Corps history, especially during the Battle of July Two, a short engagement of the Vietnam War that took place along Route 561 between Gia Binh and An Kha.

On the morning of July 2, 1967, two companies made their way up north and secured a crossroad as their first objective. As they went further north, they made contact with the elements of the North Vietnamese 90th Regiment when sniper fire began to burst, enemy fire intensified as efforts were made to suppress it. The North Vietnamese Army caused heavy casualties on the A and B Companies and prevented them from linking up. When the fighting ended, the Marines had suffered 84 dead, 190 wounded and 34 missing. Alpha and Bravo Companies were badly mauled during the battle.

The battalion was engaged in combat for 47 months and 7 days, from June 15, 1965 to October 19, 1966 and December 11, 1966 to July 14, 1969. 1/9 sustained casualties during its entire Vietnam service.

2/3 – Second Battalion, Third Marine Regiment is an infantry battalion in the Marine Corps based out of Marine Corps Base Hawaii consisting of approximately 1000 Marines and Sailors. 2/3 deployed to Da Nang in April 1965. They fought in Vietnam from April 1965 until October 1969, operating from DaNang, Camp Carroll, Quang Tri, Cam Lo, the A Shau Valley and Khe Sahn. The battalion made a night helicopter assault in the Elephant Valley south of Da Nang on 12 August 1965, shortly after Marine ground troops arrived in country. In October 1969, the battalion relocated to Marine Corps Base, Camp Pendleton.

2/4 – Second Battalion, Fourth Marine Regiment. Also known as the Magnificent Bastards. 2nd Battalion 4th Marines was committed to ground combat operations in Vietnam. In May 1965 the battalion landed at Chu Lai. The first major engagement for the battalion was Operation in August 1965.

The 1968 Tet Offensive resulted in an increase in tempo of combat activity for 2/4. Clashes between the battalion and NVA broke out near Dong Ha. 2/4 moved forward to seize the fortified village of Dai Do.

Late in 1969, 2/4 was withdrawn to Okinawa as part of the United States policy of gradually turning the war over to the South Vietnamese.

In the early 1970s, 2/4 participated with other units from the 3rd Marine Division in providing Battalion Landing Teams as part of the Special Landing Force off the coast of Vietnam. During the 1972 Easter Offensive, 2/4 actively supported Vietnamese Marines, U.S. Army Rangers and U.S. advisors ashore, from nearby amphibious ships.

During the summer of 1972 the battalion participated in a massive disaster relief effort, Operation SAKLOLO conducted in the northern part of the Philippines. In April 1975, 2/4 took part in Operation Eagle Pull, the evacuation of Americans from Phnom Penh, Cambodia. Less than 15 days later they took part in Operation Frequent Wind, the evacuation of Saigon, followed, a short while later, by the recovery of the SS Mayaguez.

2/9 –

Second Battalion, Ninth Marine is an infantry battalion of the Marine Corps also known as Hell in a Helmet. The battalion distinguished itself in the defense of Khe Sanh during the Vietnam War, and later participated in an ill fated invasion of Koh Tang Island in Southeast Asia, with the intention of rescuing the crew of the *SS Mayaguez*.

When the 3d Marine Division began operating in Vietnam on May 6, 1965, opening a Marine Compound at the Danang Air Base. On July 4, 1965, 2nd Battalion, 9th Marines were ordered to Vietnam from Okinawa. 2nd Battalion, 9th Marines fought battles in or around Danang, Hue, Phu Bai, Dong Ha, Camp Carrol, Cam Lo, Con Thien, Than Cam Son, Quang Tri, Cua Viet, Vandergrift Combat Base and Khe Sanh.

Khe Sanh security was manned by the 2nd Battalion, 9th Marines from 1967. It was used as a staging ground for a number of attacks on North Vietnamese troop movements down the Ho Chi Minh Trail.

In April and May 1967, various "Hill Fights" on Hills 061, 881 North and 881 South between the 2nd Battalion, 9th Marines and NVA occurred. In 1968, Khe Sanh Combat Base came under heavy attack in what is known as the Battle of Khe Sanh. Despite being outnumbered, 2nd Battalion, 9th Marines held their ground and the North Vietnamese were driven out of the area experiencing heavy casualties.

From January 22 to March 18, 1969, 2/9 participated in a sweep of the A Shau Valley, the last major offensive by the Marine Corps in Vietnam.

In August 1969, 2nd Battalion, 9th Marines was ordered to return to Camp Schwab, Okinawa. During this period the unit was assigned to sea duty in and around the waters of Vietnam and continued to receive combat training at Camp Fuji, Japan and Subic Bay in the Philippines.

2/26 –   Second Battalion, Twenty Sixth Marine Regiment is a deactivated infantry regiment of the Marine Corps. They fought during the Battle of Iwo Jima in World War II and were activated again during the Vietnam War. The Regiment was composed of three infantry battalions and one headquarters company.

3/3 –   Third Battalion, Third Marine Regiment is also known as America's Battalion. In 1965, 3/3 was deployed to Vietnam. The battalion continued to see major action through the Vietnam War and was rotated back to the United States in 1969.

    In January 1965, the 2nd Battalion, 1st Marines at Marine Corps Base Camp Pendleton, California deployed for a tour on Okinawa, Japan, where they were redesignated the 3rd Battalion, 3rd Marines. At the time the Marines of 3rd Battalion expected a typical 13-month deployment followed by a quick return to the states. However 3/3 found itself caught up in the initial deployment of Marine units to Vietnam, and landed on May 12 along the coast south of Danang at an airfield called Chu Lai.

    The battalion's first major operation in the Vietnam War was Operation Starlite, which was also the first major American action in the war. Starlite was an attempt by three Marine battalions, including 3/3, to clear the area just south of Chu Lai of the 1st VC Regiment. The fighting began on August 18, 1965.

    In the summer of 1966 3/3 returned to Okinawa. In October 1966, 3rd Battalion was deployed to combat the threat from the North Vietnamese Army in the Quang Tri province. While deployed in Quang Tri, 3/3 fought in such places as the Rockpile, Highway 9, Cam Lo, A-3, Gio Linh, Khe Sanh, and Con Thien. In the spring of 1967, 3rd Battalion participated in a series of bloody engagements near Khe Sanh known as the Hill fights, culminating in the Battle of Hill 881, where 46 Marines from 3/3 were killed. The fighting in the area continued to increase throughout 1967, culminating in 1968's Tet Offensive

    In early 1969, 3rd Battalion was sent south for several months to join Task Force Yankee in Operation Taylor Common near An Hoa. This operation focused on destroying the primary base for North Vietnamese Army forces operating across several provinces and 3/3 was awarded a Navy Unit Commendation for its actions during the operation. American forces captured numerous quantities of North Vietnamese arms and supplies. 3/3 returned to the DMZ for the summer of 1969 and were ordered back to the United States in the fall.

3/3 Battalion spent over 1600 days in Vietnam and conducted 48 combat operations, the most of any Marine battalion in the conflict. 547 3/3 Marines lost their lives during the Vietnam War. Nearly 2,800 others were wounded.

3/4 – Third Battalion, Fourth Marine Regiment is an infantry battalion of the Marine Corps. Also known as the Thundering Third. The battalion deployed during April 1965 to Vietnam. They re-deployed during December 1965 to March 1966 to Camp Schwab, Okinawa. They were deployed back to Vietnam and participated in action from April to December 1965 and March 1966 to November 1969.

3/9 – Third Battalion, Ninth Marine Regiment is an infantry battalion of the Marine Corps.

3/9 became the first battalion-sized ground combat unit to be deployed to Vietnam when they landed on March 8, 1965 in Da Nang. Over the course of the next four and a half years, the battalion operated from Da Nang, An Hoa and Quang Tri and participated in over 40 combat operations. The battalion redeployed in August 13, 1969, after four years of continuous combat operations.

6-by – A vehicle in the M35 family of trucks in the 2-1/2 ton weight class, it was one of many vehicles in US military service to have been referred to as the "deuce and a half." The basic M35 cargo truck can carry 5000 pounds across country or 10,000 pounds over roads. Trucks in this weight class are considered medium duty by the military and Department of Transportation. The M35 series formed the basis for a wide range of specialized vehicles.

An M35A2 cargo truck with winch is 112" tall, 96" wide and 277" long, and 13,030 pounds empty (13,530 pounds empty when equipped with the front mount winch, according to dashboard dataplates). The standard wheelbase cargo bed is 8'x12'. The M35A2 was available with a canvas soft top or a metal hard top.

The M35A2 is popularly powered by a LDT 465 engine made by either: Continental Motors,Hercules, or White. It is an in-line 6 cylinder, turbocharged multifuel engine, 478 cubic inches, with 134 bhp (100 kW) and 330 lb·ft (447 N·m) of torque. This is coupled with a 5-speed manual transmission and divorced 2-speed transfer case (Either a sprague-operated transfer case (Rockwell 136-21) or air-operated selectable transfer case (Rockwell 136-27). Multifuel engines are designed to reliably operate on a wide variety of fuels, including diesel fuel, jet fuel, kerosene, heating oil or gasoline. The curb weight of an M35 is between 13,000 and 16,000 pounds empty, depending on configuration (cargo, wrecker, tractor, etc.). Its top speed is 56 mph (90 km/h), though maximum cruising speed is approximately 48 mph (77 km/h). Fuel economy is 11 MPG highway and 8 MPG city, giving the deuce a 400-500 mile range on its 50 US gallon single fuel tank. On average, most operators experience tank averages of 8-10 mpg for an unladen vehicle.

Brake system is air-over-hydraulic six wheel drum with a driveline parking brake, although gladhands exist on the rear of the vehicle for connection to trailers with full air service and emergency brakes. Braking performance of the truck is similar to other power drum brake vehicles of this size. Each drum was designed with maximum efficiency in mind, and individual drums can dissipate up to 12 kW of braking heat. Due to this brake system and GVWR under 26,001 pounds, the big deuce can be driven without a commercial driver's license in most states. California, however, requires a CDL to operate an M35 on public roads.

The electrical system is 24 volt, using two 12 volt 6TL-series military grade batteries run in series.

Many deuces are equipped with a 10,000 pound power take off driven front winch manufactured by Garwood.

AK-47 – A Warsaw Pact or Chinese made 7.62x39mm semi – or fully automatic assault rifle with a 30-round magazine. The AK-47 was the standard weapon for VC main force battalions and NVA units. The AK was a reliable rifle with a high rate of fire. The AK-47 (contraction of Russian: *Avtomat Kalashnikova obraztsa 1947 goda*; "Kalashnikov's automatic rifle model of year 1947") is a 7.63 mm assault rifle developed in the Soviet Union by Mikhail Kalashnikov. Design work on the AK began in 1944. In 1946 the rifle was presented for official military trials, and a year later the fixed stock version was introduced into service with select units of the Red Army (the folding stock model was developed later). The AK-47 was officially accepted by the Soviet Armed Forces in 1949. It was also used by the majority of the member states of the former Warsaw Pact. The AK-47 was also used as a basis for the development of many other types of individual and crew-served firearms.It was one of the first true assault rifles and, due to its durability, low production cost and ease of use, remains the most widely used assault rifle in the world – so much so that more AK-type rifles have been produced than all other assault rifles combined.

AFRN –   Armed Forces Radio Network or American Forces Network (AFN) is the brand name used by the United States Armed Forces Radio and Television Service (AFRTS) for its entertainment and command internal information networks worldwide. It was formerly known as Armed Forces Network. American Forces Network (AFN) is the operational arm of the Armed Forces Radio and Television Service (AFRTS), an agency of the American Forces Information Service (AFIS), and is under the operational control of the Office of the Assistant Secretary of Defense for Public Affairs (OASD-PA). Editorial control is by the Department of Defense.

This broadcasting service employs primarily military broadcasters, but there are some civilians employed as engineers or operations personnel. Service personnel hold broadcasting occupational specialties for their military branch.

ao dai –   A Vietnamese national costume primarily for women. In its current form, it is a tight-fitting silk dress worn over pantaloons. *áo* refers to an item of clothing that covers from the neck down. *Dài* means "long."

In Vietnamese, the word *áo dài* was applied to various garments historically, including the *áo ngũ thân*, a 19th century aristocratic gown influenced by Manchu Chinese fashions. Inspired by Paris fashions, Hanoi artist Nguyễn Cát Tường redesigned the *áo ngũ thân* as a dress in 1930. In the 1950s, Saigon designers tightened the fit to produce the version worn by Vietnamese women today. The dress was extremely popular in South Vietnam in the 1960s and early 1970s. The communists, who have ruled Vietnam since 1975, disapproved of the dress and favored frugal, androgynous styles. In the 1990s, the ao dai regained popularity.

ARVN – Army of the Republic of Viet Nam was the military of the Republic of Vietnam (South Vietnam). They are estimated to have received 1,170,000 casualties during the Vietnam War.

Just after the end of the Vietnam War, after the fall of Saigon and the North Vietnamese takeover, the ARVN was dissolved. While some members had fled the country to the United States or elsewhere, hundreds of thousands of former ARVN soldiers were sent to reeducation camps by the newly-unified Vietnamese communist government.

AWOL – Absent Without Official Leave, absence from a post without a valid pass or leave. The United States Marine Corps and United States Navy generally refer to this as Unauthorized Absence, or "UA." Such people are dropped from their unit rolls after 30 days and then listed as *deserters*. However, as a matter of U.S. military law, desertion is not measured by time away from the unit, but rather:

- by leaving or remaining absent from their unit, organization, or place of duty, where there has been a determined intent to not return;
- if that intent is determined to be to avoid hazardous duty or shirk important responsibility;
- if they enlist or accept an appointment in the same or another branch of service without disclosing the fact that they have not been properly separated from current service.

People who are away for more than 30 days but return voluntarily or indicate a credible intent to return may still be considered *AWOL*, while those who are away for fewer than 30 days but can credibly be shown to have no intent to return (as by joining the armed forces of another country) may nevertheless be tried for *desertion* or in some rare occasions treason if enough evidence is found.

In the United States, before the Civil War, deserters from the Army were flogged, while after 1861 tattoos or branding were also adopted. The maximum U.S. penalty for desertion in wartime remains death, although this punishment was last applied to Eddie Slovik in 1945.

AWOL/UA may be punished with nonjudicial punishment (NJP; called "office hours" in the Marines). It is usually punished by Court Martial for repeat or more severe offenses.

Also, "Missing Movement" is another term which is used to describe when a particular serviceman fails to arrive at the appointed time to deploy (or "move out") with his assigned unit, ship, or aircraft; in the United States military, it is a violation of the 87th article of the Uniform Code of Military Justice. The offense is similar to AWOL, but considered more severe.

Less severe is "Failure to Repair," consisting of missing a formation, or failing to appear at an assigned place and time when so ordered.

BAS – The Battalion Aid Station is a medical section within a battalion's support company in the military of the United States, specifically, the Army and Marine Corps. As such, it is the forward-most medically-staffed treatment location. During combat, a commissioned medical doctor assumes leadership of the platoon and direct medical operations. The primary mission of the Battalion Aid Station is to collect the sick and wounded from the battalion, stabilize the patients' condition, and provide emergency medical evacuation to the combat support hospital or other medical treatment facility.

The Battalion Aid Station belongs to, and is an organic component of, the unit it supports. It may be split into two functional units for up to 24 hours, the BAS rear consisting of the medical doctor and corpsmen and a BAS forward consisting of the Physician Assistant corpsmen. This allows the section to support more than one unit or care as the unit advances or withdraws.

According to the Geneva Convention, military medical facilities, equipment and personnel are non-combatants and may not be attacked as long as they remain in a non combatant role. Medical personnel are allowed weapons for the purpose of self-and patient-defense.

battalion surgeon – The chief medical officer of a battalion in the Marines. Despite the name, most battalion surgeons are primary care physicians or general medical officers, and not actual surgeons who perform invasive surgical operations. The battalion surgeon is a special staff officer who advises the battalion commander on matters pertaining to the health of the battalion. Chief duties include managing a battalion aid station (BAS), performing sick call for members of the battalion, and medical planning for deployment. The battalion surgeon is usually a junior staff physician, and typically carries the United States Navy rank of Lieutenant (O-3).

betel nut – "Beetle-nut" – Vietnamese chew the leaf of a vine belonging to the Piperaceae family, which includes pepper and kava. It is valued both as a mild stimulant and for its medicinal properties. The betel plant is an evergreen and perennial creeper, with glossy heart-shaped leaves and white catkin. In Asia they are used to relieve toothache.

In Southeast Asia, the leaves are chewed together in a wrapped package along with the areca nut (which, by association, is often inaccurately called the "betel nut") and mineral slaked lime (calcium hydroxide). The lime acts to keep the active ingredient in its freebase or alkaline form, thus enabling it to enter the bloodstream via sublingual absorption. The areca nut contains the alkaloid arecoline, which promotes salivation (the saliva is stained red), and is itself a stimulant. This combination, known as a "betel quid", has been used for several thousand years. Tobacco is sometimes added.

Some Vietnamese men chewed betel, but women, especially in the countryside, more often use it.

The betel and areca also play an important role in Vietnamese culture. In Vietnamese there is a saying that "the betel begins the conversation", referring to the practice of people chewing betel in formal occasions or "to break the ice" in awkward situational conversations. The betel leaves and areca nuts are used ceremonially in traditional Vietnamese weddings. Based on a folk tale about the origins of these plants, the groom traditionally offer the bride's parents betel leaves and areca nuts (among other things) in exchange for the bride. The betel and areca nut are praised as an ideal combination to the point that have become important symbols of the ideal married couple bound together in love. Therefore in Vietnamese the phrase "matters of betel and areca" (*chuyện trầu cau*) is synonymous with marriage.

Bru – An ethnic group living in Vietnam, Laos, and Thailand. They speak Bru, a Mon-Khmer language, which has several dialects. Their total population is estimated at 129,559. In Vietnam, most Bru live in the Quang Binh, Quang Tri, Dak Lak, and Thua Thien-Hue provinces.

C4 – Composition C4 is a common variety of military plastic explosive. C4 is 1.34 times as explosive as TNT. C4 is made up of explosives, plastic binder, plasticizer and, usually, marker or taggant chemicals such as 2,3-dimethyl-2,3-dinitrobutane (DMDNB) to help detect the explosive and identify its source. A major advantage of C4 is that it can easily be molded into any desired shape. C-4 can be pressed into gaps, cracks and voids in buildings, bridges, equipment or machinery. Similarly, it can easily be inserted into empty shaped-charge cases of the type used by military engineers.

C4 is very stable and insensitive to most physical shocks. Detonation can only be initiated by a combination of extreme heat and a shockwave, as when a detonator inserted into it is fired. C4 cannot be detonated by a gunshot or by dropping it onto a hard surface. C4 burns with a bright, hot flame and a golf ball-sized chunk will heat a canteen cup full of water to a low boil for coffee or soup.

C-130 – The Lockheed C130 Hercules is a four-engine turboprop military transport aircraft. It is the main tactical airlifter for many military forces worldwide. Over 40 models and variants of the Hercules serve with more than 50 nations. In December 2006 the C130 became the fifth aircraft after the English Electric Canberra, B52 Stratofortress, Tupolev Tu-95, and KC135 Stratotanker – to mark 50 years of continuous use with its original primary customer, in this case the United States Air Force. The C130 remains in production as the updated C-130J Super Hercules.

Capable of takeoffs and landings from unprepared runways, the C130 was originally designed as a troop, medical evacuation, and cargo transport aircraft. The versatile airframe has found uses in a variety of other roles, including as a gunship, for airborne assault, search and rescue, scientific research support, weather reconnaissance, aerial refueling and aerial firefighting. The Hercules family has the longest continuous production run of any military aircraft in

history. During more than 50 years of service the family has participated in countless military, civilian and humanitarian aid operations.
- Capacity:
- 92 passengers *or*
- 64 airborne troops *or*
- 74 litter patients with 2 medical personnel

CAC –   A Combined Action Company. A military unit made up of American and Vietnamese personnel operating and living in villages. See CAP.

CAP –   Combined Action Program. Drawing from previous experience in "small wars", the Marine Corps operated CAPs during the Vietnam War, from 1965 to 1971. "The Combined Action Platoon's (CAP) genesis was not a deliberate plan from a higher headquarters, rather, it was a solution to one infantry battalion's problem of an expanding Tactical Area of Responsibility (TAOR). The concept of combining a squad of Marines with local Popular Forces (PFs) and assigning them a village to protect proved to be a force multiplier."

While the exact implementation varied with the war and time, the basic model was to combine a Marine squad with local forces to form a village defense platoon. It was effective in denying the enemy a sanctuary at the local village level. The pacification campaign seemed to work under the CAP concept, and the Marines fully embraced it. Objectively, there is no solid proof that the CAP concept was a resounding success; however, subjectively the evidence suggests otherwise.

CH-34 –   The Sikorsky CH34 Choctaw was a military helicopter originally designed by American aircraft manufacturer Sikorsky for the United States Navy for service in an anti-submarine warfare role.

French evaluations on the reported ground fire vulnerabilities of the CH34 may have influenced the U.S. Army's decision to deploy the CH21 Shawnee to Vietnam instead of the CH34, pending the introduction into widespread service of the Bell UH1 Iroquois. However, the approximately twenty Army CH-34s that did eventually reach Vietnam proved no more vulnerable to ground fire than any other rotary-wing aircraft in the theater, and the CH34 successfully carried out missions ranging from combat assault to aeromedical evacuation and general cargo transport.

The Marine Corps continued to use the CH34 even after the U.S. Army had phased it out. Even after the Marines adopted their own version of the UH-1, the UH1E, the CH34s continued to be used up to and for a period after the Tet Offensive in 1968.

U.S. Marine Corps CH34s were also among the first gunship helicopters, being fitted with the Temporary Kit-1 (TK-1), comprising two M60C machine guns and two 19 shot 2.75 inch rocket pods. The operations were met with mixed enthusiasm, and the armed CH-34s, known as "Stingers" were quickly phased out. The TK-1 kit would form the basis of the TK2 kit used on the UH1E helicopters of the USMC.

Most of the twenty surviving CH34 helicopters were turned over to the South Vietnamese during the course of the war, though a few were ultimately reclaimed by the Army prior to the final collapse of the Saigon government.

CH-46 – The Boeing CH46 Sea Knight is a medium-lift tandem rotor cargo helicopter, used by the United States Marine Corps to provide all-weather, day-or-night assault transport of combat troops, supplies and equipment. Assault Support is its primary function, and the movement of supplies and equipment is secondary. Additional tasks include combat support, search and rescue, support for forward refueling and rearming points, CASEVAC and Tactical Recovery of Aircraft and Personnel

C-Rats – C rations. Individual ration consisting of packaged precooked foods, which could be eaten hot or cold. It could be carried and prepared by the individual Marine. The ration was designed for feeding combat troops from a few days to an extreme of three weeks. Due to the required individual portability of this ration, maximum nourishment had to be provided in the smallest physical unit.

The "Meal, Combat, Individual," or MCI, was very similar to the C Rations in concept and packaging but had more nutritionally balanced meals and greater variety. Because of the similarities it was often called "C Rations" even if it was technically a new ration. MCI the main field ration used during the Vietnam War and was still in service until the 1980s.

A case of "Meal, Combat, Individual" rations contained 12 individual meal packages. The case was made up of a variety of menus. Each of the twelve inner boxes contained cans and accessory packages that made up the meal according to the menu plan. Each meal came with a bagged Accessory Packet (matches, chewing gum, toilet paper, instant coffee, cream substitute, sugar, salt and a plastic spoon).

Chesty Puller – A Marine Icon, Lieutenant General Lewis Burwell "Chesty" Puller (June 26, 1898 - October 11, 1971) was an officer in the United States Marine Corps and the only Marine to receive five Navy Crosses, the United States Navy's second highest decoration after the Medal of Honor. During his career, he fought guerrillas in Haiti and Nicaragua, and participated in some of the bloodiest battles of World War II and the Korean War. Puller retired from the Marine Corps in 1955, spending the rest of his life in Virginia.

Chi Com – A term used to for NVA and VC hand grenades, an abbreviation for Chinese Communist.

chloroquine primaquine – A Large orange pill used for Malaria prophylaxis. Usually administered every Sunday by medical personnel to the troops.

corpsman – Hospital Corpsman (HM) is a rating in the United States Navy and a member of the Navy's Hospital Corps. Hospital corpsmen serve as enlisted medical specialists for the United States Navy and United States Marine Corps. The Hospital Corpsman serves in a wide variety of capacities and locations, including shore establishments such as naval hospitals and clinics, aboard ships as the primary medical caregivers for sailors while underway, or with Marine Corps units. The colloquial form of address for a Corpsman is "Doc".

CP – Command Post, a command and control center that is used by a military unit in a deployed location is usually called a "command post."

Command and control is defined as the exercise of authority and direction by a properly designated commander over assigned and attached forces in the accomplishment of the mission. Command and control functions are performed through an arrangement of personnel, equipment, communications, facilities, and procedures employed by a commander in planning, directing, coordinating, and controlling forces and operations in the accomplishment of the mission.

Corporal –

Corporal is the fourth enlisted rank in the Marine Corps, ranking immediately above Lance Corporal and immediately below Sergeant. The Marine Corps, unlike the Army, has no other rank at the pay grade of E-4. Corporal is the lowest grade of non-commissioned officer in the U.S. Marine Corps, though promotion to Corporal traditionally confers a large jump in authority and responsibility compared to promotion from Private through Lance Corporal.

Theoretically, Marine Corporals generally serve as "fire-team leaders," commanding a 4-man team or unit of similar size. In practice, however, the billet of fire team leader is generally held by a Lance Corporal, while Corporals serve in the squad leader billet that would normally be held by a Sergeant (E-5) in infantry units. In support units, they direct the activities of junior Marines and provide technical supervision. Because of its emphasis on small-unit tactics, the Marine Corps usually places Corporals in billets where other services would normally have an E-5 or E-6 in authority. Similarly, the term "Strategic Corporal" refers to the special responsibilities conferred upon a Marine Corporal.

dai uy –

The Vietnamese rank of Captain.

DDT

An insecticide used for malaria control. DDT (from its trivial name, Dichloro-Diphenyl-Trichlorocthane) is one of the best-known synthetic pesticides. It is a chemical with a long, unique, and controversial history.

First synthesized in 1874, DDT's insecticidal properties were not discovered until 1939. In the second half of World War II, it was used with great effect among both military and civilian populations to control mosquitoes spreading malaria and lice transmitting typhus, resulting in dramatic reductions in the incidence of both diseases. The Swiss chemist Paul Hermann Müller of Geigy Pharmaceutical was awarded the Nobel Prize in Physiology or Medicine in 1948 "for his discovery of the high efficiency of DDT as a contact poison against several arthropods." After the war, DDT was made available for use as an agricultural insecticide, and soon its production and use skyrocketed.

In 1962, *Silent Spring* by American biologist Rachel Carson was published. The book catalogued the environmental impacts of the indiscriminate spraying of DDT in the US and questioned the logic of releasing large amounts of chemicals into the environment without fully understanding their effects on ecology or human health. The book suggested that DDT and other pesticides may cause cancer and that their agricultural use was a threat to wildlife, particularly birds. Its publication was one of the signature events in the birth of the environmental movement. *Silent Spring* resulted in a large public outcry that eventually led to most uses of DDT being banned in the US in 1972. DDT was subsequently banned for agricultural use worldwide under the Stockholm Convention, but its limited use in disease vector control continues to this day in certain parts of the world and remains controversial.

Along with the passage of the Endangered Species Act, the US ban on DDT is cited by scientists as a major factor in the comeback of the bald eagle in the contiguous US.

DMZ – Demilitarized Zone. The Vietnamese Demilitarized Zone was established as a dividing line between North and South Vietnam as a result of the First Indochina War.

During the Vietnam War it became important as the battleground demarcation separating North Vietnamese territory from South Vietnamese territory.

The DMZ ran east-west near the center of present-day Vietnam (spanning more than a hundred kilometers) and was a couple of kilometers wide. It reached across into a beach on the east. An island nearby was controlled by North Vietnamese forces during the Vietnam War. Although it was nominally described as being at "the 17th parallel," almost all of the zone lies to the south of the parallel, with only a small portion of the zone near the eastern shore actually including the parallel. It was around a hundred kilometers north of the city of Hue.

The Geneva Conference on July 21, 1954, recognized the 17th parallel as a "provisional military demarcation line" temporarily dividing the country into two states, Communist North Vietnam and South Vietnam.

The Geneva Accords promised elections in 1956 to determine a national government for a united Vietnam. However because Ho Chi Minh and the Communists immediately began trying to destabilize the free and democratic south, these elections were never held. Emperor Bảo Đại, from his home in France, appointed Ngô Đình Diệm as Prime Minister of South Vietnam. With American support, in 1955, Diệm used a rigged referendum to remove the Emperor and declare himself president of the Republic of Vietnam.

Thus the competition for the whole of Vietnam began; Diệm's military was unable to prevail in the civil war which escalated, as a result of international intervention, into the Vietnam War, which is also referred to as the *Second Indochina War*.

Doron Plate – A strong fiberglass-based laminate that was first used by the United States military as personal body armor for infantry in the Battle of Okinawa in 1945. The plates were approximately 1/8th inch thick and cut into five inch squares then inserted into pockets on a nylon vest that covered the front and back portions of the torso as well as the shoulders. The vest weighed approximately 8 pounds. The plates consist of fiberglass filaments bonded together with resin under pressure. The plates could be molded to fit the contours of the chest or back. Dow Company discovered the technology for the doron plate in May 1943 because a shortage of metal during World War II had stimulated research into non-metallic forms of body armor. The doron plate could not stop direct fire from bullets but was effective at stopping relatively slow moving flak and shrapnel. The plates were named after General G.F. Doriot who was chief of the Research and Development Branch, Office of The Quartermaster General of the Army during World War II. The doron plates were used in the Korean War in the M-1951 and T-52-2 vests and the Vietnam War in the M69 vest. Stronger and lighter materials such as Kevlar-based body armor eventually superseded the doron plate.

Duster – An army tank with twin forty millimeter guns. See M42 A1.

E-tool –   The M-1951 Entrenching Tool was a combination shovel, hoe and pick ax, with a wooden handle and folding blade and a hinged pick, and attached to the same pivot as the shovel so it too could be folded out or laid flat for storage. It could be easily carried, assembled, and required almost no instructions for use. These were issued starting in 1943.

The M-1951 had a one piece handle that was permanently attached to the blade via an adjustable hinge. Using a large nut to loosen or tighten the connection, the hinge could be freed so the shovel and handle could be set up in a line (used as a shovel), at a right angle (used as a hoe), or folded over to store in its cover.

fam fire –   Familiarization Firing is training to ensure that all Marines are thoroughly instructed in the proper use of the weapon for which training is conducted. Particular emphasis is placed on safety procedures and proper handling of the weapon. Marines are not allowed to fire any weapon until they have received appropriate safe handling instructions.

field jacket –   The M1965 jacket had four large cargo pockets and an internally tied drawstring waist, wrist closures were provided with Velcro (hook and loop) fasteners. The pockets used metal snaps to close. The front fly tab closed with snaps over a heavy zipper. A zipper along the back of the collar hides an attached hood that could be pulled out when needed. A storm flap could be closed over the throat with a Velcro tab. Most jackets had an information label sewn into the back at the top, just under the collar.

first sergeant –   First Sergeant in Marine Corps, is one level below Sergeant Major and Master Gunnery Sergeant and is the next rank above Gunnery Sergeant. It is equal in grade to Master Sergeant, although the two ranks have different responsibilities.

First Sergeant have a command responsibility while Master Sergeants have technical responsibilities. Unlike the First Sergeant and Master Sergeant programs in the U.S. Army, no lateral movement is possible between the two ranks in the Marine Corps. In their annual performance evaluations, called "fitness reports," eligible Gunnery Sergeants indicate whether they wish to be considered for promotion to Master

Sergeant or First Sergeant. A First Sergeant is then eligible to be promoted to a Sergeant Major while a Master Sergeant would be on the promotional track for Master Gunnery Sergeant.

four-holer – A prefabricated four-seat latrine box. This box can be collapsed for shipment. A four-hole burnout field-type latrine is used at most temporary bases. Camp maintenance personnel keep the latrine in an orderly condition. Two people can effectively and efficiently dispose of the excremental waste of 500 people. There are two easy ways of maintaining the burnout latrine. They are as follows: by spreading lime over the waste material or by using diesel fuel to burn the waste material. The burning pit for the waste material should be located so resulting smoke, fumes, odors, and blowing ashes do not interfere with operations or the health and general well-being of personnel.

FMSS – Field Medical Service School. A training course for Navy Corpsmen to prepare them for service with the Marine Corps focusing on medical situations encountered in combat and in field situations. Students are also required to meet the same rigid physical conditioning requirements set by the Marine Corps.

Frag – The fragmentation grenade is an anti-personnel weapon that is designed to disperse shrapnel upon exploding. The body is made of hard plastic or steel. Flechettes, notched wire, ball bearings or the case itself provide the fragments. When the word "grenade" is used without specification, and context does not suggest otherwise, it is generally assumed to refer to a fragmentation grenade.

These grenades were sometimes classed as defensive grenades because the effective casualty radius of some matched or exceeded the distance they could be thrown, thus necessitating them being thrown from behind cover.

fragging – A term from the Vietnam War, used primarily by U.S. military personnel, most commonly meaning to assassinate an unpopular officer of one's own fighting unit, often by means of a fragmentation grenade.

A grenade was often used because it would not leave any fingerprints, and because a ballistics test could not be done as it could to match a bullet with a firearm. The grenade would often be thrown into the officer's tent while he slept.

Sometimes the intended victim would be 'warned' by first having a smoke grenade thrown into his tent. If he persisted in antagonizing his men, this would be followed by a stun grenade, and finally by a fragmentation grenade.

A fragging victim could also be killed by intentional friendly fire during combat. In this case, the death would be blamed on the enemy, and, due to the dead man's unpopularity, the perpetrator could assume that no one would contradict the story.

Fragging most often involved the murder of a commanding officer (CO) or a senior noncommissioned officer perceived as unpopular, harsh, inept, or overzealous. Many soldiers were not overly keen to go into harm's way, and preferred leaders with a similar sense of self-preservation. If a CO was incompetent, fragging the officer was considered a means to the end of self preservation for the men serving under him. Fragging might also occur if a commander freely took on dangerous or suicidal missions, especially if he was deemed to be seeking glory for himself.

The very idea of fragging served to warn junior officers to avoid the ire of their enlisted men through recklessness, cowardice, or lack of leadership. Junior officers in turn could arrange the murder of senior officers when finding them incompetent or wasting their men's lives needlessly. Underground GI newspapers sometimes listed bounties offered by units for the fragging of unpopular commanding officers.

During the Vietnam War, fragging was reportedly common. There are documented cases of at least 230 American officers killed by their own troops, and as many as 1,400 other officers' deaths could not be explained. Fragging incidents were more common in the Army than in the Marines. Incidents of fragging have been recorded as far back as the 18th century.

friendly fire –

Non-hostile fire, a term originally adopted by the military, refers to fire from one's own side or allied forces, as opposed to fire coming from enemy forces.

Use of the term "friendly fire" is appropriate where there was intent to do harm to the enemy which caused injury to one's own side. 8,000 such incidents have been estimated for the Vietnam War.

Friendly fire is often seen as an inescapable result of combat. Attempts to reduce this effect by military leaders generally come down to identifying the causes of friendly fire and overcoming repetition of the incident through training, tactics and technology.

A death resulting from a negligent discharge is not considered friendly fire. Murder, whether premeditated or in the heat of the moment, or deliberate firing on one's own troops for disciplinary reasons is not classified as friendly fire.

The primary cause of friendly fire is commonly known as the "fog of war" which attributes friendly fire incidents to the confusion inherent in warfare. Friendly fire that is the result of apparent recklessness or incompetence may fall into this category. The concept of a fog of war has come under considerable criticism, as it can be used as an all-encompassing excuse for poor planning, weak or compromised intelligence and incompetent command. Fog of war incidents fall roughly into two classes:

Errors of position where fire aimed at enemy forces accidentally ends up hitting one's own. Such incidents were relatively common during the First and Second World Wars, where troops fought in close proximity to each other and targeting was relatively inaccurate. As the accuracy of weapons improved, this class of incident has become less common but still occurs.

Errors of identification where friendly troops are mistakenly attacked in the belief that they are the enemy.

A number of situations can lead to or exacerbate the risk of friendly fire. Poor terrain and visibility are major factors. Soldiers fighting on unfamiliar ground can become disoriented more easily than on familiar terrain. When being fired upon by enemy troops, the direction from which shots are coming isn't easy to find, confusing troops. The addition of poor weather conditions and combat stress can lead to separation of forces, and its easy to see how a soldier mistakenly believes that he or she is shooting at the enemy, especially when fire is exchanged. Accurate navigation and 'fire discipline' are vital.

In high-risk situations, leaders need to ensure units are properly informed of the location of friendly units and to issue clear, unambiguous orders, but they must also react correctly to responses from soldiers who are capable of using their own judgement. Miscommunication can be deadly. Radios, field telephones, and signalling systems can be used to address the problem, but when these systems are used to co-ordinate multiple forces such as ground troops and aircraft, their breakdown can dramatically increase the risk of friendly fire. When allied troops are added to the mixture, maintaining lines of communication can be even more difficult, especially if language barriers need to be surmounted.

GCT/ARI – General Comprehensive Test / Arithmetic Tests. In the vavy recruits are given many examinations, but the sum of the scores of these two test are used to determine a sailor's eligibility to enter a training category or rating. Courses have a minimum score to accept trainees. The larger the number associated with the course, the more difficult the course.

gook – A derogatory term used by the military referring to indigenous Asians used especially for enemy soldiers. Its use as an ethnic slur has been traced to U.S. Marines serving in the Philippines in the early 20th century. The earliest recorded use is dated 1920. Prior to the Vietnam War, "gook" was U.S. soldiers' jargon used to refer to any non-American. A slang dictionary published in 1893 defines "gook" as "a low prostitute." Marines fighting in the Philippine-American War (1899-1902) and the Moro Rebellion (1902-13) used the word to refer to Filipinos. This alteration of meaning may reflect contempt for native women and an accusation of promiscuity. Early usage may have been influenced by the word "goo goo" or "gugu," also applied to Filipinos by the Marines. "Gugu" originated as a mocking imitation of Filipino speech (ompared to "barbarian".)" The Marines who occupied Nicaragua in 1912 took to calling the natives gooks. In 1920, U.S. Marines in Haiti were using the term to refer to Haitians.

In the U.S., gook refers most particularly to Communist soldiers in the context of the Vietnam War. It is generally considered highly offensive, on a par with "nigger".

A folk etymology suggests that during the Korean War, Korean children would point at U.S. soldiers and shout "mee-guk" the Korean word for "America." Soldiers heard the word as "me gook," as if the children were defining themselves as "gooks." This explanation ignores the fact that there are many examples of the word's use that pre-date the Korean War.

GySgt. – Gunnery Sergeant is the seventh enlisted rank in the United States Marine Corps, just above Staff Sergeant and below Master Sergeant and First Sergeant, and is a staff non-commissioned officer (SNCO). It has a pay grade of E-7.

A Gunnery Sergeant in the infantry is typically in charge of coordinating logistics for a company-sized group of Marines, or about 180 personnel. Junior Gunnery Sergeants usually serve as platoon sergeant for weapons platoons. A Gunnery Sergeant's job is to be the operations chief of a company of Marines.

Gunnery Sergeants are commonly referred to by the informal abbreviation "gunny." This nickname is usually regarded as a title of esteem and/or camaraderie, and is generally acceptable for use in all situations except formal and ceremonial ones. Use of the term by lower-ranking personnel, however, remains at the Gunnery Sergeant's discretion.

H&S – Headquarters and Support Company. In Marine Corps units, a Headquarters and Service Company is a company sized military unit, found at the battalion level and higher. In identifying a specific headquarters unit, it is usually referred to by its abbreviation as H&S. While a regular line company is formed of three platoons, H&S is made up of the headquarters staff and headquarters support personnel of a battalion, brigade, division, or higher level unit. As these personnel do not fall inside one of the regular line companies of the battalion, brigade, or division, the H&S Unit is the unit to which they are administratively assigned. The typical personnel strength of an average H&S Company is 80 to 110 personnel.

Inside a battalion H&S, the headquarters staff will usually include the following key officers and primary staff officers:
- A battalion commander, usually a lieutenant colonel
- A battalion executive officer, usually a major
- An administration and personnel officer (S1), usually a captain

- An intelligence and counterintelligence officer (S2), usually a captain
- An operations and training officer (S3), usually a major
- A logistics officer (S4), usually a captain
- A plans officer (S5), usually a captain
- A communications and information officer (S6), usually a captain

Depending on the unit, extra support officers would round out the staff, including a Navy medical officer, Judge Advocate General (legal officer), and a battalion chaplain (Naval Officer) (often collectively referred to as the "special staff"), as well as essential non-commissioned officers and enlisted support personnel in the occupational specialities of the staff sections (S1 through S4 and the S6), and a battalion sergeant major, who is principal advisor to the battalion commander on matters regarding enlisted personnel. Additionally, H&S will contain further personnel assigned to support and sustain the mission of the battalion headquarters, including maintenance and motor transport, field mess, and supply.

H&S itself will be commanded by a company commander (usually a captain) who is supported by a company executive officer (usually a first lieutenant) and a company first sergeant. All personnel in H&S fall under the administrative command of the H&S company commander, but in practice, the primary and special staff officers report directly to the battalion commander, and while the battalion commander is administratively assigned to H&S, he or she is the H&S company commander's higher commander and thus the H&S company commander operationally answers directly to the battalion commander. The mission of the H&S company commander is to run the administrative and Marine training aspects of H&S, and to support the battalion primary staff by facilitating the environment in which they operate and in turn support the battalion commander in commanding the battalion.

head – A nautical term from the days of sailing ships when the designated place to defecate and urinate was forward, at the bow or "head" of the ship. The term derives from sailing ships in which the toilet area for the regular sailors was placed at the head or bow of the ship. In sailing ships this position was sensible for two reasons: first, since most vessels of the era could not go to weather particularly well, the winds came mostly from the quarter, placing the head essentially downwind; secondly, if placed somewhat above the water line, vents or slots cut near the floor level would allow normal wave action to wash out the facility. Only the captain had his private toilet near his quarters, below the poop deck.

In many modern ships, the heads look similar to a seated, land-type toilet, but have several technical differences. Rather than using a cistern and gravity to flush the waste away through a plumbing trap to a drain, there is a system of valves and pumps that brings sea water into the toilet and pumps the waste out through the hull. In small boats the pump is often hand operated.

HMM-262 – Chinook helicopter Squadron out of Quang Tri. A Marine Corps helicopter squadron consisting of CH-46E Sea Knight transport helicopters. The squadron, known as the "Flying Tigers", is based at Marine Corps Air Station Futenma, Okinawa, Japan and falls under the command of Marine Aircraft Group 36 (MAG-36) and the 1st Marine Aircraft Wing (1st MAW).HMM-262 was deployed to the Republic of Vietnam in December 1966 and subsequently reassigned to Marine Aircraft Group 36, 1st Marine Aircraft Wing. The squadron supported operation during the Vietnam War and operated from Ky Ha, Marble Mountain Air Facility, Quang Tri, Phu Bai and the *USS Tripoli* while participating in numerous operations throughout the country.

hooch – A generically used term to describe a dwelling. On base, a hooch was usually a rectangular building made of 2x4s and plywood with a corrugated tin roof. Also used in reference to Vietnamese civilian houses.

HST – The Helicopter Support Team is a unit of organization within the Marine Corps that manages the activities of a helicopter-landing zone (LZ). It consists of a team of eight Landing Support Marines who are trained to hook up external loads to the hooks of primarily military helicopters. All kinds of gear can be lifted by helicopter and taken to locations with terrain that is not suited for other kinds of vehicles. For example communications equipment can be placed on top of a mountain within a few minutes of flight instead of a few hours of driving, if one could even drive the equipment to the designated location. The HST is a valuable resource to the Marine Air-Ground Task Force (MAGTF)), as it provides an expedient manner of transportation for gear and supplies.

Within the HST there is the *HST* commander whose job is to coordinate the mission between the airwing, the supporting unit, and the Marine Logistics Group who provides the HST. The HST Commander is usually a Staff Sergeant and sometimes a Gunnery Sergeant. Subordinate to the HST Commander is the HST Safety NCO, the job of the safety NCO is to ensure that the gear or supplies are rigged properly, and to ensure that everyone underneath the Helicopter are doing their job in a safe manner. The Safety NCO is normally a Corporal or Sergeant. The primary members of the HST are the Leg-men and the inside and outside directors along with the hookman and the Static Man. The inside and outside directors direct the pilot of the aircraft as he centers his helicopter over the load that is being lifted. The leg-men ensure that the slings used to lift the gear do not get caught on anything and lift in a straight manner as to not disturb the load being lifted. The job of the Static man is to use a grounding rod to attach to the hook so that the static electricity conducted by the helicopter is grounded out and does not end up killing a Marine. The Hook Man the hooks up the load to the hook of the aircraft in a safe manner.

I Corps – "eye-core" South Vietnam was divided into four military regions called "corps." I Corps was the northernmost followed by II Corps, III Corps and IV Corps in the far south.

immersion burner – A gas burner designed to heat water in a 30-gallon GI can. Used primarily for cleaning and sterilizing eating utensils and trays, but can be used whenever small quantities of hot water are needed. The unit attaches to the side of the can with the heating unit near the inside bottom of the can. It uses gas or diesel which drops from a holding tank into the heating element, where it burns, heating the water.

ITR – Infantry Training Regiment is the school that Marines attend to learn basic infantryman skills after graduating from boot camp.

jungle boots –

At the outset of the Vietnam War, U.S. advisors wore leather combat boots. These continued to be used throughout the war period, but in the early 1960s, perhaps as early as 1962, Army and Marine field troops began to use a black leather and olive drab nylon-webbing tropical combat boot with a cleated sole (the "Jungle Boot" with nomenclature "Boot, Combat, Tropical, Mildew Resistant" or "Boots, Hot Weather"). One of the major contractors, Wellco, produced 5000 pairs per day in the mid-60s. Two versions of leather boots remained in service in rear areas, or where there was a fire hazard that precluded the use of nylon (e.g. for pilots and other aviators), or wherever the Jungle Boot was not desirable for any reason.

All new Jungle Boots came with an "information tag" attached that provided instructions for use. The key points on the tag were:
- Wear with one pair "socks, wool, cushion sole". Carry extra socks and change often.
- How to choose your size.
- How to pull the boots on. Check for snakes and insects.
- Wear trousers on outside of boot.
- How to keep boots clean.

KA-BAR –

Ka-Bar (trademarked as KA-BAR) is a knife-manufacturing company most known for its 11-3/4-inch fighting and utility Bowie knife used by the United States Marine Corps and United States Navy in World War II. A typical Ka-Bar knife has a 7" clip point blade. The Ka-Bar fighting knife is made of 1095 carbon steel and features a leather-washer or synthetic handle made of Kraton (a non-slip rubber substitute).

The Ka-Bar fighting knife was originally designed as a hunting knife in 1898, and would have been considered unremarkable at that time. In 1942, soon after the United States' entry into World War II, American troops experienced the problematic nature of the M1917/1918 and Mark I trench knives that they were issued initially and, realizing the need for knives suited to trench warfare, Ka-Bar's design was chosen from a catalog of hunting gear. The Marines bought many different knives and designs from a large number of suppliers during World War II, but it was the Ka-Bar fighting knife that was most common and popular. It was chosen for continued purchase and issue after the war was over. The final shape was decided upon by the Marine Corps. The changes included a slightly longer blade for combat use, introduction of a small fuller to make the blade lighter, and the pinned pommel and stacked leather handle as standard. In addition, the blade, guard, and pommel were all finished in a non-reflective matte black or gray phosphate finish instead of the brightly polished steel of the original.

Millions were made during World War II by Ka-Bar, Ontario Knife Company, Camillus Cutlery, Case Knives, and several other knife companies. The knife is inexpensive, easy to replace, and adequate for most tasks. It was also used as a diving knife in World War II, though the model in use at the time disintegrated rapidly in saltwater.

LAW – Light Anti-tank Weapon, see M72

LCpl. – Lance Corporal is the third lowest enlisted rank in the Marine Corps, just above Private First Class and below Corporal. It is not a non-commissioned officer rank. The Marines are the only component of the U.S. Armed Forces to have Lance Corporals.

The US Army had the rank of Lance Corporal from 1965-1968 with an insignia of one stripe up and one rocker stripe down before the rank was changed to Private First Class.

From the earliest years of the Corps, the ranks of lance corporal and lance sergeant were in common usage. Marines were appointed temporarily from the next lower rank to the higher grade but were still paid at the lower rank. As the rank structure became more firmly defined, the rank of lance sergeant fell out of use. Lance corporals served in the Corps into the 1930s but this unofficial rank became redundant when the rank of private first class was established in 1917. The lance corporal fell out of usage prior to World War II, before it was permanently established in the sweeping rank restructuring of 1958.

Because it is not an NCO status, only ranks equal to or above call a Lance Corporal by last name.

LSU – Landing Ship, Utility now called Landing Craft Utility (LCU) is a type of boat used by amphibious forces to transport equipment and troops to the shore. They are capable of transporting tracked or wheeled vehicles and troops from amphibious assault ships to beachheads or piers.

The LCU 1610, 1627 and 1646 class vessels are operated by the United States Navy. They are a self-sustaining craft complete with living accommodations and messing facilities for a crew of fourteen. They have been adapted for many uses including salvage operations, ferry boats for vehicles and passengers, and underwater test platforms. Each LCU is assigned an officer-in-charge (Craft Master) who is either a Chief Petty Officer or Petty Officer First Class in the Boatswain's Mate, Quartermaster, Operations Specialist or Culinary Specialist rating. These vessels have bow ramps for onload/offload, and can be linked bow to stern gate to create a temporary pier-like structure. Its welded steel hull provides high durability with deck loads of 800 pounds per square foot. Arrangement of machinery and equipment has taken into account built-in redundancy in the event of battle damage. The craft features two engine rooms separated by a watertight bulkhead to permit limited operation in the event that one engine room is disabled. An anchor system is installed on the starboard side aft to assist in retracting from the beach. These vessels are normally transported to their areas of operation on board larger amphibious vessels such as LHDs and LHAs.

LZ –

A Landing Zone is a military term for any area where aircraft land.

In the United States military, a landing zone is the actual point where aircraft land.

Landing areas are most commonly marked by colored smoke. The standard procedure is for those at the landing area to "pop smoke" (set off a smoke grenade) and declare this over the radio. The pilot says when smoke is seen and what color the smoke is. Those on the ground then respond with what color the smoke should be. Smoke of a different color can mean the landing area has been discovered and compromised by enemies, and the pilot will usually have the authority to cancel any landing.

LZs were used to a greater extent in the Vietnam War than in other wars because of the widespread use of helicopters. Helicopters were usually the fastest way around Vietnam, and as such, there needed to be Landing Zones where they could land. LZs allowed troops to be moved to closer positions near the front. While many LZs were temporary, being little more than a clearing in the jungle or a clearing made using defoliant bombs that cleared everything in a diameter of 150 feet, many others were semi-permanent.

M1 steel helmet – A steel helmet is designed to protect the user from flying fragments of exploded ordnance. Each M-1 helmet shell was stamped from a single sheet of manganese steel. The helmet has a chinstrap loop on each side attached with either a hinge or welded directly to the helmet. The helmets were painted with standard matte finish olive drab paint with shredded cork or sawdust grit mixed in to reduce glare, giving a bumpy finish.

A second component was the M-1941 helmet liner, a removable inner helmet constructed of resin-impregnated cotton canvas. The liner had an internal adjustable suspension system and its own leather chinstrap so it could be worn without the steel shell for duty that did not involve combat or combat training.

The steel outer helmet had a chinstrap made of cotton webbing attached using the bail, its only attachment. The chinstrap was often left undone (or buckled on the back of the helmet) with the unfounded idea that the force of an explosion could catch the helmet and cause injury from the jerk of the chinstrap. Although the interior suspension system of the liner was adjustable and would keep the helmet on the soldier's head even without the chin strap, there were times when an unstrapped soldier would have to hold his helmet on by hand. In some units commanders had to order the men to fasten their chinstraps at all times.

In Vietnam, the M-1 steel helmet was the standard headgear. A cloth helmet cover was designed with a disruptive camouflage pattern. The cover was reversible with leaf patterns in green or brown for fall or winter operations. The helmet cover also contained small slots for inserting natural foliage. The camouflage helmet band was designed to hold foliage in order to blend the helmet shape and color into the surrounding vegetation. In Vietnam, this band more commonly held cigarettes, insect repellent, or an extra rifle magazine. Early in 1967, writing on helmet covers began. Most commonly seen were nicknames, names of girl friends, names of home states or towns, or a short time list of dates of return to "The World".

In addition to its mission as head protection, the M-1 steel helmet was used for boiling water to make coffee, for cooking and shaving, as an entrenching tool, to bail water from a landing craft, or as a hammer.

M3A1 – The M3 Grease gun is a .45 caliber submachine gun that uses the .45 ACP (11.43 x 23mm ACP) pistol cartridge. It weighs 7.65 lb. It entered US Army service on December 12, 1942 as the United States Submachine Gun, Cal. .45, M3 and began to replace the .45 caliber Thompson series submachine guns: the M1928A1, M1 and M1A1 that were slowly being withdrawn from use. The weapon's designer was G. Hyde, while F. Sampson – GM's Inland Division chief engineer – was responsible for preparing and organizing production. Even at the development stage, the weapon's design was focused on simplified production, ease of use and the ability to convert the weapon to the 9x19mm Parabellum pistol cartridge. The weapon is commonly referred to as the "grease gun", owing to its similarity in appearance to the common mechanic's tool.

The M3 is an automatic only, blowback-operated firearm (the weapon's bolt is assisted by two parallel wire-guide action springs) that fires from an open bolt. A spring extractor is located inside the bolt, while the ejector is located in the trigger housing group. The weapon is striker fired with the firing pin contained inside the bolt, the return springs act as the striker spring. The weapon is secured from accidental firing by closing the spring-loaded ejection port cover, which has a lug that engages notches in the bolt assembly's surface, locking it in both its forward and rear positions. The firearm is fed from a double-column, single-feed 30-round detachable box magazine patterned after the British Sten gun.

The gun employs metal stamping and pressing, spot welding and welding. The bolt rides on two rods that are simultaneously the return spring guide rods. The weapon has a removable rifled barrel. A conical flash hider (developed later) could be attached. The fixed iron sights consist of a rear aperture set for firing at 100 yards (approx. 91 m) and a blade foresight. The M3 is equipped with a folding (telescoping) metal wire stock, that can be removed and used to load rounds into the magazine. The stock also features threads at both ends used to attach a bore brush that creates a cleaning rod.

The M3 was originally designed as a disposable small arm, to be used and discarded once it became inoperative. However, in 1944, a shortage of new M3 weapons forced U.S. Army Ordnance workshops to fabricate pawl springs and other parts in order to keep existing weapons operational.

The M3 and M3A1 were mostly withdrawn from U.S. service in 1957; however they continued to be used until the mid-1990s by armored vehicle crews and truck drivers. For example, during the Gulf War of 1991, drivers of the 19th Engineer Battalion, attached to the 1st Armored Division, were deployed with the M3A1.

M14 –

The M14 rifle, formally the United States Rifle, Caliber 7.62 mm, M14, is an American selective fire battle rifle firing 7.62x51mm NATO ammunition. Although largely superseded in military use by the M16 rifle, it remains in limited front line service with the United States Army, Marine Corps, and Navy, and as a ceremonial weapon. The M14 also provides the basis for the M21 and M25 sniper rifles. It was the last so-called "battle rifle" (a term applied to weapons firing full-power rifle ammunition) issued in quantity to U.S. troops. The rifle served adequately during its brief tour of duty in Vietnam. Though it was unwieldy in the thick brush due to its length and weight, the power of the 7.62 mm NATO cartridge allowed it to penetrate cover quite well and reach out to extended range, developing 2,470 ft·lbf (3,350 J) of muzzle energy. However, there were several drawbacks to the M14. The traditional wood stock of the rifle had a tendency to swell and expand in the heavy moisture of the jungle, adversely affecting accuracy. Fiberglass stocks were produced to resolve this problem. However, the rifle was discontinued before very many could be distributed for field use. Also, because of the M14's powerful 7.62x51 mm cartridge, the weapon was virtually uncontrollable in fully automatic mode. The M14 was developed as a means of taking the place of four different weapons systems – the M1 Garand, the M1 Carbine, the M3 "Grease Gun" and the M1918 Browning Automatic Rifle (BAR). It was thought that in this manner the M14 could simplify the logistical requirements of the troops if it took the place of four weapons. Although it proved to be an impossible task to replace all four, the weapon excelled as a replacement for the M1 rifle, fixing many of the previous rifle's shortcomings. The cartridge was too powerful for the submachine gun role and the weapon was simply too light to provide as a light machine gun replacement for the BAR. The M60 machine gun better served this task.

The M14 remained the primary infantry weapon in Vietnam until it was replaced by the M16 in 1966-1969. The M16 was ordered as a replacement for the M14 by direction of Secretary of Defense Robert McNamara, over the objection of those Army officers who had backed the M14. Though production of the M14 was officially discontinued, some disgruntled troops still managed to hang on to them while deriding the M16 as a frail and underpowered "Mattel toy" or "poodle shooter". In January 1968 the U.S. Army designated the M16 as the "Standard A" rifle, and the M14 became a "Limited Standard" weapon. The M14 rifle remained the standard rifle for US Army Basic Training until 1970.

M16 –

M16 (more formally Rifle, Caliber 5.56 mm, M16) is the U.S. military designation for a family of rifles derived from the ArmaLite AR-15 and further developed by Colt starting in the mid-20th century. The M16 rifle family including the M16/A1/A2/A3/A4 has been the primary infantry rifle of the United States military since the 1960s. With its variants, it has been in use by 15 NATO countries, and is the most produced firearm in its caliber. The M16 entered Army service in 1964. The M16 was an initial version first adopted in 1964 by the United States Air Force. The U.S. Army began to use the XM16E1 in 1965 with most going to Vietnam. The US Marine Corps also adopted the system during this period. The XM16E1 was standardized as the M16A1 in 1967. This version remained the primary infantry rifle of the United States military from 1967 until the 1980s, when it was supplemented by the M16A2. During the early 1980s a roughly standardized load for this ammunition was adopted throughout NATO. When the XM16E1 reached Vietnam with U.S. troops in March 1965, reports of jamming and malfunctions in combat immediately began to surface. Although the M14 featured a chrome-lined barrel and chamber to resist corrosion in combat conditions (a danger learned from WWII Pacific theatre combat experience), neither the bore nor the chamber of the M16/XM16E1 was chrome-lined. Several documented accounts of troops killed by enemy fire with jammed rifles broken-down for cleaning eventually brought a Congressional investigation. Later investigations also cast doubt on the veracity of the original 1962 reports of the alleged stopping effectiveness of the 5.56 mm bullet, as well as criticism of inadequate penetration (in comparison to the Soviet 7.62x39mm round) when firing at enemy personnel through light cover.

On February 28, 1967, the XM16E1 was standardized as the M16A1. Major revisions to the design followed. The rifle was finally given a chrome-lined chamber (and later, the entire bore) to eliminate corrosion and stuck cartridges, and the rifle's recoil mechanism was re-designed to accommodate Army-issued 5.56 mm ammunition. Rifle cleaning tools and powder solvents/lubricants were issued. Intensive training programs in weapons cleaning were instituted, and a comic book style manual was circulated among the troops to demonstrate proper maintenance. The reliability problems of the M16 diminished quickly, although the rifle's reputation continued to suffer. Moreover, complaints about the inadequate penetration and stopping power of the 5.56 mm cartridge persisted throughout the Vietnam conflict.

M37 –   The 3/4 ton rated M-37 family of trucks were built by Dodge. The M37 is a custom military design developed starting in 1948 and produced is several groups and models from 1950 to 1968. The M37 series was used by all the U.S. services from the early 1950s through the 1980s and exported widely around the world. Although a little sluggish, this is one of the toughest and most reliable trucks ever built.

M42A –   The 40 mm Self-Propelled Anti-Aircraft Gun, or "Duster" as it is known, is an armored light air-defense gun built for the U.S. Army from 1952 until December 1959. Although the M42 Duster was initially designed in the anti-aircraft role, it found great success when used in the Vietnam War against unarmored ground forces. Armament consists of fully automatic twin 40 mm M2A1 Bofors, with a rate of fire of 240 rounds per minute (rpm) and either a .30 caliber or a M-60 Machine Gun. It used components from the M41 light tank and was constructed of all welded steel. The 500 hp six cylinder air-cooled gasoline engine is located in the rear of the vehicle. A total of 3,700 M42s were built. The vehicle has a crew of six and weighs 22,500 kg (49,500 lb) fully loaded. Maximum speed is 45 mph with a range of 100 miles.

M48A3 – The M48 Patton was the third and final US medium tank. The M48 served as the U.S. Army and Marine Corp's primary battle tank during the Vietnam War.

M50 Ontos – Officially the Rifle, Multiple 106 mm, Self-propelled, M50, was a light armored tracked anti-tank vehicle developed in the US in the 1950s. It mounted six M40 106 mm recoilless rifles as its main armament, which could be fired in rapid succession against single targets to guarantee a kill.

Originally conceived as a fast tank killer, it was employed by US Marines who consistently reported excellent results when used for direct fire support against infantry during the Vietnam War. Its mobility and firepower were proven in numerous battles and operations. Produced in limited numbers and largely expended towards the end of the conflict, the Ontos was always considered an "ugly duckling" and was removed from service in 1969.

M60 – Formally the United States Machine Gun, Caliber 7.62 mm, M60 is a family of American general-purpose machine guns firing 7.62x51mm NATO cartridges from a disintegrating belt of M13 links. It can fire three types of ammunition, ball, tracer, and armor piercing. In a normal combat situation, The M-60 is loaded with ball and tracer in a 4:1 ratio.

Introduced in 1957, until recently it remained in use in every branch of the U.S military and still serves in other armed forces.

The M60 is an air-cooled and gas-operated machine gun firing from an open bolt. It chambers the 7.62x51mm NATO cartridge and feeds from a disintegrating belt of metallic M13 links. In most variants, it has an integrated folding bipod and can be mounted on the M122 Tripod and some fixed mounts.

The M60 is considered effective up to 1,100 meters when firing at an area target and mounted on a tripod; up to 800 meters when firing at an area target using the integral bipod;

up to 600 meters when firing at a point target; and up to 200 meters when firing at a moving point target. United States Marine Corps doctrine holds that the M60 and other weapons in its class are capable of suppressive fire on area targets out to 1,500 meters if the gunner is sufficiently skilled.

The M60 is generally used as crew-served weapon and operated by a team of two or three men. The team consists of the gunner, the assistant gunner (A-gunner in military slang), and the ammunition bearer. The gun's weight and the amount of ammunition it consumes when fired make it difficult for a single soldier to carry and operate. The gunner carries the weapon and, depending on his strength and stamina, anywhere from 200 to 1000 rounds of ammunition. The assistant carries a spare barrel and extra ammunition, and reloads and spots targets for the gunner. The ammunition bearer carries additional ammunition and fetches more ammunition as needed during firing. The basic ammunition load carried by the crew is 600 to 900 rounds and theoretically allows approximately two minutes of continuous firing at the maximum rate of fire. All crews carry more than the basic load, sometimes three or more times the basic amount if they can get it. In many U.S. units that used the M60 as a squad automatic weapon in Vietnam, every soldier in the rifle squad would carry an additional 200 linked rounds of ammunition for the M60, a spare barrel, or both, in addition to his personal weapon and equipment.

The M60 can be accurately fired at short ranges from the shoulder due to its design. This was an initial requirement for the design and a hold-over in concept from the Browning Automatic Rifle. It may also be fired from the M122, the integral bipod, and some other mounts.

M61 – The M61 grenade is a fragmentation hand grenade that was used by the US Armed Forces in the Vietnam War. The M61 has a thin sheet steel wall enclosing a notched steel coil and explosive core. When the grenade detonates, the coil shatters into high-velocity fragments that can cause casualties up to 15 metres away. It is sometimes referred to as a "lemon" grenade, because its explosive shell is shaped like a lemon fruit. Many millions of the M61 and its clones have been manufactured over the years. The explosive in a M61 grenade is Composition B.

M72 –   The M72-series Light Antitank Weapon (LAW) is a lightweight self-contained anti-armor weapon first fielded in the early 1960's. Although the M72-series LAW was mainly used as an anti-armor weapon, it has also been used against other targets such as buildings and light vehicles, effective to about 200 meters for stationary targets, and 165 meters for moving targets. It can penetrate up to 14 inches (350 mm) of armor.

The M72-series Light Antitank Weapon (LAW) consists of a rocket packed in a launcher that fires with open chamber and almost no recoil. It is man-portable, may be fired from either shoulder, and is issued as a round of ammunition. It requires little from the user, only a visual inspection and some operator maintenance. The launcher, which consists of two tubes, one inside the other, serves as a watertight packing container for the rocket and houses a percussion-type firing mechanism that activates the rocket, a fin-stabilized, fixed shaped charge round.

The M72-series LAW contains a nonadjustable propelling charge and a rocket. Every M72-series LAW has an integral high-explosive antitank (HEAT) warhead. The warhead is in the rocket's head (or body) section. The fuse and booster are in the rocket's closure section. The propellant, its igniter, and the fin assembly are in the rocket's motor.

Due to effect of cold temperatures on its ammunition, the M72-series is particularly susceptible to hang fires (delay between the triggering and the ignition of the propellant) in the cold. Back blast danger area is also doubled for the LAW under cold conditions.

M79 –   The M79 grenade launcher is a single-shot, shoulder-fired, break open grenade launcher. It fires a 40 x46 mm grenade and first appeared during the Vietnam War. Because of its distinctive report, it earned the nicknames of "Thumper", "Thump-Gun" "Bloop gun" and "Blooper" among American soldiers;

The M79 can fire a wide variety of 40 mm rounds, including explosive, anti-personnel, smoke, buckshot, flechette, and illumination. Its single-shot nature was a strong drawback; having to reload after every shot meant a slow rate of fire and therefore an inability to keep up a constant volume of fire during a firefight. Also, for close-in situations, the minimum arming range (the round must travel 30 meters to arm itself) and the blast radius meant a grenadier would have to either resort to a backup pistol, if he had one to begin with, or fire and hope that the grenade would not arm itself and act as a giant slow bullet. Specialty grenades for close-in fighting were created to compensate, though a Marine did not always have the luxury of being able to load one in the heat of battle. Moreover, its size meant that a Marine with an M79 would be dedicated to being only a grenadier, and if he ran out of ammunition had nothing but a pistol and knife to contribute to a fight.

M108 howitzer – A self-propelled 105 mm howitzer, first introduced in the early1960s.The M-108was powered by a Detroit diesel turbocharged 8V-71T 8-cylinders 405 hp engine. It used the same hull and turret as the 155m M109 self-propelled howitzer, and components of the M113 armored vehicle. The M108 was phased out soon after the American intervention in the Vietnam War, as the M109's 155 calibre was considered better fitted for the modern war.

M274 – The "Truck, Platform, Utility 1/2 Ton, 4x4" or the "Carrier, Light Weapons, Infantry, 1/2 ton, 4x4", known as the Mechanical Mule, was developed in the 1950s as a light weight cargo carrier to replace both the 1/4-ton jeep and 3/4-ton trucks in infantry and airborne infantry battalions. The M274 family could be fitted for many infantry tasks including transport of personnel or cargo (slowly – keeping up with foot soldiers), for stringing wire with a cable reel, for carrying patients on stretchers, and as a weapons platform for a recoilless rifle or TOW anti-tank missile. Each wheel had shackles for lifting by helicopter or parachute airdrop. The seat and the foot basket can be detached and stored underneath the platform, which can then be rigged as a steerable trailer. The steering column could be set in multiple positions so the driver could operate the vehicle from almost any position, including crouching down. The M274 vehicles were phased out by 1980.

M274 are 4x4 with a platform, a transmission with 3 forward speeds and one reverse, and a two-speed transfer case. The full-time four-wheel drive is further enhanced by locked differentials – the Mule will move even when only one wheel has traction.

M1911A1 –   The M1911 is a single-action, semi-automatic pistol (handgun) chambered for the .45 ACP cartridge. It was designed by John M. Browning, and was the standard-issue side arm for the United States armed forces from 1911 to 1985, and is still carried by some U.S. forces. It was widely used in World War I, World War II, the Korean War and the Vietnam War. Its formal designation as of 1940 was Automatic Pistol, Caliber .45, M1911 for the original Model of 1911 or Automatic Pistol, Caliber .45, M1911A1 for the M1911A1, adopted in 1924. The designation changed to Pistol, Caliber .45, Automatic, M1911A1 in the Vietnam era. In total, the United States procured around 2.7 million M1911 and M1911A1 pistols during its service life.

The M1911 is the most well known of John Browning's designs to use the short recoil principle in its basic design. Besides the pistol itself being widely copied, this operating system rose to become the pre-eminent type of the 20th century and is found in nearly all-modern center fire pistols.

M1936 pistol belt –   The M-1936 Pistol Belt was intended for soldiers who were not riflemen such as officers or crews of tanks or other equipment. In the field, at least a canteen and a first aid pouch were added. Many other items were optionally attached to the pistol belt.

M1951 flak jacket –   The M-1951 weighed 7.75 lbs. and was a zippered sleeveless jacket constructed of water-resistant nylon containing two types of armor. The first was a nylon basket-weave flexible pad, which covered the upper chest and shoulders. The other consisted of overlapping curved Doron plates covering the wearer's lower chest, back and abdomen. The M-1951 vest also featured an exterior breast pocket and a reinforced eyeleted waistband allowing equipment with the M-1910 hook fasteners to be attached to it, instead of a pistol belt.

MACV –   The U.S. Military Assistance Command, Vietnam, MACV, (*mack vee*), was the United States' unified command structure for all of its military forces in South Vietnam during the Vietnam War. Because of the many headquarters units in its locale, Tan Son Nhut Air Base (near Saigon) MACV was called Pentagon East. The MACV was created on February 8, 1962, in response to the increase in U.S. military assistance to South Vietnam. MACV was first implemented to assist the Military Assistance Advisory Group (MAAG) Vietnam, controlling every advisory and assistance effort in Vietnam, but was reorganized on May 15, 1964 and absorbed MAAG Vietnam into its command when combat unit deployment became too large for advisory group control. The first commanding general of MACV, General Paul D. Harkins, was also the commander of MAAG Vietnam, and after reorganization was succeeded by General William C. Westmoreland in June, 1964, followed by General Creighton Abrams (July 1968) and General Frederick C. Weyand (June 1972). The MACV was disbanded on March 29, 1973. Major component commands of MACV were:

- United States Army Vietnam (USARV)
- Naval Forces Vietnam (NAVFORV)
- Seventh Air Force (7AF)
- III Marine Amphibious Force (III MAF)
- I Field Force, Vietnam (I FFV)
- II Field Force, Vietnam (II FFV)
- XXIV Corps
- 5th Special Forces Group
- Civil Operations and Rural Development Support (CORDS)
- Studies and Observations Group under Joint "High Command" (Joint Chiefs of Staff & Commander in Chief) covert

MARS – The Military Affiliate Radio System (MARS) is a United States Department of Defense sponsored program, established as a separately managed and operated program by the United States Army, Navy, and Air Force. The program is a civilian auxiliary consisting primarily of licensed amateur radio operators who are interested in assisting the military with communications on a local, national, and international basis as an adjunct to normal communications. The MARS programs also include active duty, reserve, and National Guard units; Navy and National Oceanic and Atmospheric Administration ships, and Coast Guard cutters and shore stations.

MARS has a long history of providing worldwide auxiliary emergency communications during times of need. The combined three-service MARS programs (Army, Air Force, and Navy-Marine Corps) volunteer force of over 5,000 dedicated and skilled amateur radio operators provide the backbone of the MARS program. Their main benefit of MARS membership is enjoying the amateur radio hobby through an ever-expanding horizon of MARS service to the nation. MARS members work by the slogan "Proud, Professional, and Ready".

During the Korean War, Vietnam War and Gulf War, MARS was best known for its handling of "Marsgram" written messages and providing "phone patches" to allow overseas servicemen to contact their families at home.

MATS – Military Air Transport was a command of the U.S. Air Force from 1948-65, which superseded the Army Air Force's Air Transport Command, its direct predecessor, shortly after the Air Force became an independent service branch in 1947. MATS was succeeded by Military Airlift Command (MAC) in January 1966, and by Air Mobility Command (AMC) in June 1992, each of which broadened its mission.

MedCAP – Medical Civilian Action Programs were periodic medical clinics held for the Vietnamese in their villages. The corpsman treated everything from headaches to jungle ulcers, lancing boils, and stitching cuts. On occasion doctors and specialists with equipment and supplies set up a temporary field clinic to provide limited medical treatment to the local population.

medevac – Medical Evacuation. Removing casualties from the field by helicopter or truck for treatment at a medical facility.

MGySgt. – Master Gunnery Sergeant is the ninth and highest enlisted rank in the Marine Corps (along with the grade-equivalent ranks of Sergeant Major and Sergeant Major of the Marine Corps). Master Gunnery Sergeants are staff non-commissioned officers (SNCOs), and are assigned a pay grade of E-9.

Master Gunnery Sergeants are sometimes referred to by the nickname "Master Gunns" or "Master Gunny". These nicknames are unacceptable in formal or ceremonial situations, and, at the rank holder's discretion, may also be unacceptable for use by lower-ranking Marines.

The rank was derived from another rank unique to the Marine Corps, the Gunnery Sergeant, and has been in use (though not continuously) since the time of the Spanish-American War.

Establishment of the rank in its current form and paygrade occurred during sweeping reorganization of ranks and paygrades in 1958 and 1959. The rank was included, along with the rank of Master Sergeant, in a new program for the paygrades of E-8 and E-9 which allowed senior SNCO billets to be filled by occupational specialists. This move was designed to officially acknowledge the ever-increasing complexity of modern warfare, while still maintaining the First Sergeant and Sergeant Major programs, with their historic command prestige. During and prior to World War II, this was reversed; the Sergeant Major was an administrative position while the Master Gunnery Sergeant was part of the S-3 section and enforced discipline.

One of the major differences between the two E-9 ranks is that Master Gunnery Sergeants retain their Military Occupational Specialty (MOS), while Sergeants Major are given a new MOS to reflect their general command focus. This reinforces the Master Gunnery Sergeant's role as a provider of technical military leadership.

Montagnard – Indigenous peoples of the Central Highlands of Vietnam, the Degar were referred to by French colonists as Montagnard. The term Montagnard means "mountain people" in French and is a carryover from the French colonial period in Vietnam.

In Vietnamese, they are known by the term *thuong* (highlanders). *Thuong* is the Vietnamese adaptation of the Chinese "Shang". Montagnard was the term, typically shortened to "Yard", used by U.S. military personnel in the Central Highlands during the Vietnam War.

The Degar have a long history of tensions with the Vietnamese majority. While the Vietnamese are themselves heterogeneous, they generally share a common language and culture and have developed and maintained the dominant social institutions of Vietnam. The Degar do not share that heritage. There have been conflicts between the two groups over many issues, including land ownership, language and cultural preservation, access to education and resources, and political representation.

Originally inhabitants of the coastal areas of the region, they were driven to the uninhabited mountainous areas by invading Vietnamese and Cambodians beginning prior to the 9th century AD.

Although French Catholic missionaries converted some Degar in the nineteenth century, American missionaries made more of an impact in the 1930s, and many Degar are now Protestant. Of the approximately 1 million Degar, close to half are Protestant, while around 200,000 are Catholic. This made Vietnam's Communist Party suspicious of the Degar, particularly during the Vietnam War, since it was thought that they would be more inclined to help the predominantly Christian American, mainly Protestant forces.

The 1960s saw contact between the Degar and the U.S. military, as American involvement in the Vietnam War escalated and the Central Highlands emerged as a strategically important area, in large part because it included the Ho Chi Minh trail, the North Vietnamese supply line for Viet Cong forces in the south. The U.S. military, particularly the U.S. Army's Special Forces, developed base camps in the area and recruited the Degar, roughly 40,000 of whom fought alongside American soldiers and became a major part of the U.S. military effort in the Highlands.

Thousands of Degar fled to Cambodia after the fall of Saigon to the North Vietnamese Army, fearing that the new government would launch reprisals against them because they had aided the U.S. Army. The U.S. military resettled some Degar in the United States, primarily in South Carolina, but these evacuees numbered less than two thousand. In addition, the Vietnamese government has steadily displaced thousands of villagers from Vietnam's central highlands, to use the fertile land for coffee plantations.

Before the Vietnam War, the population of the Central Highlands, estimated at between 3 and 3.5 million, was almost exclusively Degar. Today, the population is approximately 4 million, of whom about 1 million are Degars. The 30 or so Degar tribes in the Central Highlands comprise more than six different ethnic groups who speak languages drawn primarily from the Malayo-Polynesian, Tai, and Mon-Khmer language families. The main tribes, in order of population, are the Jarai, Rhade, Bahnar, Koho, Mnong, and Stieng.

Outside of Vietnam, the largest community of Montagnards in the world is located in Greensboro, North Carolina.

MSgt. – Master Sergeant is the eighth enlisted rank in the United States Marine Corps, just above Gunnery Sergeant, below Master Gunnery Sergeant, Sergeant Major, and Sergeant Major of the Marine Corps. It is equal in grade to First Sergeant. Master Sergeants in the Marine Corps provide technical leadership as occupational specialists at the E-8 level. General command leadership at this paygrade is provided by the separate rank of First Sergeant. Master Sergeants may be referred to by the nickname of "Top". This usage is an informal one, however, and would not be used in an official or formal setting. Use of this nickname by Marines of subordinate rank is at the rank holder's discretion.

Mule – A small 4x4 vehicle used to move supplies. See M274

mustang – A commissioned officer who worked his way up from the enlisted ranks.

NCOIC – Non-commissioned Officer In Charge

NSA – Naval Support Activity

number 1 – Military slang. Number one was the best, number ten was the worst. Really bad was number ten thousand.

NVA – The Vietnam People's Army (VPA) is the official name of the armed forces of the Socialist Republic of Vietnam. During the Vietnam War (1957-1975), the U.S. referred to it as the North Vietnamese Army (NVA). During the war, the NVA was distinguished from the Vietcong, although current practice is to consider the Vietcong as a branch of the VPA. During the war against the French (1946-1954), the VPA was often referred to as the Viet Minh even though Viet Minh was the name of the overall independence movement that preceded the founding of the Democratic Republic of Vietnam in 1945.

The predecessor of the VPA was the Armed Propaganda Unit for National Liberation, an organization that was formed by President Ho Chi Minh on December 22, 1944 to drive the French colonialists and Japanese occupiers from Vietnam.

General Vo Nguyen Giap was the first Commander and commander-in-chief of the VPA and the fourth Minister of National Defence. This force launched many offensives, and eventually survived counter-attacks by United States. During the 1968 and 1972 the VPA sustained heavy losses.

They also participated in incursions into Cambodia, toppling the genocidal Khmer Rouge.

During peaceful periods, the VPA has actively been involved in Vietnam's workforce to develop the economy of Vietnam, in order to coordinate national defense and the economy. The VPA has regularly sent troops to aid with natural disasters such as flooding, landslides etc. The VPA is also involved in such areas as industry, agriculture, forestry, fishery and telecommunications.

The VPA has numerous small firms which have become quite profitable in recent years. However, recent decrees have effectively prohibited the commercialisation of the military.

Payable –	Radio call sign designated to 3/3 Battalion Command
PC –	Personnel Carrier, See M-37
PFC –	Private First Class (E2) in the Marine Corps is the second lowest rank, just under Lance Corporal and just above Private.
platoon –	A platoon is a military unit typically composed of two to four squads and containing about 30 to 50 soldiers. Platoons are organised into a company, which typically consists of three, four or five platoons. A platoon is typically the smallest military unit led by a commissioned officer (the platoon commander) usually a lieutenant. He is usually assisted by a senior non-commissioned officer – the platoon sergeant.

In the United States Marine Corps, rifle platoons are commanded by a *Platoon Commander*, usually a Second or First Lieutenant. The billet of Platoon Sergeant is a position intended for a Staff Sergeant, but it can be held by a Marine ranking from Corporal to Gunnery Sergeant. In a Marine regiment, rifle platoons usually consist of three rifle squads of 13 men each, usually led by a Sergeant, with a Navy corpsman, a Platoon Commander, and a Platoon Sergeant. Each squad is further divided into 3 fireteams. A weapons platoon replaces the 3 squads with a 60mm mortar section, an assault section, and a medium machine gun section. The assault section consists of dual-purpose rockets.

Pogue – A derogatory term used to describe those individuals who are not infantry or not regularly engaged in combat. For example, clerks, motor pool, supply, cooks. Derived from the Irish word for "punk".

poncho – A garment designed to keep the body warm, or if made from a watertight material, to keep dry during rain. The poncho was first used on a regular basis in the US military on the U.S. Western Plains in the 1850s. During the Civil War, Ponchos made of rubber coated cloth were officially adopted, both as rain clothing and as a ground sheet for sleeping. While originally intended for cavalry forces, they were widely used by infantry as well. In World War I, Marines in France wore the poncho; it was preferred over the raincoat for its ability to keep both the wearer and his pack dry, as well as serving as a roof for a makeshift shelter. During the 1950s, new lightweight coated nylon and other synthetic materials were developed for military ponchos. The poncho has remained in service ever since as a standard piece of military field equipment. Today, the United States Armed Forces issue ponchos that may be used as a field expedient shelter.

poncho liner – A military issue warm weather "blanket" designed to be tied to the grommets in a waterproof military poncho and used as bedding. Poncho liners consist of a thin sandwich of polyester batting between camouflage nylon covers. They dry quickly and provide some warmth even when damp.

PRC25 – Radio Set AN/PRC-25 was the state-of the-art FM tactical radio for the Vietnam War. The mostly solid-state design brought weight down to less than 20 pounds

The first AN/PRC-25's in Southeast Asia (mid-1965) were intended for advisers. With their initial distribution came the first NET Team (new equipment training) from the

Electronics Command to begin instruction on the operation and maintenance of the PRC-25. Those radios soon became the mainstay of tactical communications in Southeast Asia. In three and a half years, 33,000 PRC-25 radios were delivered to Southeast Asia. The PRC-25 was, according to General Creighton Abrams, "the single most important tactical item in Vietnam."

The PRC-25 was the radio that made military tactical communication reliable and the basis of tactical command. The PRC-25 was organic to battalion-size units and was issued through the platoon level.

The PRC-25 design had many firsts, all intended to make it much easier to carry and use than previous models. It was the first solid state FM backpack radio but also incorporated new ideas for radio circuits (such as "150 Hz squelch feature") that made it easier for the average soldier to use by reducing controls to a minimum.

Radio Set AN/PRC-25 had 920 channels spaced 50 kHz apart, operating in the 30-75.95 MHz spectrum. It transmitted about 1.5 watts of power. Operating distance was typically three to seven miles with the standard antenna. The radio could be carried with a web suspender rig or mounted on the LC-2 pack frame.

PTSD – Post Traumatic Stress Disorder is an anxiety disorder that can develop after exposure to one or more traumatic events that threatened or caused grave physical harm.

It is a severe and ongoing emotional reaction to an extreme psychological trauma. This stressor may involve someone's actual death, a threat to the patient's or someone else's life, serious physical injury, an unwanted sexual act, or a threat to physical or psychological integrity, overwhelming the individuals psychological defenses.

In some cases it can also result from profound psychological and emotional trauma, apart from any actual physical harm. Often, however, incidents involving both things are found to be the cause.

PTSD is a condition distinct from traumatic stress, which has less intensity and duration, and combat stress reaction, which is transitory. PTSD has also been recognized in the past as railway spine, stress syndrome, shell shock, battle fatigue, traumatic war neurosis, or post-traumatic stress syndrome (PTSS).

Diagnostic symptoms include reexperience such as flashbacks and nightmares, avoidance of stimuli associated with the trauma, increased arousal such as difficulty falling or staying asleep, anger and hypervigilance. By definition, the symptoms last more than six months and cause significant impairment in social, occupational, or other important areas of functioning (problems with work and relationships.)

Members of the Marines and Army are much more likely to develop PTSD than Air Force and Navy personnel, because of greater direct exposure to combat.

Untreated Post Traumatic Stress Disorder can have devastating, far-reaching consequences for sufferers' functioning in relationships, their families, and in society.

punji stick – The Punji stick or punji stake is a type of booby-trapped stake. It is a simple spike, made out of wood or bamboo, generally placed upright in the ground. Punji sticks are usually deployed in substantial numbers.

Punji sticks are placed in areas likely to be passed through by enemy troops. The presence of punji sticks may be camouflaged by natural undergrowth, crops, grass, brush or similar materials. They were often incorporated into various types of traps; for example, a camouflaged pit into which a man might step or fall. They were often smeared with human feces to increase the risk of infection.

Some pits would be dug with punji sticks in the sides pointing ***downward*** at an angle. Anyone stepping into the pit would find it impossible to remove his leg without doing severe damage, and injuries incurred by the simple fact of falling forward while one's leg is in a narrow, vertical, stake-lined pit. Such pits would require time and care to dig the soldier's leg out, immobilizing the unit longer than if the foot was simply pierced.

Punji sticks were sometimes deployed in the preparation of an ambush. Soldiers lying in wait for the enemy to pass would deploy punji sticks in the areas where the surprised enemy might be expected to take cover, thus soldiers diving for cover would impale themselves.

The point of penetration was usually in the foot or lower leg area. Punji sticks were not necessarily meant to kill the person who stepped on it; rather they were designed to wound the enemy and tie up his unit while the victim was evacuated to a medical facility.

In the Vietnam War, the Viet Cong would also use this method to force the wounded soldier to be transported by helicopter to a medical hospital for treatment, which was viewed as being more damaging to the enemy's cause than death.

Punji sticks were also used in Vietnam to complement various defenses, such as barbed wire.

Pvt. – In the Marine Corps, Private (Pvt) refers to the lowest enlisted rank, just below Private First Class. A Marine Corps Private wears no uniform insignia. Most new, non-officer Marines begin their military career as a Private.

PX – Post Exchange. Exchanges sell consumer goods and services to active, reserve, national guard, and retired United States Uniformed Services members and their dependents. Authority to use these facilities is normally determined by presentation of the individual's military member or military family member identification (ID) card, either when entering the store or when paying for goods and services.

A typical exchange is similar to a department store, but other services such as military clothing sales/uniform shops, barber shops, hair care, beauty, laundry/dry cleaning, gas stations, fast food outlets, convenience stores ("Shoppettes" or "Mini Marts"), beer and wine sales, liquor stores ("Class Six"), lawn and garden shops, movie theaters and even vehicle maintenance and repair services are commonly available. Most (but not all) sales by exchanges are free of state and local sales taxes as the sales take place on U.S. military reservations (exceptions may include gasoline sales in the U.S. and sales by concessionaires licensed by the exchange).

Unlike commissaries (military grocery stores), exchanges, for the most part, do not receive any subsidies from the federal government and must operate on a for-profit basis. With the exception of a small number of military personnel detailed for duty with the exchange services, exchange service employees' salaries are paid from revenues generated from sales of merchandise and not from funds appropriated by Congress. This leads to their often being referred to as non-appropriated fund (NAF) activities.

Exchanges play an important role for U.S. military and Government personnel assigned overseas as they are often the only local source for American retail merchandise, such as clothing, electronics, books and magazines, fast food.

Smaller field exchanges are established to provide military personnel with comforts and everyday items while deployed in combat zones.

Most profits earned by the exchange services, after paying operating expenses, are used to support community activities aimed at improving morale among service members and their families.

R&R – Rest and Relaxation (or rest and recreation), is a term used for the free time of a military man. R&R takes and have taken various forms, including mail, sports, film screenings, using the services of prostitutes and leave time.

RF – The South Vietnamese Regional Forces were roughly akin to militias. Recruited locally, they fell into two broad groups – Regional Forces and Popular Forces. During the early 1960's the Regional Forces manned the country-wide outpost system and defended critical points, such as bridges and ferries. There were some 9,000 such positions, half of them in the Mekong Delta region. In 1964, the Regional Forces were integrated into the Army of the Republic of Vietnam (ARVN) and placed under the command of the Joint General Staff.

When U.S. forces began to withdraw from South Vietnam during 1969 and the ARVN began the task of fighting the communist main force units, Regional forces took on a new importance. For the first time, they were deployed outside their home areas and were sometimes attached to ARVN units. By 1973 the Regional Forces had grown to 1,810 companies. Charged primarily with local defense, they were too lightly armed and equipped to withstand attack by regular People's Army of Vietnam units supported by tanks and artillery.

Rockpile – The Rockpile, located in Quang Tri Province of Viet Nam, known in Vietnamese as Thon Khe Tri, is a karst rock outcropping near the former demilitarized zone of South Vietnam. It rises 690 feet above the surrounding terrain. Its relatively inaccessible location (the top can reached only by helicopter) made it an important Marine observation post and artillery base from 1966 to 1968.

round-eye –   A non-Asian person.

salty –   In the Marines and Navy, one who is an old salt or a salty dog is one who is very experienced, having traveled much and seen more than his fair share of things. Used more in the lower enlisted ranks to establish some kind of credibility regardless of rank.

sappers –   Skilled VC or NVA infiltrators sent to damage fixed defenses before an attack.

NVA and Viet Cong sappers are better described as commando units. In fact, the Vietnamese term "dac cong" can be literally translated as "special task". Thousands of specially trained elite fighters served in the NVA and Viet Cong commando/sapper units which were organized as independendent formations. While not always successful, at times they inflicted heavy damage against their enemies. These elite units served as raiders against American/ARVN troops, and during the final Ho Chi Minh campaign in 1975 they seized key road and bridge assets, destroyed installations, attacked command and control nodes in the enemy rear, and otherwise helped NVA fast mobile forces to advance. The raiding force was usually grouped into assault teams, each broken down into several 3-5 man assault cells.

seabag –   A large canvas duffle bag serving as a container to carry clothing and possessions. The military (all branches: Army, Navy, Air Force, Marines, Coast Guard) issue the duffle bag to recruits at the reception depot as the primary way to carry the other items issued. The duffle bag is made from olive drab canvas in a cylindrical shape with a sewn in round bottom and open top with a circle of grommets. It has a cotton duck carrying handle and a shoulder strap that extends from the center of the bag, ending in a snap hook. The size is about 36-38 inches long and 12-15 inches in diameter.

The closure system of the duffle bag consists of a metal loop that extends through one of the grommets at the opening. A canvas flap is pulled over the contents and then each of the grommets is nested onto the metal loop in sequence. When all the grommets are nested onto the loop, the snap link on the shoulder strap is clipped to the loop to secure the closure. There is room for a padlock to add further security, although a thief could easily cut the canvas duffle bag open.

Sgt. – The Marine Corps has several ranks, which carry the title of Sergeant, the lowest of which is Sergeant (Sgt). Marine Sergeants are the fifth enlisted rank in the Marine Corps, just above Corporal and below Staff Sergeant. They typically serve as squad leaders in an infantry company, or section commander in a weapons platoon.

Sgt. Maj. – Sergeant Major In the Marine Corps, is the ninth and highest enlisted rank, just above First Sergeant, and equal in grade to Master Gunnery Sergeant, although the two have different responsibilities. Sergeant Major is both a rank and a military "billet" (a personnel position, assignment, or duty station which may be filled by one person). Marine Corps Sergeants Major serve as the senior enlisted Marine in the Corps' units of battalion, squadron or higher echelon, to assist the unit's commander and to handle matters of discipline and morale among the enlisted Marines.

The Marine Corps' first sergeant major was appointed on January 1, 1801. This was originally a solitary post, similar to the modern Sergeant Major of the Marine Corps, but by 1899 there were five Sergeants Major. The title was abolished in 1946, but re-introduced as a rank in 1954.

SgtMajMarCor – Sergeant Major of the Marine Corps (official abbreviation is, sometimes informally abbreviated as SMMC or SgtMajMC) is a unique non-commissioned rank and billet in the Marine Corps. The holder of this rank and post is the senior enlisted member of the Marine Corps. The post of Sergeant Major of the Marine Corps was established in 1957, as the senior enlisted advisor to the Commandant of the Marine Corps.

SSgt. – Staff Sergeant is E-6 rank in the Marine Corps, just above Sergeant and below Gunnery Sergeant. A Marine staff sergeant is a staff non-commissioned officer rank. This grade is normally achieved after 10 to 13 years in service. He may also be tasked as a company gunnery sergeant, or a platoon commander if required. He is the senior tactical advisor to a platoon commander by virtue of time in service, previous deployments, and experience and is responsible for the proficiency, training and administrative issues of his Marines. He is always to be referred to by his complete rank (i.e. "Staff Sergeant Jones" or simply "Staff Sergeant,").

The rank of Staff Sergeant in the USMC was created in 1923 to coincide with the U.S. Army's ranks. Until the end of WW2, the insignia of Platoon Sergeant was three chevrons and a rocker, with Staff Sergeant having a horizontal stripe instead of a rocker below the chevrons. After the separate rank of Platoon Sergeant was eliminated, the Staff Sergeant rank switched over to the rocker insignia and staff sergeants held the platoon sergeant's billet.

shelter half –

The fundamental unit of shelter for the Marine in the field is the two-man pup tent. Each pup tent is made up of two shelter half pieces that fasten together with snaps along the ridge line and, with poles, ropes and stakes, make up one pup tent. The snaps are two sided. Any pair of shelter half pieces can be fastened together with a watertight closure along the top line. The shelter half is approximately 7' long by 5' wide.

The tent half with its stakes and poles weighs about five pounds each. The rectangular part of the shelter half forms the pitched roof of the tent while the triangular end forms a back wall at one end and a flap door at the other. Grommets along the base of the tent have loops of cord, which attach to the tent stakes.

The unit of issue consists of :
- One shelter half
- Three pole sections to make one pole.
- Five stakes, stamped aluminum
- Rope guy line, approx. 7 feet, loop on one end.

In Vietnam, the tropical climate did not encourage use of the pup tent. It was issued and carried but was more likely to be used with a poncho to keep the rain off, or as a ground cloth, than pitched as a tent.

short –   Military slang meaning you had only a few days or a couple of weeks left on your tour in Vietnam. If you had nine months left in your tour, and your buddy had 10 months left, you were "shorter" than him. There were many common riffs on this theme, i.e., "I'm shorter than Tom Thumb." "But I'm shorter than Tinkerbelle". When Marines got down to their last few days, it was considered bad luck for them or anyone else to talk about them being short. There were many tall stories about guys killed when they were short.

sick bay –   A nautical term for the compartment in a ship used for medical purposes. The term is also applied ashore by the Navy and Marine Corps to treatment clinics on Naval stations and Marine bases.

smoke –   Smoke grenades are used as ground-to-ground or ground-to-air signaling devices, target or landing zone marking devices, and screening devices for unit movement. The body is a sheet-steel cylinder with emission holes in the top and bottom. These allow the smoke to be released when the grenade is ignited. Two main types exist, colored smoke (for signaling) and screening smoke. In colored smoke grenades, the filler consists of 250 to 350 grams of colored smoke mixture (mostly potassium chlorate, lactose and a dye). Screening smoke grenades usually contain HC (hexachloroethane/zinc) smoke mixture or TA (terephthalic acid) smoke mixture. HC smoke is harmful to breathe, since it contains hydrochloric acid.

tangle foot –   Barbed wire used to construct a tangle-foot obstruction either outside a single perimeter fence or in the area between double fences to provide an additional deterrent to intruders. The wire is supported on short metal or wooden pickets spaced at irregular intervals of 3 to 10 feet and at heights between 6 and 12 inches. The wire or tape should be crisscrossed to provide a more effective obstacle. The space and materials available govern the depth of the field.

Tangle foot is used where concealment is essential and to prevent the enemy from crawling between fences and in front of emplacements. The obstacle should be employed in a minimum depth of 10 meters (32.8 ft.). The pickets should be spaced at irregular intervals of from 75 cm to 3 meters

(2.5 to 10 ft.), and the height of the barbed wire should vary between 9 to 30 in. Tangle foot should be sited in scrub, if possible, using bushes as supports for part of the wire. In open ground, short pickets should be used. Growth of grass should be controlled to help prevent the enemy from secretly cutting lanes in, or tunneling under, the entanglement.

Third Shore Party – Now designated Combat Logistics Regiment 3 (CLR-3) is a transportation, landing support and logistics unit of the Marine Corps and is headquartered at Camp Foster, Okinawa. The unit falls under the 3rd Marine Logistics Group and the III Marine Expeditionary Force. Also known as the Red Patches because of the red patches sewn onto their trouser legs and utility cap designating them from other Marines deploying on a beach.

Its mission is to provide both general and direct transportation and landing support to Marine Air-Ground Task Forces (MAGTFs) in order to support Arrival and Assembly operations

- Support of the ship to shore movement during amphibious operations, terminal operations and subsequent operations for throughput of supplies, equipment and personnel sustainment.
- Medium and heavy lift transportation support for throughput and sustainment operations
- Distribution of bulk Class I(water) and bulk Class III(fuel). 3rd Shore Party Participated in the Vietnam War, April 1965-November 1969, Operating from Da Nang, Chu Lai, Phu Bai, Dong Ha, and Quang Tri

UH1E – The Bell Helicopter UH-1 Iroquois, commonly (or officially in the U.S. Marine Corps) known as the "Huey", is a multipurpose military helicopter, famous for its use in the Vietnam War.

The UH-1 was developed from 1955 US Army trials with the Bell Model 204. The initial designation of HU-1 (helicopter utility) led to its nickname, Huey. The nickname became so popular that Bell started putting the Huey name on the anti-torque pedals.

The aircraft was first used by the military in 1959 and went into tri-service production in 1962 as the UH-1. The last were produced in 1976 with more than 16,000 made in total, of which about 7,000 saw use during the Vietnam War.

In Vietnam, 2,202 Huey pilots were killed and approximately 2,500 aircraft were lost, roughly half to combat and the rest to operational accidents.

Unit One –

Combat medic bag carried by hospital corpsmen and was their primary source of medical supplies in field environments.

Relatively light weight (9 pounds fully loaded), it can be opened without removing it from the shoulder. Although it comes equipped with standard supplies, these are often modified by individual corpsmen to meet their tactical situation and personal preferences.

Specifications:
- Weight 9 pounds
- Volume: 236 cubic inches
- Compartments: 4
- Shoulder Strap: Adjustable

Contents:
- One roll wire fabric, 5" x 36"
- Two bottles of aspirin, 324 mg, 100s
- Three packages of morphine inj. 1/4 g, 5s
- One bottle tetracaine hydrochloride ophthalmic solution
- Three bottles povidone-iodine sol. 1/2 fl oz.
- Two packages atropine inj., 12s
- Two muslin triangular bandages
- Two medium battle dressings, 7 1/4 x 8
- Eight small battle dressings 4 x 7
- One roll adhesive tape, 3" x 5 yds
- Six packages of Band-Aids, 6s
- One pair scissors, bandage
- One tourniquet
- One airway, plastic adult/child
- One thermometer, oral
- One card of safety pins, medium, 12s
- One surgical instrument set, minor surgery
    - 1 Scalpel (handle and several blades)
    - 2 Scissors (large and small)
    - 2 Hemostats (curved and straight)
    - 2 Forceps
    - 1 Probe

- Suture material
- Gauze pads
- Two books field medical ID cards
- One pencil, black lead
- Two packages gauze, roller, 3 " x 5 yds

utilities – Fighting uniform of the Marines, Army calls theirs fatigues. The Marine Corps Combat Utility Uniform or MCCUU is intended for wear in the field or for working parties, but has become the typical working uniform for all deployed and most garrison Marines. To distinguish the uniform from the Army the Eagle, Globe, and anchor is stenciled on the left breast pocket.

V-12 Program – The V-12 Navy College Training Program was designed to supplement the force of commissioned officers in the United States Navy during World War II. Between July 1, 1943 and June 30, 1946, over 125,000 men were enrolled in the V-12 program in 131 colleges and universities in the United States.

V-12 participants were required to carry 17 credit hours and 9-1/2 hours of physical training each week. Study was year-round, and the number of terms for a trainee depended on his previous college background, if any, and his course of study. From the V-12 program, most of the Navy candidates went on to a four-month course at a reserve midshipmen's school, and the Marine candidates went to boot camp and then to the 12-week Officer Candidate Course at Quantico, Virginia. The curriculum was heavy on math and science for "regulars" (those entering college for the first time). Those students who already had some college credit, or "irregulars," were allowed to continue in their majors with the addition of courses in mathematics and science.

VC – Viet Cong or the National Liberation Front was an army based in South Vietnam that fought the United States and South Vietnamese governments during the Vietnam War (1959-75). It had both guerrilla and regular army units, as well as a network of cadres who organized peasants in the territory it controlled. Many soldiers were recruited in South Vietnam, but others were attached to the regular North Vietnamese army. The Viet Cong was closely allied with the government of North Vietnam. The group was formed in the 1950s by former members of the Viet Minh acting on orders from Hanoi. Many of its core members were southern communists who had resettled in the North after the Geneva Accord (1954). Hanoi gave them military training and sent them back to the South along the Ho Chi Minh Trail in the late 1950s and early 1960s. The Viet Cong's best-known action was the Tet Offensive, a massive assault on more than 100 South Vietnamese urban centers in 1968. The offensive riveted the attention of the world's media for weeks, but also overextended the Vietcong. Later communist offensives were conducted primarily by the North Vietnamese army. The group was dissolved in 1977 after North and South Vietnam were officially unified under a communist government.

American troops referred to the Viet Cong as Victor Charlie or VC. "Victor" and "Charlie" are both letters in the NATO phonetic alphabet.

Willie Peter – WP – White Phosphorus, a flare- and smoke-producing smoke-screening agent or incendiary device agent. It that is made from a common allotrope of the chemical element phosphorus. The main utility of white phosphorus munitions is to create smokescreens to mask movement from the enemy, or to mask his fire. In contrast to other smoke-causing munitions, WP burns quickly causing an instant bank of smoke. As a result of this, WP munitions are very common, particularly as smoke grenades for infantry; loaded in defensive grenade dischargers on tanks and other armored vehicles; or as part of the ammunition allotment for artillery or mortars.

However, white phosphorus has a secondary effect. While much less efficient than ordinary fragmentation effects in causing casualties, white phosphorus burns quite fiercely and can set cloth, fuel, ammunition and other combustibles on fire. It also can function as an anti-personnel weapon with the compound capable of causing serious burns or death. The agent is used in bombs, artillery, and mortars, short-range missiles which burst into burning flakes of phosphorus upon impact. White phosphorus is commonly referred to in military jargon as "WP". The slang term "Willy(ie) Pete" or "Willy(ie) Peter", dating from World War I and common at least through the Vietnam War, is still used by infantry servicemen to refer to white phosphorus.

White phosphorus weapons are controversial today because of their potential use against civilians. While the Chemical Weapons Convention does not designate WP as a chemical weapon, various groups consider it to be one. In recent years, the United States, Israel, and Russia have used white phosphorus in combat.

Willie Peter bag – A waterproofed canvas bag originally designed to keep a rolled up sleeping bag dry.

Index

A

Abraham, Joseph, 187
Abramovich (corporal), 318
Abrew, William, 303
Agent Orange, 337
Air America, 121
AK-47s, 237
aka-chan, 60
Alamo Hill, 151
Alpha Company, 122, 127
Alpha Med, 319, 326-27
Althoff, David, 13
Alves, Ed, 25
American Heroes, 338
American Red Cross, 23
Ames, Arthur, 187
Anderson, Jennings, 187
Anderson, Jerry, 297
Anderson Valley, 16
Arpin, Edward, 302
Ash, Charles "Chick," 30
Ashbaugh, Jack, 302
Atlantic City, 17
Ayd, Jacques "JJ" J., 261, 274

Ayd Station, 274, 291

B

Baca, Isidro, 296
bacitracin, 255
Baires, Marcial, 302
Balboa Naval Hospital, 41
Ba Ngao River, 242, 245
Banks, Richard, 153, 165, 292
Barker, John, 196
Barry, John, 196
Baryo, Gerald "Gerry," 296
Ba Thanh, 246
Battalion Aid Station (*see also* BAS), 12, 149, 176, 221-22, 261, 265, 270, 272, 349-50
battalion surgeon, 177
Beach, Tommy, 302
Beardsley, Gordon, 187
Beck, Martin, 233
Belmore, Michael, 172
benjo ditches, 59
Bennett, Joseph, 198
Bennett, Larry, 198
Benny Decker Theater, 64

401

Benson, Howard, 302
Berry, Don, 196
Bigelow, Alphonso, 187
Blackburn, Charles, 191
blackout curtains, 155
Blinder, Richard, 196
Bluejackets' Manual, The, 26
Blue Star Company, 227
Bob Hope Christmas Show, 116
Bodzash, James, 196
Bostick, Norvel, 303
Bradburn, James, 236
Branock, Willaim "Bill," 184
Bravo Company, 135
Bridge at Dong Ha, The (Miller), 338
Broaddus (commander), 39
Brooks, Edward, 297
Brune, Albert, 172
Bryant, Raymond, 297
Budd, Leonard, 297
Burgess, Craig, 302
Burgess, Edwin, 235

C

calendar, short-timer's, 322
Ca Lu, 241, 243, 246, 255, 268, 274
Camacho, Patricio, 187
Cam Lo, 178, 191, 232-33, 235-36, 282, 291
Camp Carroll, 150, 286, 301
Camp Fuji, 90, 343
Camp Navarro, 21, 25
Camp Pendleton
  final day in, 107
  training in, 95, 101
Camp Smedley D. Butler, 328
Casualties, 12, 68-69, 76, 125, 150, 184-87, 193-96, 198, 227, 233, 243, 250, 281, 295-96, 299-301, 326
  Killed (KIA), 12, 68-69, 76, 125, 150, 184-87, 193-96, 198, 227, 233, 243, 250, 281, 295-96, 299-301, 326
  Wounded (WIA), 12, 68-69, 76, 125, 150, 184-87, 193-96, 198, 225, 227, 233, 243, 281, 295-96, 299-301, 326
Cathy, John, 13
Chancey, Eugene, 235
China Beach, 316, 318-19
chloroquine primaquine, 110, 276, 354
Chrisman, Timothy, 302
Chris Noel Show, 288, 314
Churchill, Paul, 13
Cinderella Liberty, 60
Cinnamon Cinder, 102
Citadel, 136
Clark, Charles, 196
Cleveland, Nettie, 17
Cleveland, William Dexter, 17
code, radio brevity, 157
Company, Mike, 197-99, 227, 289
Con Thien, 233, 309
Cook, James, 302
Cook, Lewis, 265
Cook, William, 302
Covelo Rancheria Indian Reservation, 16
C rations, 227
Crosser, Jackson, 196
Crow, Roger, 196
Cruz, John, 303
Cub Scout Pack 85, 20

D

Da Nang, 119, 142, 261, 264, 318
Darden, Ronald, 303
Darsey, Carl, 65-66, 76, 229
Daytona Beach, 335
del Grosso, Nello, 49
Delong, Stephen, 303
Delta Med, 306
Derosier, Joseph, 196
Detora, Ernest, 215, 303
Devine, Freddie, 196
Devivo, Neil, 297

Dias, John, 99
Disch, Willis, 187
Donati, Bruno, 25
Dong Ha, 119, 121, 124, 127, 146, 149, 177, 234, 305-6
　casualties, 264
Donovan (commander), 107
Dorsey, John, 303
Dusters, 12, 177, 258
Dylan, Bob, 77, 82
Dzikowski, Raymond, 243

E

Ebling, Louise Johnson, 9, 13
Eisenhauer, Jackie, 297
El Camino College, 335
Eleventh Engineers, 249, 257
Elmendorf Air Force Base, 98
Enlisted Men's Club Alliance, 58
Enoshima, 63
"Eve of Destruction" (McGuire), 77

F

Fall, Bernard, 12
fam fire, 174
Feeny (nurse), 56
Field Medical Service School, 100, 105, 333
First Platoon, 176, 183
Fish Bowl, 151
Fleet Activities Hospital, 56
Fleet Marine Force, 333
Fort Bragg, 15, 17, 21
Forward, Robbie, 102
fragging, 315, 359-60
Franch, Bruno, 196
Freed, Robert, 197
Freedom Hill PX, 115
Freeland, Bruce, 302
Fuji Laundry, 57
Fuji Stick, 90

Fuss, Dan, 176, 194, 245

G

Gallegos (sergeant), 186
Galli, Anita, 40
Gamma Globulin (GG), 307
Garrison, Norman, 196
garrison boots, 124
Gent, Robert, 302
Glover, Randall, 196
Glover Gardens, 86
Goggin, Charles, 243
Golden Pavilion, 88
Goodwin, Forest (lieutenant), 228
Gorey, John, 302
Gotemba, 80, 90
Graham, Richard, 196
Gray, Denver, 153, 155, 163
Green, James, 302
Green Parrot, 17
Greenwood Flyer, 16
Grenny, Guy, 337
Grey Ghost, 41

H

Hairpin, 257-58
Hall, Ed, 30
Halsey, Bull, 18
Halstead, Chuck, 327
Hamilton, Hance, 198
Hanna, James, 303
Hanscom, John, 196
Harrington, Michael, 302
Harris, Jackie, 193
Hebert, Joseph "Ron," 153, 218
Heekin, Terry, 196
Helm, Richard, 265
Hice, Robert "Bob," 241
Higashi Honganji, 88
Hiroshima, 87

Hirt, Al, 140
Ho Chi Minh, 185
Holcombe, Richard, 297
Holt, Robert, 297
Honky Tonk, 59
Honolulu International Airport, 52
hooches, 113
Horner, Mike, 324
Horsley (HMC), 318
Hoskie, Raymond, 297
Hospital Corps quarters, 57
Hotel Company, 229
Howard, James, 191
Hoy, Chris, 9, 337
H&S, 149
HST (helicopter support team), 137
Hubert, Charles, 265
Hudson, John, 303
Hue, 135, 143
Hue University, 142
Hulbert, Charles, 16
Hulbert, Lola, 30
Hulbert, Lola Belle, 16
Hunter, Robert, 297

I

I Corps, Military Assistance Command, Vietnam, 143. *See also* MACV-I
immersion burners, 113
India Company, 181, 195, 197, 301
Infantry Training Regiment, training with, 104, 366
Italian Gardens, 77

J

Jaqua, Michael, 302
Jarvis, Lee, 301
Jarvis, Scott, 41
Jewett, Bruce, 99
Jewett, Carol Louise, 17
Jewett, Edward Fletcher, 16-17, 19
Jewett, George Orrington, 16
Jewett, Norman, 17-18
Jewett, Russell
  arriving in Japan, 54
  arriving in Vietnam, 112
  Christmas in Vietnam, 137
  climbing Mount Fuji, 90
  Corp School graduate, 48
  dating Louise, 29
  dealing with war casualties, 76
  divorce, 336
  flying to Vietnam, 111
  getting home, 330
  going on R&R, 261
  joining the Navy Reserve, 26
  learning Japanese, 82
  leaving for Japan, 49-50
  meeting Louise, 28
  meeting Mariko, 262
  motorcycle accident, 99
  motorcycle traffic violation, 83
  naval reserve boot camp, 35
  naval reserve cruise, 35, 35-37
  performing chricothyroidotomy, 194
  promotion to hospital corpsman, 293
  Purple Heart, 321
  rescuing point man, 234
  smoking pot, 314
  swimming instructor, 23
  twenty-first birthday, 283
  working in sick bay, 122
Jewett, Steve, 21, 23, 98
John, Noel, 301
Johnson, Effie, 49
Johnson, Leslie *See also* LBJ
Johnson, Louise, 65, 74, 80, 99, 105, 107, 331, 336
Jokilehto, Sophia, 17
Jones, Emma Ava Nella, 16

K

Kaden, Carlton, 73
Kaden, Steve, 30, 72, 74, 77
Kadena Air Base, 328-29
Kamakura, 62-63
Kelsey, John, 12, 153, 176, 197
Kelsey, Orville, 265
Kerlin, Stanley, 297
Key West, 332
Khe Sanh, 249
kiddie cruiser, 333
Kilo Company, 242, 296
King, Russell, 224, 289
Kinkakuji Temple, 88
Kirin Beer, 63
Klemanski, Charles, 296
Knabe, Wayne, 176
Knight, JC, 58-59, 62
Knights of Columbus, 20
Kobayashi, Mariko, 97, 262, 270
Kotoku-in Temple, 62
Kyoto, 88

L

Lake Yamanaka, 80
Lang Caht, 246
Langdon, Michael, 297
Lang Ruou, 246, 253
Larson, Jerome, 172
Lawler, Thomas, 302
Lawson, Albert, 301
LBJ, 11-12, 296
LCU-1624, 318, 321
Leblanc, Ross, 302
leeches, 166-67
Lehrack, Otto J.
  No Shining Armor, 12
Lewis, David, 243
Leyva, Frank, 297

Liberati, Peter, 184
Lima Company, 150, 152, 155, 176, 179,
  191, 244, 258, 301
Lima Hill, 151, 158, 173
  leaving, 176
Linda (Carl Darsey's girlfriend), 65
Little Rockpile, 151
Living Children, 99
Lloyd, Eddie, 297
Longo, Nicolas, 274, 283, 285-86, 299
Lothringer, Floyd, 196
Lynn, Richard, 182

M

M14, 174
M16, 174, 227
M48A3 tank, 177
M60, 171
M1914, 104
MacDonald, Kevin, 12
MacKenzie, Richard, 184, 186
Mackey, Clifford, 297
MacPartland, Guy, 12
MACV-I, 143
Madfes, Kenneth, 291, 299, 319, 326
Main, Warren, 178
Maize, Jose, 93, 96
malaria, 276-77
Marble Mountains, 318-19
Marine Corps Air Station El Toro, 329
Marine transient center, 112
Marlin, Steven, 172
MARS (Military Affiliate Radio System),
  273, 322, 380-81
Martin, Michael, 303
Martin, Morris, 196
Martin, Robert, 196
Martin, Samuel E.
  Basic Japanese Conversation Dictionary, 52
Marx, John, 172

Mason, Johnnie, 184
Mason, Perry, 302
Masonic Lodge, 20
MATS, 108. *See also* Military Air Transport Service
Maxwell, Manny, 235
McBride, David, 302
McClary, Donald, 196
McCormick, Kenneth, 303
McGowin, Francis, 13
McGuire, Barry
  "Eve of Destruction," 77
Meat Grinder, 309
MedCAP, 254, 282
medevac, 126
Medical Civilian Action Program, 254. *See also* MedCAP
Mendocino Woodlands, 20-21
Meredith, Gary, 198
Mertle, Bill, 26
Military Air Transport Service, 48
Miller, John Grider
  Bridge at Dong Ha, The, 338
Miller, John P., 279-80, 285
Mohedano, Jack, 297
Montagnards, 178, 246-47, 250, 274, 283, 291, 299, 339
Morales, Victor, 297
Mount Fuji, 90
Muehlenberg, Clifford, 302
Mules, 124
Muskett, Thomas, 302
mustang, 153, 384
Mutter's Ridge, 151

N

Nagasaki, 86
National Defense Ribbon, 328
National Museum of the Marine Corps, 14
Naval Air Station Key West, 310
Navarro River, 45

Nellie's Tit, 151
Nelson, Theodore, 265
Nickerson, Nellie May, 17
night ambush, 155
Nijo Castle, 88
Ninth Marines, 190, 343
North, Oliver, 338
No Shining Armor (Lehrack), 12
Nowak, Peter, 196
Noyo River, 21
NVA (North Vietnamese Army), 195, 197, 199, 290, 298-301, 307, 309

O

Oak Knoll Naval Hospital, 229
Oakland Induction Center, 39
Odonnell, John, 196
Ofuna Kannon, 96
Okinawa, 328
Olympia, 64
operation, search-and-destroy, 191, 241
Operation Cimarron, 286
Operation Deep Freeze, 93
Operation Hickory, 289
Operation Prairie, 180
Operation Starlite, 68-69, 344
Orloski, Michael, 297
Osaka Castle, 87
Osborne, Hansel (lieutenant), 162
Outlaw, Elliot, 297
Overmeyer, Mel, 101-2, 127, 229-30

P

Palmer, Roger, 302
Palmieri, Salvatore, 265
Paoli, Bobby, 44
passing the helmet, 315
patrol protocol, 157
Patterson, Carol, 40
Payable, 151, 176, 191, 270

Percherke, Chuck, 157
Perfume River, 127, 133, 142
Perkins, Byron, 12, 265
   account of rocket attack in Dong Ha, 265-66
Peroutka, Frank, 196
Perry, Paul, 302
Petri, George, 243
Phu Bai, 120, 130, 133, 136
Pierce, Richard, 235
Pinchon (senior corpsman), 140
plague vaccine, 316, 318-19
Poe, Otto, 17
Pogues, 296, 386
Pommier, James, 302
Presidential Unit Citation, 328
Price, Alfred, 196
Puller, Chesty, 125, 354
Punch Bowl, 151
Purple Heart, 234, 328

Q

Quan (captain), 223, 244, 274
Quang Tri River, 241, 243, 248, 253

R

Rantala, August "Kig" A., Jr., 17
Razorback, 151, 153, 158, 162, 164-66, 170, 173, 190
   Marine casualties, 171
Record Searchlight, 153
Redwood Coast Printers, 19
Reed, Sylvester, 302
Reiss, Robert, 302
Remington, Michael, 302
Rice, Terrance, 297
Richardson, Herbert, 187
Richardson, Thomas, 302
Riddles, James, 265
Ripley, John W., 11, 14-15, 152, 192, 195, 237, 268, 274, 296, 338

Ripley's Raiders, 199, 338
Rizley, Billy, 196
Rockpile, 150-51, 162, 270
Romero-De-Jesus, Benjamin, 296
Rozzi, Steve, 316, 322
The Russians Are Coming, the Russians Are Coming, 74, 105

S

Saigon, 143
Salazar, Jimmy, 303
Salmon, Ronald, 297
Salt Lake City, 35
sappers, 156, 391
Sasebo, 86-87
Schlerf, Dave, 332, 335
Schwirian, David "Tiger," 13, 245
Second Battalion Third Marines, 233
Second Platoon, 183, 258
Sexton, Jack, 303
Sexton, Merlyn, 297
A Shau Valley, 137
shelter halves, 124
Shindelus, Theodore, 243
shit birds, 273
Shore Party, 133, 142
Shore Party compound, 133
Sibilly, John, 301
Skunk Train, 99
Smith, Noble, 12
Smith, Paul, 72-73
Smith, Rodney, 336-37
Solbach, John, 236
Special Services Division, 80
Stars and Stripes, 199
Strahl, Richard, 196
Submarine Alley, 59
Sui Soi River, 258
Swoyer, Richard, 303

T

Tachikawa Air Base, 50, 54, 98
tangle foot, 156
Taubold, Mark, 44
Third Battalion Third Marines, 149, 176, 181, 199, 309
Third Medical Battalion, 146
Third Platoon, 153, 162, 176
Third Shore Party, 117, 121, 151
Thon Bai An, 198
Thornton, William, 302
Thuan An, 127
Tijuana, 102
Tokyo, 261
Tokyo Bay area, 57
Torres, Jesus "Jesse," 296
Torres, Jose, 302
Totsuka, 96
training area 6577, 104-5
Travis Air Force Base, 48, 98
Treasure Island, 34
Tressa, Edward, 297
Tsurugaoka Hachiman-gu Shrine, 63

U

Union Lumber Company, 17, 20
Unit One, 180, 242, 291
Upton, Wade, 235
USS *Essex*, 18

V

V-12 Program, 18
Vandergrift, 244
Vietnam, 137, 276, 338
  casualties, 187, 195, 198, 233, 235-36, 243, 296, 301
  climate, 288
  discovering NVA weapons, 197
Vietnamese Service Medal, 328

W

Wackerly, James, 303
Wake Island, 53
Walters, Shirley, 40
Wardell, Edward, 198
water buffalo, 246
Wawrzyniak, Stanley J., 125
Webb, George, 197
Webb, Roy, 235
West, Pierce "Chris," 288, 300
Westover, Delwin, 235
White, Tony, 301
Whited, Kent, 44
Whited, Ray, 44
Wickersham, Austin, 16
Wilder (colonel), 199
Williams, Frank, 297
Williams, Tony, 245, 255
Willits, 107
Wingard (lieutenant), 228, 234
Witch's Tit, 151
Witkoski, Gerald, 196
Wolfe, Don, 12
Wolfe, Eric, 303
Wright, Darrel, 235

Y

Yobb, Louis, 302
Yokohama, 55
Yokohama Dreamland, 96-97
Yokosuka, 26, 42, 48, 55, 58-59, 263, 312
Yorkville, 30
Young, B. A., 332

Z

Zebley, Frank, 98, 326
Zwiefelhofer, Joseph, 187